STANDING ON COMMON GROUND

Standing on Common Ground

The Making of a Sunbelt Borderland

Geraldo L. Cadava

HARVARD UNIVERSITY PRESS
Cambridge, Massachusetts
London, England

To my family, for Tucson
And to my father, for the world

Printed in the United States of America

First Harvard University Press paperback edition, 2016
First Printing

Library of Congress Cataloging-in-Publication Data

Cadava, Geraldo L., 1977–
Standing on common ground : the making of a Sunbelt borderland / Geraldo L. Cadava.
pages cm
Includes bibliographical references and index.
ISBN 978-0-674-05811-8 (cloth : alk. paper)
ISBN 978-0-674-97089-2 (pbk.)
1. Arizona—Relations—Sonora (Mexico : State) 2. Sonora
(Mexico : State)—Relations—Arizona. 3. Borderlands—Arizona.
4. Borderlands—Mexico—Sonora (State) 5. Mexican-American Border Region.
I. Title.

F815.C34 2013
972'.1—dc23 2013006904

CONTENTS

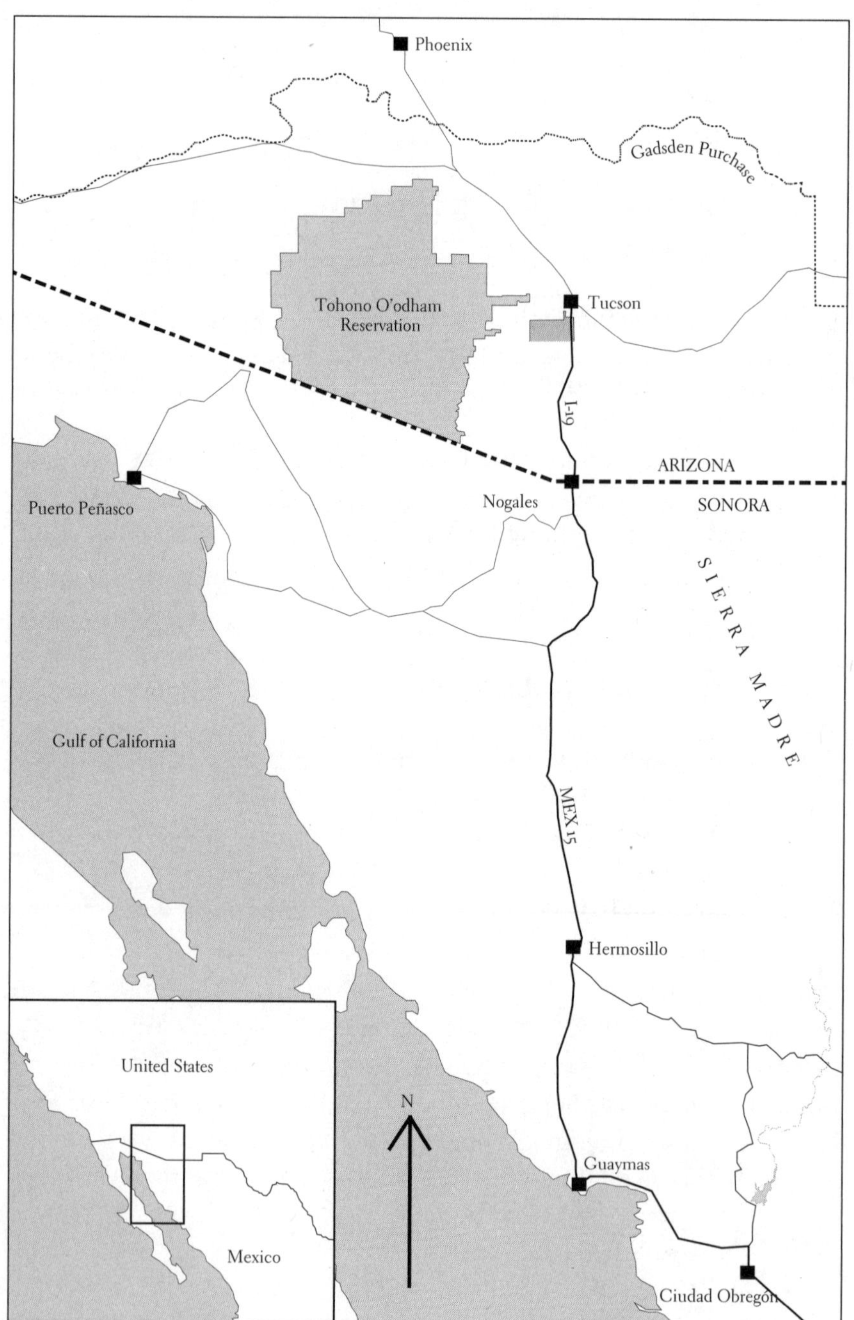

The Arizona-Sonora borderland.

PROLOGUE: TUCSON, *ARIZONA*

For three days in November 1940, Tucson hosted the world premiere of Columbia Pictures' epic film *Arizona,* a romance portraying the tenacity and entrepreneurial spirit of the territory's first white settlers. Except for a brief hiatus in 1939, after World War II broke out in Europe, the motion picture company worked furiously to complete its screen adaptation of Clarence Budington Kelland's best-selling novel. American Airlines flew to Tucson for the first time so that curious tourists could watch *Arizona*'s filming. Tucsonans planned premiere festivities. Invitations printed on "genuine Arizona copper" enticed more than a hundred movie stars and directors to the desert. According to newspaper accounts, the influx of tourists temporarily doubled the size of the city. The movie not only foreshadowed the Southwest's rise as an iconic film location and tourist destination but also offered a snapshot of racial and cross-border dynamics in Arizona on the eve of World War II.[1]

Arizona promised authenticity. Director Wesley Ruggles chose Tucson over Los Angeles for the film's location, arguing that his movie had to be shot in the desert, where it was set. Columbia Pictures spent almost one million dollars on *Arizona,* half of that amount on the biggest set ever constructed outside of California. The set became the Old Tucson Movie Studios, which, until the late twentieth century, produced dozens of famous westerns. The company created a model of Tucson in 1860 based on maps, memoirs, and photographs housed at the Arizona Historical Society. Streets had their original names; a replica Santa Cruz River made water flow in Tucson for the first time in decades; dogs, pigs, chickens, horses, and turkey buzzards roamed freely; and actors rode wagons rented from the Tucson Rodeo Parade Committee, which collected old buggies for its annual procession. "We don't dare slip up on one tiny detail," said a crewmember, because "we want this film to be authentic history."[2]

Authenticity also became the metric of success for premiere celebrations and worldwide screenings of the film. *Arizona*'s lead actress, Jean Arthur—of Calamity Jane fame—initiated the festivities by turning back the hands of an "enormous neon-lighted clock" from 1940 to 1860. All subsequent events, reported Tucson's Spanish-language newspaper, *El Tucsonense*, sought to achieve "an atmosphere that revives or reproduces Tucson in the 1860s." In the months after the premiere, as the film made its way from New Jersey to Hawaii and from Mexico to Canada to Hong Kong, Governor Sidney Osborn wrote letters to officials in those places that praised *Arizona*'s accuracy. Film critics helped Osborn make his case by writing reviews that called *Arizona* a "shining example of authenticity in pictures today." Osborn and other boosters assured viewers that what they saw on the screen was what they would see if they visited. But instead of an authentic representation of Tucson's past, moviegoers witnessed a tale based on frontier myths about the advance of white civilization, legends that cast the area's people of Mexican and Native American descent as outsiders and downplayed the city's connections with Mexico.[3]

By the time *Arizona* premiered, many white newcomers to the Southwest had spent almost a century rewriting regional history, placing themselves at the center of stories about frontier settlement. The Columbia Pictures film about Tucson was hardly any different. Arthur played the role of Phoebe Titus, the first white woman in the state who gave birth to its first white baby, a plotline that equated the arrival of whites with the birth of Arizona itself. Even though many white settlers were con men and criminals, as the Native American novelist Leslie Marmon Silko portrayed them in *Almanac of the Dead*, the industrious ones among them, *Arizona* suggested, civilized the state and developed it economically. Titus said they would "scramble along, and make this country, and tear gold 'n' silver 'n' copper out of the hills." Because of their efforts, Arizona "trembled" on the "verge of a boom."[4]

Seen in 1940, *Arizona* was a celebration of white ingenuity since the mid-nineteenth century. The film was set shortly after the 1854 Gadsden Purchase, a follow-up to the Treaty of Guadalupe Hidalgo, the document that formally ended the U.S.-Mexico War in 1848 and forced Mexico to cede half of its territory to the United States. Tucson sat at the center of Gadsden Purchase land. Even though mid-nineteenth-century visitors often called the area a wasteland, it became home to some of North America's most profitable copper-mining centers, ranches that bred millions of cattle shipped to markets throughout the hemisphere, and rich agricultural lands made productive by new dams and irrigation techniques, not to mention Mexican and native labor. Tucson became a commercial center, where merchants imported goods and distributed them to the area's mines, ranches, and farms via wagons and then railroads. As white land speculators, merchants, and financiers entered the area, they, like their peers throughout the American West, called themselves pioneers. *Arizona* told their story; they were the people who shaped the "destiny of a great new territory."[5]

If *Arizona* dramatized the original moment of white entrepreneurship in Tucson, the movie also pointed to its legacies for the present and the future. Movie promotions cited the portion of script that Titus delivered before a crowd of Tucsonans gathered in the town plaza. "We built what we have out of desert and mountain," she claimed, and "some day folk'll come flocking to the West again." Arizona, she concluded, was a "territory to invest in for the future." For early settlers, the future arrived during the late nineteenth century with the development of mining, ranching, and railroad industries, while for moviegoers in 1940, it would arrive during World War II, which transformed the region again. Even before the war, with the gradual recovery of industry following a decade of depression, boosters like the Tucson Chamber of Commerce and the Sunshine Climate Club promoted Arizona as fiercely as Arthur's character did. Tucson again stood at the edge of history. On the eve of World War II, whites in Tucson saw themselves as the inheritors of a world forged by the area's first white settlers. They, too, were pioneers who would bring progress and modernization.[6]

Arizona's narrative of white innovation, of course, depended on a fictionalized version of the border region's ethnic and racial past. Instead of history, the film traded in well-worn stereotypes. Cameras portrayed Mexicans and Native Americans napping, setting wagons on fire, bathing in a pool of muddy water, and stomping on hay and mud for adobe. Such shots halfheartedly acknowledged their labor, but the core message was that Mexicans were vagrants who groveled for a few cents in exchange for menial tasks and that Native Americans were warmongers who wreaked havoc on Arizona's nascent white communities. In the film's silent ethnographic opening sequence, white settlers entered Tucson on horseback and gazed down at the city's Mexican and Native American inhabitants, expressing wonder and disgust. Actor Paul López was a professional from Hollywood who played Estevan Ochoa, a merchant, freighter, and educator who immigrated from Sonora after the Gadsden Purchase. He was one of only a few Mexicans with speaking parts.

Even if the movie failed them, the production of *Arizona* revealed the greater vitality of the border region's Mexican and Native American communities. After studying Tucson's "labor situation," Columbia hired hundreds of Mexican and Native American laborers to construct the set. They laid 350,000 bricks to reconstruct the wall that once surrounded the presidio of Tucson. One article marveled at how quickly the set went up, comparing the forty days it took them with the 100 years it took "Indians" and "Spanish padres" to build the original. Columbia's casting agents also approached people "on the streets of Tucson" to play roles as extras. According to *El Tucsonense*, the company hired a Mexican American man to interview almost two thousand people "of our race" for bit parts. The area's Tohono O'odham also worked as extras, earning ten dollars per day for their services. These Mexicans and Native Americans signed up for six months of employment, which helped them provide for their families. Many likely were seasonal agricultural workers between jobs or individuals who chose jobs as extras instead of working in the fields.[7]

Arizona's premiere celebrations made the work of Mexicans and Native Americans even more visible. Mexican Americans selected by the Tucson Chamber of Commerce organized a "día mexicano," which displayed "times when a Mexican atmosphere pervaded Tucson." One man traveled to Mexico to commission entertainment that was "distinctly Mexican." *El Tucsonense*'s founder, Arturo Moreno, was in charge of publicity, and a Mexican consular official handled correspondence related to the premiere. Their "Comité Hispano-Americano" (Hispanic American Committee) crowned Irma Aros as the queen of the premiere and served more than three thousand helpings of *menudo*, a tripe soup. Meanwhile, five hundred Tohono O'odham, Pima, and Apache temporarily resided in teepees set up in downtown Tucson after "tons of dirt" were dropped there to replicate their desert homelands. They wore ceremonial dress, displayed crafts, performed traditional dances, and sold native foods, while the cowboys among them did riding and rope tricks. Organized by Mexican and Native American leaders, premiere events—along with set construction and roles as extras—demonstrated the social and class diversity of these communities.[8]

Arizona also entirely ignored Tucson's connection to Mexico. In the movie, the city was linked with markets in the Midwest and California

Building the set of *Arizona*. (Arizona Historical Society, Motion Picture Photograph Collection, PC 090, Folder 11, 51559.)

but not those across the border. Peter Muncie, played by William Holden, headed east with $15,000 to buy five hundred head of cattle from Kentucky (in the book) or Nebraska (in the movie) and then deliver them to Tucson. In fact, Columbia Pictures purchased the cattle that appeared in the film, all five hundred of them, from Mexico. This difference between *Arizona*'s narrative and production not only revealed the ongoing connections with Mexico erased by the film—indeed, Arizona and other U.S. states remained one of Sonora's most important markets for cattle and other goods, and Arizonans and Sonorans maintained a wide range of social and cultural relationships—but also highlighted an emerging tension between narratives of Tucson that emphasized its character as a Sunbelt city in the American West and as a regional node of the U.S.-Mexico borderlands.

Although many in Tucson wished to imagine the city only in relation to the United States, its destiny nevertheless remained tied to Mexico, both when *Arizona* was set and filmed and well into the future. Commercial firms on both sides of the border relied on business from the other side. Railroads linked Arizona and Sonora. Transnational mining corporations invested in mines and created demand for financing, labor, and goods in both states. Tucson supplied Sonoran businesses, and Sonoran farms and ranches sent produce and livestock north. During the Mexican Revolution, many Sonorans, including laborers who worked in Arizona's mines and fields and land-owning intellectuals and military leaders in exile, settled in Arizona. When workers on both sides of the border rebelled against low wages and difficult working conditions, political leaders, authorities, vigilantes, bankers, and mine owners met threats to their cross-border capitalist order with violence. Finally, the financial crisis in the United States also rocked Sonora, sending repatriates back to Mexico, halting the flow of exports to the United States, and leaving thousands unemployed.[9]

Undeniably, cross-border relations shaped Arizona and Sonora, as well as the diverse communities that lived and moved within and between the two states, but the stories told in *Arizona* persisted into the post–World War II era and beyond. A new generation of white settlers would drive economic growth as the bringers of manufacturing, high-tech, and service industries. Although a few Mexicans and Native Americans would profit from this new social and economic order, most would struggle to survive; like the extras in *Arizona,* they remained marginal community members. At the same time, forces within Arizona alternatively denied Mexico's influence, as had the film, or viewed it with disdain. Vigilantes trained their binoculars on the border, believing that they protected U.S. sovereignty against dangerous invasions, and chroniclers of Tucson called it an "American City," spinning yarns about its evolution in the twentieth century only in relation to U.S. history. This book tells a different story—of a city still defined by its connection with Mexico and two states profoundly transformed by their relation to one another.[10]

INTRODUCTION

Arizona's Interstate 19 connects Tucson with the border city of Nogales, Arizona, one hundred kilometers due south. It is the only highway in the United States that, for its entire length, measures distance in kilometers, making it familiar to thousands of Mexicans who travel the road every day and highlighting the area's long history of cross-border exchange with Sonora. The road parallels the Santa Cruz River, which flowed north from Mexico until it dried up in the early twentieth century, and also U.S. Route 89, the Old Nogales Highway. These were older pathways of exchange within the Pimería Alta—the name given the Arizona-Sonora borderland during the Spanish colonial period—and then between the United States and Mexico. Although Interstate 19 dead-ends at the border, Mexico's Federal Highway 15 picks up where it leaves off, continuing south from Nogales through Hermosillo, the state capital of Sonora, and on to the port city of Guaymas.

As they have for more than a century, the paths connecting Arizona and Sonora still transport thousands of soldiers, politicians, tourists, businesspeople, shoppers, students, family members, and others back and forth across the border. Yet by the twenty-first century, this north-south corridor—and its vast deserts to the west and east of the highways—was seen primarily as one of the most violent, narco-trafficked, and deadliest border crossings between Mexico and the United States. The other cross-border flows that linked Arizona and Sonora became obscured: the military officials from both countries who coordinated border defense efforts; politicians, tourists, and civic groups who organized regional celebrations; entrepreneurs who built retail businesses that relied on consumers from both sides of the border; students from Arizona and Sonora who participated in international exchange programs or pursued degrees abroad; and the Tohono O'odham who crossed reservation and international borders to seek work, observe religious ceremonies, and connect with family. Even as conflict strained cross-border relations in the late twentieth century, many Arizonans and Sonorans continued to believe that their futures were intertwined and that they lived in a single region defined by movement between their countries.

Even though transnational relationships still shape the Arizona-Sonora borderland, Arizona's sharp anti-immigrant politics—along with actual border fencing—heightened the divide between the United States and Mexico. An increasingly harsh tone infused Arizona from the 1970s forward, and beginning in the 1990s, the state peddled laws that sought to limit access by undocumented immigrants to government benefits, forbid citizens from offering them assistance, and make English the official language. Vigilante groups launched efforts to deter undocumented immigration, and Maricopa County Sheriff Joe Arpaio relentlessly raided Mexican and Mexican American communities. Still, many saw Senate Bill 1070 (S.B. 1070) as the pinnacle of state-sponsored discrimination. Signed by Governor Jan Brewer in April 2010, it required local and state police to verify the immigration status of suspected "illegal aliens"; authorized police to arrest them without warrants; criminalized their failure to carry identification; and prevented them from working in the state.[1]

Drafted by Arizona Senator Russell Pearce and Kansas Secretary of State Kris Kobach, the "show me your papers" law became a blueprint for other states to follow. Civil rights groups called Arizona a "laboratory for anti-immigrant experimentation." Pima County sheriff Clarence Dupnik called the law an "embarrassment," adding that it was "stupid" and "racist." Mexican officials called it a "violation of civil rights" and a "kind of apartheid." Months after Brewer signed S.B. 1070, Mexican border governors, including Sonora's, boycotted a binational conference that had been a yearly gathering for decades and, in 2010, was held in Phoenix. In 2012, the U.S. Supreme Court rejected most of the law but upheld the provision authorizing police to demand papers from suspected undocumented immigrants. Proponents argued that the law only aimed to defend U.S. sovereignty, but Latinos in the United States and Mexicans south of the border believed that the law profiled them racially.[2]

Arizona may have become "ground zero" for national debates about immigration and the border, but this book reveals the postwar Arizona-Sonora borderland as a more dynamic and complicated landscape of cultural and commercial exchange. It serves as a counterpoint to narratives by historians who have claimed that the border and its meaning had hardened or become fixed by the mid-twentieth century, as a space of conflict and a clear dividing line restricting the flow of Mexican immigrants into the United States. It also broadens the work of Arizona historians whose field of vision ends at the international line, and challenges the arguments of Americans who boldly pronounce sharp divisions between the United States and Mexico. Each misses the dense web of connections between Arizona and Sonora that have shaped the post–World War II history of each state and the region as a whole. Guided by this understanding of postwar borderlands, future policy debates that will affect the region must adopt as their frame of reference not only the protection of U.S. sovereignty against undocumented Mexican immigrants but also the full range of transnational connections that define borderland life. Considering these cross-border relations will not by itself lead to good policy making, but it offers the only hope of limiting the violence and injustice that had become endemic by the twenty-first century.[3]

In addition to the interlocked histories of U.S. and Mexican states, this book also brings together the postwar histories of diverse peoples in the Arizona-Sonora border region. Transnational relationships shaped the evolution of Mexican, native, and white communities throughout the postwar era. These are, of course, imperfect ways of describing the ethnic and racial identities of borderland residents. Many Mexicans and Mexican Americans considered themselves to be white, while many Tohono O'odham living on both sides of the border had Spanish surnames, and therefore were misidentified as Mexican. Yet by the mid-twentieth century, these ethnic labels became foundations for the articulation of shared identities among some borderland residents and also revealed the fault lines that divided many members of these groups from each other. Ever since the establishment of the present-day border, borderland residents have crossed it as a way of life. They have carried with them ideas about politics, international relations, and regional identities, demonstrating how their migrations included the movement of culture and beliefs in addition to bodies. Their crossings after World War II transformed how they saw themselves as social, political, and economic actors. The postwar histories of communities on both sides of the border, therefore, were forged in the crucible of cross-border exchange.

Transnational exchanges between Arizona and Sonora unfolded in the context of the growth and modernization of two national frontiers. Just as World War II led to the explosive militarization and demographic and economic boom of the American West, it had similar effects on Mexico's northern border region. Social, cultural, and political landscapes were reshaped every bit as much as economic and demographic realities. Comprehensive changes on both sides of the border gave rise to Arizona's and Sonora's Sunbelt borderland, which, instead of developing in the context of separate national histories, extended beyond a Sunbelt Southwest or northern Mexican frontier.

All of these things together—cross-border exchanges between Arizona and Sonora, their shaping of communities throughout the region, and the rise of a Sunbelt borderland characterized by postwar development of the U.S. Southwest and northern Mexico—demonstrated how Tucson inhabited the center of several overlapping geographies. The city stood as an important regional core of the U.S.-Mexico borderlands, the Latino Southwest, and the American West. Its connections with Sonoran cities like Nogales, Guaymas, and Hermosillo demonstrate how, during and after World War II, multiple historical trajectories collided in the Arizona-Sonora borderland. Strands of local, regional, national, and international history merged as one.

In unanticipated ways, the postwar evolution of Arizona's and Sonora's Sunbelt borderland led to the rise of immigration and border debates in the late twentieth and early twenty-first centuries. The economic growth that borderland businesspeople and politicians promoted as a universal benefit caused the migration of many thousands of Mexicans and native people into and between Sonora and Arizona. Several industries relied on their labor. Pro-business ideologies and policies at the state and national levels—in Arizona and Sonora, as in the United States and Mexico more generally—favored industry and corporations over workers, which led to inequalities that caused many laborers to leave home out of necessity, often for another country. In the context of shifting political and economic circumstances decades after the war, migrants experienced increasing discrimination and violence. Even though racism had plagued the Arizona-Sonora borderland for more than a century, its twenty-first-century forms have roots in these postwar economic, political, and social formations.

Although many have doubted the existence of a Sunbelt—because it lacks clear geographic boundaries and because certain areas considered part of it are more different than alike—it remains extremely useful as a concept highlighting regional connections that have shaped Arizona and

Sonora since World War II. Like Sunbelt areas elsewhere, this region benefited from federal investment in economic-development programs. Arizona and Sonora urbanized as their cities became regional hubs that relied on the extractive and productive economies of their hinterlands, as well as new manufacturing capabilities and transportation networks that delivered their goods to local, domestic, and international markets. In Arizona and Sonora, like other states identified as part of the Sunbelt, the line between business and politics became increasingly blurred by the collaborations of politicians and pro-business organizations like chambers of commerce and branches of the Rotary Club. Moreover, elected officials in Arizona and Sonora, with notable exceptions, held "pro-growth," "pro-defense," and "antilabor" positions representative of many Sunbelt politicians. As Arizona and Sonora evolved in the postwar era, they, like other Sunbelt areas, played increasingly important roles in the political economies of both nations. Defense, mining, agriculture, livestock, and manufacturing industries increased their influence within the United States and Mexico, which in turn boosted their political stature. To situate the ideas of historians of the American Sunbelt within a transnational context, some of the "most heated and significant political struggles" of the postwar era "played out" in the borderland between Arizona and Sonora. Finally, Arizona and Sonora's Sunbelt shared with other Sunbelt regions the experience of financial tumult from the 1970s forward as a result of neoliberal economic policy.[4]

The Arizona–Sonora Sunbelt borderland rose as businesspeople and politicians worked across the border. They hatched schemes to promote economic growth. They became close family friends and sometimes intermarried. They came together in Tucson and Hermosillo to dance or rub elbows with the leaders of both states. While they moved within national circles, they also articulated regional identities that heightened their influence on both sides of the border. Alex Jácome and Ignacio Soto were representative of a generation of postwar businesspeople and politicians who promoted cross-border relationships. The president of Jácome's Department Store in Tucson, Jácome was one of the city's most successful businesspeople. He held official and honorary diplomatic posts. He belonged to several business and civic organizations, served as president of the Tucson Rotary Club, and was a member of the state university system's board of regents. Meanwhile, Soto founded Sonora's leading cement company, Cemento Portland Nacional, and also was a member of the

Chamber of Commerce and the Rotary Club. He served as governor of Sonora from 1949 to 1955 and, in the 1960s, as president of the board of trustees of la Universidad de Sonora. Jácome and Soto became close friends, and Soto served as godfather to one of Jácome's sons. They and others like them spent lifetimes building cross-border relationships. Their successors—the supporters of economic and cultural exchanges between Arizona and Sonora into the twenty-first century—carried their work forward even as rising conflicts over immigration, drugs, and other issues overshadowed their efforts.

The ideologies of profit, progress, and modernization motivating Arizona's and Sonora's businesspeople and politicians had significant consequences for the area's ethnoracial groups and working-class communities. State leaders benefited from their political relationships with counterparts on the other side of the border. Arizona's leaders courted Mexican American voters by cultivating friendly relations with Sonora, and Sonoran leaders claimed elite status because of their professional and personal connections with prominent Arizonans. They pronounced the benefits of economic development for the social and cultural advancement of both states. Yet the benefits of the Sunbelt borderland did not lift all Arizonans and Sonorans. Despite an increase in educational and work opportunities, many borderland residents—especially Mexicans and Mexican Americans living north of the border and native communities on both sides—remained poor, marginalized, and ill equipped to take advantage of the Sunbelt borderland's economic-development initiatives, which tended to favor already wealthy investors rather than workers and small landholders. This book accounts for these multiple, often competing strains of the Sunbelt borderland's postwar history—its rise and decline, its causes and effects, its riches and growing inequalities.[5]

Arizona's and Sonora's borderland economies, like others along the U.S.-Mexico border, grew dramatically in the three decades between World War II and 1970. Both national governments invested heavily in defense, manufacturing, mining, agriculture, and ranching industries, prioritizing one or the other of these at different moments according to perceived domestic and international interests. During the war, for example, borderland economies were geared toward national and hemispheric defense efforts. But during the postwar era, they became privatized and converted into businesses that met the demands of growing populations, increasing the wealth and living standards of businesspeople and middle-class consumers on both sides of the border. Borderland economies intertwined not only because Sonora and Arizona relied on international markets across the border but also because regional industrial growth led to the rise of cross-border tourism and shopping, which kept retail and other businesses afloat. Coinciding with an extended period of national economic growth often referred to as a "miracle," Sonora's postwar development did not lead to economic parity with Arizona or the United States in general, but Sonoran business interests—in good financial times and bad—nevertheless tied themselves to their northern neighbors.[6]

New economic and cultural opportunities led to the explosion of cities throughout the region, drawing large pools of migrants from both countries into the border area and particularly to its rapidly growing metropolises. Between 1940 and 1960, Tucson's population grew from 35,000 to 213,000, while Hermosillo's leapt from 18,000 to 118,000. Those numbers translated into a twenty-year population increase of 495 percent for Tucson and an even more impressive 554 percent for Hermosillo. At the same time, the population of Nogales, Sonora, more than doubled (from 15,400 to 39,800), as did that of Guaymas (from 20,500 to 53,700). Cities in Arizona and Sonora continued their brisk growth over the following decade. By 1970, Tucson had 263,000 residents, while Hermosillo became a city of 208,000. Notably, the beach town of Puerto Peñasco grew by 117 percent between 1960 and 1970, taking it from a small town of 5,700 to a city of 12,400, because of the increased development of Sonora's coastline for tourism. Such figures formed part of a broader demographic trend that made the entire U.S.-Mexico border region the fastest-growing area of both countries and demonstrated how World War II unleashed economic and demographic changes that shaped the borderlands for decades to come.[7]

Arizona's and Sonora's political landscapes also transformed in the decades after World War II, as pro-business interests in both states increasingly became regional power brokers. Beginning in the 1950s, Arizona turned solidly Republican as a result of intense recruitment efforts by the state's business leadership. In 1948, only 18 percent of voters registered as Republicans, but within four years, by 1952, that number had risen to 32 percent. Even though Arizona industries benefited from federal investment, Barry Goldwater and other conservatives railed against government regulations and the New Deal state. Goldwater, who won a U.S. Senate seat in 1952 after years of grassroots organizing as a member of Phoenix's

Charter Government Committee, was only one outspoken representative of Arizona's conservative turn. Voters across the state chose Republican presidential candidates in every election until 1996, even when Republicans lost national elections in 1960, 1964, 1976, and 1992. Tucson may have been less conservative than Phoenix, but a majority of voters there, too, supported Republican presidential candidates. Between 1940 and 1970, Pima County bucked state trends only once, when it went for Lyndon Johnson instead of the Arizona native Goldwater. Like Phoenix, a city controlled by business-friendly politicians, Tucson's Chamber of Commerce dominated city politics during the postwar era despite the opposition of antigrowth candidates. The efforts of unions notwithstanding, antilabor measures like the 1946 right-to-work law created an oppressive atmosphere for workers in the state.[8]

Politics in Sonora also became the domain of elite businesspeople and politicians, often synonymous. After the Cárdenas-era agrarian reforms—between 1934 and 1940, when the Mexican government turned over more property than ever before (or since) to collective landholders in Sonora—national and state governments reversed gains made by these *ejidatarios* by offering them incentives to privatize and crafting laws that benefited already wealthy landowners. According to one Sonoran historian, the aftermath of the Cárdenas era signaled the end of the Mexican Revolution for landless peasants and unemployed workers and "drowned the hopes" they had for a more equal society. One political party did not embody liberalism or conservatism in Sonora, as was the case in Arizona. Instead, a single party, the Partido Revolucionario Institucional (Institutional Revolutionary Party, or PRI) controlled national and state politics for several decades after 1940. Like Arizona's political leaders, PRI leaders in Sonora supported pro-growth initiatives that concentrated power in the hands of a few agricultural, ranching, and manufacturing elites, demonstrating how conservative business practices linked both sides of the border. Sonora's leaders saw World War II as Mexico's "big opportunity" to transition from a "weak, poor, underdeveloped, and uncivilized" nation to a modern and industrialized one. They spent the decades after the war making that dream a reality, while at the same time making it difficult for most poor native peoples and *mestizos*—the mixed-race population glorified by the postrevolutionary Mexican State—to enjoy the full benefits of their economic vision. As in Arizona, the labor organizations that represented these groups protested government policies and their own diminishing influence, although some became co-opted by the government and ultimately worked on its behalf.[9]

In order to smooth the way for cross-border commercial relations between Arizona and Sonora, regional politicians and businesspeople relied on the language of Franklin Roosevelt's Good Neighbor policy and other ideologies of Pan-American friendship and goodwill. Originally conceived as a mechanism to encourage hemispheric unity against rising international threats including Fascism and Communism, the Good Neighbor policy became an idea that motivated politicians and businesspeople to engage in cross-border trade or develop regional tourism. For Arizona's politicians, the language of the Good Neighbor policy also aimed to encourage the loyalty of Mexican American voters. International threats and labor migrations during the Bracero Program—a binational accord establishing a temporary guest worker program that, between 1942 and 1964, brought to the United States millions of Mexican laborers—gave rise to increased border-enforcement efforts and nativist backlash. Yet businesspeople and politicians were more interested in opening the border than closing it. They built new gateways to promote international trade; celebrated national holidays of the United States and Mexico; supported organizations that developed cross-border ties; and expanded tourism and retail industries catering to international consumers. If financial profit was their intended result, businesspeople and politicians on both sides of the border uniformly claimed that friendship and goodwill inspired their pursuit of cross-border relations.[10]

The transformation of Arizona's and Sonora's economic and political relationships also affected the border region's demographic and racial landscape. Both states increasingly urbanized as cities like Tucson and Hermosillo became home to defense-industry manufacturers, construction companies that built irrigation canals, canneries that processed goods from ranches and fields, and railroad depots and highway interchanges that provided vital links to other areas inside and outside the region. Arizona's and Sonora's business and political elite clustered in cities, as did thousands of new immigrants of various class backgrounds, most of them workers from rural areas within the region. In Tucson, these migrations recast the city's racial balance. A majority of the city's Mexicans and Mexican Americans were of Sonoran descent; in the mid-twentieth century some two-thirds of them traced their family's roots to the Mexican state. Their number increased in the decades after World War II, as did the number of Tohono O'odham from both sides of the border. More O'odham came to live in Tucson than anywhere else. Yet whites immigrated to the city at a faster pace than either of these groups. Because of the influx of whites, Mexicans and Mexican Americans in Tucson accounted for a little more than 20 percent of the city's total population in 1960, their lowest proportion ever—either before or since.[11]

The Sunbelt borderland created both opportunities and consequences for people of Mexican and native descent. Tucsonans navigated the city's new demographic mix by participating in regional celebrations like the Tucson rodeo and parade, which helped to establish a racial order for the postwar era. Mexicans, Mexican Americans, and Native Americans held new jobs and received college degrees. Some of them acquired relative wealth and status as members of civic organizations like La Alianza Hispano-Americana (La Alianza) or the tribal council of the Tohono O'odham. A greater percentage of Mexican Americans held professional, clerical, and service positions than before the war, while the percentage doing farm work and unskilled labor decreased. Yet most people of Mexican and native descent remained marginalized in poor neighborhoods or on reservations; received lower levels of education than whites; and were more likely to live in poverty and in more crowded homes. Nevertheless, in order to establish a sense of solidarity in the face of the difficult circumstances that the Sunbelt borderland's political economy had helped to create, they forged communities by joining labor unions, church groups, veterans' associations, and mutual-aid societies that stretched across the Arizona-Sonora border.[12]

The Sunbelt borderland forged during and after World War II experienced shocks beginning in the late 1960s that led to the unraveling of the world imagined by men like Jácome and Soto and, ultimately, to the rise of heated debates about immigration and the border in general. The cross-border exchanges they saw as hallmarks of the Arizona-Sonora borderland continued into the twenty-first century, as more money, people, and goods crossed the border than ever before. Businesspeople and politicians continued to proclaim deep friendships. Yet they struggled to maintain the region's dramatic economic growth. Agriculture, ranching, and mining industries continued to operate, although they experienced several booms and busts. The businesspeople who grew wealthy from them racked up debt, as did Mexico itself. The country devalued its currency several times, leading to the instability of borderlands economies. To meet manufacturing needs, U.S. companies, including several from Arizona, turned toward Mexican border factories called *maquiladoras,* which offered cheap labor and tax loopholes. Arizona's economy, meanwhile, shifted toward construction and service industries like tourism, retail, and finance. Businesspeople and politicians on both sides of the border sought to diversify the economies of their states so they would not have to rely on a handful of industries, but regional and global market fluctuations created great volatility.[13]

The transformation of domestic and international politics from the 1960s and 1970s forward also demonstrated the move toward a more contentious period of Arizona-Sonora borderland history. In both states, businesspeople and politicians had spent decades preaching the benefits of economic growth and pro-business policies, which promised to create jobs, increase living standards, and offer cultural and educational opportunities for borderland residents. Arizona's and Sonora's universities became symbols of postwar progress by training generations of students in fields that would benefit them and their home region. But they also became spaces for articulating criticisms of the border region's postwar economic order. Students on both sides of the border, many of them with parents who had worked in mines, ranches, and fields, waged campaigns for social, economic, and political justice. Arizona's and Sonora's native communities also continued to claim that *mestizo* farmers in Sonora and whites in Arizona encroached on their land. They joined indigenous communities throughout the Americas that called for greater sovereignty. Throughout Mexico, including in Sonora, opposition parties challenged the PRI's legitimacy. At the same time, the shifting politics of the Cold War heightened cross-border tensions. Throughout the region, the United States backed oppressive military dictators who sought to crush leftist groups that gained power in several Latin American countries. Many Sonoran students expressed solidarity with the leftist leaders who opposed U.S. intervention—which they saw as a replay of earlier imperialist adventures in their country—but state and federal governments still articulated a desire for cross-border friendship.[14]

Shifting transnational economies and politics led to new employment and demographic patterns that heightened tensions both within and between Arizona and Sonora. The end of the Bracero Program in 1964 forced Mexican laborers to return to their country. Many of the workers sought employment in Sonora. The lure of jobs in internationally owned factories called *maquiladoras* also led to the arrival of a growing number of migrants from other Mexican states. Tellingly, the population of Nogales—where most of the state's *maquiladoras* were located—increased by 59 percent between 1980 and 1990, much higher than the rate of growth in other cities. Nogales then grew by 48 percent between 1990 and 2000 and 38 percent between 2000 and 2010—faster than either Tucson or Hermosillo. Demonstrating how *maquiladoras* recruited workers from all over Mexico, Nogales experienced greater immigration from other areas of the country than anywhere else in Sonora, although the state as a whole attracted more migrants from the Mexican interior in the late twentieth century than during any earlier period. Especially following the mechanization and relative decline of industries like agriculture, ranching, and mining, increased immigration to Sonora created economic pressures and high rates of unemployment, leading many Mexicans to cross into the United States. Because the 1965 Immigration and Nationality Act capped at 120,000 per year the number of immigrants from all Western Hemisphere countries who could enter the country legally, many Mexicans arrived in the United States without papers. Certain sectors of Arizona's new service economies relied on undocumented workers who earned less than other employees in Arizona but more than laborers in Mexico. Meanwhile, during the 1970s and 1980s, Arizona and Sonora received waves of Central American refugees from civil wars in their home countries, altering traditional patterns of migration back and forth between the two states.[15]

The rising number of Latin American immigrants—entering legally or not—coincided with periodic economic downturns on both sides of the border, and these two factors together ignited a prolonged period of anti-immigrant sentiment and violence from the 1970s forward. Arizonans had targeted Mexican immigrants during earlier periods as well, but this new wave of persecution stemmed from the making and unmaking of Arizona's and Sonora's Sunbelt borderland, both because the area's unfettered drive for growth and profit relied on Mexican and native immigrant labor and because slumps that came about, in part, as a result of transitions in postwar borderland economies led many borderland residents to direct blame toward Mexican and other Latin American migrants. In this climate, white ranchers and vigilantes kidnapped, harassed, and tortured Mexican immigrants, and Arizonans considered Central American refugees Communist threats and economic burdens even though many of them were middle class and merely sought to escape violence in their home countries. Immigrant and civil rights organizations defended both groups. Debates about immigration and the border spread across the country in the 1970s and 1980s, leading to passage of the Immigration Reform and Control Act (IRCA) in 1986. Arizona was not an irrelevant "backwater" when it came to these debates, as one immigration scholar described it, but rather a state that shaped national and international conversations about violence against immigrants and immigrant rights into the twenty-first century.[16]

The immigration and border debates that swept across the Arizona-Sonora borderland deeply affected the region's communities of Mexican and native descent. Postwar borderland economies had offered mobility to some Mexican Americans and Native Americans. More Mexican Americans held political office than ever before, in part because of civil rights successes. The number of Mexicans and Mexican Americans in Arizona working as managers or professionals increased, while the percentage working as laborers dropped. Still, the rate of unemployment among Mexicans and Mexican Americans was double that of whites, and between 1970 and 2000, the poverty rate among them climbed from two to four times as high. These inequalities became magnified as whites in Arizona targeted Mexicans and Mexican Americans, regardless of their immigration status, as threats and community outsiders. Employers discriminated against them. Mexican immigrants became victims of violence. Politicians regurgitated stereotypes of Mexican and Mexican American culture as clannish, violent, lazy, and gang-ridden. Border Patrol officers and other law-enforcement agents raided neighborhoods with high concentrations of Mexicans and Mexican Americans. They policed the Tohono O'odham reservation, making it increasingly difficult for O'odham to cross back and forth across the international border, which divided their homelands. As the number of Latinos as a percentage of Arizona's population climbed from just over 20 percent in 1970 to more than 40 percent in 2010, white Arizonans fretted about their future as a minority, which they will become sometime before the mid-twenty-first century.[17]

The history of Arizona's and Sonora's Sunbelt borderland since World War II makes clear that the pressing question about the border is not whether it opened or closed as a result of particular immigration laws, an expanded Border Patrol, or fence construction, but rather how communities on either side of it negotiated their relationship to the international line and to one another, as well as how their interactions shaped and reshaped the border's meaning into the twenty-first century. Communities continued to imagine their world in a way that extended beyond borders. This book therefore argues for an understanding of recent borderlands history defined less by the international line itself and more by the range of economic, political, social, and cultural relationships that transcended the line. It also reveals a world of transnational migration beyond the back-and-forth movements of undocumented laborers, including shoppers, students, businesspeople, politicians, artists, and families, whom we must account for in debates about cross-border relations and the causes and effects of immigration between Mexico and the United States. Finally, it demonstrates that all border issues have deeply transnational roots grounded not only in the arenas of cross-border economic, political, and diplomatic relations but also in a regional culture forged through the institutions and traditions of the U.S.-Mexico borderlands.[18]

1

DEFENDING THE BORDERLAND

In the summer of 1940, Tucson's Spanish-language newspaper, *El Tucsonense*, published an editorial lamenting the paranoia that swept across the border region after the outbreak of war in Europe. Written by a Mexican American resident of Nogales, Arizona, the letter responded to the formation of a vigilante group that viewed Mexicans and Mexican Americans as dangerous enemy aliens. The group's efforts, the author explained, exposed a "border problem" that stemmed from the failure of whites in Nogales to understand the "hearts" of Mexicans and Mexican Americans living on both sides of the international line. They had inhabited the area for a long time and were also concerned about its security; it was home, and they sought to protect it, too.[1]

The letter demonstrated several wartime dynamics, including how the residents of Arizona and Sonora shared a concern for border security and the security of their region during World War II. It channeled longtime fears that a vulnerable U.S.-Mexican border posed a grave threat to international security. Government officials and ordinary citizens alike suspected that Axis enemies would enter the Sea of Cortez, land along the Sonoran coast, and invade the United States by crossing the Arizona-Sonora border. These fears led to cooperation between the United States and Mexico, including increased immigration controls and border enforcement, and ramped-up military mobilizations, information sharing, and surveillance. Cooperative border-defense efforts transformed communities on both sides of the border through the construction of defense plants, army bases, and highways, as well as a militarized social, cultural, and political atmosphere. Published more than a year before Japan attacked Pearl Harbor, the editorial in *El Tucsonense* foreshadowed how the rhetoric of border security would shape the Arizona-Sonora borderland throughout the twentieth century.[2]

If wartime necessity drove the militarization of Arizona and Sonora, it also mobilized the politicians and businesspeople who saw the war as an opportunity to fulfill their dreams of profit. By the end of the 1930s, industries on both sides of the border had begun to recover from the Great Depression, but during World War II they grew exponentially. The United States and Mexico forged the Arizona-Sonora Sunbelt borderland by supporting several industries there. They offered direct investments, credit, and subsidies that created incentives for businesses that improved warplanes, built dams, extracted minerals, grew crops, raised cattle, farmed shrimp, and developed harbors, bridges, and roads that met military objectives. Commercial activity during the war laid the foundation for postwar economic development on both sides of the border. Arizona's new defense and manufacturing capabilities eased the state's dependence on extractive industries, while Sonora's investment in agriculture and livestock aided Mexico's transition from a "weak, poor, underdeveloped, and uncivilized" nation, as Governor Abelardo Rodríguez put it, to a modern and industrialized one. The economic transformation of both states depended on their proximity, cross-border exchanges between them, and the shared goals of regional business and political leaders.[3]

Progress and modernization became the mantra of the businesspeople and politicians who established Arizona's and Sonora's Sunbelt borderland. The struggle for liberty abroad led them to imagine new possibilities for economic growth at home. In Arizona, boosters, businesspeople, and elected officials created a climate favorable to capitalist investment by lowering corporate taxes and restricting labor rights. In Sonora, state leaders encouraged capitalist development by supporting the large-scale privatization of land and resources. Business and government on both sides of the border became virtually indistinguishable. State governors were successful businesspeople before their election to office. In Sonora, they marked a departure from the generation of political leaders defined by their service in the Mexican Revolution, instead representing the state's new "bourgeoisie." Pro-development platforms linked Arizona and Sonora through the participation of leaders in transnational business organizations and diplomatic promotions of international friendship and harmony, which shaped cross-border relations throughout the twentieth century.[4]

The language of President Roosevelt's Good Neighbor policy infused the rhetoric of state officials and ordinary borderland residents. Virtually all gestures by Arizonans and Sonorans toward their neighbors on the other side of the border became demonstrations of friendship and goodwill, including Fourth of July celebrations in Sonora and Mexican independence celebrations in Arizona. Such acts demonstrated a sincere desire for international harmony, especially in the context of World War II. Arizona politicians also used Good Neighbor rhetoric in order to win the support of Mexican American voters, and Sonoran politicians used it to appeal to business leaders seeking strategic partnerships with U.S. businesspeople. Finally, Good Neighbor rhetoric offered a patina of smooth cross-border relations despite political, racial, and class tensions within and between these states. It revealed a rift between leaders and ordinary citizens, who suffered the consequences of the Sunbelt borderland's economic development.

The wartime conditions that enabled great benefits for Arizona's and Sonora's leading businesspeople posed challenges for marginalized communities on both sides of the border. Concerns about border security led to profits for some and discrimination against others. Authorities harassed, imprisoned, and removed Japanese and Mexicans seen as subversive threats. Moreover, the large-scale development of mining, agriculture, and livestock industries displaced longtime residents from their land and forced them to migrate domestically and internationally in search of work. New industries also created jobs for individuals of Mexican and native descent, but these paid low salaries and offered little opportunity for advancement. Members of these communities served in the military and articulated patriotic claims to U.S. and Mexican citizenship, demonstrating the ubiquity of ideas about unity and their belief that the war presented an opportunity for increased rights and economic mobility. But they experienced racial prejudice all the same. World War II therefore signaled the rise of Arizona's and Sonora's Sunbelt borderland but also had negative consequences for Mexicans, native peoples, and others.

Altogether, mobilizations against perceived threats, wartime economic development, and persistent racial discrimination demonstrated multiple understandings of what it meant to defend the Arizona-Sonora borderland. Defending the border meant protecting U.S. and Mexican regional and national interests against enemy invasion and in support of economic growth, yet the enactment of protective measures on a local level revealed other meanings as well. Mexicans and native peoples crossed the border daily as a way of life, and many had lived in the area for generations, but vigilantes cast them as foreigners. Defending the borderland therefore signified the need for Mexican Americans, Mexicans, and native peoples to defend their histories and themselves against physical and discursive attack. Multiple meanings of defending the borderland crystallized during World War II, both in the name of international security and of securing the borderland as a homeland where people of Mexican and native descent could pursue economic, social, and cultural equality.

Defending the Border

Arizonans and Sonorans feared for their safety during World War II, leading to widespread calls for increased border defense. Tucson newspapers issued alarming statements like "Democracy has its back to the wall . . . Totalitarian influence is spreading throughout the civilized world." Many imagined that, at any moment, enemies of the United States and Mexico could attack the border region. Tucson teachers discussed the war in classrooms. Sirens rang throughout the city to ensure preparedness for bombing raids. Homeowners built private bomb shelters. Schools held bomb drills. Signs hung around town that read "Watch what you say; the enemy is listening." Sonorans expressed similar concerns. Editorials in Hermosillo's *El Imparcial* emphasized precautions against German and Japanese subversives lurking in border cities and along Mexico's Pacific Coast. Mexican government spies sent reports to superiors in Mexico City, offering accounts of threats ranging from arms smuggling to political dissidents—the individuals and groups that did not support the Partido Revolucionario Mexicano (PRM), a precursor to the Partido Revolucionario Institucional (PRI), established in 1938. For Arizonans and Sonorans alike, the specter of enemies in their midst haunted them because of their proximity to the U.S.-Mexico border.[5]

Even Hollywood filmmakers considered Tucson's location near the border before they filmed *Arizona* there. According to a 1940 article in *Collier's* magazine, Columbia Pictures and city officials argued that the construction of a movie set west of downtown would, in fact, enhance Tucson's preparedness for war. "Tucson lies a few miles north of [Mexico]," the author wrote, and "enemy bombers could leave foreign soil and drop their eggs on Tucson within twenty minutes. It's that close." He described the movie-set replica of Tucson as the "only camouflaged city in America." It was a "phony Tucson, about seventeen miles due south of itself, and in case of military activity the bombers are expected to leave [Mexico], fly north and mistakenly drop their bombs on the imitation Tucson, thus sparing the real city." As residents of a border city in a border state, Tucsonans were scared, but a movie-set simulacrum did not help them feel safe. Fears spread throughout the U.S.-Mexico borderlands that enemies would infiltrate the area; many suspected that they already had.[6]

Mexican politicians also demonstrated how the rhetoric of border security infiltrated their country's domestic and international politics. Manuel Ávila Camacho, the PRM candidate for president in 1940, spoke about the need for cooperative border-defense efforts. At a rally in Hermosillo, he discussed the "World War, and fears in the United States that totalitarians plan to invade America." As a former general and secretary of national defense, he confidently stated that, because of Mexico's commitment to defending the border, any such invasion "would not be successful for whoever might try it." His campaign-trail proclamations convinced the United States that his administration would focus on international security, but they also addressed the concerns of Sonorans seeking reassurance in the face of danger. In part because of Camacho's vocal support for border defense, the United States backed him instead of Juan Andreu Almazán. In July 1940, Camacho won the hotly contested election, sparking months of bloody street battles that only intensified wartime anxieties.[7]

In the wake of Almazán's defeat, Mexicans themselves—not Germans, Italians, or Japanese—became enemies of the state and targets of surveillance. Government spies bunkered in Nogales, Sonora, sent intelligence reports to their superiors in Mexico City about the dealings of *Almazanistas*—the loyal followers of Almazán who, the spies claimed, agitated against the government and had extensive support throughout southern Arizona. *Almazanistas*, they reported, were planning an armed uprising that would take place in early November 1940. In a Tucson bakery, they stored guns and ammunition that female smugglers would traffic across the border. Disrupting the domestic and cross-border harmony that politicians said the war had inspired, fears of mobilization by *Almazanistas* led one spy to report that, at "all points along Sonora's border with the United States, there is news unfavorable to future tranquility."[8]

Fears of violence and upheaval after Mexico's 1940 presidential election were only the latest instance of potential conflict along the U.S.-Mexico border. In some ways, tension had defined U.S.-Mexico relations for more than a century, leading Sonorans to debate the merits of a strategic alliance with the United States. During the 1830s, one Sonoran journalist wrote, the United States "treacherously" wrenched Texas from Mexico. Only a decade later, the U.S.-Mexico war resulted in Mexico's "humiliation." Mexico and the United States defended the border against attack throughout the nineteenth century. They sought to prevent raids by indigenous groups and white cowboys from one side to the other. The governments of both countries tried to quell challenges to state authority posed by Mexican exiles revolting against the dictator Porfirio Díaz from within the United States. Following Pancho Villa's 1916 raid against Columbus, New Mexico, in which eighteen U.S. citizens died, residents of other border communities, including Tucson, feared that Villa would attack their hometowns. Then, during the 1920s, landowners in Arizona and Sonora railed against the so-called Yellow Peril, a perceived "Asiatic 'empire'" that had conquered their fields and communities.[9]

Until World War II, land disputes, payment of outstanding debts, water distribution from rivers that flowed across the border, and Mexico's nationalization of petroleum reserves riddled relations between the United States and Mexico. So did arms trading, anti-Mexican racism, unauthorized migration, drug smuggling, and compensating U.S. companies and individual landowners for the expropriation of their properties in Mexico. Mexicans, therefore, were wary of alliance. Before the countries entered into a formal military and economic partnership, *El Imparcial* explained, they worked to resolve these "problems along the border." In the end, many borderland residents argued that the global scale and potential consequences of World War II demanded U.S.-Mexican cooperation.[10]

Ezequiel Padilla—Mexico's foreign relations secretary and staunch supporter of a U.S.-Mexican alliance—assured Mexicans that he would protect their sovereignty. He concluded that the gravity of world events trumped past grievances and that Mexico could not remain neutral. Many Sonorans agreed. Mexico "cannot remain indifferent before the coming crisis," one wrote, because the "flag raised by the United States is the same as our own, that of democracy." Mexico had legitimate, long-standing grievances against the United States, but, many Sonorans believed, the Good Neighbor policy had improved international relations, and they faced common threats. The solution was as "clear as day: to be allied with the United States." Mexico entered into commercial treaties; committed to do whatever it took to defeat "fifth columnism" in the Americas; and proposed to construct new military bases for use by all American countries—even though they were never built.[11]

For many Mexicans, participation in the war even signaled a kind of revolution—the transition from old to new, past to present, and primitive to modern. President Camacho had blamed the war on Europe's old-style politics, and the Americas offered a fresh solution. America was new, different, and in many ways antithetical to Europe. Germany and Italy fought not only against "freedom and democracy," he said, but also against the "historical purity of the Americas and the generosity of its peoples." Mexico was a "young country, without hatred, without selfishness, and free of all unjust appetite for hegemony." Despite its romanticism, Camacho's speech rallied many in Sonora to support the war. *El Imparcial* called it the "most transcendental moment of the past thirty years," dating back to the beginning of the Mexican Revolution.[12]

If the United States and Mexico stumbled toward an alliance in the early years of the war, Japan's attack on Pearl Harbor led the governments of both countries to march forward together. Forming a unified front against Axis powers, Mexico cut diplomatic ties with Japan, Germany, and Italy. German and Italian ambassadors fled Mexico, and Mexican diplomats in those countries returned home. Military officials from the United States traveled to Mexico to assess the risk of an attack against the country's west coast. Along the Arizona-Sonora border, U.S. and Mexican militaries sent soldiers to patrol the Sonoran desert and train at U.S. military installations. The United States allowed Mexican troops to pass through Arizona and California on their way to Baja California, which they defended against any "foolhardy" attempts by Japan to invade Mexico or the United States. Governor Sidney Osborn immediately doubled the number of guards at the Arizona border, sent there to defend water and electric plants, railroad stations, telegraph offices, and other "vital points" in Nogales, Arizona. They had the same mission as Mexican troops, to defend the border against any "act or circumstance" propagated by "Japanese Agents or the Berlin-Rome Axis."[13]

Arizona and Sonora continued to negotiate threats to their cooperation throughout the war, but a spirit of friendship and goodwill overwhelmed episodes of conflict. Labor strikes on both sides of the border temporarily disrupted production and corporate stability, particularly in the mines of Nacozari and Cananea in Sonora. The mayor of Nogales, Sonora, sought to prevent "unruly" American soldiers from entering his city, particularly at night, when they partook in illicit activities. Mexican immigration officials charged American visitors an extralegal fee, or

Mexican soldiers entering Arizona by train. (Arizona Historical Society, Tucson Photo Files, 59441.)

mordida, for goods transported from Mexico to the United States, causing Arizonans and Sonoran businesspeople to decry such behavior as a "vicious and national shame." Finally, American consular officials stationed in Sonora monitored potential subversives and local opinions about the war. They found that some Sonorans remained "passive" or "apathetic," while others maintained anti-American sentiments and worked "in the dark" to support the Axis. However, state leaders, wealthy Sonorans, and most others, they concluded, supported the Allied war effort and formed groups like the "Pan-American Service Club" and the "Municipal Committee for the Fight against Nazi-Fascism."[14]

In addition, U.S. government officials—persuaded by politicians and boosters—settled on the Arizona-Sonora border region as a base of operations because of the area's ideal climate for training pilots and ground troops for desert warfare in North Africa and other theaters of war. Arizona also had abundant resources and labor, and it formed part of the international border with Mexico, a bulwark against invasions from the south. The U.S. military therefore established several bases throughout the Southwest, including Arizona's Davis-Monthan Army Air Field in Tucson (later called Davis-Monthan Air Force Base), Luke Air Field in Phoenix, and the Marana Army Air Field. Another installation, the Desert Training Center/California-Arizona Maneuver Area, covered twenty thousand square miles of southern California and western Arizona and soon became the largest military training center in the world. When General George Patton first surveyed the training area, he called it "the best I have seen." Approximately 17,500 pilots and one million troops from the United States and allied countries trained in Arizona. Because of the state's prominent role in the war, one article claimed, Arizona had a "special share in the results" whenever a "stick of bombs is dropped or an enemy plane is sent spiraling down in flames by America's amazingly accurate young triggermen of the air forces."[15]

Arizona's centrality to national security and to border defense in particular became a key theme of Osborn's correspondence with military personnel and officials. In 1942, Osborn wrote a letter to Lieutenant General John DeWitt, seeking budgetary appropriations for his state. Arizona is "most important" to war production and "defense of the West Coast," he wrote. He cited the state's production of one-third of all copper mined in the United States; crops of long-staple cotton and other agricultural goods; and the roads, railroads, and bridges that facilitated evacuation from the Pacific coast and the distribution of war materials. He also described the threat posed by air attacks, warning that the United States would face dire consequences if warplanes taking off from the Gulf of California—only 150 miles from Phoenix—destroyed one of Arizona's military bases, dams, bridges, or smelters. Implying how Arizona's modernization had led to significant advancement over the past century, Osborn wrote, the state would "revert to desert waste."[16]

Particularly troubling about Mexico's Gulf Coast, Osborn explained, was its remoteness, which enabled enemies to operate freely if left unmonitored. There were "literally hundreds of square miles" of "ideal places" to hide gasoline supplies, bombs, and troops. He therefore recommended construction of a military highway between Arizona and Sonora for the transportation of troops and supplies; improvement of the harbor at Puerto Peñasco; and the deployment of patrol boats that would work with air and ground patrols to protect against a "sneak Jap attack" through

Sonora. In a brief response to Osborn, DeWitt assured him that the military was "not unmindful" of Arizona's "contribution to the war effort" and that the United States and Mexico had already mobilized to address Osborn's concerns by conducting secret military operations south of the border.[17]

Defending Arizona's border became a preoccupation not only for politicians and military strategists but also for numbers of Arizona citizens who formed vigilante groups that would allegedly protect border communities. In 1942, Tucson resident Jack van Ryder informed Osborn of his plan to establish an organization for the "protection of this border." Its members would include "all cowpunchers and ranchers over the military age." During the same year, Albert Shropshire Jr., of Douglas—the border town just across the international line from Agua Prieta, Sonora—wrote to Osborn and Roosevelt to suggest a similar plan. He proposed to call his group the United States Roving Rangers and explained that it would comprise "Western Men" from southern Arizona who aimed to defend "this border of ours" against "the infiltration of undesirable and dangerous aliens." Ignoring their legacy of racial violence, he cited the Arizona Rangers as a model for his group. Osborn responded that he sympathized with their concerns but could not sanction their civilian defense organizations. Only Arizona's state legislature could do that. Nevertheless, Van Ryder's and Shropshire's plans revealed a link between ranchers and border vigilantism, foreshadowing later episodes of conflict.[18]

Instead of vigilante organizations, Arizona's and Sonora's political and military leaders coordinated regional border-defense efforts. Governors Osborn and Anselmo Macías Valenzuela worked together to ensure military preparedness. Shortly after Pearl Harbor, Osborn wrote a letter to Macías, in which he offered to send training pamphlets from Washington, D.C., that contained detailed information about blackouts during air raids and the training of civilians for emergency work. Such "mutual protective efforts" by officials in Nogales, Arizona, and Nogales, Sonora—together called Ambos Nogales—would be "highly desirable," Osborn believed, because such "close cooperation with you and your people" would advance "our mutual desire for solidarity and friendship." Macías responded simply that he "would be pleased" to receive the materials and would forward their instructions to Sonora's highest-ranking military officers.[19]

The U.S. border-defense efforts spread far beyond the border itself, all along Mexico's west coast. Several Mexican governors wrote to their Arizona counterparts to ask for financial assistance. In 1943, on behalf of Governor Rodolfo Loaiza of Sinaloa, Osborn lobbied the American Steel Company for help with the improvement of Sinaloa's radio and telephone communications systems, claiming that these infrastructures were vital to wartime security. Loaiza prompted Osborn to act by explaining that the construction of communications systems between Culiacán, the state capital, and municipalities throughout Sinaloa was an "indispensable necessity" given "the state of war in which we find ourselves." Osborn then wrote the American Steel Company directly, asserting that the "maintenance of efficient communications" between Culiacán and other areas of the state would further the "war effort." Defending Mexico, he suggested, was tantamount to defending the United States.[20]

The interplay among militaries, governments, and businesses on both sides of the border demonstrated how profit—in addition to military necessity—motivated the joint efforts of the United States and Mexico. The two countries entered into treaties designed to secure their economic cooperation and investment in defense, mining, agriculture, and livestock industries. "Top business leaders" in the United States and Mexico formed the Mexican-American Commission for Economic Cooperation (MACEC) to promote Mexico's industrialization and development. The United States also financed Mexican food and health programs, as well as construction, transportation, communications, and public works projects. Direct investments, subsidies, loans, production quotas, guest-worker programs, and other arrangements encouraged the establishment of new businesses. With the support of their governments, chambers of commerce in Arizona and Sonora also clamored for economic development. As a result, industrialists, ranchers, and farmers constructed dams and irrigation canals, raised herds of cattle, and produced cotton, rice, linseed, and sesame, primarily to meet the wartime demands of the United States. These forces combined to transform borderland economies during World War II and beyond.[21]

State officials and publications on both sides of the border described the modernization of the region in terms that were familiar to one another, telling invigorating tales about the World War II era that echoed themes of frontier development, freedom of spirit, and an entrepreneurial way of seeing the world. Tucson transitioned from an Old Western town to a modernized and technologically advanced city through the same hard work that cowboys had applied to taming cattle. "Arizona is rallying to the task of smashing the Axis," one article said, "with the same spirit that the cowpokes formerly displayed in ridding the range of rustlers." Governor Rodríguez similarly described Sonora's progress during World War II. Like pioneer heroes north of the border, Sonorans, too, were "pioneers" who had inherited from their ancestors a "steely composure," an "indomitable character," and a sense of independence that predisposed them to think of "big projects" and to make "strong investments."[22]

Wartime economic policies signaled important turning points for the United States and Mexico. In 1941, President Camacho announced the return of land expropriated during the Cárdenas *sexenio.* Governors Román Yocupicio, Macías, and Rodríguez oversaw this process in Sonora, intending to support the "productive euphoria unleashed by the war." Government officials and banks favored individual landowners over collective *ejido* societies, which had a hard time securing loans. As a result, the ownership of Sonoran land became concentrated in the hands of a small percentage of the state's anti-agrarian business and commercial elite. Sonora's wartime governors comprised a conservative generation of state leaders known not for their role in the Mexican Revolution, as one historian has written, but rather as representatives of the "new agricultural and industrial bourgeoisie." They had been financially successful businesspeople before they were elected to the position. While in office, they supported agriculture and livestock industries, which transformed Sonora and facilitated increased levels of cross-border commercial exchange. One U.S. consular official said that Yocupicio's "point of view" was, fundamentally, "that of a prosperous cattleman" with close ties to U.S. businesspeople.[23]

Economic policies favoring the private development of national and cross-border commerce led to the establishment of businesses that generated profits for each state separately and the region as a whole. The Sonoran port cities of Puerto Peñasco and Guaymas became prime examples of cross-border economic development. Ever since the mid-nineteenth century, U.S. businesspeople had sought access to a port that would help them reach markets around the world. World War II seemed to present an ideal moment to revisit the issue since the development of Sonoran ports would help prevent an attack launched from the Gulf of California. However, they would also provide a spectacular opportunity for the "energetic man" to develop "prosperous" port towns and tourist resorts. Businesspeople suggested leasing the port in Guaymas and establishing a naval academy there, arguing that it would be the perfect "strategic location" between the Panama Canal and other bases along the Pacific Coast. Sonoran officials did not go along with their plan for a military academy, but they were open to the city's economic development by U.S. business interests. Sonora governor Rodríguez invited the California businessman Lucian Small to revamp Sonora's fishing industries. Small bought twelve boats and offered them as credit to fishing cooperatives, which also received support from newly established state-financing agencies. Fishing in turn created hundreds of jobs in packaging, refrigeration, and freezing plants. Sonora put promotional muscle behind the new fishing operations by organizing a fishing festival every spring. Mexican and U.S. businesspeople similarly worked together to develop regional agriculture and ranching industries.[24]

Financiers, growers, and small business owners on both sides of the border therefore benefited most from federal and state economic policies during World War II. The owners and operators of Sonora's factories, construction companies, ranches, and banks became the wealthiest and most influential people in the state. Perhaps no Sonoran gained more than Ignacio Soto. His cement company, Cemento Portland Nacional—established in 1930 with U.S. and Mexican financing—received several million pesos from Mexican and Sonoran governments to build the library and museum at the new Universidad de Sonora, as well as dams and canals that stored water and funneled its flow to Sonora's cities and fields. The government granted his company the land for the construction of a new plant and repaired or replaced machines that produced 350 tons of concrete every day. The company's growth during the war led to mounting profits during the postwar era and solidified Soto's reputation as an international businessman with deep connections in the United States. He was a member of the Chamber of Commerce and Rotary Club International and was an associate of Alex Jácome, the Tucson department store owner. Sonoran newspapers described him as a man representative of his time: dynamic, tenacious, and spiritually and physically strong.[25]

The economic transformation of Arizona and Sonora also reshaped the physical landscape of each state. Construction companies dug canals and built dams, military installations, and food-processing plants. These establishments led to dramatic population redistributions from rural areas to cities, spurring a wave of domestic and international migration into the cities of the Arizona-Sonora borderland. Tucson's urbanization began before World War II as the University of Arizona grew, tuberculosis patients occupied sanitariums, and Mexican American ranchers sold their properties and moved to the city. But the pace of growth increased during the war and would explode in the postwar period. Meanwhile, Sonora's rural areas remained population and economic centers until World War II. Mining, agriculture, and livestock industries were located around Nogales and the Sierra Madre Occidental. However, as federal and state governments developed lands between Hermosillo and the Sea of Cortez, the Mayo and Yaqui Valleys, and Sonoran port cities, Mexicans and native peoples migrated to cities such as Hermosillo, Ciudad Obregón, Puerto Peñasco, and Guaymas. The owners and operators of Sonora's new industries purchased homes in desirable areas like Hermosillo's Colonia Pitic, an expensive neighborhood developed by investors with political ties. Tucson's commercial elite, meanwhile, settled primarily in El Encanto Estates and Colonia Solana.[26]

Highways themselves became manifestations of Arizona's and Sonora's physical transformation. They were symbols of the modernization and progress that, according to politicians and businesspeople on both sides of the border, characterized development during the World War II era. The Pan-American Highway, which initially ran from the Texas-Mexico border to the Panama Canal, was but the grandest example. After the attack on Pearl Harbor, Mexican and U.S. officials argued that the highway facilitated the circulation of troops, arms, and other materials across the Americas. But highways constructed at the local and state levels connected all areas along the U.S.-Mexico border. In Sonora, a U.S. company completed a highway connecting Nogales, Hermosillo, and the fishing port of Guaymas, while smaller roads branching from this larger one linked more remote areas. Like the Pan-American Highway, these Sonoran roads were originally envisioned as part of the wartime defense effort, but they also paved the way for smooth commercial exchanges during and after the war. Winter produce moved from Sonora to Arizona, tourists traveled in both directions, and goods flowed to ports, from which they found their way to markets around the world.[27]

Surely Rodríguez's own experience informed his interpretation of Sonoran character. He rose through the ranks of the Mexican military to become the governor of Baja California, where he invested in hotels, casinos, and fishing industries. Then he served as the interim president of Mexico from 1932 to 1934 and next as the head of a Sonoran economic-development agency. He held that position until he became the governor of Sonora, an office he won, according to one historian, through support from business associates on both sides of the border. World War II was Sonora's moment of frontier development, and Sonoran pioneers like Rodríguez stood ready to profit. But if Rodríguez was a man of great accomplishments, he was not singular in his rise as a prominent businessman and politician who promoted cross-border economic and cultural relationships. He represented a cohort of individuals and organizations that would constitute Arizona's and Sonora's growth machine from World War II forward.[28]

Businesspeople and politicians promoted economic growth on both sides of the border through several institutions. Like their counterparts in Phoenix, the Sunshine Climate Club, the Optimist Club, and the Chamber of Commerce led Tucson's growth machine. Sonoran officials, meanwhile, established the "Pro-Sonora Committee" and *El Imparcial* fed readers throughout the region the government's messages about progress and prosperity. Echoing state politicians, the columnist Enriqueta de Parodi referred to Sonora as Mexico's "state of the future." World War II was a pivotal moment, she argued, when Sonora teetered between a primitive past and a modern future. The transition from one to the other depended on industrial production and Sonora's relationship with the United States. Sonora had everything, Parodi wrote, "vast territory, dormant riches," and "men of vigorous energies." The state's new cadre of business leaders and its proximity to the most powerful country in the world, she concluded, poised Sonora to realize its full economic potential.[29]

To benefit from the state's natural advantages, Sonorans had to dedicate themselves to progress. According to Parodi, Sonorans had to invest in Sonora's future with their "minds, thoughts, and arms":

> With their minds, elevating Sonoran culture, decimating illiteracy, fighting social blots—with their thoughts, making the sight of Sonora's flag signify a powerful state in all aspects, and with their arms seizing every opportunity to develop Sonora's riches.

She and others pointed to the 1942 establishment of la Universidad de Sonora, the spread of electricity throughout the state, and hundreds of miles of newly paved highways as important symbols of Sonora's modernization. The "path of work," she wrote, would "carry us to success." Sonorans and all Mexicans, she hoped, would dedicate themselves to work as farmers, ranchers, and industrialists. President Camacho echoed the sentiment, proclaiming that, rather than on battlefields, "our fight will be waged in the factories and in the fields." The war would stimulate a "new consciousness" that motivated all segments of Sonoran society.[30]

If national and state officials focused on large-scale transformations in agriculture, livestock, and manufacturing industries, local merchants on both sides of the border also capitalized on wartime economies. Sonoran merchants specialized in the trade of goods that were of limited supply in the United States. Many Tucsonans traveled to Sonoran border cities to purchase sugar, meat, shoes, oil, and other rationed items. A Mexican American man from Arizona remembered lining up at the border to buy Mexican gasoline. Gas stations south of the border raised prices, but gas was still cheaper in Mexico than it was on the U.S. black market. Sonorans also bought shoes, clothing, and food in Arizona stores despite their rationing north of the border. As much as 80 percent of all commerce in Nogales, Arizona, was due to "Sonoran buying power." Moreover, because Jácome's department store did not want to lose its Mexican clientele during the war, it often gave Sonorans ration stamps for Levis, shoes, nylons, sheets, and other items instead of reserving them for American shoppers. Whereas the U.S. government tried during the war to place restrictions on cross-border trade, arguing that rationed provisions were to be reserved for the war effort, local merchants and officials maintained that commerce between Arizona and Sonora "constituted an important basis for friendly and cordial relations" and should remain uninterrupted.[31]

The opportunities for cross-border commerce during World War II in fact launched the careers of several merchants and export-import brokers. Mario "Mike" de la Fuente, for example, attended the University of Texas at Austin and worked for Standard Oil in Mexico City before becoming a customs broker and bull-fighting impresario in Nogales, Sonora. In his memoir, *I Like You, Gringo—But!*, he described the profits he reaped during the war. Because "American industry was geared almost completely to producing goods needed for the war effort," he wrote, many Arizonans turned to Mexico for curios, jewelry, liquor, and other goods. He hired two English-speaking salesmen who bought jewelry from southern and central Mexico and then sold it in Arizona and throughout the American Southwest. Small shops and military base exchanges formed his customer base. Buying the goods wholesale, then adding a 40 percent markup plus whatever duties U.S. Customs charged, he earned approximately $15,000 per month during the war.[32]

Meanwhile, U.S. and Mexican politicians, diplomats, and businesspeople rhetorically cultivated international cooperation, friendship, and goodwill. As followers of Roosevelt's Good Neighbor policy, they attended the inauguration ceremonies of their counterparts on the other side of the border. They recognized national holidays that demonstrated their shared love of freedom and held local, cross-border celebrations like "Good Neighbor Day" in Ambos Nogales. In addition, U.S. consular officials in Sonora hosted gatherings with "Mexican citizens as the guests of honor," aiming to "promote friendship and good will between Americans and Mexicans." Through such gestures, Osborn and other U.S. officials also sought to demonstrate their support for Arizonans of Mexican descent. Their efforts paid political dividends, as Mexicans and Mexican Americans from throughout the state wrote appreciative letters that thanked them for their "sincere friendship." Osborn, one letter claimed, had been the "only candidate" to grasp the "spirit of mutual understanding" between Mexicans and Americans. He had earned their votes.[33]

Mexican and U.S. officials and businesspeople during World War II, in La Caverna, a restaurant dug into a hillside in Nogales, Sonora. (Arizona Historical Society, Tucson Photo Files, 59440.)

Communications between diplomats and politicians in Arizona and Sonora followed a script, offering one pleasantry after another. In letters to Mexican journalists, Osborn wrote, "old prejudices and barriers of race and nation are fast disappearing," and "mankind possesses a mutuality of interests that is not confined by national boundaries." Although officials made similar proclamations after the war, during the war they conveyed a heightened sense of solemnity because both countries faced perilous threats. Arizonans and Sonorans no doubt issued proclamations of friendship and goodwill with the best of intentions, yet the wishful and self-congratulatory tone of much official correspondence elided difficult issues, including the racial, economic, and political discrimination that in many ways stemmed from the development of Arizona's and Sonora's Sunbelt borderland. Courtesies like the observance of national holidays and awards for diplomatic service superficially sidestepped frequent reports in newspapers, letters to politicians, and complaints to labor officials of racism, neglect, and other grievances, which, according to one Mexican consular official, were "contrary" to the Good Neighbor policy. Instead of feared enemy aliens, these realities threatened many borderland residents and shaped their experience of the war.[34]

Defending Homelands

While cross-border militarization, economic development, and goodwill diplomacy characterized the international relations of Arizona and Sonora during World War II, these dynamics also affected each state separately. One reporter said that Arizona became an "armed camp." His statement portrayed the state's military buildup and the experience of the war for people of Mexican, Japanese, and native descent on both sides of the border. Members of these communities served the Allied war cause as soldiers, migrant laborers, and defense workers. Discrimination against them despite their service—seeing them as security threats or invoking much older ideas about their racial inferiority—was the height of hypocrisy given the professed war aims of the United States and Mexico, including harmonious inter-American relations. The governments of Arizona and Sonora listened to their grievances but ultimately stood with regional businesspeople. Marginalized communities were forced to defend themselves against injustice.[35]

Local communities on both sides of the border responded to the threat of enemy invasion by militarizing the landscape. In Tucson, armed guards ringed Davis-Monthan Air Force Base. City officials ordered the placement of a barbed-wire fence around the city's main water plant. A local civic organization brought in a graduate from West Point to teach women how to use brooms and shovels in Tucson's defense. University of Arizona dormitories, dining facilities, and athletic fields became barracks, mess halls, and training grounds. In Sonora, Mexican spies bunkered in the border city of Nogales sent reports to Mexico City about potentially threatening Japanese, German, and Italian merchants. They monitored the activities of Japanese fishermen in Guaymas, as Governor Macías himself patrolled the Sonoran coastline in his Buick station wagon, looking out for subversive behavior of all sorts.[36]

Davis-Monthan Air Force Base embodied Tucson's wartime militarization. The base was established during the early twentieth century as a municipal airport, but it served no military purpose until World War II. Heeding the solicitations of the Tucson Chamber of Commerce and other boosters, the U.S. government provided Works Progress Administration funds to convert the airport into an army air force base by adding more than a thousand acres—leased at a dollar per year—and six miles of runways that could accommodate the "heaviest types of bombers in existence or even proposed." According to Washington, Tucson had the "finest 12-months-a-year flying climate in the United States," and the city's proximity to the "international border and the Pacific Coast" also made it an ideal location. After the base expansion, according to one historian, the entire city became a "military-aviation center."[37]

Davis-Monthan grew dramatically after the attack on Pearl Harbor. In 1940 and 1941, only 163 officers and approximately two thousand airmen held posts there. By January 1942, the U.S. military had invested $3 million in a base-expansion program. The result, according to one reporter, was that "pilots, co-pilots, navigators, bombardiers, radio men, aircraft gunners and engineers flocked to Tucson to be molded into war-ready B17 and B24 crews." Within three weeks of the Japanese attack, more than nine thousand army personnel were stationed at the base, including Mexican Americans and African Americans. The military also hired civilians to work as cooks, secretaries, and janitors; they considered their work "satisfying" because it introduced them to "people from different parts of the country . . . and people of different ethnicities." Deactivated only briefly at the end of the war, Davis-Monthan remained an important part of Tucson's social, cultural, political, and economic life into the postwar era.[38]

As the city militarized, Tucsonans developed mixed feelings about the base in their midst. Prominent residents such as Estela Jácome, the wife of department-store owner Alex Jácome, believed that the base had a positive impact on the city. Military personnel and civilians got along wonderfully, she recalled, adding that the arrival of Davis-Monthan was "one of the nicest things that ever happened" to Tucson. Servicemen stationed at the base patronized downtown businesses. Officers mingled with Tucson's middle and upper classes while dancing at the Pioneer Hotel, hosted parties to which they invited community leaders, and held other social events to which they bused the city's single women (and their chaperones) to play cards, bowl, and dance with soldiers. These social events led one soldier to call Davis-Monthan the "country club" of the Air Force. Many servicemen enjoyed their time in the city and settled there permanently, occupying positions with local newspapers, car dealerships, and other businesses. The city government honored Davis-Monthan's top brass—and the military's presence in Tucson more broadly—at the annual rodeo and other community celebrations.[39]

Nonetheless, the increased military presence troubled others, who "did not want the military to be part of our community," as Tucsonan Josie Huerta Herrera put it. Eventually civilians and military personnel "learned to live in peace," yet some remained afraid of servicemen throughout the war years. Herrera cited the rape of a schoolgirl as a particularly troubling incident. Although she offered few details, she likely referred to the highly publicized case of Francis Albert Line, a white soldier from Michigan stationed at Davis-Monthan, who raped a twelve-year-old girl at knifepoint in a Southern Pacific boxcar on August 11, 1942. He was court-martialed and sentenced to death. On March 26, 1943, he was hanged from gallows constructed at Davis-Monthan for his execution. At the end of the war, Herrera recalled, Tucsonans celebrated the Allied victory and hoped that the war's end would relieve tensions between the military and civilians.[40]

Even though the U.S. government claimed that wartime restrictions applied equally to all, minorities suffered the greatest consequences of regional militarization. People of Mexican descent were under siege across the Southwest. Mexican and Mexican American intellectuals, labor leaders, and youth gangs from Los Angeles to El Paso, many Americans believed, were under the influence of totalitarianism or Communism. In accordance with the Good Neighbor era's spirit of nondiscrimination, U.S. officials tried to correct this notion, but many in Arizona had made up their minds: people of Mexican descent constituted a threat.[41]

In response to the potential dangers posed by Mexican border crossers, U.S. authorities substantially increased border enforcement. The U.S. Border Patrol policed the U.S.-Mexico borderlands as never before. The U.S. government required Mexicans who were living in the United States to register with U.S. authorities. Likewise, Mexican officials required the registration of U.S. citizens who were living in their country. Mexicans in the United States had to declare their political activities, the organizations they belonged to, and whether they endorsed the politics of an enemy nation. Mexican Americans who read *El Tucsonense* feared that their activities would be monitored as well since many whites indiscriminately grouped them with Mexicans. Recall the editorial that described how Mexicans and Mexican Americans in the Arizona border city of Nogales became victims of vigilantism even though they were U.S. citizens and had lived in the city for a long time. The FBI rounded up thousands of suspected enemy aliens along the Arizona-Sonora border during the war and more than sixteen hundred in 1940 and 1941 alone. Even as they sought to apprehend potential enemies, officials assured tourists that they would still be able to fish in Guaymas, shop in Nogales, and visit Tucson.[42]

Despite promises that commerce would remain unaffected by the war, border restrictions had negative consequences for Arizona communities that depended on business from Sonora. The Mexicans and Mexican Americans living there suffered as a result. In 1940, the mayor of Nogales, Arizona, wrote a terse telegram to Governor Robert Jones, which read, "U.S. Immigration ruling which will cancel crossing cards for Mexicans living in Nogales Sonora promises to have paralyzing effect on business here as most of our business comes from Mexico." Crossing cards had allowed for the relatively easy passage of Sonorans who shopped, worked, or visited family members in Arizona. By doing away with the cards, the new restrictions temporarily interrupted the discretion of immigration officials to skirt federal laws and sanction border crossings by local residents. They required instead that all Mexicans entering the United States carry passports, which many of them did not have. Passports were expensive, and border-crossing cards had satisfied their need to travel across the international line. Such restrictions led Arizona businesspeople to complain that they violated the "custom, since the settling of this country, for citizens of both countries to exchange trade and seek employment and business enterprise on each side of the border without respect to citizenship or race."[43]

Racism also shaped the experiences of people of Japanese descent in the Arizona-Sonora borderland and throughout the Americas. The Allied struggle for freedom meant little to Japanese in the United States and Mexico, as spies, consular officials, and other government agents closely monitored and imprisoned them. Building on anti-Asian sentiments dating back to the late nineteenth century—which stemmed from the rising perception that Japanese were fierce economic competitors, as well as fears of Japanese imperial ambitions—U.S. and Mexican citizens during World War II saw anyone of Japanese ancestry as a dangerous threat, particularly after Pearl Harbor. Governor Osborn speculated that the Japanese would infiltrate Mexico through Sonora's Gulf Coast. They had carried out such operations in Singapore, Hong Kong, and the Philippines, he claimed, and were more than capable of delivering Sonora and Arizona a "devastating surprise blow . . . from the rear." Alarmingly, Osborn claimed that such operations were already under way. Arizonans who hunted and fished in Puerto Peñasco claimed to have seen Japanese soldiers disguised as tuna fishermen and Japanese engineers developing railroads, harbors, and "drilling operations." Fears of political upheaval and anti-Americanism, rather than the conquest of territory, motivated anti-Japanese agitation not only in the U.S.-Mexico borderlands but also in the Panama Canal Zone and the Caribbean.[44]

In Arizona, following President Roosevelt's Executive Order 9066, the U.S. government established Japanese internment camps at Rivers, Poston, and Leupp, all within a few hours of Tucson. Interns of Japanese descent lived in tarpaper-covered barracks without heating, cooling, or plumbing. The United States also held German and Italian prisoners of war at Florence, Papago Park, and, for a brief period, at Davis-Monthan Air Force Base. Before the war, only four hundred Japanese lived in Arizona, but that number grew to more than thirty-one thousand as a result of their internment. More Japanese were interned in Arizona than in any other state. Recalling the devastation of internment decades after his family's relocation to Poston, Edwin Fujinaka said he wanted to "urinate" on the gravesite of Earl Warren, the former attorney general of California who ordered their removal from Los Angeles. Thousands of Japanese remained in Arizona after their release, farming and operating small businesses; they were freed from internment but still victims of discrimination. Cast as economic threats, the Japanese "farmhand and clerk," Governor Osborn said, would become the "cutthroat competitors of tomorrow." Another Arizonan asserted that a single person of Japanese descent was "worse than a thousand rattlesnakes."[45]

The policing of Japanese communities in Sonora revealed how Mexicans could simultaneously be victims of discrimination on one side of the border and perpetrators on the other. Even though they experienced racism in Arizona, Mexicans, like many white Americans, feared the Japanese and believed them to be working in Mexico as subversives. They cooperated with the United States to jointly persecute Japanese communities in Mexico. Two thousand of five thousand Japanese Mexicans were arrested and, at the request of the U.S. government, sent to internment camps in Texas and New Mexico. Mexico imposed travel restrictions, banned meetings of more than ten Japanese, and froze Japanese bank accounts. By law, Japanese could not live within two hundred kilometers of Mexico's coastlines or one hundred kilometers of Mexico's border with the United States. Mexican authorities therefore vowed to remove them from Sonora and Baja California and to relocate them to Mexico's interior—especially Guadalajara and Mexico City—or deport them from the country. In practice, many managed to stay in their homes by bribing Mexican officials or making use of influential connections.[46]

Many Japanese lived in Sonora for years, married Mexican women, and started families there, yet Governor Rodríguez and other Sonorans had worked for decades to expel them. Following the removal of Japanese ambassadors and intellectuals in the wake of Pearl Harbor, the majority who remained in Mexico were small farmers and merchants. In Sonora, as in Arizona, they lived "in poverty" and did not constitute a threat to Mexico or the United States. Their wives worked as "laundresses," "domestic servants," street vendors, and shopkeepers to support them. Nevertheless, Sonorans praised how their removal led to the reclamation of Mexican land for Mexicans. "Now Mexicans have recovered their lands," one article said, which "affirmed in a decisive manner the nationalization of lands that once were controlled by foreigners." The relocation of Japanese and the repossession of their land marked a significant transition in northwestern Mexico and recalled Sonora's earlier wave of anti-Chinese persecution from the early 1900s through the 1930s. With support from state leaders, Sonorans expelled hundreds of Chinese and took over their businesses. In neighboring Baja California, foreigners—including Chinese, Japanese, and Americans—owned 85 percent of the state's land in the 1930s. By early 1942, that number had plummeted to 5 percent.[47]

Discrimination against Arizona's and Sonora's minority communities, because of their wartime service, struck many as despicable. Nearly half of all males in Arizona served in the war. Among young adults, that percentage was even greater. In total, more than sixteen hundred soldiers from Arizona died in the war, and approximately 240 of them came from the Tucson area. At least 40 percent of Pima County's war dead had Spanish surnames, a proportion greater than their overall representation in the county. Many died at tragically young ages: Reinaldo Urquides was 24 years old, Manuel Olguín was 21, and Ramón Chaparro was 20. Although some individuals of Mexican descent evaded the draft by crossing the border to move in with family members in Sonora, many others entered the war as soldiers. One Mexican American from Tucson recalled how *pachucos*—allegedly rebellious youth identified by their language and style of dress—were rounded up as officials yelled, "All the *pachucos*, let's go." Mexican Americans also served in other ways by collecting rationed goods like rubber bands and scrap metal or buying and selling war bonds. Jácome's Department Store employees, half of whom were Mexican American, proudly announced that they sold five times more war bonds than all other department stores in Tucson combined.[48]

Serving alongside Mexican Americans, African Americans and Native Americans proved themselves to be "good Americans," but they also experienced discrimination. Southeast of Tucson, all of Fort Huachuca's soldiers were African American, whereas all of the base's officers were white. During periods of acute labor shortages, black soldiers were asked to pick cotton, sparking the ire of the National Association for the Advancement of Colored People. Even as members of the military, they could not eat at white-owned restaurants, could swim in public pools only on the day before cleaning, and were required to sit in movie theater balconies, commonly referred to as "the crow's nest." One woman whose husband served at Fort Huachuca believed that such racism revealed how a "few bigots" brought to Arizona the "same ideologies as Hitler, Mussolini, and Tojo." Meanwhile, many Arizonans viewed Native American soldiers with a high degree of sensationalism. Arizona reporters propagated well-worn stereotypes about their warlike character. One article explained how, only a few decades earlier, they had fought bitter struggles against the United States, but now they fought for "Uncle Sam" in his "hour of need." They were "on the warpath once more," but this time in common cause with the United States.[49]

The discrimination they experienced led Arizona's Mexican Americans and Native Americans, in particular, to offer diverse, often conflicting reasons for their service, demonstrating complicated ideas of race and national belonging. Some Mexican Americans said they served because the United States was their country, and they fought for its freedoms and opportunities despite the racism they experienced within its borders. Tucsonan Manuel Herrera Jr., the son of a butcher from Mexico, enlisted because his "country had been wronged." Likewise, a Yaqui named Mariano Tapia fought because America "is my country and I am willing to go to war to defend it because this is where I was born." Tohono O'odham Patrick Franco, however, claimed that he was pressed into service unwillingly. "We didn't want to go into the service, but we had to go," he said. Other O'odham refused to serve as well. Pia Machita, an O'odham leader who called himself a Mexican citizen despite his residence in Arizona, would not permit the O'odham under his authority to enlist in the war. When U.S. agents entered the reservation to arrest him and his followers for draft evasion, a skirmish broke out. Herrera, Tapia, Franco, and Machita did not represent all of the members of their communities, but they articulated diverse attitudes toward patriotism during World War II.[50]

Regardless of their mixed feelings about the war, Mexicans and minority communities in the United States honored their members who served in the military. In Tucson, families and friends lit votive candles at El Tiradito, the wishing shrine, where they prayed for the safety of soldiers. A group of mothers and wives formed La Asociación Hispano-Americana de Madres y Esposas (Hispanic-American Association of Mothers and Wives). They wrote letters, established a recreation center for Mexican American soldiers, and bought and sold war bonds. They also published a newsletter called *Chatter*, which provided the community with information about Mexican American soldiers serving abroad and soldiers with news about happenings back home. Sonoran families also paid tribute to Mexican soldiers by organizing a "Day of the Soldier," during which they invited young servicemen into their homes for a visit. Mexicans greeted soldiers who returned home and arranged ceremonies for those who died in battle, some of whom received Purple Heart medals for having made the "supreme sacrifice." One article in *El Imparcial* called them "defenders of the country, keepers of institutions, and guarantors of society." Finally, O'odham veterans formed a new generation of tribal leadership as they gradually replaced community elders.[51]

Early civil rights organizations also praised the service of Mexican-descent soldiers as part of their strategy to defend them against discrimination. Founded in 1894 by a group of Mexican-descent community leaders, La Alianza originally served as a fraternal insurance organization that offered health and death benefits to its paying members. By the 1930s, however, it had become one of the largest and most significant mutual-aid societies and civil rights organizations in the U.S.-Mexico borderlands, claiming more than twelve thousand members who belonged to lodges on both sides of the border. Throughout World War II, in nearly every issue of its monthly publication, La Alianza spread the news about the decoration of Mexican American soldiers and the wartime bravery of Mexican citizens. One article described how these young men, even though they were "born beyond our borders," have "spilled" their blood for the United States. La Alianza also praised Mexican and Mexican American laborers by explaining how they mobilized and advanced like an "army of productive workers." Finally, the organization hosted dances at its downtown headquarters for Mexican American soldiers stationed at Davis-Monthan. Celebrations of Mexican and Native American soldiers and veterans demonstrated not only how deeply the war permeated family, social, and civic life on both sides of the border but also, by contrast, how insulting and degrading discrimination against them could be.[52]

Because they believed World War II to be a period of progress, federal and state officials claimed to have "never heard" of discrimination against people of Mexican descent even though it was widespread. Economic disparities, housing discrimination, de facto segregation, employment inequalities, and high rates of malnutrition and illiteracy defined reality for Mexican Americans throughout the United States, including Tucson. Until litigation and pressure from the International Union of Mine, Mill, and Smelter Workers (IUMMSW) forced them to end the practice, mining companies encircling Tucson continued the dual-wage system, which paid Mexicans and Mexican Americans less than whites. A Mexican American coworker was still just a "damn Mexican!" Signs hung in restaurants that announced their refusal to serve "Mexicans and Negroes," and only a few Mexican American students enrolled at the University of Arizona. Mexican American women found work at jobs that previously had excluded them, but these low-paying positions held little promise of promotion. Tucson built its first housing project for low-income workers, many of them Mexican American, but a wartime housing crunch gave priority to military and civilian defense workers, preventing them from moving in. Homebuilders and neighbors even sought to bar wealthier families like the Jácomes from moving into El Encanto or Colonia Solana. One Mexican American soldier lamented the persistence of such "un-Americanism" and "narrow-minded" discrimination.[53]

People of Mexican and native descent nevertheless believed that participation in Sunbelt borderland economies was the only way for them to secure better lives for their families on both sides of the border. They pursued jobs on military bases and railroad tracks or in mines, factories, and fields. Southern Arizona's mining industries were located in towns that ringed Tucson, such as Bisbee, Clifton, and Silverbell, while those in Sonora centered in Cananea and smaller towns throughout the Sierra Madre Occidental. Areas of agricultural production in both states also surrounded cities, while railroads and new highways linked rural areas with city depots that processed, consumed, and shipped goods throughout the United States and Mexico and around the world.

Regional publications cited the Arizona-Sonora border region's supply of cheap, racialized labor as one of the best reasons for companies to do business in the area. O'odham from Arizona and Sonora filled Pima County's cotton fields during harvest season and worked as domestics in Tucson homes. More Mexican Americans worked at Consolidated Vultee and the Southern Pacific railroad company than anywhere else. Consolidated Vultee outfitted airplanes to make them war ready. Company employees worked three shifts a day to modify fifty-three hundred B-24 bombers between 1943 and 1945, when the plant closed just a few days after Victory over Japan Day. Of Consolidated Vultee's 3,000–4,000 employees, approximately 25 percent were Mexican American; many of them arrived from Colorado and New Mexico, while others were from Tucson. According to company reports, "minority" laborers could be "found in all parts of the plant," working in the cafeteria, as janitors, or as machinists. Most had never done industrial work before, and some had never worked away from home.[54]

The Southern Pacific railroad—a civilian company that performed vital wartime services, including the transportation of troops and war materiel regionally, nationally, and internationally—also employed many Mexican Americans during World War II. Only twenty years earlier, in 1920, the "SP," as it was known popularly, was the single largest employer of Mexicans and Mexican Americans in Tucson. Twenty-five percent of the city's Mexican male workforce labored there, and during World War II, 65 percent of SP employees were of Mexican descent. Company managers believed that Mexican incompetence and their use of Spanish barred them from skilled track work, and as a result most worked in low-paying, unskilled positions. Labor unions filed grievances on their behalf, but government hearings on "unfair practices in railroad employment" were postponed because of the war. The company never acknowledged discrimination.[55]

Even as Consolidated Vultee and Southern Pacific hired Mexican Americans into low-wage, unskilled positions, the opportunity to work at these companies was still new for women. Like industries across the Southwest—canneries, shipyards, weapons manufacturers, and others—Tucson's railroad and defense operations hired Mexican women to replace men serving in the military or working in new jobs themselves. These positions marked women's entrance into "lower white-collar" positions, where they earned less than men but more than they had earned before. One woman, Lily Valenzuela Liu, was a single mother who worked as a chambermaid at the Santa Rita Hotel and cleaned houses before she accepted a job with the railroad. Jennie Benítez was another single mother who worked for the SP. Donning blue overalls, button-down shirts, steel-toed boots, and caps that hid their long hair, Benítez and Liu maintained trains when they arrived in the station, earning between $50 and $60 every two weeks. The grueling work demanded that they climb precariously balanced ladders while carrying buckets of boiling oil. They also pushed heavy wheelbarrows of sand across the rail yard. After three years, Liu quit when she suffered a hernia at work.[56]

The telegraphers and telephone operators who worked at SP demonstrated the migratory nature of Mexican American labor and the forging of wartime social networks for women. One telegrapher, Juanita Villegas Bernal, recalled how SP hired women "right off the street" during the war. "If you could use a telephone," she said, "they hired you." Born in

Las Cruces, New Mexico, in 1926, Bernal moved during World War II to El Paso, where SP trained women telegraphers. She was only seventeen and had never been away from home. Her father had left her mother with three children, so Bernal wanted to help. While she trained in El Paso, she worked from 6:00 a.m. to 2:00 p.m. at El Minuto Café to pay her bills and send money to her mother. When Bernal got off work, she walked directly to school, where she took classes from 3:00 p.m. to 10:00 p.m. She supported the Allied war effort, but she worked primarily to meet her family's economic needs.[57]

When Bernal completed training, the SP's Tucson Division offered her a job, and over the next several decades she worked for the company in Bosque, Blaisdell, Estrella, Sentinel, Tucson, Yuma, and other cities throughout southern Arizona. Describing how the work required them to move frequently between cities, one former SP employee said, "We would finish one place, then they would send us to another." Especially in the smaller towns, where Bernal worked, she struggled to have a social life. Living alone in an SP boxcar—a common arrangement for an SP employee—Bernal wanted to get on the next train and leave Bosque during her first few days there. However, her situation improved when station foreman Rupert Ruiz and his wife took her into their own boxcar home. Despite the cramped quarters, Bernal enjoyed the companionship. Because many men served in the war, she socialized mainly with other female workers, who became some of her closest friends.

Bernal and other SP employees spent their days off riding to Tucson on passenger trains, which were free to them. They passed the day shopping and rode back in time for work the next day. Many wives of SP employees wanted to live in Tucson, Bernal recalled, so their husbands bought them houses there, worked outside the city, and were "fathers and husbands" only on "weekends." Bernal herself did not live in Tucson until she married Raymond Bernal, an SP employee whom she met while they both worked in Sentinel, Arizona. After they married in July 1945, they moved to Tucson to live with Raymond Bernal's sister. They started a family in the city and spent the rest of their lives there. Bernal worked at SP into the postwar era, but many Mexican American women "resumed their prewar routines" at home or at less remunerative jobs.[58]

Although Bernal migrated within the United States from New Mexico to Texas to Arizona, Mexican migrant workers crossed the international boundary to work near Tucson and across the United States. In 1941, Arizona farmers requested eighteen thousand Mexican laborers to harvest their crops. Rumors of the availability of work caused Sonoran miners to leave their jobs in Cananea and "rush" to Arizona. Soon afterward, Sonorans would cross the border as official participants in the Bracero Program or as undocumented migrants. The majority went to California and Texas, but many worked in Arizona as well. Before they crossed the border, *braceros* were processed at contracting centers in Empalme, Sonora. Because of the economic boom in Sonora and other northern Mexican states caused by the war, many Mexican employers criticized their government for allowing co-nationals to work in the United States when their labor was needed at home. Some Sonoran employers even circumvented the law by intercepting *braceros* and convincing them to work for them before—or instead of—crossing the border. Mexican immigration officials in Sonora exploited the *braceros'* vulnerability and their eagerness to work in the United States by illegally demanding payment from them and, if the workers refused to pay, confiscating their passports, mutilating their immigration permits, and taking saddles from the ranchers among them. One disgruntled Arizona rancher, whose contracted workers were harassed at the border, complained that Mexican officials had been "grafting in this manner for several months," thereby making it "impossible to do needed international business."[59]

A diverse range of Arizonans protested the importation of Mexican guest workers. Under pressure from local citizens, who claimed that *braceros* competed against Americans for jobs, Immigration and Naturalization Service officers in Yuma County rounded up "scores" of Mexicans thought to have entered Arizona illegally. Unions echoed the claim about job competition and added that *braceros* lowered wages for all Arizona workers. For their part, members of the Pima County Board of Supervisors and the Tucson Rotary Club—organizations that simultaneously promoted trade with Mexico—held that Mexicans would create social problems and bring diseases, that counties would have to pay for their medical care, and that U.S. citizens would do agricultural labor if they received more pay in the fields than what they could make working at other jobs. Such organizations demonstrated how some exchanges with Mexicans were acceptable, while others were not. Governor Osborn ultimately sided with Arizona growers who demanded the "immediate opening of the international border" and wrote letters to Carl Hayden, one of Arizona's U.S.

senators, pleading their case. While many Arizonans protested the importation of *braceros*, others supported their presence. Meeting wartime demands, the *braceros* were "making a substantial contribution to our food production program." Their fair treatment therefore supported Arizona's "future friendly relationship with Mexico."[60]

The common compulsion to move in order to pursue better economic opportunities linked the migrations of people of Mexican and native descent on both sides of the border, demonstrating how wartime economies of the Sunbelt borderland pushed working-class people to circulate throughout the region. The Grijalva family, for example, settled in Tucson after years of moving back and forth between Arizona and Sonora. Raúl Grijalva's mother was born in Ajo, Arizona, where her father worked as a miner. But she grew up in Sonora after her father bought a ranch there with money he saved in the United States. She remained a U.S. citizen and eventually moved back to Arizona, where she met and married Grijalva's father. He had immigrated from Sáric, Sonora, to work as a *bracero* on the Canoa Ranch, located between Nogales and Tucson. Many of Arizona's ranch hands left to serve in the military, and *braceros* who had been Mexican cowboys, or *vaqueros*, in Sonora filled the void. Most *bracero* workers in Arizona labored in Maricopa and Yuma counties, farming communities in the central and southwestern parts of the state, but others worked on the cattle ranches surrounding Tucson. They were a good fit because, as Grijalva put it, "the cowboys came from Sonora." After several years working on the ranch, Grijalva's father moved to Tucson to work at a brickyard. He received permanent legal status and spent the rest of his life working in Tucson as a bricklayer, a shovel and pick worker, and a union member.[61]

Labor migrations by the Bernals and the Grijalvas revealed how job opportunities led workers from both sides of the border to settle first in Arizona's rural areas but then move to Tucson—a small part of the story of Arizona's urbanization as a result of the war. Grijalva's father also demonstrated how Mexican migrants, once settled in cities, participated actively in community affairs by joining labor unions and other civic organizations. Finally, they showed how Tucson became an economic core of the Arizona-Sonora borderland, a hub of regional and international exchanges that shaped the city's future. Tucson became a home base, a place to pass through, a point of departure, and a destination.

In fact, cities on both sides of the Arizona-Sonora border, as in other Sunbelt areas, were transformed during the war because several industries sparked their economic and demographic growth. Into the postwar era, they played vital roles as centers of a regional economy that encompassed both states. As Grijalva said of Tucson, the surrounding borderland aided the city's development because communities on both sides of the border were "feeders" for Tucson. The flow also ran in reverse, as Tucson shaped regional cultures, economies, and politics throughout the borderland. Tucson hosted events such as the annual Tucson rodeo and parade, which drew a large local, national, and international audience to celebrate regional ranching cultures. The city also supplied mines, farms, and ranches with food, equipment, and workers. Moreover, Tucson-based radio shows, such as KVOA's *La Hora Mexicana* and programs hosted by disc jockeys Jacinto Orozco, Oscar Stevens, and Ernesto Portillo on KEVT, Tucson's first full time Spanish-language radio station, broadcast throughout the borderland. The city was pivotal in facilitating cross-border commercial and cultural exchange between Arizona and Sonora.[62]

The same was true of Nogales, Hermosillo, Guaymas, and other Sonoran cities, which also developed in relation to the Arizona Sunbelt. Wartime transformations in these places were akin to those north of the border, leading to their rapid growth. Sonoran governors invested in the modernization of cities and argued that economic and demographic transformations were part of their states' broader cultural shifts. Dams collected water that irrigated the fields surrounding Sonoran cities, which, in turn, led to massive profits for construction, cement, and land-speculation businesses. Businesspeople and governments on both sides of the border invested in mining, agriculture, and ranching enterprises that were located elsewhere but ultimately relied on cities to bring their goods to markets around the world. All of these transactions required investors and workers who relocated to cities. The long-term sustainability of these industries depended on educational, social, and cultural opportunities. New office buildings, homes, hotels, museums, schools, distilleries, stores, dams, roads, and factories offered evidence that economic and cultural modernization went hand in hand.[63]

Officials in Arizona and Sonora told themselves and the citizens of their states that growth and modernization depended on racial and class harmony. Governor Osborn said that "racial prejudices and antagonisms" undermined "national unity," so he and other Arizona officials claimed that no discrimination existed in their state. Sonoran intellectuals and officials also knew that harmony was necessary; they, too, downplayed inequalities on their side of the border. During his 1943 campaign, as the gubernatorial candidate supported by the Partido Nacional Revolucionario (National Revolutionary Party, or PNR), which succeeded the PRM, Rodríguez claimed that cattlemen worked alongside cowboys; growers labored in fields; and merchants ran their own shops. He said that Sonora had become one of the most "homogeneous" and democratic of all Mexican states, especially after Japanese removal.[64]

Such rhetoric certainly benefited the politicians and businesspeople driving the economic transformation of Arizona's and Sonora's Sunbelt borderland. For them, World War II was a "golden opportunity." But poor *mestizo* and indigenous communities experienced it differently. They suffered the consequences of the government's economic policies. Even though average salaries increased during the war, the cost of living shot up even higher. Many Sonorans did not have enough food, clothing, and other necessities. While collective *ejidos* constituted 40 percent of Sonora's arable land by the end of the Cárdenas administration, Sonoran governors during World War II scaled them back and granted the land to individual farmers and ranchers instead. Their policies displaced poor communities from their homes in mountains, deserts, and agricultural valleys. O'odham and other native peoples in Sonora tried to resist, refusing to leave their property. But new dams diverted the flow of water from their fields, and raw materials processed in city factories came from lands they once owned. They bought goods that they once had provided for themselves. Thousands of workers struck for better pay and working conditions. Some threatened to take up arms against their government. During World War II, one historian wrote, Mexico "buried" the "promise of social change" for the working poor.[65]

As World War II drew to a close, politicians and businesspeople expressed faith that the postwar era would usher in an extended period of peace and prosperity. An editorial in *El Imparcial* claimed that the border between the two states would become a "touchstone" of "mutual understanding." Artistic, scientific, and literary production on both sides of the border, the editorial suggested, would ensure peace. The histories of the United States and Latin America pointed to their shared destiny. During the war, Governor Osborn wrote, the "living generation" honored the memory of Benito Juárez, Simón Bolívar, and George Washington because of their "steadfast determination and valiant struggles to achieve and preserve human liberty." Given the long history of conflict spanning the nineteenth and early twentieth centuries, such lofty rhetoric was extreme historical revisionism. Nonetheless, it characterized a moment when Arizonans and Sonorans expected the war to positively transform cross-border relations.[66]

In economic terms, businesspeople and politicians in both states believed that wartime developments would lead to great profits in the postwar period. In Sonora, Ignacio Soto claimed that the end of the war pointed to a "most brilliant future for men of initiative and business." More dams would be constructed, agricultural production would continue to increase, and more manufacturing plants would be built. The standard of life for all Sonorans would rise, converting them into modern consumers. The whole state stood at the "threshold of a new era of development, progress, and betterment, as never seen before," he said. Businesspeople in Arizona had reason to be just as optimistic. The number of manufacturing firms in the state had nearly doubled from 300 in 1939 to 550 by 1947. The number of people employed by these firms increased from eight thousand to more than fourteen thousand, and their value to local economies skyrocketed from $32 million to $104 million. Elected officials, chambers of commerce, and branches of the Rotary Club devised plans to build on Arizona's industrial base by recruiting high-tech industries that would reshape its economy for years to come.[67]

The economic development of Arizona and Sonora established a foundation upon which both states continued to build into the postwar era. Defense, agriculture, ranching, and manufacturing industries continued to expand and were largely responsible for the region's growth. Cross-border tourism developed as well. Tourists traveled between Tucson and Guaymas. They partook in La Fiesta de los Vaqueros in Tucson, shopped in the city's department stores, and visited Sonoran border cities and beach towns. In the United States, the Southwest was representative of the nation's postwar growth. In Mexico, economic development along the country's northern border became a crux of the so-called miracle of the mid-twentieth century. However, these national developments were, in fact, a product of cross-border relationships between the United States and Mexico. Both countries developed in relation to one another through the development of a Sunbelt borderland that transcended the borderline itself.

If the postwar Arizona-Sonora borderland seemed to politicians and businesspeople to be full of promise, it circumscribed the lives of many people of Mexican and native descent, who continued to experience economic inequality and social and racial persecution. Given the long history of borderlands conflict, some Sonorans remained wary of the United States, noting the persistence of anti-Mexican racism. During the war, soldiers of Mexican descent had mixed their blood with the "blood of all races and nationalities from freedom-loving countries," an editorial in *El Imparcial* noted. Discrimination against them therefore stood as the "most powerful obstacle" to "friendly, cordial, and reciprocal understanding between our two countries." Wartime necessity and economic opportunity intensified rhetoric about international cooperation, but Mexicans feared that pragmatism and profits motivated the United States, not a commitment to fairness and equality between the two nations.[68]

It would take several decades before the full scope of the war's social, economic, and cultural effects were realized. In Sonora, wartime economic development converted public and communal lands into privately held, large-scale commercial agriculture and livestock operations that displaced thousands of small farmers—many of them from poor *mestizo* and indigenous communities—who then sought work in Arizona's and Sonora's cities. In Tucson, growth, industrialization, and modernization increasingly dominated city politics and economies, with great consequences for people of Mexican and native descent. Some acquired valuable technical skills through their military service, which also opened doors to higher education and home ownership, but most did not receive better treatment as a result of the war. They continued to struggle for equality.[69]

At the outset of the war, the film *Arizona* projected a narrative of Tucson that cast whites as the creative forces in the region, while people of Mexican and native descent were peripheral community members or leaders of their own communities but never leaders of the city as a whole. This narrative found even greater purchase after the war, as business-friendly politicians and organizations like the Chamber of Commerce wielded more and more influence over the city and the region. La Fiesta de los Vaqueros, an annual celebration of regional ranching traditions, became a way for them to lure white settlers and tourists to Tucson and to display their own version of the area's history, one that hewed closely to the white pioneer's tale in *Arizona* and many other stories about the American West. But La Fiesta de los Vaqueros also appealed to Sonoran politicians, businesspeople, and boosters, who saw in the celebration an opportunity to network with their counterparts in Arizona and grow cross-border tourism industries. Ranching had linked Arizona and Sonora for centuries, and the rodeo symbolized an era when ranching dominated regional economies, as well as vibrant cultural and commercial cross-border exchanges. At the same time, La Fiesta de los Vaqueros became for people of Mexican and native descent a way to make sense of their changing circumstances, maintain their community histories, and demonstrate their belonging in the Arizona-Sonora borderland.

2

LA FIESTA DE LOS VAQUEROS

As in other Sunbelt areas, astounding growth defined the transition from World War II to the postwar era in Arizona's and Sonora's Sunbelt borderland. Sustaining the economic development unleashed by the war became a core concern for politicians and businesspeople in both states. With support from federal governments on both sides of the border, manufacturing, tourism, agriculture, and livestock industries expanded dramatically. In the United States, the war marked the beginning of economic, political, and cultural transformations that reshaped the Southwest, while in Mexico, the war signified the beginning of an extended period of growth that shaped Mexican society into the late 1960s. These national histories crossed the border in both directions and were narrated through La Fiesta de los Vaqueros, Tucson's annual rodeo and parade, which took place every February from 1925 forward. After World War II, La Fiesta de los Vaqueros became the single biggest event of Arizona's and Sonora's winter tourism season and fashioned a cultural identity for a city in the process of becoming the center of Arizona's and Sonora's Sunbelt borderland.[1]

Many considered rodeo—the triumph of man over beast—to be the essence of rodeo week, but other events made La Fiesta de los Vaqueros a window into the Arizona-Sonora borderland during the mid-twentieth century. One newspaper article proclaimed, "the rodeo is strictly the cowboy's show." There were "a few special events," but "they are merely the icing on the cake." Like other festivals and celebrations throughout the border region, La Fiesta de los Vaqueros "transcended mere spectacle." Much more than a display of horse and rope tricks, Tucson's rodeo and parade highlighted the cultivation of harmonious international relations as a way of nurturing regional economic development; the intimate ties between transnational business and civic organizations and regional politics; the rise of cross-border tourism; and shifting demographic and racial realities on both sides of the border.[2]

Tucson's rodeo and parade promised to unify Arizona and Sonora through celebrations of borderland horse and cattle cultures, which had shaped the region for centuries. On both sides of the border, early ranchers like Eusebio Francisco Kino, the Jesuit missionary credited with establishing cattle industries in the area, became icons of regional history. The cattle trade was a cornerstone of the area's economy and, after the border between Arizona and Sonora was drawn, became an enduring symbol of cross-border trade. Even as other industries during the twentieth century replaced ranching as main engines of economic growth, Arizona and Sonora still depended on the cattle trade, and cowboys and *vaqueros* endured as symbols of the region's masculinity, independence, and industriousness. As outsiders settled in the Arizona-Sonora border region, many among them—including several conservative businesspeople and politicians—adopted cowboy personae in order to claim oneness with regional culture.[3]

As it had during the war, the rhetoric of the Good Neighbor policy and inter-American solidarity shaped U.S.-Mexico relations into the 1960s and was on full display during rodeo week. With the escalation of Cold War competition, the United States sought Latin American allies to curb the spread of Communism throughout the Americas. Tensions caused by immigration and racism threatened to undermine the U.S.-Mexican alliance. Fears of Communism led many Americans to label people of Mexican descent as potential subversives and also to the deportation of more than a million of them as a consequence of the Internal Security Act of 1950, the Immigration and Nationality Act of 1952, and Operation Wetback in 1954. An increased number of undocumented immigrants led many Arizonans to express unfounded concerns that Mexicans spread disease, depressed wages, and stole jobs from U.S. citizens. Politicians and businesspeople often considered such discriminatory sentiments as obstacles rather than injustices. They believed that their vision of smooth cross-border relationships would prevail over these tensions because, for them, regional economic development was the key to cross-border harmony.[4]

Transnational business and civic organizations with strong political ties to leaders on both sides of the border promoted their vision of postwar development through rodeo celebrations and year-round collaboration on a wide variety of other activities. Tucson's Chamber of Commerce sponsored the rodeo and, as in Phoenix, swayed city politics during the postwar era. Through its association with chambers of commerce on both sides of the border it promoted economic development locally and on a transnational scale. The Tucson Rotary Club joined Rotary International clubs in Sonora to hail the virtues of cross-border investment and trade. Even La Alianza, the Tucson-based mutual-aid society and civil rights organization whose leaders served as cultural brokers between the city's Mexican and white communities, shared with Alianza lodges in Sonora the belief that economic development would lead to the social and cultural advancement of Mexicans in both countries. Businesspeople and politicians like Hermosillo's Ignacio Soto and Tucson's Alex Jácome—either as individuals or through their membership in one or all three of these organizations—capitalized on the postwar spirit of economic exchange and international friendship, in part through the relationships they cultivated at La Fiesta de los Vaqueros.[5]

Cross-border tourism became a mantle of economic and cultural exchange, and for many boosters, businesspeople, and politicians, La Fiesta de los Vaqueros was its centerpiece. Tourists traveling through the Southwest visited Tucson during rodeo week. Some of them continued south into Mexico, passing Mexicans headed in the opposite direction, on their way to Tucson. Automobile road trips from the 1920s forward sparked the development of U.S.-Mexico borderlands tourism, which maintained a significant influence on regional economies into the twenty-first century. In Mexico, tourism formed part of the country's postrevolutionary modernization, as public-private partnerships enhanced roadways and established hotels, restaurants, and stores that catered to visitors. However, borderlands tourism grew exponentially during and after World War II, aided by increased investments in highways and the global conflict itself, which temporarily diminished travel to Europe. Like boosters from California to Texas, those in Arizona and Sonora portrayed their borderland as a region defined by warm weather, leisure, and the romance of the area's indigenous, Spanish, and Mexican cultures.[6]

If La Fiesta de los Vaqueros offered a lens for viewing postwar cross-border relations between Arizona and Sonora, it also shaped and reflected the shifting demographic, racial, and political landscapes of each state separately. From the 1940s onward, the U.S.-Mexico border region was the fastest-growing area of both countries. Staggering economic growth was both cause and effect of the population boom that began during the war years and continued for the remainder of the twentieth century. The vast majority of newcomers to the area settled in cities. Whites and people of Mexican and native descent followed the promise of economic opportunity into the area. Tucson's white population grew faster than the city's Mexican or native communities, which, by 1960, formed barely 20 percent of the city's population. A handful of Mexican American and Native American leaders found inclusion within the inner circles of Tucson's business, political, and social elite. They served on rodeo-planning committees and negotiated relationships between their communities and Tucson's predominantly white leaders. Nonetheless, the vast majority of Mexican and native peoples remained segregated in Tucson's barrios or in the villages of the Tohono O'odham reservation. They continued to work in low-paying jobs and remained some of the state's most marginalized citizens. Postwar economies had devastating consequences for poor people in Sonora as well. Sonoran governors promoted large-scale industrial development that was, by and large, incompatible with the aims and capabilities of collective *ejidal* societies. As a result, members of poor *mestizo* and indigenous communities were forced to leave their land to find wage work in cities on both sides of the border. La Fiesta de los Vaqueros celebrations deemphasized these postwar disparities and instead highlighted the horse and cattle cultures that brought binational communities together. While ranch work entailed its own divisions and hierarchies, the shared romance of ranching traditions superficially united Arizonans and Sonorans of all backgrounds for one week every year.[7]

Participation by people of Mexican and indigenous descent in the events of rodeo week therefore revealed the paradox of La Fiesta de los Vaqueros: at the same time that they affirmed the language of regional togetherness, they also displayed the city's inequalities during the mid-twentieth century. In fact, regional growth required projects like La Fiesta de los Vaqueros, which event sponsors used to shape how new Tucsonans and tourists understood the area's ethnic and racial diversity. According to rodeo planners, Tucson had been a sleepy Mexican town plagued by Indian raids that hampered its economic development until entrepreneurial white settlers during the late nineteenth century introduced railroads, mines, and industrialized ranching and agriculture. Mexican Americans and some Native Americans were friends and neighbors, but they were not city leaders. Considering such racial hierarchies, their participation in

La Fiesta de los Vaqueros reasserted their role in the creation of regional history and their continued influence on Tucson's traditions.[8]

Cowboys, Capitalists, and Good Neighbors

La Fiesta de los Vaqueros celebrations offered a glimpse of the interplay between Tucson's changing domestic landscape and relations between Arizona and Sonora. At the same time that the rodeo provided a cultural identity for a rapidly growing city in the American Southwest—one that was based on exceptional myths about cowboys and westward expansion—it gestured toward unity with Sonora through celebrations of the ranching traditions that were critical to the development of borderland histories and economies. For Arizona's and Sonora's politicians and businesspeople, rodeo events offered an opportunity to solidify these historical and commercial relationships and to promote emerging tourism industries that joined defense, manufacturing, ranching, and agriculture as another engine of regional growth. Rodeo events also became a form of diplomacy, as Good Neighbor rhetoric filled Tucson's air during rodeo week. In the context of postwar U.S.-Mexico relations, which increasingly focused on the containment of Communism, boosters hoped that friendly gatherings of Arizonans and Sonorans would help unify the region in the name of free enterprise and increased understanding between the two countries.

La Fiesta de los Vaqueros began in 1925 but remained a minor event until the postwar era, when it eclipsed all of Tucson's other gatherings and celebrations in size and significance. Businessman and Pennsylvania native Leighton Kramer received credit for founding the event. Like many settlers in Tucson, he first visited the city to seek a cure for respiratory illness. As president of the Arizona Polo Association and member of Tucson's Chamber of Commerce, Kramer planned La Fiesta de Los Vaqueros as a fundraiser to send the University of Arizona's polo team east for a match against Princeton. In 1924, he hosted a luncheon to pitch his idea to a group of local businesspeople, including Chamber of Commerce officers, a car dealer, a newspaper reporter, and cattlemen Jack Kinney and Bud Parker. Tucson held its first rodeo the next year.[9]

Kramer's luncheon demonstrated how La Fiesta de los Vaqueros, from its inception, linked culture and business in the Arizona-Sonora borderland. He and his associates saw it as a chance to entice winter visitors—Tucson's snowbirds—to nest in southern Arizona. The city, they believed, should capitalize on its unique culture, picturesque mountains, saguaro cacti, dude-ranch lifestyle, and year-round sunshine. A brief history of Tucson's rodeo made plain the event's profit-driven motivations by offering on almost every page a summary of how much the Chamber of Commerce spent and earned. An emphasis on the bottom line may have been an important consideration for businesspeople and boosters, but it was a failing formula for encouraging popular participation in rodeo celebrations. For that purpose, sponsors needed an event that highlighted the city's relation to regional traditions.[10]

To make La Fiesta de los Vaqueros seem authentic and organic to the Arizona-Sonora borderland, boosters crafted an origin story that downplayed Kramer's part while highlighting the role of local cattlemen. Newspapers reported that Kramer's eastern roots stripped the event of its authenticity. "This'll take the starch out of your Levi's," one wrote, bracing his readers for what followed: "La Fiesta de los Vaqueros, Tucson's most western event—and just maybe the last thing left to yippie-ti-yi-yo about in this town—was started by a polo-playing Eastern industrialist." The new tale spun by Kramer and the Chamber of Commerce held that three amigos—Kramer and cattlemen Ed Echols and Kinney—sung the rodeo's first notes while sitting on a corral fencepost at Echols's ranch. The scene proved perfect: two longtime cowboys and a booster with money and business connections inventing a tradition that tapped simultaneously into the border region's horse and cattle cultures and the area's potential for economic growth.[11]

The new story inserted cattlemen into the foundational moment of an event essentially about business, but it ignored the influence of Mexican traditions altogether. Rodeo-like events were held in Jalisco, Mexico, during the early Spanish colonial period. The first rodeo in the United States was held centuries later. Some say rodeo began in Santa Fe, Mexico, in the early 1840s, before that city became part of New Mexico. Others say it began in Prescott, Arizona, in 1888. All agree that Spanish and Mexican ranchers shaped the sport. Even the name "rodeo" derived from the Spanish verb *rodear,* to "round up." Other words from the white cowboy vernacular have roots in Mexican ranch work as well, including buckaroo *(vaquero),* lariat *(la reata),* chaps *(chaparreras),* and dally *(dar la vuelta).* Mexican *vaqueros* competed informally during the eighteenth century, and when they introduced white ranchers to their trade during the nineteenth century, these cowboys began to compete as well. By the early twentieth century, Mexican and white horsemen on both sides of the border feared the passing of their traditions, so they established professional organizations for rodeo and *charrería*, the Mexican sport from which U.S. rodeo was derived. The Mexican Federation of Charros was established in 1933 and set up headquarters in Mexico City to govern local *charro* associations across the country. North of the border, the Cowboys' Turtle Association was established in 1936, after which affiliated organizations formed throughout the United States.[12]

By the time that *charrería* and rodeo associations were established, Mexican and white ranchers in the Arizona-Sonora borderland had worked alongside one another for decades, and cattle ranching had shaped the area for hundreds of years. Francisco Vásquez de Coronado first brought cattle into the Pimería Alta during the 1540s in order to provision his expedition's search for the legendary Seven Cities of Cíbola, which Spanish colonizers believed were filled with riches. During the next century, cattle spread from the Gulf of Mexico near Veracruz to El Bajío in Central Mexico and then to Chihuahua's Mesa del Norte and the Pacific Coast. Regularly managed herds became a part of the region's political economy only during the 1690s, after the arrival of the Jesuit missionary Eusebio Francisco Kino. Spaniards and their mixed-race followers brought hundreds of thousands of cattle into the area. They distributed many of the animals to native communities, thereby establishing not only patterns of dependence that often resulted in the religious conversion of indigenous peoples but also communities of indigenous cattlemen who bred animals and owned or worked on ranches from the Spanish colonial period forward. During the eighteenth and nineteenth centuries, borderland residents raised herds despite the revolts and raids that, according to most historians, impeded the development of large-scale commercial ranching until decades after the Gadsden Purchase.[13]

During the late nineteenth century and beyond, cattle ranching became as much a business as a way of life and entailed class divisions like other big industries in the area. In Arizona, cowboys had little upward mobility and rarely became landowners. In Sonora, *vaqueros* and other ranch hands lived "very poorly, in adobe huts with dirt floors," while bosses and foremen were given "better-than-usual" accommodations. Land speculators and government bureaucrats on both sides of the border consolidated small ranches, in part through the dispossession of Mexican and native landholders. They introduced more durable breeds to the area's desert grasslands and developed trade networks with Texas, California, and, of course, northern Mexico. Finally, they managed boom-and-bust cycles caused by unpredictable weather patterns, fluctuating global economies, the threat of cattle-borne illnesses, and the degradation and recovery of ranges. The global economic crisis of the 1930s crippled ranchers who relied on international markets, requiring massive federal subsidies and other forms of support. Regional cattle markets again boomed, and Sonoran exports to Arizona increased as a result of wartime demands but crashed in 1947 following the outbreak of foot-and-mouth disease, or *fiebre aftosa*.[14]

Even though the disease did not travel as far north as Sonora, the United States halted all cattle imports from Mexico, painfully reminding Sonorans of their ongoing dependence on U.S. markets. The ban caused a surplus of livestock that competed for scarce resources. Without enough water to drink or pasture to graze, thousands of animals were slaughtered, canned, and refrigerated at the new Frígorifica y Empacadora de Sonora, a meatpacking and refrigeration plant in Hermosillo built as a solution to the crisis. The *fiebre aftosa* also shaped broader debates, leading to calls for the construction of a border fence even though birds carrying the disease could easily fly over such barriers. Seeing it as an impediment to the flow of people that would damage international relations, Mexicans and Americans alike called the proposed fence a "repulsive" symbol of "division." They echoed Good Neighbor rhetoric, arguing that the United States and Mexico, "today more than ever," were "friends and good neighbors." In the end, the panic only temporarily hampered the cross-border cattle trade, and by the 1950s hundreds of thousands of cattle crossed yearly from Sonora to Arizona.[15]

Despite the resurgence of the cattle trade, the episode urged Sonorans to develop domestic protections and international markets beyond the United States. In addition to refrigeration and meatpacking plants that could store and can beef in the event of a market downturn, the Sonoran government relied on the Unión Ganadera Regional de Sonora (Sonoran Regional Livestock Union), an organization headquartered in Nogales—the core of the state's cattle-ranching industries—to lobby for the domestic and international interests of ranchers. Still, Sonoran ranchers depended on exports and therefore maintained close cross-border relationships.

Sonoran ranchers and officials attended conventions in Arizona, and vice versa. Conventions in Sonora featured an "Arizona Day," which highlighted these transnational relationships. When exports to Arizona waned, Sonoran ranchers sent their cattle to Mexico City and other Latin American countries. By and large, however, Sonoran cattle economies depended on U.S. markets into the late twentieth century even though ranching represented a decreasing proportion of regional economic activity as a whole.[16]

The state of Arizona, according to one historian, experienced its "most explosive decade of growth" during the 1950s, as economic development focused less on agricultural and livestock production and more on manufacturing and high-tech industries. Despite Democratic Party and union opposition to business-friendly policies like Arizona's 1946 right-to-work law, which dealt a severe blow to the ability of labor unions to organize workers anywhere but in mining towns, politicians in both parties and at all levels of government—city, county, and state—invested in the rhetoric of growth and modernization. With the help of local chambers of commerce, they attracted the Goodyear Aircraft Company, Sperry Rand, and Motorola to Phoenix and the Howard Hughes Aircraft Company to Tucson. Hughes had a payroll of more than $10 million per year, mining income leapt from $11.5 million in 1940 to $50 million by the late 1950s, and, because of Davis-Monthan, Tucson's annual military payroll shot up from $5,000 to $30 million between 1940 and 1954. New and expanded industries created thousands of jobs and pumped hundreds of millions of dollars into regional economies, leading to a rise in spending on homes, groceries, clothes, and other goods.[17]

In Sonora, the period between 1940 and 1955 was the "golden age" of agricultural production and a time of great economic growth in general. Oil production increased off the coast of Guaymas, cattle breeding continued apace, and more areas of the state received paved highways and new schools. But no industry transformed Sonora more than agriculture. Like ranching, agriculture was geared toward markets across the border and paralleled agriculture's relative decline in Arizona. Mexico's national and state governments consolidated landholdings and supported independent, individual farmers instead of collective *ejidos*, primarily through credit, subsidies, and grants of land. Five dams were constructed between 1942 and 1955, providing electricity and irrigating hundreds of thousands of hectares of land throughout the state. These developments benefited prominent Sonoran companies and individuals, including Cemento Portland Nacional, the Frígorifica y Empacadora de Sonora, and Hermosillo retailers such as the Mazón brothers. Together they received thousands of hectares of irrigated land, demonstrating the increasingly close links between business and government in Sonora. Growers, industrialists, and financiers headed state agencies and Sonoran chambers of commerce, cultivating trade partnerships in the United States. Ties between business and government became even more intimate through the intermarriage of prominent Sonoran families during the late 1940s. In the decade after the war, agricultural output in Sonora more than tripled. Economic centers shifted from the mineral-producing regions of the Sierra Madre Occidental to the agriculturally rich valleys and coastlines, where one-third of Sonora's population, 75 percent of manufacturing businesses, and 90 percent of crop values were located. The state's wealthiest and most powerful landowners relocated there, constituting a growing Sonoran business class with a taste for American fashion and music.[18]

Even though the economies of Arizona and Sonora relied less and less on ranching during the mid-twentieth century, cattle cultures and cowboys themselves remained an important part of the region's cultural identity. Businesspeople during the mid-twentieth century saw themselves as akin to the ranchers of yesteryear, claiming that they, like cattlemen, were the bringers of progress and modernization. Even the religious figure Kino was described as equal parts businessman and missionary. The borderlands historian Herbert Eugene Bolton, in his book about Kino, called *The Padre on Horseback*, wrote, "The work which Father Kino did as a ranchman" made him the "cattle king of his day and region." The languages and histories of Arizona's and Sonora's horse and cattle cultures therefore were translated into ideas about postwar economic development, suggesting how La Fiesta de los Vaqueros was both a lament for a bygone era and a tribute to its latter-day manifestations.[19]

Arizonans and Sonorans therefore reinforced cultural and commercial ties by celebrating regional ranching traditions. Good Neighbor rhetoric became the driving force behind the rodeo's transnational elements. In the name of goodwill, politicians and businesspeople mediated conflict, provided humanitarian aid, and requested concessions from their counterparts across the border. Osborn scolded an Arizona importer who refused to pay a Mexican grower for tomatoes, claiming that such negligence threatened Arizona's and Mexico's "friendly and amicable relations." Ignacio Soto praised the "Good Neighbor principles" of farmers on both sides of the border who shared information and technology. A Sonoran official asked Arizona to lower fees for Mexican children who attended school in the United States; his request was part of the "Good Neighbor" effort, he argued, because "ties of friendship" first formed in school. Then, after a disastrous flood in Sonora, Arizonans helped with relief efforts. The state's Mexican American community, in particular, made a "spontaneous" show of support, driving car- and truckloads of goods to the border. Governor Horacio Sobarzo thanked Arizona, and the head of the Comité Pro-Damnificados del Mayo, a Sonoran committee that supported flood victims, said that the donation efforts "cemented good relations" between the United States and Mexico.[20]

If the Good Neighbor policy shaped U.S.-Mexico relations, drug trafficking and immigration threatened to cause tensions between the two countries. Government officials on both sides of the border monitored the production and sale of marijuana, opium, and heroin, as well as drug-related arrests along Mexico's west coast. They also debated increased crossings by Mexican laborers. Arizona employers accustomed to the supply of *braceros* argued for their continued importation after the war, citing work shortages caused by the return of veterans who had received training for industrial and technical jobs. Many Sonorans resisted the guest-worker program because Mexico's economic boom required workers to stay home. Nevertheless, Arizonans persisted, claiming that they intended to recruit only Sonorans "who may be unemployed." They argued that Sonora's cooperation would reaffirm Good Neighbor relations.[21]

The appeal of jobs in the United States was more powerful than Mexican efforts to keep *braceros* at home, luring Mexican workers to the border region and Sonoran recruitment centers. As during the war years, fraud delayed their journey or ended it entirely. Unscrupulous Sonoran officials and employers lied to the migrants and demanded a fee in exchange for the required paperwork. Most migrants did not have the money, so they worked in Sonora's fields to raise it. Many ended up broke and never made it to the United States, often assembling at the Governor's Palace to seek redress. Sonoran governors rebuked Mexicans who duped *braceros* and compelled officials to distribute thousands of fliers that warned workers about the scam, but ultimately they sent the *braceros* back to the recruitment centers. For these migrant laborers, their encounter with the

Bracero Program ended before it began and left them worse off than when they left home.[22]

Even when migrant workers made it to Arizona, the experience was more difficult than they imagined. Perhaps they did not encounter the "bloodthirsty dogs" that Sonoran newspapers said awaited them on the other side of the border, but neither did they find fair wages or decent housing. Labor unions and individual farm workers protested the importation of Mexican guest workers. These critics, including many Mexican Americans, claimed that migrants stole their jobs and, because they were willing to work for so little, threatened their "living standards." More disparaging critics added that migrants spread disease, committed crime, and lived on charity. Employers, however, insisted that they were unable to find American workers and that they paid Mexican laborers the same wages they paid U.S. citizens. Arizona governors supported their claims, arguing that Mexican guest workers were vital to the success of Arizona's agriculture industries. Tensions caused by Mexican immigration and drug smuggling increased in the late twentieth century, but into the late 1960s borderlands politicians focused obsessively on growth, modernization, and international harmony.[23]

Because immigration and racism threatened to undermine Cold War relations between the United States and Mexico, acts and expressions of goodwill had broad international and domestic significance. North American independence holidays, for example, became anti-Communist celebrations. Cinco de Mayo, Governor Dan Garvey claimed, signaled Mexico's love of liberty and a "firm determination" to maintain "democratic institutions." Likewise, Fourth of July celebrations, Soto said, recognized struggles by the "Americas and other democratic countries" against "totalitarian regimes." In Arizona, celebrations of U.S. and Mexican holidays also sought to convince Mexicans and Mexican Americans in the United States of the country's antidiscriminatory values and therefore to reinforce state authority against Communist influence. For this reason, governors and other state representatives, such as Phoenix city councilman Barry Goldwater, spoke at Mexican Independence Day celebrations in Tucson and throughout the state, where they expressed a "tremendous debt of gratitude" to "our citizens of Spanish-speaking origin."[24]

The desire for smooth U.S.-Mexico relations also justified the profit motives of entrepreneurs in Arizona and Sonora, who deployed Good Neighbor rhetoric when they collaborated with fellow "captains of finance" on the other side of the border. After the war, Mexican growers shipped bigger and bigger loads of shrimp, fruits, and vegetables to Arizona, and entrepreneurs in Tucson lobbied for their city to become a storage and distribution center for Mexican produce. When businesspersons advocated for cross-border commercial exchanges, they claimed to serve broader political aims. Tucson entrepreneurs hatched plans that simultaneously would make them money and "cement, strengthen and perpetuate good relations" between the United States and Mexico. Theirs was not an "out-and-out commercial proposition" but rather one that was "principally designed to bring about better understanding between the peoples of the two countries." The same held true for cross-border dealings by Rotary Club, Chamber of Commerce, and Lion's Club members, as well as university administrators, newspaper executives, and tourism boosters. They all crossed the border as "ambassadors" who promoted international "goodwill" as a path toward cross-border economic exchange.[25]

When Governor Howard Pyle wrote, then, that La Fiesta de los Vaqueros was "designed for the purpose of promoting goodwill between our two great countries," he referenced the multiple meanings of Good Neighbor relations in the postwar era. The Rodeo Committee enshrined Good Neighbor relations as an important part of rodeo celebrations through Good Neighbor Day, also called Mexico Day or International Day. Politicians and businesspeople from Arizona and Sonora also used Good Neighbor relations as their pretense to network at the rodeo. Sonoran governors, municipal presidents, treasurers, secretaries, and tourism officials all attended. Governor Soto met there with Governor Pyle to discuss interstate affairs. Gonzalo Guerrero Almada, the municipal president of Nogales and member of the Rotary Club, proclaimed that the "innumerable attentions" he received while at the rodeo gave him "complete assurance" that "goodwill and friendship" would lead to "better international comprehension." From horse-drawn buggies, these guests and their families smiled and waved at throngs of paradegoers, all in the name of Good Neighbor relations.[26]

Chambers of commerce, branches of the Rotary Club, and La Alianza lodges in Arizona and Sonora, in particular, promoted Good Neighbor relations through La Fiesta de los Vaqueros. Chamber of Commerce members from Arizona traveled to Hermosillo, where Sonoran chambers of commerce held banquets in their honor and took them on tours of the state's dams, ranches, and warehouses. Arizona's chambers of commerce

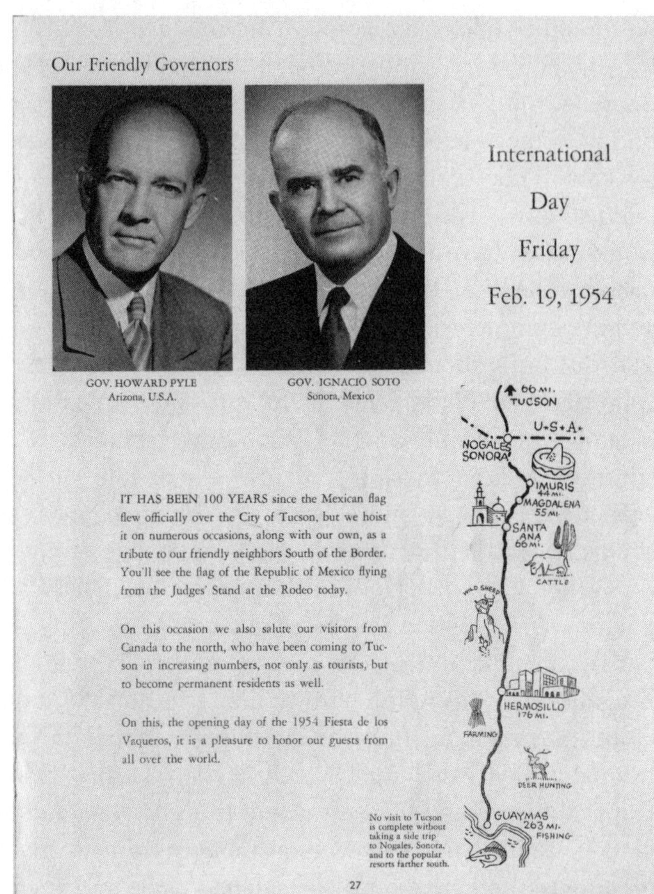

Our Friendly Governors

GOV. HOWARD PYLE
Arizona, U.S.A.

GOV. IGNACIO SOTO
Sonora, Mexico

International

Day

Friday

Feb. 19, 1954

IT HAS BEEN 100 YEARS since the Mexican flag flew officially over the City of Tucson, but we hoist it on numerous occasions, along with our own, as a tribute to our friendly neighbors South of the Border. You'll see the flag of the Republic of Mexico flying from the Judges' Stand at the Rodeo today.

On this occasion we also salute our visitors from Canada to the north, who have been coming to Tucson in increasing numbers, not only as tourists, but to become permanent residents as well.

On this, the opening day of the 1954 Fiesta de los Vaqueros, it is a pleasure to honor our guests from all over the world.

No visit to Tucson is complete without taking a side trip to Nogales, Sonora, and to the popular resorts farther south.

27

"International Day" at La Fiesta de los Vaqueros, 1954. (Arizona Historical Society, Tucson Ephemera Files, La Fiesta de los Vaqueros.)

returned the favor when Sonorans traveled to their state. They hosted dinners at Tucson's Pioneer Hotel and showed them some of the state's factories and fertilizer- and insecticide-distribution centers. Moreover, chambers of commerce enjoyed close relationships with the political leadership of both states. Governors attended Chamber of Commerce events, delivered speeches at their meetings, and traveled to their international gatherings. Many state leaders had themselves been Chamber of Commerce executives before they held office; the business relationships they formed through organizational activities had, in fact, facilitated their rise as politicians. Ignacio Soto, for example, had founded the Nogales, Sonora, Chamber of Commerce before he became the head of Cemento Portland Nacional and then governor of Sonora. When Chamber of Commerce members from both sides of the border gathered at La Fiesta de los Vaqueros, they promoted cross-border business relationships, as they had for decades.[27]

In addition to chambers of commerce, Rotary Club branches also cultivated cross-border business relationships. Rotary clubs in Arizona and Sonora claimed philanthropic service as their main objective. The Rotary Club in Hermosillo raised money for flood victims, established fellowships for Sonorans to study in the United States, and founded organizations like the Casa Hogar del Niño Pobre, a children's home in Sonora. In a speech to a gathering of Sonoran Rotarians, Governor Soto—a founding member of the Nogales, Sonora, Rotary Club—called on all members to continue their good works and to commit themselves to the "progress of their communities." But Rotary Club rosters also were filled with "distinguished businessmen" from both sides of the border. Their mutual interest in the profits to be earned through cross-border economic development had brought them together. Arizona Rotarians visited Sonora, where Sonoran Rotarians hosted them, took them to the state's "principal industrial centers," fed them "Sonoran-style food," held golf tournaments that matched locals against visitors, and organized fashion shows to introduce them to regional clothing from Sonora and other Mexican states. Sonoran Rotarians received the same treatment when they visited Arizona. Like chambers of commerce, Rotary Club branches were also deeply connected to the political leadership of both states. After Governor Soto spoke at a fiftieth-anniversary celebration of Rotary International in Nogales, Sonora, he headed straight to Tucson to celebrate La Fiesta de los Vaqueros. There he joined other Rotarians, whose business connections formed the basis for their friendship as they participated in the events of rodeo week.[28]

La Alianza in Arizona and Sonora rounded out the efforts of organizations to nurture cross-border relationships through La Fiesta de los Vaqueros. From one lodge in Tucson, La Alianza grew during the early twentieth century into a regional mutual-aid society with lodges in Arizona, California, Texas, New Mexico, and Colorado. During the 1920s and 1930s, the group became an international organization with chapters in Chihuahua, Sonora, and Mexico City. By the 1940s La Alianza had become Tucson's leading Mexican American mutual-aid society, one of the largest Mexican American societies in the United States, and one of the few to establish partner lodges in Mexico. Considering La Alianza's 12,500 members in hundreds of lodges throughout the Southwest and

Alex and Estela Jácome at 1947 rodeo party hosted by the Rotary Club. (Estela Jácome personal collection.)

northern Mexico, the organization has received surprisingly little attention despite the fact that it shaped Mexican American politics in Tucson and beyond. According to its own history, penned in the 1953 La Fiesta de los Vaqueros edition of *La Alianza*, La Alianza had become "the greatest society for the Spanish-speaking people."[29]

The connections that lodges in Arizona and Sonora formed with each other distinguished them from other mutual-aid societies, which tended to engage in political and economic activities on only one side of the border. From La Alianza's earliest years, the organization emphasized the unity of Mexicans and Mexican Americans in both countries. Many of the group's founders had moved from Sonora to Tucson after the

Gadsden Purchase. Several of its leaders were Sonorans who had settled in Arizona during the Mexican Revolution. To honor the relationships La Alianza forged with partner lodges throughout Sonora, the organization celebrated the national holidays of both countries and offered history lessons about the Mexican flag, the indigenous hero of Mexican independence, Vicente Guerrero, and former Mexican president Benito Juárez. Its monthly magazine also featured a column called "News from Mexico," which promoted fraternity with "our Good Neighbor to the south." In 1955 the group moved beyond binationalism by adopting a Cold War–inspired platform of Pan-Americanism, which preached hemispheric unity against Communism. La Alianza Hispano-Americana Internacional—the international conglomeration of La Alianza lodges—would "encompass the United States, Mexico, and all of the republics of Central and South America." This new offshoot, the group vowed, would unite and protect "through fraternalism the Spanish-speaking peoples of this continent."[30]

La Alianza lodges became some of the region's most active civic organizations with ties to business and political leaders in both states. During its gatherings at La Alianza headquarters in Tucson or at the "Alianza casino" in Hermosillo, the organization collected clothing and food to donate to flood victims, raised funds for campaigns against tuberculosis, and collected books and magazines to add to its library. Like chambers of commerce and branches of the Rotary Club, La Alianza lodges were connected to regional business and political leaders. Only Sonora's "most distinguished" families attended La Alianza functions. The governors of both states supported the group and frequently spoke at its events. Anticipating the central role La Alianza would play in Hermosillo, the organization constructed a new building in the city to host meetings and dances, which *El Imparcial* described as "elegant, spacious, modern, and comfortable." Demonstrating the regional influence of La Alianza and how state officials considered *aliancistas* to be men of importance, members from Arizona who attended a group celebration in Sonora—in 1953, shortly after the passage of the restrictive McCarran-Walter Act, no less—had only to flash an Alianza membership card when they reentered the United States at the event's conclusion, with "no other requirement from American immigration." Their easy crossings again showed how federal immigration laws could bend to accommodate local transnational relationships.[31]

La Alianza's internationalism carried over to the organization's approach to La Fiesta de los Vaqueros. During rodeo week, the Tucson

Chamber of Commerce and other rodeo sponsors relied on *aliancistas* to negotiate the city's relationships with Sonora. La Alianza leaders rallied their membership to the cause by praising the rodeo's implicit acknowledgment of Tucson's Mexican heritage. They emphasized that the governors of Sonora and Arizona rode together in one carriage; highlighted Mexico Day (or Good Neighbor Day); and noted that the "Tucson rodeo is the only event of its kind with a distinct Spanish and Indian flavor." During rodeo week, the organization hosted banquets for Sonoran governors and chaperoned visits south of the border by tourists who traveled to Tucson to attend La Fiesta de los Vaqueros.[32]

To be sure, boosters planned celebrations like La Fiesta de los Vaqueros to increase domestic tourism. From the 1920s forward, they sold Tucson as the "Old Pueblo," a city with a unique and multicultural past and present. They sent Los Carlistas—the band led by Eduardo "Lalo" Guerrero, a Mexican American musician from Tucson who became a star after he moved to Los Angeles—to the 1939 World Fair in New York to promote Tucson through music. Guerrero's father had worked in Sonoran shipyards before he moved the family to Tucson, where he took a job with the Southern Pacific. As a teenager in Tucson, Lalo Guerrero joined car clubs and learned to speak *caló*, the dialect of *pachucos*. His own family therefore reflected the experiences of many Mexicans and Mexican Americans in Arizona, influencing his songs, which combined older Mexican styles with newer American ones. Guerrero's songs helped tourists imagine the world they would enter when they traveled to Tucson to attend rodeo week events.[33]

Even more broadly, however, boosters in Tucson worked with their Sonoran counterparts to develop cross-border tourism, an alluring side attraction of La Fiesta de los Vaqueros. Sonorans established a state tourism bureau in the 1930s and placed Ignacio Soto at its head. One U.S. consular official believed that Soto was "eminently suited for the position in view of his friendship for Americans and his excellent spoken English." Officials and boosters in both states then used Europe's devastation to generate regional profits. Governor Osborn remarked that, before the war, U.S. tourists had the "European travel habit," but after it ended, as Europe and Asia faced reconstruction, there was "no doubt" that the "majority" of them would visit the American West and Mexico. In Sonora, Governor Macías sought to capitalize on their shifting preferences by establishing tourism offices in Hermosillo and Nogales, which built relationships with chambers of commerce, consular officials, travel agencies, and car clubs on both sides of the border. His government printed "propaganda brochures" and maps and, with boosters in Arizona, produced films that were distributed across the United States. His successor, Governor Rodriguez, commissioned books about Sonora's history, geography, and prominent personalities to promote travel to the state. La Alianza aided their cause by organizing a three-day trip to Sonora that would cost Fiesta de los Vaqueros participants $28.50, including lodging and transportation. The group encouraged its members to serve as "interpreters to the others on the trip"; they became cultural diplomats, the guides who introduced U.S. tourists to Mexico.[34]

Hermosillo's *El Imparcial* described U.S. tourists to Sonora as "middle-class" adventurers who enjoyed the favorable exchange rate from pesos to dollars. Buoyed by their increased purchasing power, they spent ever-greater quantities in Mexico. Between 1938 and 1939, the amount U.S. tourists spent there almost quadrupled, from $14 million to $53 million, and by 1945, U.S. tourists spent $78 million in Mexico annually. This rapid increase led Soto to echo Osborn; tourism, he said, would be a "new and important economic resource" that all Sonorans should "stimulate" and "protect." At the national level, the Mexican Association of Tourism proclaimed, the industry "deserves the greatest attention." Businesspersons and state officials on both sides of the border did everything they could to ease the passage of tourists between one country and the other by building more ports of entry, lowering crossing fees, and extending the amount of time tourists could spend in each country, as well as the distance they were allowed to travel from the border.[35]

Visits by U.S. tourists during rodeo week demonstrated how La Fiesta de los Vaqueros benefited Sonora, but even as the grandest of borderland celebrations, it was only part of the regional tourism industry, which state officials expected to play an increasingly important role in Sonora's economic future. As early as World War II, roadways that had been built for strategic-defense purposes carried tourists throughout northern Mexico. Highway construction then exploded after the war. For many Sonorans, the 1950 opening of the Nogales-Guaymas highway, which extended across the entire state from north to south, marked the beginning of Sonora's postwar tourism industry. State officials celebrated the occasion with an elaborate ribbon-cutting ceremony. Prominent Sonorans like Ignacio Soto and the municipal presidents of towns from Nogales to Guaymas attended the event. Arizonans including Governor Garvey, Alex Jácome, and Chamber of Commerce members joined them, arriving in the Sonoran port city via automobiles that *El Imparcial* called "caravans of goodwill."[36]

Sonorans immediately recognized the benefits of the highway as thousands of tourists traveled on it in 1950 to attend Hermosillo's Carnaval, a yearly celebration sponsored by national and local politicians, businesspersons, and tourism agencies, which shared much in common with La Fiesta de los Vaqueros. The Carnaval in Hermosillo was Sonora's own midwinter effort to attract domestic and international visitors. Highlighting how Carnaval had become a tradition by the mid-twentieth century, *El Imparcial* called it a "permanent attraction." A Carnaval Committee planned dances for the election of Carnaval queens and orchestrated a grand parade of themed floats that wound through city streets and ended at La Alianza casino. Sonoran breweries and student groups from la Universidad de Sonora sponsored floats that became symbols of the state's

Arizona tourists crossing into Nogales, Sonora. (Arizona Historical Society, Charles and Lucile Herbert, Western Ways Features Manuscript and Photograph Collection, MS 1255, Folder 284, O.)

industrialization and educational advancement. The "Emperor's Club" hosted a dance where partygoers grooved to popular American styles, including swing and jitterbug. Like Tucson's Rodeo Committee, Carnaval Committee members were local political and business leaders. Several were members of the city's Chamber of Commerce, Rotary Club, and La Alianza lodge.[37]

Because the 1950 Carnaval took place right before La Fiesta de los Vaqueros, tireless politicians, businesspeople, and boosters went to both, celebrating first in Hermosillo and then in Tucson. Arizonans had attended Carnaval for years, but the 1950 event was a special occasion because of the opening of the Nogales-Guaymas Highway just weeks earlier. That year's Carnaval was advertised throughout Arizona in newspapers and over radio waves. Thousands attended from the United States and Mexico. *El Imparcial* mentioned by name Governor Garvey; the proprietors of Capin's and Bracker's department stores in Nogales, Arizona; and Tucson businessman Alex Jácome, who brought together "men of enterprise from both states." At a dance held at Tucson's Santa Rita Hotel, Tucsonans elected a queen to represent them at the Carnaval, and the city itself entered a float in the Carnaval Parade.[38]

In addition to all of the fanfare it created, the Carnaval was a financial success. Five hundred U.S. tourists had spent an average of $20 each, or $10,000 total, amounting to 90,000 pesos. Three thousand "co-nationals," meanwhile, had spent a total of 150,000 pesos, or 50 pesos each. In other words, six times as many Mexican tourists barely spent more than the U.S. tourists who attended. The author called the inflow of U.S. tourist dollars a "nice injection of money for only three days." Because U.S. tourists had become so valuable to the Sonoran economy, the state's politicians and businesspeople urged all Sonorans to treat them respectfully and to recognize that they would return home to tell their relatives, friends, and neighbors about their time in Mexico. As Sonora's tourism commissioner put it, the state hoped to "do everything possible to take care of the American tourist who comes to Mexico for a good time" and "to have them leave with the best of feelings toward our state and our people."[39]

During the postwar era, ideologies of progress and modernization shaped cross-border celebrations and encouraged transnational commercial investment. Newspapers, the Chamber of Commerce, and La Alianza argued that Mexico had progressed considerably since the Mexican Revolution. The *Daily Star* peppered its special rodeo edition with articles about industry and investment opportunities in Mexico, and *La Alianza* challenged ideas about "old Mexico" as a lazy "land of mañana." The group instead recast it as a forward-looking nation that had taken its place among other modern democracies. Increased mine production, aviation innovations, advances in education, and internationally renowned artists demonstrated that Mexicans were "persons of superior culture." By reorienting ideas about Mexico, La Alianza undermined racist arguments about Mexican backwardness and reinforced the relationship between *aliancistas* on both sides of the border.[40]

Tucsonans echoed information about Mexico that Sonorans projected for domestic and international consumption. Just as Tucson's postwar politicians trumpeted their city's rapid growth, increased electrification, and new roads, Sonorans also hailed their state's new schools, libraries, sports complexes, and highways. Each governor applauded increases in land ownership, literacy, and international trade. Newspapers described the refurbished trailer parks with water, electricity, and gas hookups for recreational vehicles and cited longtime visitors to Sonora who observed less poverty in the state. Postwar leaders embodied Sonora's progress and modernization. Abelardo Rodríguez represented the "sentiment of the New," and Soto—a man who had established a bank, a cement company, and a local Rotary Club chapter and had served as president of the Nogales, Sonora, Chamber of Commerce, all before his election as governor—was the "man of Sonora, the man of Mexico, and, why not say it, the man of America."[41]

By the late 1950s, ideologies of progress and modernization had also become part of Arizona's and Sonora's urban landscapes. Tourists from every corner of the United States and Mexico streamed into Tucson, Nogales, Hermosillo, Guaymas, and Puerto Peñasco, delighting in the region's new transportation, lodging, and dining services. Sonorans began to study the impact of cross-border economies such as tourism, and increased tourist flows led to the employment of thousands of Arizonans and Sonorans. For a period in the early 1950s, more foreigners entered Mexico through the Nogales, Sonora, port of entry than anywhere else along the border. But the development of cross-border economies did not benefit all borderland residents. New regional economies left most Mexicans and native peoples impoverished and politically marginalized. While La Fiesta de los Vaqueros was an opportunity for Arizona's and Sonora's entrepreneurs and politicians to come together and celebrate Good Neighbor relations and cross-border commerce, for others the rodeo held different meanings.[42]

Tucson's Shifting Racial Dynamics

For many Mexican Americans, La Fiesta de los Vaqueros became a reminder of dispossession of the land they and their ancestors had owned for more than a century, as well as their changing relationship to a tradition that had defined their family histories. During the late nineteenth and early twentieth centuries, whites purchased much of Arizona's Mexican-owned ranchland. Many who sold their property moved to Tucson to support themselves and their families as railroad workers, agricultural laborers, miners, electricians, and custodians, helping to account for southern Arizona's urbanization during the early twentieth century. Over time the new owners converted the land into large-scale livestock operations, mechanized farms, dude ranches, housing developments, and, later, shopping centers and golf courses. There were exceptions, of course. The Amado family owned its ranch between Tucson and Nogales well into the twentieth century, and some white ranchers bought small plots of land near the U.S.-Mexico border for noncommercial purposes. Nevertheless, dispossession provided the discursive lens through which people of Mexican descent saw their lives in the Arizona-Sonora borderland.[43]

The oral histories collected by Patricia Preciado Martin in her book *Beloved Land* demonstrate how the loss of land became a traumatic event that affected Mexican families into the early twenty-first century. Those who left their ranches also left behind a way of life. Many saw themselves as *vaqueros*, Mexican cowboys who earned a living by raising and selling cattle. Carlotta Sotomayor, the daughter of a *vaquero* who migrated from Hermosillo to Tucson, narrated her family's history in the region. Reminiscing about her father, she said, "He was a cowboy. I remember a lot of old-timers like my father who were cowboys." She continued, "Once they got off their horses, they didn't seem to have interest in much of anything. '*Ay! Ese caballito!*' my mother used to sigh. 'Oh, that horse!'" Stories like Sotomayor's highlight how the creators of La Fiesta de los Vaqueros brushed aside Mexican ranching traditions, crowning Echols and Kinney as regional heroes instead.[44]

The Tucson Chamber of Commerce narrated a story of white entrepreneurship as the key ingredient in Tucson's postwar growth. Along with business-friendly politicians across the state—like the members of Phoenix's Charter Government—Tucson's Chamber of Commerce increasingly controlled city politics. The organization promoted Tucson's postwar economic growth in the *Arizona Daily Star*'s rodeo edition. Tourism and conventions, especially La Fiesta de los Vaqueros, became the city's greatest moneymakers, bringing in $58 million per year. Wholesale and retail businesses paid their employees more than $55 million, while the military paid $54 million; manufacturing, $43 million; mining, $40 million; construction, $37 million; agriculture, $20 million; and the University of Arizona, $11 million. The booming economy helped Tucson spread across the valley. New homes popped up everywhere. Hundreds of miles of new roads crisscrossed the desert floor, and a thousand new residents moved to the city every month. Promotional literature offered the impression that whites were responsible for such growth, ignoring how Mexican and native laborers, tourists, and consumers supported the city's expansion.[45]

Rodeo events linked white entrepreneurship and Arizona's pioneer history. One historian has called this phenomenon Tucson's "Anglo fantasy heritage," or the revision of regional history to highlight the experience of white pioneers as constitutive of regional history as a whole. During the mid-twentieth century, many whites in Tucson cast themselves as heirs to nineteenth-century pioneers. Their status and inclusion in the city depended, in part, on their performance of cowboy symbols, images, styles, and rhetoric. During rodeo week, they demonstrated belonging by participating in several "contests with a Western atmosphere," such as the Whiskerino, Big Hat, and bowleg competitions, which determined Tucson's most bowlegged resident and tourist.[46]

These games became ways for rodeo sponsors to shape the terms of civic engagement through participation in La Fiesta de los Vaqueros. Participants grew beards and had their bowlegs measured. Judges evaluated facial hair for its "length, softness, and style." Whiskerino, as the competition was called, followed a simple logic. Western men of an earlier era wore beards, and so should modern men during rodeo season. The bowleg contest relied on a similar premise. Cowboys had bowlegs from a life spent on horseback, so bowlegs would be fashionable once again during rodeo week. The only question was, how much Arizona sunshine shines between your knees? The award went to the man whose knees were the farthest apart with his feet together and planted flat on the ground.[47]

No rodeo performance displayed the efforts by rodeo organizers to fashion Tucson as a modern western city like the annual "Go Western" mandate, a tradition La Fiesta de los Vaqueros shared with rodeos throughout the North American West. The name referred to the proclamation by Tucson mayors urging residents and tourists in the city to wear three or more articles of western clothing for the duration of rodeo season. The only acceptable substitute was an "authentic Mexican costume" since the city was "proud of its Spanish heritage." Rodeo sponsors made western wear as compulsory as possible and even threatened a sort of "imprisonment." Those who did not comply got tossed into a hoosegow, a "commodious barred cage on wheels."[48]

Many happily complied, swaggering in step with rodeo season. Hughes Aircraft encouraged its employees to "indulge in the spirit" of rodeo week by going western. For department stores such as Jácome's, Steinfeld's, and Cele Peterson's, "Go Western" was a business opportunity. In newspapers on both sides of the border, these merchants advertised Tony Lama cowboy boots, starch-stiff Levi's, and wide-brimmed sombreros. Men wore cowboy hats, and women wore squaw dresses, popular garments designed by Peterson to resemble Native American dresses. "Nearly everyone" took pictures of themselves wearing western clothing. They held onto these photos as evidence of their adopted western identities.[49]

Although the Go Western mandate was a game, it nevertheless highlighted challenges inherent in Tucson's postwar modernization. In the 1950s, according to one Tucson reporter, "factors of rapid population growth and semi-industrialization" led to a waning interest in going western. Echols—the longtime rodeo boss who also served as Pima County sheriff from 1937 to 1946—offered another historical explanation for the rise and fall of going western. "When the cowboys began to thin out," he said, "the town folks dressed western so visitors would think the town was still full of cowboys. Then the visitors caught on and got a thrill out of dressing western themselves." However, "there came a time," he continued, "when Tucsonans got careless about putting on hats and boots, and something had to be done about it," so rodeo organizers locked up those who pooh-poohed tradition. Yearly performances of Tucson's western identity, he and other boosters believed, were the only way to maintain balance, order, and conformity with Tucson's western self-fashioning.[50]

In addition to the delicate balance between tradition and modernization, the celebrations of rodeo season became a way for Tucsonans and tourists to reinforce postwar gender dynamics. Women riders participated in some rodeo events, but mostly cowboys tamed the wild bulls and the broncos. One reporter for the *Tucson Daily Citizen* described the rodeo cowboy as "all man." But outside the rodeo arena, women played key roles in rodeo week events. They were goodwill ambassadors to Tucson, their city of beauty and charm. As one 1956 article put it, each "curvaceous beauty" did "her part as a pretty ambassador in bringing Tucson to millions of people throughout the country." Rodeo queens played this role perfectly. Each year, a current or former University of Arizona student held the rodeo-queen title. Often a native of Tucson, she always wore a full smile, invariably demonstrated "poise" and "personality," and showed that she was well adapted to the ruggedness of the West by posing in pictures with live wildcats, jaguars, and mountain lions. Most housewives who had worked at industrial jobs during World War II resumed their lives as homemakers after the war, and during rodeo season they were placed on a pedestal as waving and smiling representatives at the head of the rodeo parade and in the grandstand at rodeo events, projecting a domestic ideal that eclipsed their other labors in support of Tucson's growth.[51]

Rodeo celebrations of white entrepreneurship and modernization also revealed the Arizona-Sonora border region's postwar ethnic and racial order. Mexican Americans and Native Americans encountered new opportunities during World War II. Many served in the military at home and abroad, fighting and dying in every theater of the war. Others contributed to the war effort by working in defense, mining, agriculture, and ranching industries. Their wartime service led veterans, on behalf of all members of their communities, to demand fair treatment during the postwar era. They believed that their training in the military had prepared them for skilled jobs and that the GI Bill, which primarily benefited men, would help them attend school and own homes. But for most of them, the war changed little. In Tucson, they saw their political and economic power decline.[52]

Mexicans and Mexican Americans experienced multiple discriminations. Because the very word "Mexican" signaled lower-class status, many Mexican Americans distanced themselves from Mexican immigrant workers. Mexican Americans and Mexican immigrants nevertheless remained segregated in *barrios*. The legal rejection of race-based residential covenants during the late 1940s notwithstanding, whites still tried to prevent people of Mexican descent from living in neighborhoods north and east of Tucson's railroad tracks, especially the exclusive El Encanto Estates and Colonia Solana. Before the successful school-desegregation cases brought by La Alianza during the early 1950s, Mexican Americans in Arizona attended separate schools and were allowed to use swimming pools, dance halls, and other facilities only on certain days of the week. The greater employment opportunities they hoped for rarely materialized. Mexican American employment with the Southern Pacific Railroad had declined, and only 200 to 250 Mexican Americans worked at Hughes, which, as the city's largest employer, had a total workforce of about three thousand employees. Many worked as "common laborers" building the "new streets, new shopping centers, and new subdivisions" representative of Tucson's postwar growth. They opposed the privileging of pro-business policies that drove economic development in the Sunbelt borderland, including low taxes for corporations, low wages for workers, and few opportunities for promotion. Mutual-aid societies, civil rights organizations, and some labor unions combated discrimination and inequality by fighting for better jobs, equal pay, and desegregation.[53]

Further demonstrating how modernization and progress did not benefit all borderland residents, inequalities and staggering poverty characterized the postwar experience of indigenous communities in Arizona and Sonora as well. At the same time that the U.S. government adopted termination and relocation policies to encourage Native American assimilation and tribal self-determination, the Bureau of Indian Affairs (BIA) and the Tohono O'odham Tribal Council established a "Papago Development Program," which they expected to improve O'odham economic circumstances. In sync with government policies, the program called for an end to "federal supervision . . . special to Indians" and for O'odham to "become a part of the general community." O'odham lagged behind whites, the report said, only because they lacked proper schools, hospitals, transportation, homes, clothing, nutrition, and economic opportunity. With $23 million in federal support, the program sought to increase the carrying capacity of rangelands, improve irrigation techniques, and develop new soil-conservation methods. Officials estimated that O'odham income would double as a result of these new initiatives. Improved ranches and farms would support one-third of all O'odham. Another third would continue to live in the "traditional" O'odham way, through small-scale ranching and farming. The last third would find off-reservation work as wage laborers. Over time, the "Papago problem" would "cease to exist."[54]

However, the Papago Development Program failed to bring real change to the reservation. In Arizona, a small minority of O'odham ranchers and landowners who leased property to mining companies prospered. The wealthy ranchers who lived near Tucson constituted only 5 percent of the O'odham population, yet owned 80 percent of all cattle. In general, agricultural and livestock production fell precipitously and left many O'odham without work. O'odham subsisted on an average family income of about $2,400 per year, or one-fifth the income of white families. But the median income of O'odham families was less than $1,000 per year, and 25 percent of O'odham families earned less than $100 per year. Many reservation homes had neither running water nor electricity. O'odham experienced higher rates of illiteracy and poorer health than did whites. More than seven hundred O'odham children did not attend school at all, primarily because families—and growers—relied on their labor. Twenty-five percent of O'odham infants died in their first year of life, and more than half died by the age of eighteen. Finally, they could not vote in Arizona until 1948 even though the U.S. government granted Native Americans this right in 1924. In relative terms, though, Arizona O'odham were better off than O'odham in Sonora. Throughout the postwar era, *mestizo* farmers invaded the small *rancherías* of the O'odham. As a result, many of them left their communities near the border to seek work in the cities of Arizona and Sonora.[55]

The tense Cold War climate only made things more difficult for people of Mexican and native descent. They experienced extreme pressures to display American patriotism and its corollary, anti-Communism. Newspapers claimed that more than one hundred Communists crossed the border every day. Moreover, the Communist parties of the United States and Mexico cooperated to undermine established governments in both countries. According to Hermosillo's *El Imparcial*, such facts constituted a "grave threat" to regional security. New immigration laws such as the Internal Security Act and the McCarran-Walter Act—even as they sanctioned cross-border tourism, economic exchange, and student-exchange programs—targeted suspected Communists for deportation. Although these laws supposedly singled out individuals who threatened security, they also led to widespread anti-Mexican sentiment that spread across the United States and culminated in Operation Wetback, a mass deportation campaign that expelled more than a million Mexicans and Mexican Americans. This campaign and other episodes of discrimination and violence inspired emerging struggles for civil rights and equality.[56]

Many Mexican American and Native American organizations responded to the inequalities, discriminations, and pressures of the 1940s and 1950s by demanding inclusion in borderland society, in part through their annual participation in La Fiesta de los Vaqueros. If desegregation cases, labor activism, emerging youth cultures, and other movements for justice have offered important lenses for viewing Mexican American and Native American histories of the postwar and Cold War eras, the participation of these groups in Tucson's rodeo and parade also revealed how they struggled for inclusion by inserting themselves within narratives of regional history offered by the Chamber of Commerce and other event organizers. Instead of accepting these narratives, Mexican Americans and Native Americans complicated them by placing themselves before rodeo and paradegoers to assert their influence on both the past and the present of the Arizona-Sonora borderland.

Members of La Alianza were representative of the Mexican American community's participation in La Fiesta de los Vaqueros. As an organization, La Alianza played a pivotal role in the development of Mexican American social and political life in Tucson and negotiated relations between Tucson's Mexican American community and Arizona's business and political leadership. Male and female members of La Alianza gathered at meetings convened by individual lodges or their women's auxiliaries to discuss issues that affected Mexican Americans as a community and to organize support for political candidates. La Alianza's executives, in particular, were seen as representative of respectable, middle-class Mexicans and Mexican Americans. White politicians acknowledged their influence by joining the organization and placing ads in its magazine every election season, seeking Mexican American votes. White-led corporations and banks also placed congratulatory ads in *La Alianza* every February to commemorate the group's anniversary, which happened to coincide with the rodeo.

After World War II, La Alianza sought to demonstrate that Mexican Americans shared values of progress and modernization with Arizona's white leaders. Similar to many other emerging civil rights groups that preached racial uplift, La Alianza's motto was "Protection, Morality, Instruction." The group struck a delicate balance between highlighting its patriotism and criticizing U.S. laws and customs that discriminated against peoples of Mexican descent. La Alianza bought more than $800,000 in U.S. war bonds and rejected Communism. However, when the U.S. Senate, over President Harry Truman's veto, passed the McCarran-Walter Act, La Alianza published a ten-part series criticizing the new law. By articulating positions that simultaneously preached patriotism and antidiscrimination, La Alianza resembled other Mexican American civic organizations, including the League of United Latin American Citizens (formed in Corpus Christi, Texas, in 1929) and the Community Service Organization (formed in Los Angeles, California, in 1947).[57]

As La Alianza did for Mexican Americans, the Tohono O'odham Tribal Council brokered Native American relations with Tucson's white leaders. Arizona politicians and businesspeople saw tribal chairman Thomas Segundo as a figurehead, a living example of midcentury progress and modernization and a representative of the Tohono O'odham and all Native Americans in Arizona. In their descriptions of the Tohono O'odham, the rodeo programs of the 1940s and 1950s featured photographs of Segundo, a World War II veteran and University of Arizona graduate whose short hair, spectacles, and business suit defied the aesthetic self-presentation that tourists expected of the O'odham. In 1947, the O'odham elected Segundo to succeed José Ignacio as tribal chairman. In doing so, they set a precedent by making him, at the age of twenty-six, the youngest man ever to hold the position. While older O'odham expressed surprise that the tribe had "chosen a mere boy," Segundo responded that he represented a new kind of leader:

> During the war my people talked much of giving veterans more responsibility when they returned. I believe the tribe remembered those promises to the young people during the election, and that was why I was chosen. Those of us who have gone to high schools and colleges and who served in some capacity during the war are believed to have a broader view, to have more knowledge of laws and the functions of government . . . So the tendency now is to give us more responsibility in the tribal government.

Reporters relished Segundo's words and praised his descent from a long line of "the most progressive Papago families." Segundo served as tribal chairman from 1947 to 1953 and then again from 1968 until 1971, when he died tragically in an airplane crash. During his fifteen-year hiatus from the duties of tribal chairman, he pursued graduate degrees in law and social sciences at the University of Chicago and held various positions as a liaison between federal, state, and tribal governments.[58]

Even though Segundo earned high praise as tribal chairman, he did not have the support of all O'odham. Not all members of the tribe saw the tribal council as their highest authority. Many instead placed greater stock in the decision-making powers of village councils. Of the eleven districts on the San Xavier and Sells reservations, one historian has argued, the ones closest to Tucson lent the tribal council its greatest support. The relatively wealthy O'odham families who earned a living from livestock operations and land leases to mining corporations lived in these districts and had an interest in BIA programs promoted by the tribal council. Other tribal council supporters lived in Sells, the capital of the Tohono O'odham nation, where most tribal and BIA employees worked. Still, as tribal chairman, Segundo wielded significant influence. At his funeral, the O'odham eulogized him as the "greatest man in the history of Papago people."[59]

Because of their role as cultural brokers, La Alianza and the Tohono O'odham Tribal Council received solicitations from the Tucson Chamber of Commerce to have members of their communities participate in rodeo week events. The Chamber of Commerce addressed Mexican Americans in the pages of *La Alianza* or in the city's Spanish-language newspaper, *El Tucsonense,* which published translations of articles in the *Arizona Daily Star* and the *Tucson Daily Citizen.* As the head of the Tohono O'odham Tribal Council, Segundo encouraged O'odham to attend "Papago Indian Day," which, according to rodeo programs, paid "tribute to our friendly and industrious neighbors." He also arranged for women to run in relay races and to play *tóka,* a game resembling field hockey, offering his "assurance . . . that the teams would be ready for action each day." For La Alianza and the tribal council, participation in La Fiesta de los Vaqueros was a cultural and political opportunity to have Mexican Americans and Native Americans perform their traditions and ethnicity. Their participation confounded caricatures of them and aimed for Tucsonans to reimagine civic life in a way that included them.[60]

Even though rodeo programs applied the liberal rhetoric of progress and modernization to groups like La Alianza and the Tohono O'odham Tribal Council, they did not portray Mexican Americans or Native Americans as leaders of the city as a whole. An image of a Mexican man

Tohono O'odham women playing *tóka* at La Fiesta de los Vaqueros. (Arizona Historical Society, Charles and Lucile Herbert, Western Ways Features Manuscript and Photograph Collection, MS 1255, Folder 410, B.)

pictured him wearing a serape and a sombrero pulled down over his eyes, napping against an adobe wall. Others showed a Mexican boy drawing water from a well and a Tohono O'odham mother staring into the distance, seemingly out of place on a downtown street corner. They were depicted as lazy, antimodern, common laborers.[61]

Such representations of Tucson's racial order leapt from the pages of rodeo programs in the celebrations of rodeo week. Although event organizers intended rodeo celebrations to be fun, the events often held serious implications for those who participated and for those excluded from participation. The 1953 Whiskerino competition, for example, played off racial stereotype as hoax. Two "redskin chieftains," who were, in fact, white men dressed as Native Americans, interrupted a meeting of the Jaycee "vigilantes"—Junior Chamber of Commerce members who went by this name only during rodeo week—and threatened to cut off their facial hair. "Indian No Grow Beard, Scalp Big White Chief for Whiskers," read one headline describing the event. Keeping the joke alive, the article continued, "Indians, you know, can't grow beards, but that isn't going to stop these determined hatchet men." Their performance enacted several stereotypes at once. If donning a beard during rodeo season was the duty of men, then wisecracks about the supposed inability of Native American men to grow one stripped them of their masculinity. The prank also hearkened back to ideas of Apache Indians as violence-crazed savages, or "hatchet men," who were said to have terrorized whites in Tucson and other settlements into the late nineteenth century. The Jaycee performers pacified Native Americans again, reasserting authority over them by reenacting a playful scalping in the contained, ordered context of their meeting.[62]

Considering these stock examples of prejudice against them, it is perhaps surprising that people of Mexican and native descent participated in the events of rodeo week at all. It was an event planned by the same city boosters who benefited from Tucson's maintenance of racial hierarchies. Most rodeo planners were middle- and upper-class whites; rodeo celebrations could be inside jokes for their amusement. Nevertheless, Mexican Americans and Native Americans, through their participation, defended themselves against World War II– and Cold War–era attacks by seeking inclusion within the community, asserting their Americanism and their central role in the creation of the Arizona-Sonora borderland. The leaders of La Alianza and the Tohono O'odham Tribal Council displayed one form of ethnic and racial politics, while the individuals who entered the rodeo parade performed another. But all identified with regional horse and cattle cultures because their ancestors had been *vaqueros*, they themselves were ranchers, or they recognized boosterish performances of regional traditions as the border region's emerging language of status, power, and inclusion.

While thousands of Mexican Americans and Native Americans attended or participated in rodeo celebrations, a much small number attended the rodeo itself, perhaps because seats at the rodeo cost money, whereas other events were free. Lists of rodeo entrants from the 1940s and 1950s revealed that less than 5 percent of them had Spanish last names. Only a few names appeared more than once. Even by the 1980s, the National Rodeo Hall of Fame included only three Mexican American rodeo cowboys: Leopoldo Carrillo, Vicente Oropeza, and Juan Salinas. In addition, Native American cowboys rarely competed in rodeo competitions. They performed in the events of rodeo week, but they also held their own "Papago Indian Fair and Rodeo" in Sells, the capital of Arizona's O'odham reservation, where they rode instead. Their limited competition in the Tucson rodeo mirrored their almost total absence from the committees that planned La Fiesta de los Vaqueros. Only select leaders of La Alianza—and no Native Americans—served on the Rodeo Committee.[63]

Mexican Americans also planned parallel rodeo events that demonstrated their social and cultural separation from whites. La Asociacíon Progresista de Hombres de Negocios del Lado Oeste de Tucson (The Progressive Association of West Tucson Businessmen) sponsored a Mexican American rodeo-queen competition and hosted dances at the meeting hall of La Alianza, where attendees voted for their favorite of five or six women. *El Tucsonense* offered brief profiles of the candidates, calling them "the queens of our race." Like the white rodeo queen, the Mexican American queen had to be comfortable in the saddle and at home in the rough-and-tumble culture of ranch life. The 1940 queen, one article claimed, tamed even the "bravest of horses." She rode in the rodeo parade as the guest of the white queen, revealing how the racial hierarchies of La Fiesta de los Vaqueros mirrored those of the city as a whole.[64]

The annual rodeo parade drew greater Mexican American and Native American participation than any other event during rodeo week. It was the biggest single gathering of Tucson's winter tourism season and certainly of La Fiesta de los Vaqueros. Boosters described it as the longest nonmechanized parade in the world. As many as one hundred thousand spectators lined city streets to watch more than two hundred horse-drawn buggies and parade floats wind their way through downtown, carrying 300–600 participants in any given year. The wagons transported paradegoers to a bygone era. "During that short two-hour period," one article explained, "the usual traffic noises of motor vehicles, honking horns, and squealing brakes gives way to the sounds of the frontier days."[65]

One of several elements of La Fiesta de los Vaqueros that highlighted Arizona's connections with Mexico, the jewel of the rodeo parade was a carriage given to the Rodeo Parade Committee in 1934 by Rodolfo Elías Calles, Sonora's governor from 1931 to 1935. He was the son of Plutarco Elías Calles, who governed Sonora during the Mexican Revolution, from 1915 to 1919, and served as Mexico's president from 1924 to 1928. According to Tucson lore, a Paris company fabricated the wagon in 1864 specifically for Emperor Maximilian's use in Mexico. In almost every rodeo parade since the mid-1930s, the Maximilian carriage carried parade dignitaries such as the mayor of Tucson and the governors of Arizona and Sonora. It became a symbol of the close relationship between the neighboring states and of Mexico's postrevolutionary modernization. Legend held that Mexican leaders from Maximillian's time forward used the carriage during their inauguration processions—until 1924, when Plutarco Elías Calles ceremoniously stepped out of the carriage and into an automobile in the middle of his own inauguration, thereby declaring Mexico a motorized nation.[66]

The rodeo parade displayed the Arizona-Sonora border region's postwar dynamism and ethnic and racial diversity. Bands, individuals, and floats sponsored by banks, department stores, utility companies, schools, dude ranches, and social organizations formed the line of parade participants. Following the white cowboy, Native American, and Mexican color guard, all who marched in the parade chose some combination of these three characters for their costumes. Mexican Americans and Native Americans competed for designation as the "most typical Mexican cowboy," "most authentic Indian female," "best-attired Indian man," and "best-attired Indian female," for which they could win overalls, a jean jacket, a leather jacket, or a pair of cowboy boots. To be considered for a prize, participants had to fill out a form, including the name and description of the entry; number of participants; particular prize they hoped to win; and whether they would furnish their own horses. After entering the competitions, they chose how to represent their race and ethnicity and spent a great deal of time preparing their costumes. Surely the expectations of others constrained their performances; judges had their own ideas about what a "Mexican cowboy" or well-attired "Indian" should look like, and so would an entrant's family and friends. However, they also made decisions for themselves that reflected their feelings not only about their ethnic and cultural heritage but also about the histories of their communities in the Arizona-Sonora borderland.[67]

Parade floats designed by Mexican Americans demonstrated how they and their ancestors had shaped borderland histories. The themes, symbols, and costumes of some floats reflected the narrative of progress told by rodeo boosters. For the 1948 parade, Ernesto Navarro, a supervisor at the Santa Rosa playground, helped the Mexican American and Native American children he cared for design a float that paid tribute, as one article put it, to the "contribution of Father Kino in Arizona history as a missionary to the Indians." Their creation won that year's "grand sweepstakes prize" for the best overall float. Arizona-Sonora borderland residents saw Kino as either a civilizer or a colonizer. For paradegoers who viewed Kino as a colonizer, the performance was an example of conquest theater, which one historian described as a "well-choreographed political drama" that taught Native Americans about the "meaning of their own defeat." Understood in these terms, the Kino-themed float displayed the extent to which Mexican American and Native American residents of the Arizona-Sonora borderland, honoring Kino's legacy, had internalized narratives of the region's colonization. However, the children's performance also inscribed them within a celebrated episode of local history and regional cattle culture, signaling their inclusion within Tucson's civic life.[68]

The float of the Amado Farms and Cattle Ranch was another entrant in the 1948 parade and also lent itself to ambiguous interpretations of the Arizona-Sonora border region's Mexican past and present. Like other ranches owned by the Aguirre, Aros, Carrillo, Elías, Gil, Robles, and Otero families, the Amado ranch was passed down from generation to generation of Amado family members. The Amado family highlighted this history with the float itself. By the mid-twentieth century, most other Mexican American ranches had long since been sold to white ranchers, who during the early decades of the twentieth century bought up as much land in Arizona and Sonora as they could, with plans to industrialize ranching and agriculture on both sides of the border. Many of the ranchers who lost their land moved into cities, hoping to build new lives there. The Amado family's float therefore rolled through Tucson both as a kind of hearse, carrying within it the passing of an era, and as a vehicle that represented and celebrated the lasting influence of Mexican and Mexican American cattle ranchers on the border region's past, present, and future.[69]

Meanwhile, Native Americans who entered rodeo-parade competitions satisfied tourist desires to see something unfamiliar and, paradegoers believed, authentic from Arizona's past. Describing his reaction to one Native American parade performance, a visitor from Ohio explained, "It was colorful and interesting and what one wants to see in the Southwest." Tourists regurgitated clichéd narratives: Apaches were the fiercest Native Americans that "ever roamed this country," while the Navajo, Pima, Tohono O'odham, and Hopi were more "peaceful nations." Local newspapers reinforced this idea. Charles Geronimo, who claimed to be the grandson of the famed Apache chief, competed for the "most authentic Indian male" prize, which he won several times. His 1952 performance reminded onlookers of his grandfather, the "famous warrior who left a trail of blood across southern Arizona." Just seeing Charles Geronimo walk through downtown Tucson "bristled the hair on many a young western movie fan," who may have learned of his grandfather's exploits from fantasy-filled films such as *Stagecoach* (1939), *I Killed Geronimo* (1950), or *Apache* (1954).[70]

Even beyond Charles Geronimo's performances, "authentic" became the buzzword most commonly applied to all Native American parade participants. Feeding the cravings of viewers left unsatisfied by modernity in the postwar era, "authentic princesses," the "authentic St. Johns Indian Band," and "authentic Indian dancers" who wore "feathers and bells" that "caught everyone's fancy" marched in the rodeo parade. Moreover, the only parade prizes labeled as "authentic" were the "most authentic Indian male" and the "most authentic Indian female." The labeling of Native American performances as authentic hoped to convey something like accurate, truthful, or real. But use of the term also revealed tourist desires to witness something exotic, strange, and out of the ordinary in the context of their daily lives. Rodeo programs claimed that O'odham performers knew what "white men like to see," which, according to tourists, was a glimpse of an essentially unchanged, ancient, and mysterious past. In many cases, such desires led them to the Southwest in the first place.[71]

La Fiesta de los Vaqueros participants had confidence in the "history on parade" in Tucson. Having seen it, they believed they could return home to tell their friends and families the true history of the American Southwest. As one tourist from Minnesota exclaimed, "Gee, will I be able to tell them about the pioneer days now. I know everything!" Local newspapers primed their expectations by explaining how they would "see beneath the trappings and the tinsel of the holiday the authentic history of one of the last frontiers of our nation." If tourists relayed what they learned in Tucson, they likely explained how the brawn and perseverance of white pioneers triumphed over the area's Mexican American and Native American communities. Perhaps they thought that this history unfolded before them in the form of postwar economic, political, and social transformations. Yet Mexican Americans and Native Americans demonstrated their influence on regional histories and traditions and their active involvement in Tucson's civic life into the present. Tucson's leading politicians and businesspeople solicited their participation because postwar domestic and international politics demanded interracial harmony. The inequalities experienced by these communities, however, revealed that claims to unity were as romantic as rodeo performances themselves. The rhetoric of harmony reached across the border as well. Tucson's rodeo linked Arizona and Sonora through celebrations of the area's horse and cattle cultures even though the events of rodeo week highlighted the transnational business and political relationships that forged the Sunbelt borderland and marginalized a majority of Mexicans and native peoples.[72]

Mexican and Mexican American horse riders eventually celebrated their influence on regional horse and cattle cultures independently of La Fiesta de los Vaqueros. The first Mexican *charro* association in the United States formed in 1970 and was followed by the Asociación de Charros de Tucson only three years later. These *charro* associations abided by the same rules and guidelines as those in Mexico, and members participated in the same gatherings. Their formation during the 1970s became a prime example of how Mexicans and Mexican Americans in Tucson, as one scholar has written, celebrated their identity while at the same time connecting with *charrería* and Mexican traditions in general.[73]

But during the 1940s and 1950s, Mexican Americans and Native Americans participated in La Fiesta de los Vaqueros in order to claim their place within the rapidly changing Arizona-Sonora borderland. They had witnessed an unprecedented influx of white immigrants who reshaped regional culture and politics, in part through rodeo celebrations that fashioned an identity for Tucson as a modern, white-led city in the American West. Different interests in rodeo celebrations suggested a fundamental divide within the city over issues of race, ethnicity, and culture. As the desert became industrialized, La Fiesta de los Vaqueros became a way to grapple with the social and cultural meanings of change. Tucson's rodeo celebrations included people of Mexican and native descent in a unified vision of Tucson's civic life even as it reinforced a racial hierarchy with whites on top. Within this context, La Alianza, the Tohono O'odham Tribal Council, and parade entrants sought inclusion within Tucson's civic society by adopting values of progress and modernization, and endeavored to remind newcomers that people of Mexican and native descent shaped the border region's past and present and would shape its future as well.

In broad terms, the Arizona-Sonora border region's postwar growth brought hundreds of thousands of people to the area, and La Fiesta de los

Vaqueros provided them with a sense of Tucson's cultural identity and historical traditions. Despite the declining importance of cattle-ranching economies relative to other industries, cowboys and other horsemen remained important figures in regional imaginaries for decades to come. They were envisioned as role models for politicians who saw themselves as fiercely independent; purveyors of frontier justice for vigilante groups; and progenitors of regional economic growth for late-twentieth-century businesspeople. Meanwhile, through their sponsorship of La Fiesta de los Vaqueros and their participation in various rodeo events, businesspeople and politicians from both sides of the border cultivated regional economic exchanges and reaffirmed the spirit of Pan-Americanism, which characterized early Cold War relations between the United States and Mexico.

The prominent Mexican American businessman Alex Jácome participated vigorously in La Fiesta de los Vaqueros. The business he owned—Jácome's Department Store—benefited from transnational commercial exchange and the Sunbelt borderland's general economic expansion. Both led to the rise of middle- and upper-class consumers on both sides of the border who had the money to shop at his store. Like the promoters of La Fiesta de los Vaqueros, Jácome was deeply involved in building the network of cross-border business and political relationships that shaped the Sunbelt borderland.

3

JÁCOME'S MISSION

Demonstrating how they had profited from Arizona's and Sonora's postwar growth, the Jácomes expanded their family's department store and opened a new location at the corner of Stone Avenue and Pennington Street in downtown Tucson. They threw a huge block party to celebrate. On June 30, 1951, more than twenty thousand people from both sides of the border crowded the stage set up for the occasion. Attendees listened to speeches by the governors of Arizona and Sonora, Howard Pyle and Ignacio Soto, respectively, praising the store and its president, Alex Jácome, for promoting peaceful and prosperous international relations. Other attendees included fellow department-store owner and Phoenix City Council member Barry Goldwater, Tucson mayor Fred Emery, and the mayor of Ures, Sonora, where store founder Carlos Jácome was born.

Tucson newspapers said the celebration displayed the "gaiety of a Mexican fiesta." A ten-piece mariachi band, the bells of San Agustín Cathedral, and the Tucson Boys Chorus provided the music. Children swung a stick at a seven-foot clown piñata brought from Sonora and filled with candies, pennies, nickels, and dimes. Before going home, attendees took a tour of the new store, where Alex Jácome—Carlos Jácome's son—greeted them with open arms and a warm smile. He invited them to peruse the latest styles and admire the Spanish- and Mexican-themed murals that adorned the store's balconies. The celebration offered a window—a department store window—into the Arizona-Sonora borderland after World War II.[1]

Like cities across the United States, Tucson's downtown shopping district became a hive of activity during the postwar era, as people from Arizona and Sonora filled its streets, sidewalks, and stores. Like La Fiesta de los Vaqueros, Jácome's expansion demonstrated the Sunbelt borderland's spirit of postwar growth and progress. The Jácomes expanded their consumer empire just as Tucson became an urban center. Wartime economic development and the efforts of booster organizations to attract tourists and new settlers to the area positioned Jácome's to achieve unprecedented success. Between 1950 and 1970, new mass consumerism driven by the expansion of middle classes on both sides of the border led the Jácomes to conclude that a renovation of their store would increase profits even more.[2]

Jácome's promotion of cross-border exchange demonstrated how Arizona and Sonora, to his mind, constituted one borderless region defined by kinship between businesspeople and politicians. Indeed, the elite Sonorans who formed a core constituency of Jácome's clientele—considered to be "más agringado," or more like gringos, than other Mexicans—demonstrated that privileged middle- and upper-class Mexicans enjoyed entitlements such as social clout, the ability to spend luxuriously, and access to power that many Mexican Americans in Tucson did not experience in their own city. These Sonorans pumped millions of dollars into Tucson's economy each year, challenging descriptions of migrants as economic burdens. Rather than portraying Mexican migrants as impoverished workers or potential criminals, which was all too common during the Cold War era, newspapers in Arizona and Sonora represented Jácome's Mexican clientele as part of a regional elite. The direct beneficiaries of Sonora's postwar industrialization, they formed part of a business and political class whose travels back and forth across the border went relatively unencumbered despite increasing border restrictions.[3]

Furthermore, Jácome's Sonoran clientele comprised several state governors, other political leaders, and businesspeople whose economic, social, and cultural views aligned with those of the department store owner and other conservatives in Arizona. They couched their views in the language of Cold War Pan-Americanism, which held that U.S.–Latin American relations should be based on sincere friendship, the promotion of democracy, and cross-border business opportunities. Jácome's department store enacted these principles on a local level, but Jácome also sought to export and apply them to U.S.–Latin American relations more broadly. While their mutual dependence blurred the international line dividing the United States and Mexico, Jácome and his Mexican associates did not bridge the inequalities and tensions that stymied U.S.-Mexico relations during the Cold War. In fact, the spectacle of their wealth and, in many cases, their politics highlighted the multiple fault lines that divided borderland residents.[4]

Through his promotion of cross-border commercial exchange, Jácome allied himself closely with conservative politicians, businesspeople, and boosters on both sides of the border who played central roles in the creation of Arizona's and Sonora's Sunbelt borderland. Jácome defied dominant narratives of Mexican American political activism focused on new racial identities, discrimination in schools, workplace inequalities, political disenfranchisement, and the war in Vietnam. The department-store owner instead supported proposals to abolish the minimum wage, saw little use for labor unions, railed against César Chávez, criticized Chicano activism, supported Goldwater's 1964 presidential bid, and opposed passage of both the 1964 Civil Rights Act and the 1965 Voting Rights Act. He fomented conservative Cold War politics by criticizing organized labor, promoting limited government intervention in the economy, and denouncing Communism. His staunch conservatism earned him much criticism from many Mexican Americans and Chicanos. Jácome was not a "Cold War pragmatist" who fought for civil rights despite increasingly narrow pathways toward progressive change. He was a Cold Warrior who resisted change.[5]

Jácome's conservatism, at first glance a product of Cold War America, also revealed deeper histories of Mexican and Mexican American conservatism in the Arizona-Sonora border region. He inherited political and economic views from his father's generation during the late nineteenth and early twentieth centuries. Carlos Jácome and other elite Mexicans cited their bootstrapping work ethic as the reason for their individual success. Moreover, several conservative Mexicans who fled Sonora during the Mexican Revolution and settled in Tucson became close associates of the Jácomes, and Jácome affiliated with *priísta* businesspeople and politicians. These loyal followers of Mexico's PRI had organized Chinese and Japanese expulsions from Sonora, opposed Cárdenas-era agrarian reforms, and encouraged—and benefited from—the growth of privatized commercial agriculture. These relationships shaped Alex Jácome's politics during the 1950s and 1960s as he came to embody conservative Mexican American politics during the Cold War and civil rights eras. Jácome and his department store, therefore, represented not only shifting commercial relationships but also the origins and development of Mexican American conservatism in the U.S.-Mexico borderlands.

Jácome's success led regional businesspeople and politicians to view him as a leading representative of his ethnic group, but his wealth and conservative politics alienated many Mexicans and Mexican Americans. Those Sonorans who were increasingly marginalized and displaced by Mexico's postwar economic development could not afford to shop at his store. They opposed the policies of Jácome's associates in Sonora, and their struggles for land and fair labor practices clashed with his core beliefs in private property, unrestrained capitalist enterprise, and nonunionized labor. In Arizona and across the Southwest, Mexican Americans confronted Cold War–era discrimination by shifting away from civil rights strategies that emphasized American patriotism and assimilation. Alex Jácome, on the other hand, embraced these strategies. He either rejected ethnic and racial politics altogether or demonstrated a chameleon-like ability to shift his allegiances according to his audience's tastes. He was, after all, a department-store owner who made a living by selling carefully crafted representations of himself and his store. In Tucson newspapers, he referred to himself as Spanish American or American of Mexican descent, while in letters to associates in Mexico he counted himself as one of their own. In spite of such flexibility, he never identified with Chicanos, and he always rejected the idea that Mexican Americans were a distinct race within the United States.[6]

If Jácome bucked liberal ethnic and racial politics, he nevertheless saw himself as a leader of Tucson's Mexican American community. He wrote about the Mexican blood that ran through his veins. Jácome's brand of politics—simultaneously conservative and antidiscriminatory, nationalistic and supportive of cross-border exchange—defied the us-versus-them, citizen-versus-foreigner, and insider-versus-outsider mentalities that defined the Cold War for many Americans. The rift between Jácome and other community members of Mexican descent, as well as the internal contradictions of his own positions, reflected not only the social, cultural, and class divisions that riddled ethnic communities in the Arizona-Sonora borderland but also the complicated stakes of identity politics in Cold War America.

The ephemeral nature of downtown Tucson's postwar boom became clear by the early 1970s. New shopping centers serviced Tucson's radial growth away from the city center. Downtown declined as fewer and fewer shoppers visited the area. While most downtown merchants moved their businesses to the new shopping centers, the Jácomes anchored their store to the fate of downtown. Combined with these local developments, international forces also led to the city's and the store's demise. A deadly hotel fire in 1970 symbolized the ruin of downtown Tucson and also foreshadowed increasing tensions between the United States and Mexico. A few years later, Mexico's economic crises decreased visits to Tucson by wealthy Mexican shoppers, a customer base that Jácome's had relied upon to remain afloat. The decline of downtown and withering business from Mexico became insurmountable challenges for Jácome's, and the store closed in 1980; downtown Tucson's postwar boom had become a nostalgic memory. The store's expansion and closing therefore represent bookends in a tale of the rise and fall of Tucson's city center—a fate suffered by many cities across the United States—and of changing cross-border relations that signaled emerging challenges to the Sunbelt borderland Jácome had helped create.[7]

During its heyday, Jácome negotiated local, regional, and international relationships from his perch at Jácome's department store, which he

Alex Jácome with Albert Steinfeld at the 1951 store opening, with Sonora's governor, Ignacio Soto, to their right. (Jácome's Department Store Records, MS 405, Box 10, Folder 14, courtesy of University of Arizona Libraries, Special Collections.)

occupied much like a friar at the head of a mission during the Spanish colonial period. Missions had been institutions that were critical to frontier development during the eighteenth and early nineteenth centuries—as borderlands historian Herbert Eugene Bolton famously argued—and Jácome's department store became an institution that shaped the post–World War II borderlands. The 1951 store opening made this connection clear by displaying "all the pomp of a religious pageant." At exactly 6:30 p.m., San Agustín's bells rang, the Tucson Boys Chorus sang "Ave Maria," and Tucson's Catholic leaders emerged from the Pioneer Hotel across the street to begin an "ancient ceremonial" blessing of Jácome's. They entered the store and continued their procession, "blessing the foundation, merchandise, and fixtures." Like the missions of an earlier era, Jácome's became an institution that demonstrated the nexus of Catholicism, business, and politics in the borderlands. Jácome's store was his mission. It enabled his rise to prominence as a businessman, political figure, and arbiter of international relations during the Cold War.[8]

We'll See Each Other at Jácome's!

Jácome's department store first opened in 1896, but the Jácome family had lived in the border region since the eighteenth century. After immigrating from Sonora in 1879, Carlos Jácome became a prominent figure in Arizona's territorial politics. In 1894, two years before he founded Jácome's, he helped form La Alianza, and in 1896 he became a member of the nascent Tucson Chamber of Commerce. He later served as a Republican delegate to Arizona's 1910 Constitutional Convention, became an active member of the Arizona Pioneers Historical Society, and in 1922 helped found the Tucson Sunshine Climate Club, an organization with the sole purpose of attracting tourists to Tucson. Carlos Jácome was one of a small group of people of Mexican descent to hold leadership positions in local civic organizations. Collectively they offered counterexamples to the increasing marginalization of Mexicans and Mexican Americans in Tucson.[9]

Carlos Jácome had thirteen children with Dionisia Germán, who had also immigrated from Sonora. Alex Jácome was Carlos and Dionisia's tenth child and second youngest son. Born in 1904, Alex Jácome grew up in Tucson and graduated from the University of Arizona in 1927. After receiving his degree in business administration, he worked briefly in New York City at the Arnold Constable Company and then in Laredo, Texas, at

J. C. Penney's. These jobs helped prepare him to run Jácome's after his father died in 1932. While his brothers held other executive positions at the store, Alex Jácome served as president for forty years, until 1972, and then remained chairman of the board until his death in 1980.[10]

The family patriarch cast a long shadow over the department store he founded and over his son's tenure as store president. After World War II, Jácome continued to speak of his father with reverence in speeches, newspaper articles, and store pamphlets. Homage to him became a way for the Jácomes to demonstrate their store's long history in the border region and also to yoke the store to the rise of the city itself. Alex Jácome always claimed that his father's "humble origins and strong internal values" shaped his approach to business. In touting his father's legacy, Jácome made the department store seem indispensable to postwar growth.[11]

While Carlos Jácome laid a solid foundation for the store during the prewar period, Jácome's experienced its greatest growth after World War II. The department store expanded twice during the 1950s: first in 1951 and then again in 1957. With the second expansion, which cost $200,000 and added twelve thousand square feet of floor space, Jácome's became a full-service department store, selling everything from clothing to furniture. Jácome announced the second expansion in 1956, on the occasion of the store's sixtieth anniversary, leading Tucson newspapers to muse, "growth and expansion are synonymous with the name Jácome." As Jácome put it, "expansion is in keeping with our policy to grow with Tucson." During the 1950s, the downtown business district transformed to meet the demands of thousands of new shoppers. Jácome's kept pace, and by the mid-1960s, the store enjoyed its most profitable years ever, with annual earnings of as much as $4 million. The growth of Jácome's and Tucson became mutually dependent, the store a fixture of the city's center.[12]

The postwar success of their store also reaped benefits for the Jácome family. In addition to joining organizations such as the Rodeo Committee and the Rotary Club, over which he presided, Alex Jácome also belonged to social clubs like the Elks Club, the Old Pueblo Club, and, as an avid golfer, the Tucson Country Club and the El Rio Golf Course. Estela Jácome, his wife, belonged to several organizations as well, including the Tucson Board of Visitors, which organized several tourist celebrations every year. In 1956, the family moved from a home near the University of Arizona to El Encanto Estates, where the Jácomes became the first Mexican American family to live in Tucson's most exclusive neighborhood.

Despite resistance from some of the white families living there, the Jácomes stood fast in a residential area that was home to presidents of the university, city politicians, and business leaders and became so in later years to wealthy ranchers, merchants, and former mayors from Sonora. By the 1960s, profiting from connections formed at their department store, the Jácomes had become one of Tucson's wealthiest Mexican American families and had achieved inclusion in the upper echelons of the Tucson elite.[13]

While the Jácomes and their store catered to Tucsonans who shared their social and class status, many other retail options existed in Tucson as well. Consumers from throughout the Arizona-Sonora border region crowded downtown Tucson's streets as the city boomed. A supply center for regional mines and ranches from the nineteenth century onward, postwar Tucson became a regional shopping hub for residents of Pima, Santa Cruz, and Cochise counties, in addition to Mexicans from Sonora and other northern Mexican states. Whites, Mexicans, Mexican Americans, African Americans, Tohono O'odham, and Chinese filled the city's sidewalks. Class distinctions between and within these groups became evident as crowds fanned into the stores where they could afford to shop. In general, Jácome's served a middle- and upper-class clientele from both sides of the border; so did Cele Peterson's, Steinfeld's, and Levy's. Meanwhile, Myerson's White House department store, Penney's, Woolworth's, Sears, and Montgomery Ward catered primarily to Tucson's working and middle classes. Recognizing Tucson as one of the Southwest's emerging population centers, these national chains began to open stores in the city in the 1920s and 1930s. Like Jácome's, some expanded their downtown operations, while others, beginning in the 1960s, moved their business to new malls and shopping centers east of downtown.[14]

Even as Jácome's became a gathering point for individuals from similar class backgrounds living on both sides of the border, its prices kept many out. In this sense, the store mimicked the international border itself, highlighting both the boundaries dividing certain segments of society and the nexus that brought them together. Working-class Mexican Americans sometimes shopped at Jácome's for special occasions, such as prom or graduation, but mostly they went elsewhere. Even though many of the store's customers were white, Jácome's drew a more varied clientele than its upscale competitors. An anthropologist at the University of Arizona, in a 1950 study of Tucson's "interethnic relationships," conducted a survey of the city's department stores and on one day of observation found that slightly more than half of Jácome's customers were "Anglo," while almost one-third were "Mexican," and one-fifth "Negro." Jácome's was the only store with one "Indian" customer. Fewer "Mexicans" and "Negros" visited Steinfeld's and Levy's, and no "Indians" visited either store. However incomplete, the survey nevertheless offered a snapshot of the ethnic and class composition of Tucson's consumer groups.[15]

Jácome's and other downtown stores hired a comparatively diverse workforce to serve their clientele. Storeowners knew that, given the border region's demographics, they catered primarily to a Mexican, Mexican American, and white customer base. Therefore, large department stores and smaller boutiques alike hired employees who spoke both Spanish and English. Jácome's, however, employed a more diverse workforce than did its competitors. According to the anthropologist, Jácome's workforce was 50 percent "Anglo" and 50 percent "Mexican," whereas Levy's sales staff was 75 percent "Anglo" and 25 percent "Mexican," and Steinfeld's was more than 80 percent "Anglo" and less than 20 percent "Mexican." Jácome's profit-sharing plan for employees who worked at the store for more than five years encouraged many Mexican Americans to make careers there. Several worked at the store for twenty-five to thirty years. They were a loyal group that the Jácomes called family.[16]

Nevertheless, some employees experienced discrimination. Mexican American employees with darker skin were not allowed to attend to customers on the sales floor, and some female employees experienced sexist remarks by store managers. Such a working environment, not unlike the one found in other Arizona establishments, such as Barry Goldwater's family store, reflected and reinforced both the prevalent aesthetic sensibility that white was beautiful and workplace gender dynamics typical of the 1950s and 1960s. Nevertheless, some female workers thought of their jobs at Jácome's as plum positions. One young woman who worked at the Kress department store before working at Jácome's told friends that her job at Jácome's was the best she had ever had.[17]

By the time of Jácome's expansions during the mid-1950s, national chains increasingly pressured local merchants, who redefined their role within Tucson's changing commercial landscape in order to maintain a competitive edge or simply to survive. Jácome seemed not to mind the competition, believing that it would increase the overall level of traffic downtown and therefore business. About J. C. Penney's, Jácome wrote, "our neighbors . . . opened their emporium and North Stone Avenue looks like Fifth Avenue" in New York. "People are milling all around," and "naturally" some of them stopped by Jácome's. "We really needed an attraction next to us here," he continued, "and it looks like it is going to be mutually profitable." Despite his optimism, national chains became a detriment to local merchants, and, as one business historian has written, each of Tucson's department stores responded by developing their own "blueprint for survival." For their part, the Jácomes distinguished their business by maintaining its feel as a family-oriented general store that stressed intimate customer service, while at the same time keeping up with modern fashions and marketing trends. Jácome still greeted shoppers as they entered the store, and a fleet of employees stood ready to serve them. To further distinguish the business, they emphasized the Jácome family's history in the region, something national chains could not claim.[18]

Coincident with Jácome's 1957 expansion, Jácome wrote a five-piece serial for the *Arizona Daily Star*, titled "The Jácome Story," which portrayed the store as an institution deeply embedded within the history of the U.S.-Mexico border region. The stories highlighted Jácome's strategy of merging the benefits of a modern department store with nostalgia for an earlier era. Jácome wrote about his father's work ethic; the family's dedication to customers in personal and business matters; and its cultivation of close relationships with Mexican clientele.

During the Mexican Revolution, Jácome's had been a meeting place for exiled Mexican businesspersons and revolutionaries, including supporters of the deposed dictator Porfirio Díaz. Some of them, Jácome wrote, eventually became store employees. Mexican ranchers who did not trust banks kept their hard-earned cash at Jácome's, where they could rest assured it would be waiting for them when they needed it. During the Great Depression, Carlos Jácome deferred his customers' debts until they could afford to pay them. Some Mexican and Mexican American customers, Jácome proudly wrote, even got married at the store. Jácome also claimed that his father bailed Mexicans out of jail if they found trouble in Tucson and took his employees to bullfights in Nogales, Sonora, and on picnics in Tucson's Sabino Canyon, where he sang "Cielito lindo" and fed them menudo, enchiladas, and tamales. Claiming these practices as part of Carlos Jácome's legacy, he wrote, "that kind of concern for the other person—whether he is a customer, a salesman, a solicitor, or a fellow employee—has been a part of Jacome's since our father, Carlos Jácome, founded the business in 1896." Such stories, codified when Jácome fixed them to paper, reflected and shaped narratives of the region into which Jácome inserted his family and store. At the same time, they were good for business, designed to instill trust in the store's brand among its binational clientele, which kept customers streaming into Jácome's.[19]

Jácome's placement of the store within broader narratives of regional history had its visual counterparts in the Spanish- and Mexican-themed designs the Jácomes wore to events such as La Fiesta de los Vaqueros. To this annual celebration of Tucson's horse and cattle cultures, Jácome often wore a full *charro* or *vaquero* costume, while Estela Jácome wore a lady's long, flowing, Spanish-style dress and veil. Describing her choice of Spanish outfits for such events, while at the same time implying her relation to a regional elite despite the fact that her family had come from Argentina, Estela Jácome said, "I always wore a Spanish costume because my theory was that if my family had lived here at that time this is what they would have worn." In the messy ethnic and racial landscape created by postwar politics and immigration—both from Mexico and other parts of the United States—the Jácomes offered one particular way of understanding this terrain, articulating a claim to the area's Spanish past that emphasized upper-middle-class shoppers' dignity and civilization and roots in the region. That image also emphasized that the Jácomes and other Mexican Americans in the region were themselves white—not Indians or peons—which appealed both to other white shoppers and to Mexicans who distinguished themselves from Sonora's indigenous groups.[20]

Other local merchants emphasized their relationship to regional histories as well. Cele Peterson, who was born in Bisbee and worked in Mexico City before opening her store in Tucson, became well known for her "squaw dress" design, which she described as the "first squaw dress not worn by squaws." When asked about its inspiration, she replied, "I lifted them right off the Indian women." Peterson continued, "Go down to San Xavier Mission, go down to any of these places, and what were they wearing except these full skirts"? The dress was part of her "Station Wagon Togs" clothing line, which appealed to shoppers interested in "casual Southwestern-style living." Because they combined a fascination with Native American culture, contrived conceptions of Southwestern lifestyle, and emerging forms of family leisure—the station wagon road trip—squaw dresses

Alex and Estela Jácome in tuxedo and dress. (Estela Jácome personal collection.)

became popular among tourists from across the United States, who took them home as souvenirs from their time in Tucson. Clothing worn by the Jácomes and pieces designed by Cele Peterson demonstrated how Tucson's independent merchants relied on regional symbols to establish their prominence within the city's shifting commercial environment.[21]

In addition to the clothes they wore, the symbols the Jácomes chose to represent their store highlighted their imagined relation to Tucson's Spanish colonial past. In store murals and on store letterhead, invoices, and advertisements, Jácome's used Spanish and Mexican imagery to highlight the store's roots in the region and to connect beliefs held by many in Arizona and Sonora about the industry of Spanish explorers and missionaries with Jácome's own sense of ingenuity and pioneering. Artist Dale Nichols painted murals on store walls depicting a "typical Mexican village, a family group, and a fiesta scene." Mexican artist Salvador Corona—a former bullfighter whom Jácome met at a Rotary Club dinner in Nogales, Sonora—painted a mural representing the first Europeans to enter Arizona with Fray Marcos de Niza's 1539 expedition. A store sales slip linked Jácome's and de Niza even more explicitly. Ignoring the many native peoples who lived in the region before the Spaniards, it said, "Fray Marcos discovered Arizona in 1539, Jácome's in Tucson since 1896." This imaginative link between de Niza and Jácome's placed the store in a long narrative of regional history. It also clearly reflected Jácome's idea that both de Niza and his father were pioneers in their own time. Moreover, it demonstrated how Jácome fashioned himself as a sort of postwar friar, following previous great men in regional history like de Niza and Kino.[22]

Jácome also commissioned Edith Hamlin Dixon, widow of the Western American artist Maynard Dixon, to design a new seal for the store. His only stipulation was that the seal represent Tucson's origins. Hamlin Dixon's design, which hung over the store's main entrance from 1951 forward, depicted a Spanish missionary, Spanish conquistadors, and kneeling Indians. Several characteristics distinguished the new store seal. First, three Indians pictured on the seal knelt before a Spanish missionary. Two sat cross-legged and looked up at the missionary, who was bearing a cross, ready to receive his religious instruction. The third, a woman, bowed her head before the missionary, perhaps in prayer. Invoking ideas about the civilizing mission of Spanish religious figures, who sought to convert Indians to Christianity, the seal also implied the pacification of indigenous communities through armored conquistadors. To the Jácomes, the missionary and the conquistadors represented Tucson's beginning as a Spanish religious and military outpost. The saguaro cactus in the background and the spelling of Jácome's also conveyed meaning; the saguaro made it a regional story about the Sonoran desert since that was one of the few places in the world where the cactus grew, while the spelling of Jácome's highlighted the store's location in the linguistic borderlands between the United States and Mexico. The accent over the letter *a* in "Jácome's" and the apostrophe making the word possessive were indistinguishable, appearing as the same mark. However, the accent emphasizing the name's first syllable made it distinctly Spanish, while the possessive apostrophe made it distinctly English. Through the seal and other imagery, Jácome reaffirmed the colonial order of Tucson's Spanish past: both the civilizing work of Spanish missionaries and the violence against native peoples that Spanish colonization entailed.

The Spanish-themed images and symbols used by Jácome's became a key marketing strategy that attracted shoppers in both the United States and Mexico. As evidenced by La Fiesta de los Vaqueros celebrations, the

Jácome's Department Stores, Inc., logo. (Estela Jácome personal collection.)

city's leaders self-consciously constructed Tucson as the Old Pueblo, a place where native, Spanish, Mexican, and white cultures had merged harmoniously. Highlighting Jácome's relation to the region's Spanish and Mexican past was therefore good for business. Even if the store sold mainstream fashions of the United States, its borderlands imagery and the mixture of languages spoken there appealed both to white clients from the United States, who sought an exotic, regionally authentic shopping experience, and wealthy shoppers from Mexico, who felt that Jácome's, in particular, was the store that welcomed them most. Decorating the store with images and symbols from the area's Spanish and Mexican past was also a strategy that attracted both Mexican clientele and white shoppers. For Mexican shoppers, who represented more than a quarter of the store's customer base, Jácome's projected an inclusive vision of regional history. Arizona and Sonora shared a history of Spanish Empire, and the entire region had formed part of Mexico. Jácome's store deemphasized the national histories that had divided the two states since the mid-nineteenth century.

Meanwhile, for members of Tucson's white elite, which comprised both newer immigrants and so-called pioneers, whose families had lived in the area since the nineteenth century, Jácome's department store delivered a palatable interpretation of border cultures. The store president's conservative politics, formed in the crucible of ideas about frontier independence and opportunity, were in many cases like theirs, and he had money like them. But his Mexican ethnicity also helped him mediate Arizona's and Sonora's power structures. As the city underwent a demographic transformation, Jácome stressed a shared history that transcended the international border and aligned with midcentury Pan-Americanism, not a criticism of whites. Finally, much like La Fiesta de los Vaqueros, Jácome's use of Spanish-themed imagery showed how ideas of progress went hand in hand with the maintenance of past traditions. Such images and symbols entrenched the Jácome family in the history of the region even as they paved the way for the store's future success.

Words, images, and symbols reinforced the family's social and class status in the border region. Historians have commented on the relationship between local custom and the cultivation of regional power during the late nineteenth century, when the influx of transnational capital transformed the area into one of the world's most productive copper-mining regions. Amid such rapid changes, one way for individuals to claim power was by wrapping themselves in a cloak of custom and tradition, fashioning themselves as so-called pioneers with deep connections to local practices. "Custom was a byword for local relations of power," one wrote. The argument also applied to Jácome's department store during the mid-twentieth century. If the Arizona-Sonora borderland boomed during the nineteenth century because of the discovery of rich veins of copper and other minerals, then Tucson boomed in later decades because of defense industries, manufacturing, and regional tourism. The Jácomes capitalized on these economic and demographic shifts by claiming their longtime residence in the area and familiarity with its customs.[23]

Demonstrating the success of Jácome's regional marketing schemes, the store's trade with Mexico thrived at midcentury. Business from Mexico had always been an important part of Jácome's operations, but it became even more so during the 1950s and 1960s, as Sonora's middle class grew and consumers had money to spend in Tucson. They bought homes in the city, automobiles, and home furnishings. "Conspicuous consumption" became a "way of life" in Sonora. State governors argued that all Sonorans benefited from development and modernization. Agricultural fields, urban factories, and coastal port towns had reaped great profits. Most areas of the state gained electricity and potable water. Federal and state governments spent hundreds of millions of pesos on new highways, hospitals, and schools, with much new development concentrated along the border. Businesspeople and officials in Ambos Nogales argued for the improvement and expansion of border gateways in order to facilitate the rise in cross-border traffic that flowed from regional growth. Meanwhile, the Mexican government implemented a border-development and -beautification project as part of its Programa Nacional Fronterizo (National Border Program, or PRONAF), designed to encourage greater commercial activity in the border region and other areas that had a high volume of tourism. As a result, the U.S. and Mexican governments built new customs and immigration complexes on both sides of the Nogales border. As thousands of Sonorans enjoyed greater prosperity, they visited Jácome's and other businesses in Tucson. As Estela Jácome recalled, Mexicans became "more accustomed to coming up here to shop."[24]

With the exception of Mazón's and a few other department stores—which, like Jácome's, carried American and European styles—Sonoran retailers catered primarily to working-class shoppers. Upper-class Sonorans who could afford Levi's jeans, suits, and haute-couture fashions shopped in Tucson, the closest metropolitan area to Sonoran cities such as Ciudad Obregón, Guaymas, Hermosillo, and Nogales. Doctors from Sonora made trips to Tucson to buy medical supplies; farmers and livestock breeders visited to buy ranching equipment; and parents dropped off their children at the University of Arizona or at preparatory schools such as Salpointe, St. Joseph's, and Immaculate Heart academies. As they planned these trips, they made sure to include visits to "Don Alejandro" at Jácome's department store. Oftentimes Jácome's was the first place Mexican visitors stopped after they checked into the Pioneer Hotel, conveniently located directly across the street.[25]

At midcentury, the Pioneer Hotel, like Phoenix's Westward Ho, was a central gathering place for elites from both sides of the border. Opened in 1929 by Tucson businessman Harold Steinfeld—the department-store owner and real-estate developer who leased the Jácomes their store's property—business at the Pioneer expanded with the growth of Tucson's tourism industries. The hotel hosted famous guests and meetings of Arizona's and Sonora's leading civic and business organizations. Summing up the Pioneer's place in Tucson society, one columnist wrote, "For more than four decades, cattle barons and soldiers bellied up to its bars, brides and debutantes whirled around its ballroom, and politicians and businessmen huddled in its back rooms." For all the press the hotel received during the 1950s and 1960s, newspapers rarely, if ever, mentioned the Pioneer as a popular destination for Mexicans visiting Tucson despite evidence that the hotel management itself acknowledged them. The hotel's restaurant featured a bilingual menu offering *melón y fresas en su temporada* (fresh melon and berries in season) and *hotcakes estilo Pioneer* (hotcakes à la Pioneer). Moreover, a travel agency operated by Aeronaves de México, the first airline to fly between Tucson and Mexico, adjoined the hotel's main entrance to arrange international travel.[26]

Jácome's did a great deal to encourage the loyalty of Sonoran shoppers. It was the first store to accept payment in pesos even though many Mexicans exchanged their currency for U.S. dollars at a local bank before they shopped. Jácome's set a flat exchange rate of eight pesos per dollar, for example, even if the exact rate was .795 or .796, sweeping aside whatever loss it incurred as "insignificant," just part of the store's "promotional effort." During the late 1950s, Jácome's cashed as many as three to five million pesos, or $250,000 to $400,000, each year. Finally, along with a handful of other stores in Arizona, Jácome's advertised widely throughout Sonora and Sinaloa, buying space at baseball stadiums, on billboards, and in newspapers. These advertisements called Jácome's the "home for Sonorans in Tucson." They said that women who shopped at Jácome's would create a "memory that lasts," and to the store's male clients they offered "internationally famous" brands that were "made to fit." Underscoring the class position of the Mexican clientele Jácome's targeted, the store did not advertise on Sonoran radio stations because their listeners were overwhelmingly illiterate and poor and could not afford to travel to Tucson, let alone purchase the items in Jácome's department store. Even if Jácome's did not appeal to all Mexicans, its work to attract well-to-do Mexican clientele paid off. By the time of the store's closing in 1980 it maintained thirty thousand accounts, of which approximately 25 percent, or seventy-five hundred, belonged to Mexican nationals, including many Sonoran growers who paid their bill at the end of every harvest season.[27]

José Vázquez, an engineer from Ciudad Obregón, Sonora—an agriculture and livestock stronghold in the southern part of the state—was representative of Jácome's Mexican clientele. A student at the University of Arizona's College of Agriculture from 1963 to 1967, he recalled Jácome's as a gathering place for Mexicans in Tucson. Born in Hermosillo in 1942, Vázquez shopped at Jácome's from the time he was a child. He visited

Tucson at least four times a year throughout the 1940s and 1950s. At the change of every season, his mother bought him new clothes. As soon as the Vázquez family arrived at Jácome's department store, Jácome escorted Vázquez and his siblings downstairs to the basement, where he removed change from his coat pocket and bought them a soda, leaving their mother free to shop without distraction. It was a savvy business strategy. Visits to Jácome's by Vázquez continued on a more regular basis after he moved to Tucson in 1963 to attend the University of Arizona. At that time, Vázquez remembered, Jácome's was a rendezvous for young Mexicans studying at the University of Arizona or at one of Tucson's college preparatory schools. He visited the store weekly not only for social purposes but also for a more pressing reason. Vázquez's father, a doctor in Sonora, had arranged with Jácome for his son to receive an allowance for books and other living expenses from the store, which Jácome's charged to the Vázquez family account. Vázquez's experience at Jácome's department store and with the Jácome family blurred the line between personal and business connections. Like many of Jácome's Mexican clients, members of the Vázquez family became friends of the Jácomes.[28]

The Vázquez family was also similar to Jácome's other Mexican clientele in that they formed part of Sonora's upper class. Ranchers, doctors, developers, bankers, politicians, and other well-to-do individuals: these were the Mexicans with means to shop at Jácome's. They benefited from Sonora's postwar modernization, which increased their purchasing power at home and abroad. A July 1956 article published in a Sonoran newspaper read like a high-society gossip column, suggesting that a reunion of Mexicans at Jácome's was a see-and-be-seen affair that conferred status and influence. Describing the store, the article read, "Jácome's department store is the meeting place of the most distinguished businessmen and families from Mexico's West Coast." The article continued, " 'We'll see each other at Jácome's!' That is the saying of visitors from Nayarit, Jalisco, Sinaloa, and, above all, Sonora, who pass through the Old Pueblo on their way to the many other cities of this grand country."[29]

In addition to being an attraction for Sonora's most distinguished citizens, the author suggested that Jácome's, and Tucson in general, was a common point of departure. The city was the first stop in the United States from which Mexican visitors continued their travels throughout the Southwest; it was the city that linked them to other regions much like a hub linked spokes to a larger wheel. The article also offered an illustrious history of Jácome's and of the influence of Jácome in particular. "Of all of Carlos Jácome's children," it read, "Alejandro is the most well connected with Mexican bankers, farmers, and industrialists." Finally, the author offered the names and vitae of the Sonoran visitors he saw at Jácome's on just one day. The list included Rodolfo Elías Calles, the governor of Sonora from 1931 to 1935; René Gándara, who in 1956 was the mayor of Ciudad Obregón; and Guillermo Acedo Romero, the secretary general of the state of Sonora. More than mere reportage of facts, this article confirmed for readers in Sonora the elite status of those with means to shop and travel beyond their home state. Their ability to shop in Tucson and other U.S. cities reinforced their status back home, demonstrating that the maintenance of their prominence within Sonora depended upon both their professional acumen and their ability to participate in mass consumerism and high society north of the border. But if Jácome and his store had become well known on both sides of the border, he stressed that he had forged these relationships through years of hard work.[30]

Jácome explained the process of developing relationships with Mexicans in a speech he delivered at the Tucson Optimist Club in the late 1950s, which became an allegory for his vision of U.S.-Mexico relations more broadly. He told members of the club, which aggressively promoted Tucson's growth and economic development, how they and the city might profit from increased business relationships with Mexicans. In his speech, Jácome revealed several of his core ideas about progress and modernization, while at the same time positioning himself as Tucson's resident expert in international relations. Even while still in college at the University of Arizona, he said, he "could observe the business potential in customers from Mexico." Seeking to increase Tucson's international trade, he visited "towns south of the border." Traveling along Sonora's "unpaved" roads in his "trusty Chevrolet," he stopped in towns such as Santa Ana and Magdalena, where he met "most of the influential people." The purpose of these early trips was not to sell anything but rather to make the acquaintance of elite Sonorans. After "eating dust for several years," as he put it, Mexicans finally invited him into their homes, which he saw as a breakthrough. "That, in Mexico and Latin America," he said, "is the set high standard that you have been accepted as a friend—a true amigo." Business relationships developed from these personal friendships. Several acquaintances Jácome made during his travels through Sonora began to visit him in Tucson, at first, perhaps, as clients of the other stores but ultimately as loyal customers of Jácome's.[31]

Sonora's modernization paralleled Arizona's during the mid-twentieth century, and when Jácome referred in his speech to the "unpaved" Mexican roads he traveled during the late 1920s, he established a contrast between the moment of his speech and the past about which he spoke. Having experienced rapid development and incorporation within the consumer economies of Mexico and the United States, businesspeople and politicians on both sides of the border contemplated how they could move forward together. In 1959, they formed the Arizona-Mexico West Coast Trade Commission, which later became the Arizona-Mexico Commission. Prominent men in both countries had conceived of the organization; founding members included governors Paul Fannin and Álvaro Obregón Tapia, the son of former Mexican president Álvaro Obregón Salido. Governor Fannin stated that the commission sought "renewed friendship" and a "greater social, cultural, and economic relationship between our two states." Jácome's business and his customers seemed to be the perfect embodiments of these ideals. Originally a supporter of the new organization, Jácome came to believe that it merely sought financial gain rather than friendship. He forged his own path, using his department store as a platform for brokering international relations and regional ethnic politics.[32]

A Most Able Representative

As Jácome's department store played an increasingly important role in developing consumer, commercial, and political cultures between Arizona and Sonora, Jácome articulated his conviction that Mexico and the United States shared a common political future and that this belief had always guided his business dealings. In part because of Jácome's success in cultivating Mexican clientele, Arizona and Sonora borderland residents viewed him as one of Tucson's foremost diplomats to Mexico and to Latin America in general. Early in his life, he even aspired to become a U.S. diplomat, but his father's passing gave him greater responsibilities at their store. Nonetheless, Jácome had an opportunity to fill several official posts as Tucson's honorary vice consul to Mexico, U.S. delegate to the 1954 Inter-American Indian Conference in Bolivia, and U.S. representative to a trade mission in Spain. He was seen as a leader in the realm of

U.S.-Mexico relations because of his cultivation of cross-border friendship between Arizona and Sonora, yet many Mexican Americans in Tucson viewed him with disdain or ignored him completely. Because of his wealth and conservative politics, he was a controversial character who embodied tangled histories of ethnicity, class, and national belonging in the Arizona-Sonora borderland.[33]

Although Jácome observed the high-level negotiations of diplomats in Mexico City and Washington, D.C., his vision for U.S.-Mexico relations relied on the personal and professional relationships he formed during his decades as president of Jácome's department store. In a 1969 letter to Luis Echeverría Álvarez, who at the time was Mexico's interior secretary under President Gustavo Díaz Ordaz, Jácome wrote, "I have great love" for Mexico "because my parents are of Mexican descent (from Sonora), and therefore Mexican blood flows in our veins." Although he worked to strengthen relations between the United States and Latin America in general, he spent most of his energies locally, focusing his efforts on issues that affected Arizona and Sonora. From Tucson, Jácome wrote letters to admissions officers at the University of Arizona to secure spots for Mexican students; helped Mexicans find doctors in Tucson to cure their various illnesses; and arranged for the immigration of Mexicans to work at his department store. These efforts formed part of his favor exchange, a politics of personal favors that was a microcosm of his vision for U.S.-Mexico relations more broadly.[34]

During the Cold War, local and state politicians considered Jácome's counsel on ethnic politics and international relations indispensable. Believing Mexico's support critical to their mission of protecting the "security of the free world"—as officials at Davis-Monthan Air Force Base described their role both locally and internationally—they relied on Jácome's assistance in helping them counter charges of U.S. racism. He was a living example that people of Mexican descent could succeed in the United States, one of only a handful of Mexican American members of civic organizations such as the Tucson Rodeo Committee, the Tucson Rotary Club, and the Tucson Chamber of Commerce. He played host to visitors from Mexico during rodeo week, organized meetings in Sonora with Mexican Rotarians, and invited friends, including Ignacio Soto Jr., son of the Sonoran governor Ignacio Soto, to speak in Tucson. In 1950, President Miguel Alemán nominated Jácome to serve as Tucson's honorary vice consul to Mexico. In 1952, he became the only Mexican American member of the University of Arizona's Board of Regents and in 1959 served as its president. As the 1960s began, Jácome approached the pinnacle of his career as a businessman, regional power broker, and international diplomat.[35]

Jácome's department store was a successful family business, yet it also became a site for the negotiation of regionally defined relations between the United States and Mexico. Jácome developed relationships with many Mexicans who called on him for help, even those with whom he had little personal connection. Some favor seekers did not even know where exactly to mail their requests, so they generically addressed them to "Alejandro Jácome, Tucson, Arizona." One Hermosillo resident, for example, having heard what Jácome did to help the son of a mutual friend, solicited the department-store owner's help in arranging for his sixteen-year-old son to study in the United States. "Although I have not had the pleasure of knowing you personally," he wrote, "I am well aware of your reputation for caring for Mexico and her people." He argued that, if his son were "able to realize his dream" of studying in the United States, it would be a "wonderful way for him to begin his professional studies and, in a not-too-distant future, begin a distinguished profession for the honor and satisfaction of his country and his family." The urgent tone of his letter combined with the fact that he addressed it to a stranger demonstrated that Jácome had become someone whom many Mexicans solicited for help in realizing their goals in the United States.[36]

In addition to an education in Tucson, Sonorans sought Jácome's help in procuring medical services north of the border. When Jácome received letters from Mexicans explaining their various ailments or the illness of a family member, he forwarded them to a specialist and sometimes took it upon himself to call the appropriate doctor to arrange an appointment. In 1965, he made an appointment for a woman from Guaymas with an ophthalmologist whom Jácome described as a highly sought-after, first-rate doctor. He managed similar health-related requests into the last years of his life. In 1975, he responded to the request of a Sonoran official to help a friend of his, who, because of his "precarious financial situation," needed a doctor in Tucson willing to perform an operation at little or no cost. He addressed his concerns to Jácome, in particular, "because we are familiar with your spirit of service to society and for the interest you have always demonstrated in similar cases." Recognizing what Jácome did for Mexicans who solicited his help, one Tucson doctor wrote, "You seem to inherit the medical troubles of the world!"[37]

Finally, at the request of friends such as Ignacio Soto, Jácome offered the sons and daughters of acquaintances in Mexico positions at the department store. In 1957, for example, he arranged for the immigration of Hermosillo's Abelardo Betancourt León, who accepted a bookkeeping position at Jácome's that paid $200 per month, from which he would pay his own room and board. In a letter to the Tucson department-store owner, Soto listed Betancourt's proficiencies as a banker and then added, "the young man Betancourt belongs to a distinguished family from Hermosillo, whose forebears are of the best quality." Soto's letter prompted Jácome to file immigration papers on Betancourt's behalf. He made similar employment arrangements for other Mexicans as well, including individuals from Nogales and Agua Prieta, Sonora; Valle del Bravo, Mexico; and Ciudad Juárez, Chihuahua. In a letter written to support one Mexican immigrant, Jácome assured immigration authorities that the individual in question was of "good character" and would "abide by the laws of our country." By helping them immigrate, Jácome helped forge Tucson's postwar Mexican immigrant community, in addition to the efforts of *bracero* labor recruiters and others who helped arrange their migration and settlement.[38]

Each favor to Mexicans seeking employment, education, or health care demonstrated that the practice of international relations between the United States and Mexico often was a matter of informal local and regional initiative. According to Arizona's state- and federal-government representatives, Jácome exemplified this form of diplomacy. As Governor Fannin put it in a letter to Jácome, "In all my relations with the people of Mexico I have never found any Arizonan that was more admired and trusted than you and this is certainly in evidence by the number of people from Mexico that call on you when they are in Tucson." In 1956, near the end of his first term as a U.S. senator, Barry Goldwater acknowledged the same when he recommended Jácome for the position of undersecretary of state for Latin America. Goldwater wrote, Jácome was "regarded among the Mexicans as one of the most able representatives this country has in its relationship with that country." Surely Goldwater and other Arizona politicians—Republicans and Democrats alike—fawned over Jácome in order to cultivate relationships with Arizona's Mexican American voters, but they also earnestly relied upon him to provide advice in matters of U.S.-Mexico relations. Arizona's Democratic senator Morris Udall wrote in a 1962 letter to Jácome, "If I were Secretary of State I think one of my first acts would be to recruit about fifteen men with your background and ability and turn them loose in Latin America."[39]

Jácome sought to counter what he saw as a general failure of U.S. diplomacy in Latin America. His primary criticism was that diplomats from the United States had little or no knowledge of the people and countries to which they were assigned. He resented that the "diplomatic corps" was full of people who "in one day know what's wrong with the country, expressing themselves without thinking." In his view, the United States threw money at Latin American countries, but, as he said many times over, "dollars do not buy friendship." He emphasized this point in his speech at the Optimist Club, in which he argued that Latin American countries—through their provision of "tin, rubber, molybdenum, copper, tungsten, lead, silver, petroleum, hemp, sugar, coffee, quinine and hundreds of [other] items"—had helped win the war. But "what did we do after the war?" he asked. "We completely forgot our friends" and tried, once again,

> [to] buy friendship under the guise of helping the vanquished nations get on their feet and to protect ourselves against Communism by helping all the *under-developed* nations of the world! . . . We are treated with scorn in most of the countries . . . where we have dumped our billions of dollars. I am sure that Latin America does not want our dollars . . . all they would have wanted after the war is friendship and understanding, and goodwill from our fellow citizens and our great country.

A native of the border region who was well acquainted with its transnational communities and politics, Goldwater recognized this problem as well. "God knows, we may wind up with Mexico as our only friend," he wrote, "but there are times when I think our officials are even trying to lose them." Such criticisms became particularly significant during the Cold War, when the United States prioritized winning the allegiance of Latin American nations. Even though U.S. diplomats worked to cultivate U.S.-Mexico relations during the early years of the Cold War as well, only after the Cuban Revolution in 1959 did Mexico, and Latin America in general, become the "center of Washington's conceptualization of the Cold War as public diplomacy." In this context, Cold Warriors such as Jácome became highly valuable to the United States for their willingness and ability to positively represent the country.[40]

While he served the United States loyally, Jácome also confronted the difficult issues that arose between Arizona and Sonora. Even as cross-border commerce and favor exchanges provided opportunities for the two states to forge friendly relationships, bureaucratic obstacles and patterns of discrimination plagued interactions both between Arizona and Sonora and between the United States and Mexico more broadly. Jácome wrote to Goldwater when problems arose along the border. The mutual understanding they expressed in their correspondence demonstrated concern for their home region. In 1957, in the middle of debates over renewal of the Bracero Program, for example, Jácome expressed his dismay with the exploitation of *braceros* in Arizona. They were charged four hundred pesos, a lifetime of savings, just to receive interviews for jobs, and in the United States they worked on farms that were like "concentration camps" that caused "nothing but ill will toward the United States." Jácome also complained about the injustices Mexicans suffered at the border; opposed the barring of Mexican children from schools in Arizona; criticized the harassment of Mexican dignitaries as they tried to enter the United States on official business; and protested the unnecessary medical examination of Mexicans on their way to Tucson. In such instances, Goldwater responded, "I will continue to press for whatever resolution of this situation you deem advisable." Importantly, Jácome, expecting federal border policy to support transborder economic connections, based most of his grievances on the prevention of money and goods from flowing across the border rather than on complaints of racial discrimination.[41]

Jácome and Goldwater corresponded about not only U.S.-Mexico relations but also many other dimensions of culture and politics in the Arizona-Sonora borderland. For more than thirty years, from the early 1950s until his death in 1980, Jácome carried on an extensive dialogue with Goldwater, offering a window into the ways in which Mexican American conservatives negotiated power and influence during the 1950s and 1960s. Most Goldwater biographers have focused on his relationships with Washington politicians, while none have mentioned his relationship with Jácome or with any Mexican Americans. Jácome's relationship with Goldwater, however, reframes narratives of U.S. conservatism's rise during the late twentieth century, demonstrating how it evolved with support from some Mexican Americans and in dialogue with conservatives in Mexico in addition to populist activism in American suburbs and evangelical Christianity.[42]

By the mid-twentieth century, Jácome and Goldwater had known each other for decades. Both hailed from two of Arizona's most prominent merchant families. The fathers of both men, Carlos Jácome and Baron Goldwater, served in Arizona's constitutional conventions in 1910 and 1912, and Jácome and Goldwater just missed each other as students at the University of Arizona. During the 1940s, they went on joint buying trips to New York to stock their department stores. They also were members of La Alianza (Goldwater of Phoenix's Lodge 129 and Jácome of Tucson's Logia Fundadora, or Founding Lodge). During Goldwater's hiatus from national politics—between his failed presidential bid and his 1968 reelection to the U.S. Senate—the Goldwaters and the Jácomes traveled together to Guadalajara, where Jácome introduced Goldwater to friends, including the owner of Sauza Tequila. What becomes clear from their correspondence is that Jácome and Goldwater thought of one another as political confidants, coconspirators in conservative politics, and, not least, as residents of the Arizona-Sonora borderland with shared concerns about their home region. Goldwater shared Jácome's faith in cross-border commerce, which he believed would strengthen ties between the United States and Mexico well into the future. In 1962, on the fiftieth anniversary of Arizona statehood, he looked ahead to the year 2012, when Arizona would celebrate its centennial. Ignoring national debates about Mexican immigration, he wrongly predicted that the "Mexican border will become as the Canadian border, a free one, with the formalities and red tape of ingress and egress cut to a minimum so that the residents of both countries can travel back and forth across the line as if it was [*sic*] not there."[43]

Jácome and Goldwater traded letters on many subjects, from the national minimum wage, politicians' terms of office, and the Vietnam War to Goldwater's courtship of Mexican American voters, bilingualism, and U.S.-Mexico relations. When Goldwater was in Washington, D.C., Jácome advised him on many matters related to the U.S.-Mexico border and U.S.-Latin American relations. Their correspondence increased when Goldwater began his career as a U.S. senator after serving four years on Phoenix's city council and as Jácome became increasingly involved in national and international affairs. They helped each other with their respective endeavors. When Goldwater sought election to the U.S. Senate in 1952 and 1958, Jácome tried to persuade Democrats who needed convincing that "Goldwater is O.K." He served as Goldwater's unofficial political advisor in Tucson, offering advice about attracting Mexican American votes, and for

Alex Jácome with Senator Barry Goldwater (right) and Senator Carl Hayden's aide, Joe González. (Estela Jácome personal collection.)

the 1950s' campaigns, the Jácome family home became one of Goldwater's campaign headquarters.[44]

Jácome also worked to get out the vote for Goldwater. The night before elections, Estela Jácome remembered, Jácome called his "cronies" to make sure they planned to vote. He and his brothers also closed the department store for a few hours on Election Day, while they drove voters to polling locations across Tucson. While encouraging Tucsonans to vote, the Jácomes highlighted the us-versus-them mentality of the Cold War. One advertisement stated, "Remember, it isn't WHO you vote for . . . but that you DO vote! **HAVE YOUR SAY THE AMERICAN WAY,** Vote! . . . If you forget or ignore *your* right to vote, remember that enemies of good government can vote, too . . . and *THEY* will not forget!" While language like this was often deployed during the Cold War in order to red-bait people of Mexican descent, the Jácomes used it to demonstrate their family's patriotism.[45]

Jácome encouraged other Mexican Americans to be politically engaged, especially if they supported conservative candidates. Just a week before the 1958 U.S. Senate election, a rematch between Goldwater and Arizona's popular Democratic governor Ernest McFarland, Jácome sent Goldwater a letter to notify him that a leaflet in support of his candidacy had been sent to twenty-seven hundred "residents of Mexican descent" in the Tucson area. With hope that proved false—since Goldwater narrowly lost Pima County despite winning the state—Jácome added, "It looks very good in this county," but "in order to be sure" of victory, he wrote that Goldwater had "better put candles on all the saints, and don't forget the 'Tiradito,'" a folk religious wishing shrine of great importance to Tucson's Mexican and Mexican American communities. Goldwater returned the favor of Jácome's help and advice by using his Washington connections to recommend him for various diplomatic honors and posts.[46]

As their correspondence grew more prolific during the 1960s, Jácome continued to offer Goldwater political advice, particularly during the run-up to Goldwater's failed bid for the U.S. presidency. Jácome did not limit his comments to analysis of Tucson's Mexican American voters. He also offered a poignant critique of Goldwater's brash style in general, which many in the United States echoed. After Goldwater made comments about First Lady Jacqueline Kennedy that Jácome considered "a little too vituperous," Jácome wrote a letter to his friend that said, "I hope you won't mind a little fatherly advice . . . You, 'my Knight in Shining Armor from the virile West,' should always be gallant and chivalrous with the feminine sex." He continued, "Your words regarding her should only be used in places like the '*Ranchito*.' " Suggesting that there was an appropriate time and place for men to speak freely about women, such words offered a glimpse of Jácome's traditional gender politics. They also demonstrated the level of intimacy and confidence with which the two had come to regard one another. Jácome remained loyal to Goldwater even as the senator's political career reached its low point after the 1964 presidential election, in which Lyndon Johnson defeated him by a wide margin. When *Newsweek* published a piece that Jácome read as unfairly biased, he wrote a letter to the editor that read, "Senator Goldwater and the Republican convention were the victims of a vicious and mendacious diatribe. I have known Barry Goldwater most of my life and can testify that you have grossly misrepresented the man and his principles."[47]

Because Goldwater often relied on Jácome's counsel, when he ran for president, speculation was widespread that Jácome would earn a position in a Goldwater cabinet. Mindful of how such an outcome might affect their state, Sonorans observed the 1964 election closely, and some expressed excitement at the prospect of having "our friendly neighbors from Arizona" in or near the seat of national power. Enrique de Alba, a columnist whose articles appeared in newspapers throughout Sonora, wrote to Jácome months before the 1964 election to describe how Goldwater's election might benefit Mexico. In pro-government papers like *El Imparcial*, he and others wrote approvingly of Goldwater's anti-Communism and promotions of free enterprise. In his letter to Jácome, de Alba stated, "All Sonorans are thrilled that a distinguished son (Goldwater) of our neighboring state of Arizona has reached such a high political position." He continued: "We receive even greater satisfaction knowing that you, because you are a distinguished member of the Republican party, are so closely identified with Senator Goldwater." In one of his articles, de Alba referred directly to Jácome: "If Goldwater triumphs, you can already imagine how many of our Republican friends from Arizona will be appointed to high positions in his administration!" Even though Goldwater lost, their imagination demonstrated an unrecognized facet of cross-border relations between Arizona and Sonora: that conservative politics based on ideologies of free enterprise and anti-Communism linked the United States and Mexico.[48]

In Arizona, fellow Republican Mexican Americans—or Americans of Mexican descent, as Jácome preferred to call them—also admired Jácome and his family and believed him to be a leading representative of his ethnic group. After reading "The Jácome Story," Carlos Ronstadt, general manager of the Baboquivari Cattle Company and member of one of Tucson's leading Mexican American families, sent Jácome a letter that read, "The success your family has had and the contributions to a better Tucson are unrivaled." Ronstadt recognized the Jácome family's mobility and success in a city whose social, economic, political, and cultural elite was overwhelmingly white. Other admirers cited his potential to inspire the uplift of all Mexican Americans. Roy Laos Jr., a Mexican American who served on Tucson's city council, for example, felt that the family's example "contributed greatly to the future development of greater respect for the accomplishments and abilities of the Mexican-Americans of this country." All Mexican Americans, he concluded, "must admire and endeavor to pursue" the same path Jácome followed.[49]

Despite the rapid influx of white settlers who reconfigured Tucson's social, cultural, and political landscape, the Jácomes maintained their place within Tucson's power structure through the success of their store. In an interview, one of Jácome's sons commented that it was during the 1960s that Tucson transitioned from a "sleepy little pueblo" to a "thriving metropolis." He claimed that his father was as responsible for this transition as anyone else in the city. Perpetuating a narrative typical of the Arizona-Sonora Sunbelt borderland, in which businesspeople nurtured regional economic development and modernization, he said that his father had figured prominently in what seemed to be every major negotiation among city leaders, especially those involving Tucson's relationship with people of Mexican and native descent. However, there was a darker side to such stories, including the increased marginalization of Mexicans and native peoples as a consequence of the economic and political schemes that favored powerful men like Jácome and his associates on both sides of the border.[50]

It was an inescapable fact that Jácome and his family were exceptional, one of only a handful of Mexican American families to join the "inner circles of the town's business community," as one historian put it. Their wealth and conservatism placed them at odds with most Arizonans and Sonorans of Mexican and native descent. Jácome's position as a small business owner shaped his conservative views of labor, minimum wages, government spending, and other issues. He protested César Chávez's United Farm Workers, which he caricatured as a Communist-inspired organization led by an egotistical, power-hungry self-promoter. Jácome's criticism of Chávez, one historian has argued, responded to the threat Chávez and other labor organizers posed to the "established social system of which the Jácome family had become a part." But Jácome also argued that a union to represent his employees would be superfluous because he already treated them well. Store employees never wanted a union to represent them, according to Jácome's son, and when newer employees sometimes tried to raise the issue of unionization, store veterans shunned them. Jácome used a similar argument to protest a national minimum wage. He already paid his employees a fair wage, he said, and offered them plenty of opportunity for advancement. "As soon as they show any interest in their department," he wrote in a letter to Goldwater, "most of our employees . . . receive an increase in their salaries." A wage-raising amendment to the 1938 Fair Labor Standards Act, which first established the national minimum wage, Jácome argued, would hurt him as a "small independent retailer" and his employees as well, since a boost to their wages would mean that he could hire fewer of them.[51]

Even when a particular issue had no direct connection with his business, Jácome used department-store analogies to bolster his positions. He wrote a letter to Goldwater that called space exploration a waste of taxpayers' dollars: "Don't you think we've had enough trips to the moon?" Jácome asked. "Let's quit throwing our money away, pal . . . When you were in the Department Store business, you had to use your money where it would do the most good to continue paying your bills on time," he continued. He represented antiunionism, opposition to a minimum wage, and curbs on government spending as fundamentally conservative beliefs that somehow were distinct from issues of ethnicity or race. Nevertheless, these positions were inseparable from ethnic politics, and they clashed in almost every way with beliefs held by most other members of his ethnic group.[52]

People of Mexican descent in Tucson came under attack from several directions during the 1950s and 1960s, and Jácome claimed to defend their history and culture even as he rejected the increasingly aggressive tactics of Chicano youth. Mexicans and Mexican Americans remained segregated in Tucson's *barrios.* They were not permitted to speak Spanish in Arizona's classrooms. As part of their city beautification projects, efforts to build tourism industries, and baldly anti-Mexican campaigns of one sort of another, cities across the country demolished sites of importance to Mexican and Mexican American communities. Tucson's white leadership—businesspeople, politicians, and civic organizations—proposed several redevelopment plans. Jácome's and other large retail businesses remained unaffected by their proposals, and Jácome publicly voiced support for urban renewal as a whole, believing that it would expand business opportunities downtown. But he also endorsed the activities of Mexican American groups that opposed redevelopment and allowed them to set up tables outside his store to raise funds for their campaign to counter the effort. Nevertheless, as part of a federally funded urban-renewal project, the city of Tucson in the late 1960s redeveloped eighty acres of land and destroyed almost three hundred homes, businesses, and other structures that for more than a century had formed the core of the city's Mexican and Native American *barrio,* replacing them with the Tucson Convention Center and a faux Mexican village called La Placita.[53]

Sunbelt borderland–development schemes also affected the Tohono O'odham, as Jácome and others negotiated the redevelopment of their reservation lands. Arizona's economy began to shift by the late 1960s toward high-tech and service industries. This transition left fewer off-reservation farming, ranching, and mining jobs for O'odham workers, leading to renewed efforts to create jobs on the reservation and encouragement for O'odham to pursue permanent jobs away from home. Almost 40 percent of O'odham settled and found work in nearby communities like Tucson or more distant places like Chicago and Los Angeles. By the early 1960s, Tucson, as a result of these migrations, became home to the largest O'odham community anywhere. Moreover, U.S. government termination and relocation policies, purportedly designed to grant Native Americans greater autonomy, in reality reinforced O'odham dependence on tribal and federal governments and on corporations. For example, the O'odham and other Native American groups regained their rights to subsurface minerals on reservation lands, but this opened the door for many O'odham families to lease their land to mining corporations like the American Smelting and Refining Company. Leasing to outsiders caused tense debates within the tribe about how to share profits among individual landowners, districts, and the tribe as a whole.[54]

Even if Jácome's motives were less profit-driven than those of the mining companies, he, too, played a role in the leasing of O'odham land to non-Native Americans. Considering it as part of the region's development and cultural advancement, he helped negotiate a deal with the Tohono O'odham Tribal Council that allowed the University of Arizona to build Kitt Peak National Observatory on O'odham land. At a time when many Tucsonans still considered the O'odham to be antimodern relics from a distant past, Jácome prided himself and his ancestors on dealing with them fairly. His father, Carlos Jácome, spoke their language and bartered with them, accepting payment in "corn, wood, watermelons, or beans" when they could not pay in cash. According to Tucson newspapers, Carlos Jácome's O'odham customers called him a chief, but Alex Jácome used the goodwill his father had established to help the university lease O'odham land. Newspapers claimed that the O'Odham were at first reluctant because they considered the land sacred and feared that the United States would use the mountaintop to launch rockets. Members of the Tohono O'odham Tribal Council—dominated by residents of the southeastern districts closest to Tucson—conceded, the papers claimed, only after they saw the moon through telescopes at the university. They called the astronomers and their instruments "men with long eyes" and agreed to lease the land if it would be used for research purposes only.[55]

Because of the role he played as a wealthy and conservative power broker, Jácome was frequently at odds with Tucson's broader Mexican American community. In particular, he battled the Mexican American youth who, during the emerging civil rights era, called themselves Chicanas and Chicanos. Together, the Jácomes and Chicano youth represented two points on a spectrum of political activism. Describing the feeling that many Chicanas and Chicanos held toward Jácome, Guadalupe Castillo, a student and community leader during the 1960s and 1970s, recalled that he was not someone whom she or others "looked up to." Jácome's identification with the Spanish conqueror, explorer, and proselytizer contrasted with the self-fashioning of Chicanas and Chicanos, who articulated their real and imagined relation to indigenous populations throughout the Americas and protested discrimination and marginalization by defiantly asserting their history in the Arizona-Sonora borderland. Another view of Jácome held by some participants in the civil rights struggles of the 1960s was that he simply did not matter. He was so far removed from the concerns of a majority of Chicanos as to be irrelevant. He was an anomaly, an exception, and unrepresentative. Many dismissed him as a "fat cat" who had "made it." Jácome, of course, preferred comparisons with Spain's friars and conquistadors. Castillo—who attended the University of Arizona as an undergraduate in the midsixties and then as a graduate student pursuing degrees in history and education—did not think of Jácome as an adversary or as a sellout; he was just a department-store owner, "somewhere very far away."[56]

The Jácomes therefore demonstrated both the possibilities and the limits of ethnic upward mobility during the postwar era. They became widely recognized as one of Tucson's leading families, regardless of race. Particularly with the rise of the Cold War, celebrations of expansion, growth, and prosperity—or the ability to produce and consume, as one historian has posited—reinforced claims to U.S. citizenship by the Jácomes and Tucson's other ethnic leaders. In one sense, attendance at the 1951 store-expansion celebration by Thomas Segundo of the Tohono O'odham Tribal Council and Frank Wong of the Chinese Chamber of Commerce signaled the multiethnic accommodation promised by postwar civic celebrations such as La Fiesta de los Vaqueros. However, in another sense, their participation also demonstrated that ethnic upward mobility depended on the extent to which particular individuals were able to incorporate themselves as members of Tucson's business elite by articulating their faith in capitalism and economic development. Nevertheless, this inner circle excluded a majority of Mexicans, native peoples, and others who experienced economic inequality and racial discrimination.

Alex Jácome and Jácome's department store were products of the 1950s' and 1960s' borderland, a time and place defined by the cross-cutting currents of the Cold War era. At a basic level, each of these currents revealed the striking diversity of the region despite the Cold War's drive for cultural and political consensus. At the same time that mutual recriminations flew between him and Chicanos, Jácome carried on an extensive correspondence with local and national politicians that touched upon the most pressing issues affecting relations between the United States and Mexico. Meanwhile, he developed relationships with many members of Sonora's upper class. The tensions demonstrated the deep divisions that existed among Tucson's Mexican and Mexican American communities, while the friendships forged between politicians and wealthy Mexicans in Arizona and Sonora showed the possibilities of cross-border alliances based on the conservative ideologies of Arizona's and Sonora's Sunbelt borderland.

In the Cave of Terror

All the while, commerce across the Arizona-Sonora border continued as it had for more than a century. Take the year 1970, for example. Even as Jácome, in April, wrote a letter to the *Arizona Daily Star* to protest what he saw as the unpatriotic demonstrations of Chicana and Chicano students, shoppers from Mexico traveled to Tucson during the holiday season, like they did every December, to shop for gifts to take back to Mexico for Christmas celebrations. Advertisements in Hermosillo's *El Imparcial* read, "for your holiday shopping, Tucson awaits you." But a tragic fire at the Pioneer Hotel, where many Mexican shoppers stayed, made that holiday season particularly unforgettable. The fire transformed Tucson and the Arizona-Sonora border region for years to come, threatening to undo the Sunbelt borderland and foreshadowing an increasingly tense period in U.S.-Mexico relations.[57]

Twenty-eight guests died as the Pioneer Hotel burned to the ground on December 20, 1970: seventeen from carbon-monoxide poisoning, seven from severe burns, and four by leaping to their deaths in a "futile effort to escape the smoke and flames." One article called the fire "a holocaust never before experienced by the city of Tucson." More than three hundred Hughes Aircraft employees were attending the company's annual Christmas party when a fire was reported shortly before midnight, as it moved swiftly from the sixth floor to the eleventh. One Sonoran guest recalled that, from their room, she and her mother heard "terrified cries coming from the hallways." Once they escaped, they saw women throwing themselves from hotel windows and "smash[ing] into the pavement." Fire and medical trucks arrived too late to prevent these horrors. Finding him guilty of arson, a jury sentenced sixteen-year-old Louis Taylor—whose father was African American and mother was Mexican American—to twenty-eight consecutive life sentences, one for each death. Taylor had grown up in public housing in one of Tucson's Mexican *barrios*. He maintained his innocence into the twenty-first century and wondered whether a white man would have been convicted. After the fire, the hotel owners tried to resurrect their business as quickly as possible. But the Pioneer never recovered and finally closed in 1974.[58]

Articles recounting the fire, particularly those written decades after the incident, focused on its devastation of downtown Tucson rather than its impact on Sonora. They told of the suffering experienced by the relatives of hotel owner Harold Steinfeld and his wife, Peggy Steinfeld, who both perished in the fire as they slept in their penthouse on the top floor. Only a few focused on its impact on Sonoran families as well. Amid the ashes of the Pioneer Hotel were the bodies of thirteen Sonorans—three adults and ten children—who had traveled to Tucson to do holiday shopping. A total of sixty-six Mexicans were guests at the hotel that evening. All of the dead were members of the Luken, Soto, and Antillon families; they were "close friends and part of the upper class of Hermosillo and Sonora," one reporter wrote. Governor Faustino Félix Serna called acquaintances in Tucson to ask what had happened and for an update on the survivors. Sonoran officials left for Tucson immediately to investigate the scene, and when they arrived at the hotel, the bed frames in the rooms where the fire had struck were still hot. Almost unimaginably, Francisco Luken lost his wife and five of his seven children. "My life is undone," he said. Leon Levy, owner of Levy's Department Store, visited the city morgue at around 3 a.m. that night to help identify the bodies. He looked at "body after body," recognizing all of them. Then he saw the Lukens, a "Mexican family of six lined up on slabs." He and the Jácomes recalled seeing them in their stores just the day before.[59]

Demonstrating how closely linked ideas about Sonora's modernization, progress, and future prospects had become with business and politics, observers wondered what would happen to the state after the fire. Referring to the Luken, Antillon, and Soto families, one reporter lamented that the fire had "virtually wiped out" the "scions of three of the most prominent families of Sonora." Francisco Luken was a police chief; José Jesús Antillon was "one of Mexico's best-known and most skilled cardiologists and chest surgeons"; and the Soto family included some of Sonora's most powerful politicians. They would have been "assured prominent positions in the state's future." Reeling from grief, however, most Sonorans did not consider such consequences. One of the thousands who, in Hermosillo, met the airplane carrying the Soto children told reporters, "All Hermosillo is completely knocked off its emotional balance by this tragedy, no one can think about possible political effects . . . The families of all Sonora are in mourning—the country is in spiritual pain."[60]

The Sonorans directly affected by the fire were overwhelmed with grief. They tried to insulate their home state from experiencing their personal sadness. On December 22, Francisco Luken attended a mass at Tucson's San Agustín cathedral held for all of the victims, where he stood next to his only surviving children: Alejandro, age twenty-three, and Yolanda, age eighteen. Francisco and Alejandro had not made the fateful trip to Tucson, and while Yolanda did go, she decided to stay with a friend from Tucson rather than at the Pioneer with the others. One newspaper article described how Father Arsenio Carrillo said the Mass in Spanish as "rain fell quietly outside within view of the 11-floor downtown hotel where 13 Mexicans and 15 Americans lost their lives three days before." After Mass, a "60-car funeral procession formed behind six hearses" heading toward Tucson's South Lawn Cemetery, where Luken had chosen to temporarily entomb his wife and children in a stone mausoleum. He did not want to take them to Hermosillo, he explained, because "The pain and loss is mine, I don't want to bring this sorrow to the people of Sonora." In Tucson, Governor Félix Serna, Vice Governor César Gándara, Secretary of Agriculture Alfonso Reyna, Cananea mayor Roberto Elz y Torrez, Nogales mayor Octavio García, and San Luis mayor Jorge Flores all stood by

Luken's side as the grief-stricken husband and father bid farewell to his wife and children.[61]

In addition to the gatherings at San Agustín and South Lawn, several other memorials in the days after the fire indicated how the sense of mourning pervaded the Arizona-Sonora borderland. At a memorial in Tucson on December 24, altar boys carried an "American flag and the flag of the Republic of Mexico." One article, titled "Hotel Fire Brings Grief to 2 Nations," explained that the tragedy made clear the "bonds existing between the border states, this time regretfully a bond of tragedy." For days after the fire, Hermosillo's *El Imparcial* printed condolences not only from Sonoran families, businesspeople, and politicians but also from Jácome's department store, the Tucson Trade Bureau, the University of Arizona, and other Tucson retailers.[62]

In chronicles of the city, the tragedy at the Pioneer is considered one of the main causes of downtown Tucson's decline, along with the move of Cele Peterson's in 1962, Levy's in 1967, and Steinfeld's in 1971 to shopping centers east of downtown, such as El Con. As Tucson businessman Roy Drachman explained in his memoir, even though the "flight of important retail stores" hurt downtown, it was still the "heart of the city," and the "Pioneer Hotel was that heart as much as any one place could be." But "all that ended" after the fire, he continued, because Tucson "never recovered from the loss of its heart." The fire's significance for Tucson was undeniable, but the fact that its equal devastation of families from Sonora went unmentioned became a fitting metaphor for how most Tucsonans ignored Sonora's role in shaping the city. Even though Mexicans perished in the fire, only the deaths of white "pioneers" such as the Steinfelds were remembered in popular accounts.[63]

Although the fire also affected Jácome's trade with Mexico—the Lukens, Sotos, and Antillons were longtime customers of the store—other factors limited trade between Arizona and Sonora as well. These included the growing indebtedness of many Sonoran businesspeople and the country as a whole, devaluation of the Mexican peso in 1976, and an increase in violence against Mexican immigrants that threatened U.S.-Mexico relations. The decline of their currency was for a few wealthy Sonorans an opportunity to invest in Tucson real estate, which they saw as a relatively stable venture, but most Mexicans could no longer afford shopping trips to Arizona. Nevertheless, Jácome's remained open until 1980, by which time profits had declined and shareholders—various members of the extended Jácome family—contemplated ways to salvage their investment by selling the store.

The year the store closed, Jácome's eldest son carried a Mexican flag in the rodeo parade as a tribute to his father. Only a month before, on January 14, Jácome had died of a heart attack while working at his desk at the store. With his passing, *El Imparcial* proclaimed, Tucson lost one of the "pillars" of the community, "beneath whose shadow" the city had grown. The procession would be a fitting way to honor a man whose life and work helped shape Arizona's and Sonora's Sunbelt borderland. The occasion also commemorated the Jácome family's annual participation in La Fiesta de los Vaqueros. Jácome rode in the parade from the 1930s to the 1960s, when his son picked up the reins and carried forward the family tradition. In 1976, the Rodeo Parade Committee recognized Jácome's lifelong contribution to the city by naming him that year's grand marshal. He became only the second Mexican American to be so honored, following Ambassador Raul H. Castro, who was the parade's grand marshal in 1970. Praising the parade committee's selection of Jácome, Castro, who by 1975 had become Arizona's first Mexican American governor, said, Jácome "typifies Tucson and has made our neighbors to the south and southern Arizona become as one."[64]

The 1980 parade became a funeral procession for the Tucson department store that his father, Carlos Jácome, had founded eighty-four years earlier. Noting the double significance of the occasion, one reporter wrote, Jácome's son "looked splendid that day in a magnificent sombrero with a gorgeous horse dancing beneath him. He was smiling. But he carried within him not only the recent death of his father, but also the knowledge of yet another death in the pioneer Jácome family—the closing of their store." After almost a century in business, Jácome's could no longer stay afloat in Tucson's and the U.S.-Mexico border region's shifting economic environment. Throughout the 1950s, as Tucson's business core remained downtown, Jácome's department store was one of its main anchors. But as Tucson's population exploded, city government annexed expanses of land east of downtown, which over the years filled with neighborhoods, schools, and shopping centers that eventually spread across the valley. Just a week after the 1980 rodeo parade, Jácome's son prepared to announce the store's closing to more than one hundred store employees and the general public. "We're beginning to see the total collapse of commerce in the old center of Tucson," he told a Sonoran reporter. Newcomers to Tucson, he believed, were unfamiliar with the heritage of the Jácomes and their store, and he was glad that his father did not live to see the day. He thanked Sonorans one last time for their "valuable and constant support."[65]

As the Jácomes shuttered their business, another institution sought to rebuild Tucson's connections with Sonora and establish itself as an international hub in the middle of the Sonoran Desert. The University of Arizona stood less than two miles east of the Pioneer Hotel and Jácome's department store, in the new heart of Tucson, and at the center of the city's eastward expansion. It became another borderland institution representative of the city's exchanges with Sonora during the 1960s and 1970s, one that demonstrated faith in the border region's modernization, scientific advancement, and intercultural understanding and also revealed cracks in the façade of the Sunbelt borderland built by men like Jácome.

4

STUDENT MOVEMENTS

The first Arizona-Sonora conferences, held during the late 1950s and early 1960s, celebrated the postwar "civic and moral progress" of both states. Participants discussed the profits to be reaped from regional industries, including ranching, agriculture, fishing, and tourism. The first gathering took place in Hermosillo in 1959, with support from professors and students at the University of Arizona (U of A) and la Universidad de Sonora (Uni-Son). The second was held the next year in Tucson, where Ignacio Soto—the Sonoran businessman, former governor, and president of Uni-Son's board of trustees—served as its cochair with Arizona banker Lewis Douglas. Governors Fannin and Obregón attended as well, and months before he became the U.S. secretary of state, Dean Rusk, who at the time served as president of the Rockefeller Foundation, gave a speech, called "Borders and Neighbors," which detailed the history of international cooperation between the United States and Mexico. The U of A and Uni-Son sent delegations of teachers and students who sought a greater "cultural exchange" with each other, but most conference participants were not academics. Before the meeting, Soto and Douglas recruited leading bankers and industrialists. All vowed to work together for Arizona's and Sonora's mutual benefit. Summarizing the sentiment of the conference, the governors of both states proclaimed, "God made us neighbors—Let us be good neighbors."[1]

When politicians, businesspeople, students, and teachers came together at the U of A and Uni-Son, they marked those institutions as pinnacles of the Sunbelt borderland's modernization. State and national governments on both sides of the border invested in education during the mid-twentieth century. Their representatives believed that universities were symbols of postwar progress and would be engines of economic development in the future. Founded in 1885 as a land-grant institution, the U of A celebrated its seventy-fifth anniversary in 1960, when rodeo organizers selected university president Richard Harvill as the grand marshal of that year's parade. Also marking the occasion, Douglas Martin's ode, *The Lamp in the Desert,* told a tale of frontier triumph. From a "barren campus of forty acres," he wrote, the U of A became "one of the nation's great institutions of advanced education." Like Jácome's department store, the U of A by 1960 had benefited from the region's demographic expansion and high-tech industrialization, becoming a leader in anthropology, astronomy, arid land studies, and other fields. Meanwhile, Uni-Son, founded in 1942, was only twenty years old. But Sonoran politicians and businesspeople saw the institution as the height of postrevolutionary progress. The growth of Sonora's middle class expanded educational opportunities, governors lavished money on Uni-Son, and businesspeople supported programs that advanced their interests.[2]

Offering their arguments for increased collaboration, administrators, teachers, and students at both universities mimicked the Good Neighbor rhetoric of politicians and businesspeople, a hallmark of the postwar era. Interactions between universities on both sides of the border would increase international goodwill and understanding, they claimed. But they also referred to a long history of academic exchange between the United States and Mexico. University administrators received honorary degrees from neighboring countries. Professors developed cross-border research agendas. Students moved back and forth between the countries as participants in student-exchange programs or as tourists seeking pleasure. Wealthy Mexican families, including those of Sonora's leading businesspeople and politicians, sent their children to high schools and universities in the United States. The U of A and Uni-Son, therefore, served as gateways for cultural, intellectual, and economic exchanges.

As study abroad programs and the pursuit of degrees abroad demonstrated student activities beyond activism, student protests at the U of A and Uni-Son revealed widening fault lines in the Arizona-Sonora Sunbelt borderland. Students, influenced by their working-class backgrounds or middle-class aspirations, expressed their frustration with persistent ethnic, social, and economic disparities despite the promises of postwar economic development. Tucson students, especially Mexican Americans who increasingly called themselves Chicanas and Chicanos, protested the underrepresentation at the U of A of minority students and faculty. They mobilized beyond the university as well, arguing against the marginalization of Tucson's Mexican and Mexican American communities and highlighting the consequences of the city's growth and so-called progress. Businesspeople, politicians, and boosters continued to argue into the late twentieth century that economic development had benefited all of the city's residents financially, socially, and culturally. However, Mexican American journalist Leyla Cattan, writing on the U of A's one-hundredth anniversary in 1985, denied that this was the case for "Hispanic" students. They continued to struggle for equality. Students at Uni-Son also criticized state and federal claims about the benefits of postwar progress and modernization as well as the political corruption and the nondemocratic nature of their university. The expansion of agriculture, ranching, manufacturing, and mining industries had yielded great profits for a few Sonorans but left the vast majority of them in poverty. Rather than address these inequalities head-on, the purpose of the university for businesspeople and politicians, they believed, was to perpetuate the gap between rich and poor by training an aspiring class of professionals to ignore the social and economic challenges limiting opportunities for most Mexicans. In short, students on both sides of the border protested against the failures—or the gap between rhetoric and reality—of U.S. and Mexican states during the postwar era.[3]

The tensions that exploded at universities during the 1960s and 1970s reflected much deeper troubles that threatened to unravel the world envisioned by Jácome, Soto, and other businesspeople and politicians on both sides of the border. In addition to a region shaped by development, progress, harmony, and international goodwill, the borderland, students at the U of A and Uni-Son demonstrated, was riddled by economic, social, and cultural divisions. These divisions were not entirely new, of course. Mexican Americans had struggled against inequality, discrimination, and marginalization since before World War II. Likewise, Mexico's PRI spent decades trying to limit damage caused by criticisms that it did not represent the goals of the Mexican Revolution. Mexican workers, small landowners, and students organized against political corruption, policies that favored large-scale landowners, and growing economic and racial injustices.

Nevertheless, the sense that borderlands society was increasingly divided gained new urgency during the 1960s and 1970s, given the shifting currents of regional and global history. Not only did people of Mexican and indigenous descent confront the reality of undelivered, decades-old promises but youth movements, conflict around the world, and economic uncertainties for working- and middle-class residents in the United States and Mexico also created conditions that led to increased tensions and the unmaking of Arizona's and Sonora's Sunbelt borderland. Throughout the Americas, the United States backed repressive military dictatorships working to crush leftist movements. The rhetoric and violence of these conflicts, albeit on a much smaller scale, infiltrated the Arizona-Sonora borderland as students at the U of A and Uni-Son fought for change. Businesspeople and officials on both sides of the border dismissed these protestors as anarchists, radicals, and Communists. Ultimately, the turbulence of the period resulted from the failures of liberal regimes that did not improve life for—or even truly represent—a majority of their citizens. In the Arizona-Sonora borderland, the U of A and Uni-Son—like universities around the world—therefore became institutional arbiters of shifting international relations, culture, and politics.[4]

Two Universities, One Region

Between 1960 and 1980, administrators, professors, and students at the U of A engaged in a wide variety of exchanges with their counterparts at Uni-Son and throughout Mexico. For them and for the politicians of Arizona and Sonora, such cross-border connections were pivotal elements of the past and present for the U of A and Uni-Son, which also shaped Arizona's and Sonora's Sunbelt borderland. The institutions became representative of the progress and modernization of the entire region. *The Lamp in the Desert* chronicled the careers of professors who attracted capital investment in the territory's industrialization, designed the Phoenix area's Roosevelt Dam, and conceived of wartime rationing programs. President John Schaefer's annual reports highlighted the institution's leadership in astronomy, archaeology, and other fields, emphasizing the university's adoption of the "most modern" technologies. He and his successors echoed regional boosters, businesspeople, and politicians, who cast Tucson as a haven for the economic development that would light the path toward the university's future success.[5]

Meanwhile, Uni-Son quickly became a symbol of Sonora's modernization and cultural enlightenment. During the mid-1950s, Sonorans believed that their state's continued growth depended on the expansion of educational opportunities to a greater number of citizens. Federal and state governments, with additional support from private investors, built secondary schools and expanded Uni-Son. They bought desks, lab equipment, machinery, and books, including hundreds of volumes about the state's "historical, geographical, social, and economic" character that were shelved in Uni-Son's "Sonoran Library." They also established agriculture, livestock, business, nursing, and engineering schools at Uni-Son that introduced growers and ranchers to new technologies and trained Sonorans to make lasting contributions to their state's progress. For their part, Sonoran governors allocated hundreds of thousands of pesos to fellowships for university students and levied new state taxes that went directly to Uni-Son's coffers.[6]

But if the U of A and Uni-Son represented the growth of Arizona and Sonora, respectively, officials at both universities understood the success of their institutions in relation to the surrounding region. Schaefer highlighted two U of A radio programs as evidence that the university cared about international and "minority affairs." These were called *Latin American Week* and *Fiesta*, a Spanish-language program that targeted the region's Mexican and Mexican American communities. He also mentioned the university-funded "low-energy humidification-cycle desalting plant" in Puerto Peñasco, Sonora, which sought solutions to the scarcity of water in the desert. Schaefer also listed agricultural projects in Mexico alongside work in Brazil and Iraq, as well as statistics about international students from Mexico, Africa, China, Iran, and other countries. The university's internationalism helped bolster his claim that the U of A was the "most complete university in the arid or semiarid area of the world."[7]

While Schaefer highlighted these late twentieth-century programs, the U of A's relationship with Mexico, and Sonora in particular, spanned the century as a whole. In 1919, U of A president Rufus Von KleinSmid had visited Mexico City's Universidad Nacional Autónoma de México (UNAM), where he met Mexican president Venustiano Carranza and received an honorary degree. One Mexican professor observed that relations between the U of A and Mexican universities had been "forever cemented by the visit of your president to our country and our national institution." The very next year, UNAM's rector, José Macías, visited Tucson, where KleinSmid awarded him an honorary degree. Moreover, the scions of prominent Sinaloan and Sonoran families earned degrees at the U of A. These histories paved the way for continued relationships during the postwar era.[8]

Professors also conceived of research agendas intended to nurture cross-border understanding. One early effort came in 1955, when professors from multiple disciplines coauthored "An Arizona-Sonora Research Report," a systematic effort to define the relationship between the U of A and Sonora and to determine its future scope. The report envisioned dozens of cross-border research projects in the social sciences, physical sciences, humanities, and other areas. It offered a sweeping statement about the shared histories of the two states. "From the time of earliest man in the Southwest," the report stated, "the areas of Sonora and Arizona have been one geographical entity." Spanish conquistadors, Father Kino, and their followers joined in the common project of civilizing the area. "No line of demarcation divided this region," the report continued, "until the Gadsden Purchase in 1853 imposed an international boundary line between Mexico and the territory of Arizona." The work of university professors, the report implied, would continue the projects begun by Spaniards. These historical antecedents grounded their argument that the U of A should play a central role in the development of Arizona-Sonora relations.[9]

Authors of the report saw the postwar era as a particularly favorable moment to develop future projects in Sonora because of Mexico's parallel modernization. After World War II, the growth of agricultural industries and increased trade with the United States signaled to many that the region was ripe for research and economic development. After the Gadsden Purchase, the report claimed, "growth" in Sonora "was at first retarded," but the situation of the state had improved, and during the postwar era it became "apparent that the natural advantages of the area will permit its development as one of the country's major breadbaskets." In the language of economic imperialism, which emphasized what Arizona had to gain by expanding its financial investments in Mexico, the report continued, "the development of Guaymas and other seaports, the rapidly expanding commerce and traffic between the United States and Mexico via the Arizona-Sonora points of entry, the opening of the new Nogales–Mexico City highway—all indicate the economic potential of this area." The authors of the report therefore demonstrated that they shared the profit motives of the businesspeople and politicians who sponsored conferences in Hermosillo and Tucson and who financed regional economic development. They at least recognized that appealing to them was essential to gaining funding for their research agendas in Mexico.[10]

Not surprisingly, the report acknowledged Jácome as an important link between the U of A and Sonora's educational and business interests. Jácome helped arrange a visit to the U of A by faculty and administrators from Uni-Son, planning dinners at the Old Pueblo and Rotary Clubs and a tour of the U of A's Agricultural Experiment Station. According to *El Imparcial*, by the time they left Tucson to return to Sonora, they had resolved to apply at Uni-Son what they had learned in Arizona and make their university the "cultural bulwark" of Sonora and northern Mexico. Jácome also helped arrange President Harvill's trip to Jalisco, where Harvill hoped to learn Spanish and meet Jácome's business associates. Similar to the gatherings of rodeo week, these visits were both social gatherings and opportunities to develop financial relationships between the university and Mexican businesspeople. Jácome also arranged visits to Tucson by prominent Mexicans like Ignacio Soto Jr., who enrolled in a U of A course called "Business for Executives." Recognizing his work, the U of A awarded Jácome an honorary degree at its 1974 commencement exercises. A blurb about the award in the *Tucsotarian*—the newsletter of the Tucson Rotary Club—praised his "achievements in business and civic affairs" and "his distinguished service in the field of international relations."[11]

Anthropologist James Officer followed up on the Arizona-Sonora Research Report with his own study, "A Proposal for a Joint Economic Survey of Arizona and Sonora." Officer's proposal also emphasized that both states shared common histories. Both had similar geographies and faced similar environmental challenges. Mining, livestock, and agricultural industries were vital to the economies of both states; Arizona and Sonora shared similar demographic traits, including rural-to-urban migration. Finally, according to Officer, Arizona and Sonora followed similar trajectories of modernization. Both had moved from a "pioneering phase" typical of "folk society" toward industrialization. The 1955 and 1960 reports together established a framework for understanding Arizona's and Sonora's joint development. Both proposals implied that commercial interests played a key role in the U of A's relationships in Mexico. However, if Officer's proposal again demonstrated the connection between business and university interests in Mexico, it had social, cultural, and historical motivations as well.[12]

Officer's proposal envisioned a wide variety of research collaborations between academics in Arizona and Sonora, enabling the kind of "cross-cultural analysis" fundamental to his proposal. It would be a multiyear project that would involve selecting research teams, conducting general surveys of both states, and completing several research projects "on specific delimited problems common to each state." Officer explained how the "viewpoints of researchers with differing cultural backgrounds operating within the same broad framework and working in a culture other than their own should provide insights otherwise difficult to obtain." The universities would accomplish such mutual understanding by having Uni-Son researchers live and work for a month at the U of A, and then U of A researchers would do the same at Uni-Son. Even if such exchange programs never blossomed as Officer had imagined, they anticipated several later developments, including the construction of experimental stations for the production of potable water and for a joint project by marine biologists from both universities, who partnered with regional fishermen to study animals in the Sea of Cortez. Then during the 1970s, U of A professors, including Thomas Sheridan, formed small groups like the "Menudo Society," a forum for them to discuss their work on Sonora, while historians and anthropologists from the U of A and Uni-Son organized symposia on both sides of the border to share their research.[13]

At the U of A and Uni-Son, the anthropology departments in particular worked to cultivate cross-border relationships. Byron Cummings, an archaeologist at the U of A, had set a precedent during the 1920s, when he excavated Mexico City's Cuicuilco, an ancient Mesoamerican site south of Teotihuacán. Moreover, during his sixteen years as chair of the Department of Anthropology at the U of A, Raymond H. Thompson invited Mexican anthropologists to teach at the U of A and helped establish symposia on regional topics. At the first "Conference on the Anthropology and History of Northwestern Mexico," held in Hermosillo in January 1974, he delivered the keynote address. Only an "artificial" border divided Arizonans and Sonorans, Thompson said. "For us in the Southwestern United States," he continued, the "study of the anthropology and history of Northwestern Mexico is the basis of our cultural inheritance, much like it is the root of yours." In part because of their work to establish cross-border collaborations, the Mexican government chose Hermosillo for one of the first six regional centers of the National Institute for Anthropology and History, precisely because of Hermosillo's proximity to Tucson and the U of A.[14]

Because of its specialization in research on the border region, the anthropology department established itself as one of the best in the nation. During the early 1950s, the university funded the Bureau of Ethnic Research (BER) as a department subdivision, which by the 1970s had carried out studies on border health issues, local impacts of modernization on Arizona's Native American populations, and Mexican migration. The department also offered courses on the Southwest, Mexico, and Latin America in general and became an early sponsor of courses on race and ethnicity in the United States, such as "Minority Peoples of the U.S.," "Native Peoples of the Southwest," and "Mexican American Culture." Despite topics that covered their histories and cultures, few Spanish-surnamed or Native American students took these courses.[15]

At the same time that professors encouraged expanded relationships between the U of A and Uni-Son—and deeper knowledge of the U.S.-Mexico borderlands in general—businesspeople, governments, institutions of higher education, and civic organizations on both sides of the border created opportunities for students to travel and study abroad. Hosted by students at Uni-Son, U of A business and accounting majors visited Hermosillo's cement factories, cooling plants, food-processing plants, and television stations, as well as Uni-Son's museums, libraries, athletic fields, and classrooms—all symbols of Sonoran progress. They also enrolled in the university's Guadalajara Summer Program, which shaped their perceptions of Mexico and also influenced Mexican views of the United States. The program began during the immediate postwar era and for decades remained the university's only program in Mexico. Faculty and students boarded a train in Nogales, stopped in Guadalajara, and then continued on to Michoacán, Morelos, and Mexico City.[16]

The Guadalajara Summer Program gained a national reputation, and college students from across the United States with interests in international relations applied to participate, in part because of the Cold War spirit of Pan-Americanism. In 1966, students came from forty-one states and 173 different universities. For most, it was their first visit to Mexico. Many had an interest in U.S.–Latin American relations before they applied. During the 1960s, Aeronaves de México initiated direct flights from Tucson to the interior of Mexico, which made it convenient for students to embark from the U of A. But students also frequently traveled from the border by bus. After arriving, they took courses for six weeks with U of A professors, Mexican professors hired specifically for the program, and others hired summer by summer from U.S. universities. Students could take courses in law, art, music, religion, or economics; slightly more focused courses such as "Contemporary Mexican Literature," "Mexican Culture and Manners," or "Mexican Affairs"; or specialized courses such as "Colonial History," "Women in Mexico," or "The Radio and TV Industry in Mexico."[17]

Renato Rosaldo, a professor in the Spanish department at the U of A, pitched the program as a comprehensive learning experience through which participants would become intimately familiar with Mexico and Mexicans, who also got to know something about their guests. Stays with Mexican host families and the tour of Mexico that followed the coursework had a great impact on the students. The U of A took great care to ensure that their students lived with "better than average middle-class families," preferably those with college-aged children. Program administrators inspected each house before the students arrived to ensure that it met the program's standards of cleanliness, respectability, and modernity. Students "concerned about whether or not there would be plumbing," Rosaldo's successor, Macario Saldate, recalled, "arrived to find swimming pools." The program sought to give students the impression that life in Mexico could be similar to that in the United States. Students developed deep attachments to their host families—"laughing with them, crying with them," as one put it. They participated in family conversations, traveled, shopped, and prepared meals together.[18]

As guests in middle-class Mexican homes, students experienced only one small, preselected slice of Mexico's social, cultural, and economic stratum. Ncvcrthclcss, for thc program participants, thc Mcxican host families represented Mexico as a whole. As one female student wrote, the host families "were Mexico, just as for them we were the United States of America." Recognizing that national stereotypes streamed across the border in both directions—that Mexicans, too, had their own preconceptions about what it was like to live in the United States—she continued, "Most of them seemed surprised that we were not millionaires' daughters and that our parents were not divorced as they had seen in all American films." Their surprise demonstrated the power of the cinema to shape the stereotypes Mexicans held about the United States. Moreover, to the extent that stereotypes about high divorce rates among U.S. couples bolstered ideas in Mexico about the relative stability of Mexican families, exchanges between Mexican hosts and their guests led these parties to question their assumptions about both countries. For Rosaldo, this was precisely the point. Such interactions, he wrote, worked to "acquaint them first-hand with Mexican culture and manners" and "promote mutual understanding between citizens of Mexico and the United States."[19]

Their experience in Mexico led many students to see themselves as unofficial ambassadors of the United States. After six weeks in class, they traveled throughout Mexico for an additional two, visiting small towns such as Jiquilpan, Zamora, Pátzcuaro, and Janitzio; tourist destinations such as Taxco, Acapulco, and Cuernavaca; and Mexico City, where they visited the National Museum, National Palace, Chapultepec Castle, Xochimilco, and the Basilica of Guadalupe. Interacting with Mexicans and representing the United States wherever they went, students returned from Mexico believing that they had, in fact, worked to improve relations between Mexico and the United States. As one participant wrote, referring explicitly to Eugene Burdick and William Lederer's 1958 novel, *The Ugly American*, "If more young people were given such opportunities, I feel that, gradually, we Americans might become a little less ugly in the eyes of our neighbors." He continued, "This program accomplished much in the field of human relations on both sides of the fence."[20]

Sonoran students who spent a few days at the U of A also gained positive impressions of the United States and hoped that their interactions with students in Tucson might strengthen cross-border relations. One visited Arizona in December 1963 at the invitation of a group of U of A alumni. A law and social sciences student at Uni-Son, he sat in on classes at the U of A and claimed to immediately notice differences in "environment" and "custom." One "breathes" differently in Arizona, he wrote. Students in the United States had a greater range of educational experiences to choose from because there were many more universities there than in Mexico, he observed. They also had great vitality and energy and were highly interested in Mexican politics and society. Their way of thinking was not all that different from how Sonoran students thought, he noted, and their concerns, joys, ambitions, and group affiliations also were the same. Drawing a conclusion that was similar to what U of A students took away from their time in Mexico, the student explained that, if students from the United States and Mexico had even more occasions to interact with each other, their time together might "result in the removal of any problems between the United States and Mexico that might arise in the future."[21]

If the Guadalajara Summer Program helped U.S. and Mexican families and students better understand each other, it also helped Mexican Americans learn about themselves and their families. Very few Mexican Americans participated in the program—first, because few of them attended college, and second, because, for those who did, travel-abroad programs were a luxury they could not afford. Spanish major Patricia Ann

Preciado was able to participate in the program only because she received one of twenty Carnegie Fellowships awarded nationally. A native of Tucson, Preciado attended the U of A from 1957 to 1960. She went to Guadalajara the summer after she graduated. Even though she had spent her entire life near the border, she had never visited Mexico—not even Nogales, Sonora, sixty miles away. She "wasn't allowed," she recalled, because "parents of that generation were pretty strict" or at least "my father was very strict." So when she caught the bus from Nogales, Sonora, to Guadalajara, Jalisco, she had little knowledge of the wider world beyond Arizona. "Here I was," she said, "all of a sudden on a bus . . . going to Guadalajara, twelve hundred miles away from home." What unfolded, she explained, was a process of self-discovery.[22]

Describing the program's effect on her, Preciado said, in Guadalajara "this whole world about Mexico opened up to me." She had taken many courses in the Spanish department, but most of that coursework focused on the literary history of Spain rather than Mexico. Preciado recalled that Chicano studies did not exist during the late 1950s and stated that students certainly "didn't learn anything at all" about the history of Mexican Americans in Tucson. At the university, her only exposure to "Mexican culture" came through the courses she took with Rosaldo, a role model to Preciado and her older sister, who also studied at the U of A. Preciado's parents were "proud of being Mexican," she recalled, but her father's experience working in mines in Jerome, Arizona, and in California led him to encourage his daughters to assimilate and learn English. In Tucson, Preciado claimed, she was not "aware of being different." But when she arrived in Mexico, she thought, "this is my heritage . . . this is who I am." Later, Preciado became an acclaimed author of short stories and ethnographic work on the Arizona border region's Mexican and Mexican American communities. Books such as *Images and Conversations* (1983), *Songs My Mother Sang to Me* (1992), and *Beloved Land* (2004) have demonstrated Preciado's deep knowledge of Mexican culture and language. The success of interviews with Mexican elders, she said, depended on it. She attributed her biculturalism and bilingualism to the Guadalajara Summer Program. "It was Mexico that did it," she said, "I just came back a different person."[23]

For pleasure-seeking road trippers from the U of A, the idea of Mexico opening up a new world to them meant something else entirely. Instead of opportunities for ethnic self-identification, mutual understanding, or goodwill, visits to Mexico—only one hour away—provided many U.S. students an opportunity for leisure and mischief. If students who traveled throughout the Mexican interior as part of the Guadalajara Summer Program took seriously their role as junior ambassadors and watched their behavior, students who stayed closer to home, traveling to northern Mexico's beaches and border towns, seemed more likely to seek out the kinds of vices that would get them in trouble in the United States. To be sure, students who traveled to the interior of Mexico found trouble, and many students who traveled only to beaches and border towns stayed out of it. Moreover, college students also found vice in the United States. Nonetheless, pleasure-seeking students demonstrated how Mexican borderlands provided a space where U.S. students sought carnal pleasure and adventure.

Between the fall and spring semesters, during spring break, for a long weekend or even for an evening, students sought pleasure in Sonoran towns such as Nogales, Guaymas, or Puerto Peñasco, which Arizonans referred to as "Rocky Point." While there, they indulged in Mexico's younger drinking age, went deep-sea fishing in the Gulf of California, danced the Watusi to American music, sunbathed, had sex, and went to bullfights. An article in the student newspaper described a sanitized version of what awaited them: "when University students combine sun, sand, suds, and water skiing, the result is often a weekend of fun and relaxation at Rocky Point, Mexico." In addition to fun and relaxation, however, some landed in jail. In 1966, thirty of the two hundred undergrads who "invaded" the beach town of Mazatlán, Sinaloa—some fifteen hours from the Arizona-Sonora border by car—found themselves imprisoned following a "wild party in one of the beach bars." Students who witnessed or took part in the chaos failed to acknowledge their own bad behavior, thinking that Mexican authorities had set out to arrest them.[24]

Although the Guadalajara Summer Program, according to its participants, had a positive influence on U.S.-Mexico relations, leisure trips to the Mexican border and coastal cities frequently had the opposite effect. In January 1965, hundreds of students from the U of A traveled to the beach town of Guaymas, Sonora. One evening, they held an all-night party at the Hotel Miramar that led manager Juan Alcántar to threaten to report the students to university administrators. The year before, students tore sinks from bathroom walls and broke six screen doors, ten glass doors, and hundreds of glasses from the hotel bar. In 1965, they burned a beach house to the ground, set off cherry bombs in the hotel bar, and shattered

American tourists dancing in Guaymas, Sonora. (Arizona Historical Society, Charles and Lucile Herbert, Western Ways Features Manuscript and Photograph Collection, MS 1255, Folder 276, N.)

several windows, and some even refused to pay their hotel bills. Even though students were a vital source of income for Sonoran businesses, Alcántar broke up their celebration. Mexican police arrested seven. The Guaymas newspaper *El Diario* ran an article under the headline "Unpleasant Presence of Foreign Tourists in Our City; They Behave like Savages, Abusing the Hospitality Which They Are Given Here." The residents of Guaymas had shown much consideration in welcoming students into their community, yet the students did not return the courtesy they received.[25]

The unruly behavior of U.S. spring breakers visiting Mexico tarnished the reputations of both the U of A and the United States. The U.S. vice consul in Nogales insisted that "the vacation of students," despite their meddling, was in no way "troublesome" to U.S.-Mexico relations. Nevertheless, Mexicans formed their own opinions. Some claimed that the U of A "stakes its prestige very low" due to the students' conduct. Recognizing that student travel abroad carried risks, at the beginning of each break administrators warned students to mind their manners. Just before the 1965 debacle in Guaymas, the U of A's dean of men explained, "students must help build United States and University relations when visiting Mexico." He continued, "Any student in trouble reflects adversely on the University as well as the country."[26]

Instead of apologizing or demonstrating shame for their behavior, these university students cast the Mexican response as a gross overreaction. Two days after the *Wildcat* reported on the incident in Guaymas, the student newspaper ran another commentary, this time a political cartoon. It showed a college student blindfolded, arms behind his back, and bound with rope tied around his chest and legs. He stood before a firing squad taking aim at him, as a thickly mustachioed *caudillo,* or military leader, wearing a sombrero and bandoliers, raised his sword, ready to issue his order to shoot. In a final effort to save his own life, the student in the cartoon exclaimed, "FOR THE LAST TIME, IT WAS A ***PARTY***, NOT A REVOLUTION." The student seemed to have pleaded his case many times, but his defense fell on deaf ears, and now he would pay the price. Students went to Guaymas only to have fun, the cartoon implied, not to cause trouble. They may have gotten a little carried away, but certainly they intended no harm.[27]

While U of A students traveled to Mexico for a wide variety of reasons—to participate in study-abroad programs or to enjoy leisure time—Mexican students traveled to Arizona to pursue undergraduate and graduate degrees in Tucson. By the 1970s, the U of A considered itself an international university not only because of its faculty but also because of its student body. The annual President's Reports emphasized that U of A students hailed from more than seventy countries, including Turkey, China, India, Lebanon, Nigeria, and Pakistan. Nevertheless, Mexican students, particularly from Sonora, formed the University of Arizona's largest bloc of international students. They gained access to U.S. universities through a combination of political connections and financial means, and, throughout the 1960s and 1970s, the U of A remained a leading institution for the education of wealthy Mexicans. This changed slowly during the 1970s, with the establishment of Mexican government and U of A scholarship programs that democratized the pursuit of secondary degrees outside Mexico and the broader shift among elite Mexicans toward sending their children to more prestigious institutions elsewhere in the United States and Europe.[28]

Postwar economic growth enabled some Sonorans to attend U.S. universities. A new and increasingly urbanized middle class of small-business owners, professionals, teachers, and others sent their children to Uni-Son, but other students benefited from family wealth or new fellowship opportunities that paid their way at the U of A. Sonoran students chose the U of A primarily because it was close to home. As one alumnus said, "Like all Mexican families, we like to keep close to our parents or our children." Moreover, Mexican students felt that Mexican culture surrounded them in Tucson. Sonoran families with children at the U of A sometimes purchased second homes in the city. Tucson real-estate developers catered to them, advertising in Sonoran newspapers one-, two-, and three-bedroom apartments that cost between $35,000 and $50,000, or between $100,000 and $130,000 in early twenty-first century prices. Realtors called their apartments the "best investment in Tucson," highlighting their convenient location near El Con mall, medical centers, and the U of A. During their visits, Sonorans maintained family and business connections as they dropped in on their children.[29]

Another reason that Sonorans sent their children to the U of A was that agricultural industries constituted a significant part of the state's economy, and the U of A had a strong College of Agriculture. By encouraging their children to study there, owners of Sonoran farms and ranches hoped to "prolong the empire" by helping their children take over the family business, as one U of A official put it. Finally, the Mexican government's Consejo Nacional de Ciencia y Tecnología (CONACYT) scholarships, established during the 1970s, enabled Mexicans to pursue secondary degrees abroad. In addition, U of A scholarship programs specifically for students from Mexico and Latin America also created opportunities for them. Nevertheless, Mexicans who studied in the United States were still seen as privileged individuals likely to join the ranks of Sonora's professional classes after receiving their degrees. For all of these reasons, throughout the 1970s, the U of A hosted more Mexican students than any other university in the United States.[30]

Humberto Acuña and María Eugenia Flores were representative of the Sonoran students who attended the U of A during the 1970s. Their journeys from primary schools in smaller Sonoran towns to high schools in Hermosillo and then to high school and college in Tucson demonstrated postwar educational opportunities and revealed the migratory circuits that many Sonorans traveled to the United States not only as laborers but also as students. Acuña and Flores followed parallel paths from the small mining town of Cananea, Sonora, to the U of A. Both of their families worked in the mines. Originally from Bacoachi, Sonora, a small town where the Sonoran River begins to flow south toward Hermosillo, Acuña's father worked as a traffic manager for the American-owned Anaconda Copper Mining Company. After 1971, when Mexican president Luis Echeverría Álvarez nationalized the mine, it became the Compañía Minera de Cananea. Flores's father worked as a purchasing agent for the same company. Their mothers were housewives.[31]

Acuña and Flores had other experiences in common before they moved to Tucson. Acuña's parents "treasured education as the best thing for their kids," he recalled. Similarly, Flores remembered her father saying, "If there's anything I can leave you, it's a good education, and then you do whatever you want with that." As children, both Acuña and Flores attended the American school operated by the mine, which, they said, the company had established mainly to educate the American children whose parents were executives. After the eighth grade, both left Cananea for boarding schools in Hermosillo. As the valedictorian of his class at the American school, Acuña was offered a Compañía Minera de Cananea fellowship to attend Colegio Regis, a Catholic boarding school in Hermosillo. Although she did not receive a scholarship, Flores also moved to Hermosillo to study at a nun's school named Colegio Lux. Both then moved to Tucson for their final year of high school and, afterward, enrolled at the U of A during the late 1970s. According to Flores, "many, many, many" Mexicans followed similar trajectories from Sonora to the U of A.

Several Cananeans had business or family connections in southern Arizona, and their familiarity with the region became an important factor as they considered sending their children to the U of A. Two of Acuña's friends from Cananea enrolled at the university while Acuña was still in Hermosillo completing his *educación secundaria*, the equivalent of high school in the United States. They recruited him to Tucson by telling him that the U of A had a good engineering program and that he would be able to capitalize on his command of both Spanish and English. Similarly, the Flores family had a son who had studied at Salpointe Catholic High School, enrolled at the U of A, and completed a year of coursework there before returning to Mexico to finish his degree at the Technological

Institute of Monterrey. After Flores moved to Tucson, her two younger sisters followed her to the U of A. Flores's mother also had a good friend in Tucson, whose family owned a large ranch just outside Cananea and whose presence in Tucson made Flores's parents comfortable sending their daughter to study there. Another important consideration for Flores's parents was that Salpointe was a Catholic school. According to former Salpointe student Felipe Jácome, Alex Jácome's youngest son, this was the main reason that many Mexican parents sent their children to Salpointe instead of to other schools in Tucson. Jácome estimated that between five and ten of two hundred students from his graduating class in 1975 were Mexican nationals.[32]

Tucson's proximity to Mexico of course meant that Mexican parents could frequently visit their children at the U of A, crossing the border casually for a few days in the city. Acuña recalled that his parents visited him approximately once a month. While in Tucson, Acuña said, his parents liked to do the things they "could not do" in Sonora. They went to the Arizona-Sonora Desert Museum, Old Tucson Movie Studios, El Con Shopping Center, and other popular tourism and shopping destinations. The Flores family, meanwhile, was particularly eager to visit Tucson because three of their six children lived there. After her sisters followed her to Tucson, Flores moved with them into an apartment near the university. Her father sent them money for rent and food, but Flores and her sisters also held various work-study jobs in order to earn spending money. Although their visits provided opportunities to shop and socialize with friends from Cananea, they visited mainly to check in on and pamper their daughters. "They came over to help us," Flores recalled, saying that her mother cooked meals in Cananea and brought them to her "little girls."

Acuña's and Flores's different political experiences also shaped the way they remembered their time in Tucson. Acuña participated in the U of A's "New Start" program to recruit minority students, through which he became familiar with Chicano politics. The individuals who ran New Start at the U of A were members of El Movimiento Estudiantil Chicano de Aztlán (MEChA), a student group established in the late 1960s. Acuña listened to their conversations and came to believe that MEChA served only Mexican Americans. "I've always considered myself a *mexicano* from Mexico," he explained. "Maybe some of the language they talk I can identify with, but not the actual culture." Meanwhile, Flores had no connection to Chicano politics, stating bluntly, "I wasn't interested in that."

Acuña and Flores both attended the U of A during a period of transition for cross-border exchange and border politics more broadly. Acuña was there from 1977 to 1981, and Flores from 1977 to 1982. Following a 1976 peso devaluation, it became difficult for all but the wealthiest of Sonorans to send their children to universities in the United States. To make up for the decline caused by Mexico's economic situation, the U of A offered as many as twenty-five fellowships per year to students from Mexico. These paid full tuition, leaving students responsible only for their room and board. Unlike wealthier Sonorans, Acuña and Flores were able to study in the United States only because of such fellowships. Along with agriculture, mining, and business administration, engineering was one of the more popular majors for Mexican nationals, particularly men, who more often than women "went into the technical fields." These majors, Acuña believed, furnished skills Mexicans needed for successful careers in Sonora. Mexican nationals pursued other fields of study as well, including home economics, liberal arts, or foreign languages, but these "softer kinds of areas," as Flores called them, targeted women in particular. Flores was one of the few women to choose business administration as a major, demonstrating how traditional gender norms in Mexico and the United States circumscribed the experiences of Sonoran women even if the educational landscape opened up to make higher education possible for more of them during the 1970s.

Ultimately, the experience of Mexican students at the U of A helped train them for careers in business, politics, and other endeavors in both the United States and Mexico. Oftentimes their careers had an international bent, involved multiple moves across borders, and followed trends in broader transnational political economies. By the time he graduated in May 1981, Acuña had already secured a job in Tucson with an engineering firm. The company folded, however, when metal prices plummeted in the early 1980s. Because he was in the United States on a temporary work visa, he had to return to Mexico, where he found a job with a mining company near Nacozari, Sonora. He worked there for two years before moving to Hermosillo, where he accepted a job as a resident engineer at the recently opened Ford Motor Company assembly plant. After a few years he and a business associate opened a water-treatment company in Hermosillo, and Acuña finally returned to Arizona to work at a water and wastewater engineering firm in Phoenix.

Flores's career also crossed borders throughout the Americas, demonstrating the emergence of globalization in the U.S.-Mexico borderlands and throughout the Americas. After her graduation from the U of A, she accepted a job at a bank in Guadalajara. When that bank opened an office in Hermosillo, she transferred in order to be closer to her family. Like Acuña, she, too, accepted a position with Ford. She remained with the company into the twenty-first century, spending long periods in Hermosillo, Mexico City, Detroit, and São Paolo, Brazil. Even if Flores's and Acuña's experiences crossing borders were distinctive, their lives shed light on broader patterns of international migration that were ignored as the region became the focus of national debates about undocumented laborers.

The Sunbelt Borderland Unmade

Several cross-border exchanges hosted by the U of A and Uni-Son demonstrated the ways in which institutions of higher education symbolized the Sunbelt borderland's continued rise, but student activism at both universities also revealed signs that, by the 1960s and 1970s, the world envisioned and created by Arizona's and Sonora's businesspeople and politicians continued to produce tensions. Administrators held up the U of A and Uni-Son as examples of regional progress and modernization. Professors on both sides of the border argued that joint research projects would have cultural, political, and economic benefits for both states. Students from the U of A believed that their participation in the Guadalajara Summer Program cultivated greater international understanding between the United States and Mexico, and Mexican students pursued degrees at the U of A that enabled their transnational careers in business, engineering, and other fields. But at the same time, U of A and Uni-Son students offered critiques of the inequalities and injustices that characterized postwar borderland society, conditions that in many ways were the consequences of decisions made by politicians and businesspeople. Ironically, the relative democratization of educational opportunities for students of Mexican descent on both sides of the border—through the GI Bill and other fellowship programs—led to their increased representation at universities that were the product of societies that, according to them, failed to deliver on promises of postwar progress. Chicanas and Chicanos in Tucson rose up against what they saw as a racist university in a racist city, and Mexican students at Uni-Son protested a nondemocratic administration that, as they saw it, was representative of the authoritarian nature of the Mexican government.

Throughout the United States during the 1960s and 1970s, Mexican American youth increasingly identified as Chicanas or Chicanos, self-descriptions that signaled radical politics rejecting not only white racism but also the moderate or conservative political positions of an older generation of Mexican Americans, including Jácome and his ilk. As an organization, La Alianza had played a central role in the social and political life of Tucson's Mexican American community, in many ways serving as a gravitational force that held together members of different generations and class backgrounds. However, after La Alianza folded in 1965 as a result of internal and financial disputes, Tucson's Mexican American community had no organizational core. Several groups filled the void to combat local and regional labor, educational, and racial discrimination. In 1967, for example, Chicana and Chicano students at the U of A established a group that two years later became MEChA, when their peers from around the country first established that group at a conference held in Santa Barbara, California. Following MEChA's formation at the U of A, other chapters formed at Pima County Community College and local high schools. Many Chicanas and Chicanos in Tucson were the children of mineworkers and agricultural laborers. They were mindful of their parents' earlier struggles as they mobilized against injustice.[33]

Several causes animated the national Chicano movement, influencing student and community activism in Tucson. Building on both the successes and the failures of earlier efforts to achieve equality, many Chicanos in the United States organized during these decades to fight discrimination. Members of MEChA at the U of A connected with these wider movements by attending the 1969 Chicano Youth Conference in Denver, traveling to Los Angeles to participate in the 1970 Chicano moratorium protest of the Vietnam War, and supporting strikes in Phoenix in 1972 led by César Chávez in support of Arizona farm workers. But they focused primarily on local issues, especially the university's failure to recruit and retain minority students and faculty, their demand for community resource centers, and enduring educational inequalities, including the segregation of African Americans and Mexican Americans in Tucson schools well into the 1970s.[34]

In 1969, the U.S. Department of Housing, Education, and Welfare (HEW) bolstered MEChA's claims of discrimination with a report charging the U of A with institutional racism. Government researchers spent several days conducting interviews and asking university affiliates to complete surveys. Based on its findings, the agency delivered a report that accused the administration of failing to recruit minorities, a relatively new term applied to populations that, for most of the area's history, had constituted majorities. The report also charged the university with not developing a curriculum or student centers for minority affairs. "The University of Arizona, located 67 miles from the Mexican border, has always operated in a bi-cultural environment," and the "large numbers of Mexican-Americans who reside in this area and throughout the State of Arizona have contributed much to the development of every facet of life in Arizona." When "large numbers of American Indians and increasingly large numbers of Negroes and other minorities are added to this social setting," it continued, "it becomes evident that this educational institution serves an extremely diverse, multi-racial population."[35]

President Harvill defended the institution against the report's findings by claiming not only that the U of A "avoided any kind of discrimination" but also that "many special steps have been taken over the years to provide special kinds of consideration and help for minority group young people." But the evidence Harvill offered in support of his claim only underscored the accuracy of the government's report. Harvill argued that, in 1960, African Americans represented only 3.3 percent of Arizona's population and 3 percent of Pima County's population in 1960, much lower than the national averages. Their underrepresentation at the U of A, he argued, was therefore to be expected. He then took a similar tack toward the question of Native American representation, arguing that they represented only 2.8 percent of Pima County's population, while they represented 6.4 percent of Arizona's population. The largest reservations were in the northern part of the state, not near Tucson, and Native Americans, he argued, were reluctant to attend college so far from home. However, the fact that the U of A claimed to represent the entire border region made his arguments about Tucson's population seem provincial. He also offered no solutions to underrepresentation, suggesting that it was simply a fact of life, given Tucson's demographics. Harvill remained silent about the university's students of Mexican descent, who accounted for 2 to 3 percent of all students in 1960 even though they represented 15 percent of Arizona's population and 16.7 percent of Pima County's population. He could hardly have applied the same logic to them since they made up a greater proportion of Tucson than other communities, and because the percentage of Pima County's Mexican-descent population was larger than that of the state as a whole.[36]

Throughout the 1970s, community members, faculty, and students echoed the government report's findings. The struggles of African Americans, Mexican Americans, and Native Americans for equality at the University of Arizona were representative of their fight against economic, social, and political marginalization more generally. In 1970, between 20 and 30 percent of their communities lived below the poverty line despite three decades of economic growth. Almost 20 percent of Mexican and Mexican American heads of household were unemployed, and most of those who held jobs worked in construction, gardening, or mines surrounding Tucson. Many Tohono O'odham also were unemployed, while most with jobs worked in mines, cotton fields, or unskilled positions. Believing education to be key to lifting them out of this situation, they demanded that the university increase the enrollment of minority students. They argued for "parity," or a proportion of students equal to their representation in Pima County. The university never met this demand, but the enrollment of Mexicans and Mexican Americans as a percentage of the student population grew as the decade came to a close. Nevertheless, a 1978 survey revealed that only 5 percent of the twenty-four thousand degrees awarded since 1973 went to people of Mexican descent, who at the time constituted 23.4 percent of Pima County's population. By 1982, their enrollment had increased to 8 percent of all undergraduates, while Pima County's population of Mexican descent stood at 25 percent.[37]

Just as troubling, many minority students fared poorly at the university. Even though they constituted 5 percent of all undergraduates in 1978, they accounted for 11 percent of all undergraduates on probation. A 1980 breakdown of probation and dropout rates found that 57 percent of all "Hispanic," 54 percent of all African American, and 39 percent of all Native American undergraduates were either on probation or had flunked out of school. Frank Felix, who served as an Arizona state senator from 1973 to 1979 before taking an administrative post at the university, called these figures "appalling."[38]

Statistics on minority faculty during the 1970s also were "dismal." According to one newspaper article, by 1983, "Affirmative Action just hasn't taken place." That year, the university appointed a committee of eleven faculty members to author a report on the institution's minority hiring and promotion practices. It found that minorities represented only 3.5 percent of full professors, 7.5 percent of associate professors, and 8.6 percent of assistant professors. Since 1970, only one African American had been promoted to full professor, while during the same period the number of full professors of Mexican descent increased from four to seven, and the number of Native American full professors increased from one to three. These figures led the chairman of the committee to conclude, "there has been little improvement" at the U of A, and in many ways the "situation is worse than it was." President Henry Koffler, who succeeded Schaefer in 1982, attributed the university's deficit of minority faculty to the "empty pipeline" of individuals pursuing doctorates. Yet many argued instead that it stemmed from the persistence of racial discrimination. On balance, minority underrepresentation reflected poorly on the university. As one article put it, "A university that remains a white male enclave cannot adequately serve a state in which . . . minorities comprise nearly 28 percent of the population."[39]

Minority underrepresentation at the U of A was one of the main issues driving Tucson's Chicano student movement, which spread from the university throughout the community. By the late 1960s, Mexican Americans in Tucson had, in fact, worked for decades to increase the presence of students of Mexican descent at the U of A. During the 1950s, the Jácome family established the "Carlos C. Jácome Fellowship in Merchandising," named after the family's patriarch. The award went to a U of A student of "Mexican" or "Spanish" descent who majored in business and demonstrated financial need. In 1968, Tucson's League of Mexican American Women created a fund that managed to raise more than $100,000 by the late 1970s; the purpose of the fund was to offer female students "an opportunity to become a source of strength for the entire Tucson community." The next year, the Mexican American Scholarship Foundation was established to provide fellowships for seven students of Mexican descent. Other community groups such as the Tucson Coalition for Justice, Image of Tucson, La Raza Legal Alliance, the Southwest Voter Registration Project, and Chicanos por la Causa also worked to increase the number of Mexican Americans at the U of A. These efforts notwithstanding, the government report and Tucson's Mexican American community concluded that the U of A had made little progress.[40]

During the Chicano movement, U of A students ramped up recruitment efforts in area high schools, junior high schools, and even elementary schools. With modest financial support from a university administration that sought to limit negative publicity, students first reached out to Cholla, Tucson, Sunnyside, Pueblo, Salpointe, Nogales, and Douglas high schools because many of these had minority populations that exceeded 50 percent of the student body. University students visited these schools to discuss the benefits of a college education. They also met parents with the goal of developing a "healthy attitude in the home toward attending college." By the early 1980s, the university had also designed summer courses for junior high and high school students in creative writing, computers, drama, speech, and other fields. According to one reporter, these became an important way for the university to establish relationships with Mexicans and Mexican Americans in Tucson. Once students arrived at the university, they found new tutoring services, "skill centers," and cultural organizations that would help them ease their transition.[41]

Beyond offering college prep guidance, Chicana and Chicano students at the U of A encouraged high school students to become politically active. Undergraduates and MEChA members Salomón Baldenegro and Raúl Grijalva, for example, in 1969 helped organize student walkouts at Pueblo and Tucson high schools approximately one year after the famous East L.A. blowouts, during which Chicana and Chicano high school students walked out of classes at multiple Los Angeles schools to protest that city's educational inequalities. Because Tucson's superintendent of public schools had refused to meet with them, hundreds of students walked out of class in February and March 1969 to demand classes in Mexican-American history, Spanish-language classes for Spanish-speaking students, and more "Chicano" teachers and administrators in Tucson's high schools. They also contributed essays, poetry, and opinion pieces to *El Coraje* (Courage), a newsletter published by Tucson's Mexican American Liberation Committee (MALC) and distributed throughout the community.[42]

Currents of university-community exchange exposed rifts between Mexican Americans in Tucson based on different understandings of ethnicity, race, and class. Chicanos clashed with individuals like Jácome, whom they referred to as a "vendido," someone who had sold out his race. Even older Mexican Americans described their ambivalence toward the department-store owner, simultaneously admiring his success and criticizing his alleged abandonment of Mexican culture. He did not care about social, political, and economic inequality, Chicanos believed, and others like him were called "armchair generals" who felt entitled to comment on the problems of Mexican Americans, yet did nothing to alleviate the injustices they experienced. Articles in *El Coraje* echoed these claims. One praised Chicano students who gave their time and money to repair and improve homes in Tucson's *barrios*, while middle- and upper-class Mexican Americans with more resources mustered a mere five dollars and volunteered none of their time. Another article, titled "Commitment Gap," contemplated more existential divisions. The "real Mexican-Americans (Chicanos)," wrote the author of the article, "are the ones who will help their people, the ones who care about the problems of the Mexican-Americans in the area," not the ones who "think and act like they were Anglo-Americans." These divisions resulted in "a deep feeling of suspicion." There was indeed a border to be found in Tucson, and it divided people of Mexican descent from each other.[43]

Mexican Americans like Jácome experienced the division as well, but they felt that Chicano youth had betrayed *them*, not the other way around. The 1970 El Rio controversy was a telling episode. From summer through fall of that year, the El Rio Coalition Front—a group led by Baldenegro that claimed to represent more than ten thousand west-side residents—battled with the city to convert the private El Rio Country Club and Golf Course into a park and community center. Shortly after the urban renewal that razed the *barrio histórico*, they voiced a broad critique of postwar Tucson's urban development and encroachment into their neighborhoods. As a member of the golf club, Jácome opposed the initiative not only because he believed it would deprive the area of income from membership dues but also because of the manner in which the El Rio Coalition Front protested. They held public demonstrations and hearings, sometimes heckling golfers and making it "uncomfortable" for them to approach the course. On September 5, 1970, their protests turned violent. "A group of about 30 militants forced their way onto the grounds, picketed, milled [about], and finally stoned patrol cars, broke windows, and forced open the main gate." Reports claimed that "unknown vandals" returned later that evening and "damaged greens, tore up benches and ball washers, and overturned an electric drinking fountain." Borrowing redbaiting antiprotest language typical on both sides of the border, Jácome labeled their activism "anarchy" and "militancy."[44]

The incident concluded in December 1970, when the city agreed to the El Rio Coalition Front's demands by converting the course from private to public and building a community center in a small corner of the park. The whole movement defied what Jácome considered to be the civility, dignity, and respect of Tucson's community of Mexican descent. In one sense, the incident marked a generational gap between Chicano youth and their parents. But generational difference did not explain how the El Rio Coalition Front had galvanized the support of youth and adults alike. The real shift was the much broader mobilization around social, political, and ethnic issues that in a fundamental way undermined the position of Jácome—who seemed genuinely confounded by Chicano radicalism—and also the logic of growth, progress, modernization, and harmony, which had been key to almost thirty years of Sunbelt borderland development.[45]

Jácome took issue with the separatist rhetoric of Chicanas and Chicanos. Just before the El Rio incident, Jácome wrote an op-ed for the *Arizona Daily Star* that bluntly criticized Chicano student activists. "We are Americans 100 percent," he wrote, and "we should not segregate ourselves

Salomón Baldenegro with loudspeaker at El Rio protest. (Jack Sheaffer Photograph Collection, MS 435, 40463, 41, courtesy of University of Arizona Libraries, Special Collections.)

and call ourselves Chicanos, Raza, or any hyphenated names." He made the same argument when ideas for the U of A's Mexican American Studies and Research Center (MASRC) first gained momentum. Its name was still up for debate. University administrators had not decided whether it would include terms like "Chicano" or "Raza." Expressing his own thoughts on the matter, Jácome wrote in a letter to the dean, "I think the University of Arizona should eliminate" such words. During a conversation with professors Adalberto Guerrero, Macario Saldate, and Henry Oyama—a part Japanese, part Mexican American teacher who worked on minority-education issues and whose family had been interned in Arizona during World War II—Jácome launched into a tirade about the very word "Chicano." He asked, what did it mean? "¿Que chingado es, Chicano, chingado, Chicano, chingado?" Saldate recalled that Jácome became red in the face as "he kept confusing the word 'Chicano' with 'chingado,'" a crude expletive. The delegation left, having said not a word. "It was a one-way conversation," Saldate remarked.[46]

As their failure to communicate suggests, Jácome and Chicano activists spent the 1960s and 1970s caricaturing one another. Conservatives like Jácome called activists revolutionaries without a cause, Communists, and radicals, and the activists called Mexican Americans like Jácome *vendidos*, *pochos*, and other names meaning sellouts or servants to the white race. None of these characterizations accurately portrayed the ideological diversity of Tucson's communities of Mexican descent. Many Mexican Americans identified neither as conservatives nor as radicals. The Mexican American students who belonged to "los universitarios" gathered socially and raised money for scholarships. Others supported MEChA but were not members themselves. Isabel García, an undergraduate during the early 1970s, recalled participating in the regional labor struggles of Mexican and Mexican American workers in Arizona. Her father was an organizer for the International Union of Mine, Mill, and Smelter Workers (IUMMSW), and she became politically active because of her parents' influence. But she did not consider her activism part of Tucson's Chicano movement. Instead, she believed it was part of the broader fight for workers' rights. She was "beyond MEChA," she said. This broad range of activities demonstrated the diversity of Mexican and Mexican American responses to the Chicano movement.[47]

Competing understandings of class and ethnic politics not only fractured communities in Tucson but also shaped the encounters of people of

Mexican descent from both sides of the border. Even though Chicanos, as Sonoran newspapers noted, fancied their connection to Mexico and descent from a mythical homeland in the U.S.-Mexico borderlands called Aztlán, many Chicanos and Mexicans came from different economic and social backgrounds. They rarely socialized as a group at the U of A. Mexicans formed cliques of students from Hermosillo, Obregón, Cananea, and other cities. Others affiliated with Mexicans from similar class backgrounds. As Humberto Acuña put it, "the higher-up people that had a whole bunch of money to spend, they were a little group," and "then the people that really had to study because their parents were making a big effort to have them there were in another group." Mexicans at the U of A also rarely socialized with white students. They sat at particular tables in a Mexican restaurant at the student union, gossiping, making plans, and going to class as their schedules demanded. Several issues separated Chicanos from Mexicans, Mexicans from each other, and Mexicans from whites.[48]

Mexican student activism at Uni-Son rocked Hermosillo at the same time that Chicano activism deepened rifts in Tucson. Nevertheless, students at the U of A and Uni-Son worked in isolation despite their avowed solidarity with global liberation movements and common criticism of states that failed to achieve justice and equality for all of their citizens. Student activists in Arizona and Sonora were aware of efforts by their counterparts just across the international line, but they sought redress from their respective states and nations. Guadalupe Castillo recalled that a few Mexican students sought refuge in Tucson when Mexican university administrators lashed out at them. Chicano students hosted them, she said, but, according to Baldenegro, Chicano and Mexican students never organized together. Chicano students at the U of A protested against racial discrimination and their continued marginalization within Tucson, while Mexican students at Uni-Son waged campaigns against statewide political corruption, the lack of transparency at their institution, and the growing gap between rich and poor. Students at both universities claimed to support farm workers, miners, and other laborers in their respective states, but they did not offer a regional or transnational criticism of the negative effects of Arizona's and Sonora's Sunbelt borderland.[49]

The 1960s and 1970s shook Uni-Son, its administrators, and the state as a whole. Student activism in Mexico began during the 1950s with a series of strikes that merged leftist factions, including labor organizations, the Mexican Communist Party, cardenistas, and supporters of Third World–liberation movements. Together with middle-class teachers, bankers, lawyers, laborers, and others, students throughout the country criticized the government as postwar regional and national economies declined. In Sonora, student strikes led the police and the military to employ violence against them. A 1967 strike gained steam after Sonora's PRI, without consulting students or workers, imposed on them its choice of Félix Serna to run for the governorship of Sonora. In response, members of la Federación de Estudiantes de la Universidad de Sonora (the Uni-Son Student Federation) instead backed Fausto Acosta Romo, who withdrew from the race after police sprayed students with tear gas and beat them with clubs, pipes, and chains. Describing their frustration with Sonora's electoral politics, students wrote in 1973, at the time of the next gubernatorial election, that the "same circus gets staged every six years" and that all governors represent "the same thing." Students argued for the formation of political parties that were independent of the PRI and the more conservative Partido Acción Nacional (National Action Party, PAN). More strikes during the early 1970s unfolded for similar reasons, and the government again used force to squash them. During these decades of activism, Arizona's governor, Jack Williams, assisted his Sonoran counterparts by sending tear gas to Hermosillo to repel the so-called radical activists.[50]

Like Chicano students at the U of A, Mexican students at Uni-Son denounced their university's administrators, charging them not with racism but rather with cronyism, neglect, and pandering to the state's business and political leadership. Sonora's political, business, and university leaders were often one and the same. Ignacio Soto served as president of the board of trustees after serving as governor, and Luis Encinas had been the rector of Uni-Son beforehand, which struck many students as the height of political and educational corruption. Students also complained about outdated textbooks and classrooms, insisted on better teachers, and argued for "freedom of thought" in their classrooms. They believed they would achieve these reforms only if they "linked the problems of the university with the problems of society as a whole." So they called on their professors to engage global issues, including the Vietnam War, sixties counterculture, drug addiction, and growing economic inequality. Students throughout Mexico called for courses on Marx, Lenin, Stalin, and Mao. In Sonora, they demanded a "critical education," one that did not simply "justify" the "exploitative system in which we live" but rather strove for a more "humane and just society."[51]

Uni-Son students framed their criticisms of government and university within the context of Mexican society during the twentieth century, especially the Mexican Revolution and post–World War II economic growth. In its broadest terms, their activism during the 1960s and 1970s was a stinging rebuke of postrevolutionary Mexican politics in general. Students praised Pancho Villa and Emiliano Zapata as the true leaders of the revolution, but they claimed that "industrialists, landowners, merchants, and bankers"—the boosters of Arizona's and Sonora's Sunbelt borderland—had become its main beneficiaries. Through violence, briberies, and lies, the rich had removed poor farmers from their land. Students also found fault with former revolutionaries who, they believed, had become corrupted through their association with the PRI. Nevertheless, the Mexican government "exalted" the "achievements" of the revolution. From the 1940s forward, Mexican leaders cited the country's economic growth as the fruit of the revolution, clear evidence of progress. Moreover, the beneficiaries of postwar growth claimed responsibility for the "heroic gestures" that led to Sonora's economic development. Mexico had benefited from wartime production in the United States, which created opportunities for Mexico's increased production for domestic and, even more important, international consumption. However, for Uni-Son students, this narrative of Mexico's economic growth only demonstrated the "contradictions of capitalist society."[52]

Student critics wrote that the displacement of indigenous communities and other poor farmers from their land, the decline of collective farming, exploitation of agricultural workers, the ascent of a "divine caste," and subordination of politics to the interests of large landowners was the "true history" of postwar Sonora. The classes that benefited from Sonora's growth were the same ones that "defeated masses of farm workers" during the revolution and had strong ties to "North American imperialists." After reversing the gains of the Cárdenas era, the government supported new lending policies that favored individual *ejidatarios*, thereby causing collective landowners to literally lose ground. "*Ejidatario* devoured *ejidatario*" as individual landowners assimilated to a postwar economy that converted some from poor farmers into members of a "rural bourgeoisie." As a result, unemployed Sonorans migrated to cities like Hermosillo, Guaymas, and Ciudad Obregón, whose growth benefited from the "misery and exploitation of thousands and thousands of workers." At first the Mexican government "desperately" sought to alleviate tensions between the "class in power" and the "popular masses," but then repression increasingly became the government's answer to activism among students, teachers, and workers. Cycles of activism and repression during the 1950s set the stage for the violence of the late 1960s, most notably the massacre at Tlatelolco on October 2, 1968, during which Mexican government forces killed hundreds of students in the public square of Mexico City. These earlier battles, Sonoran students insisted, animated their struggles during the 1970s against federal and state governments, police, and university administrations.[53]

Although students at Uni-Son rhetorically linked their movement with others throughout Mexico, Latin America, and beyond, their positions did not neatly match up with the anti-imperialist sentiment surging among students elsewhere around the world. They observed conditions in Yucatán, Nuevo León, Chihuahua, Puebla, Sinaloa, and the capital city that were similar to those in Sonora. They hung on Uni-Son's walls pictures of Ho Chi Minh, Che Guevara, and Genaro Vázquez Rojas, a radical activist from Guerrero, Mexico. The students felt "solidarity with the Vietnamese people," one student wrote, because of the "capitalist regime" that was "drowning them." They also expressed outrage at the toppling and assassination of Chilean president Salvador Allende and called Rector Alfonso Castellanos Idiáquez the "Pinochet of Uni-Son," referring to the Chilean dictator who upended Allende with help from the United States. For Uni-Son students, the rise of Augusto Pinochet demonstrated the efforts of Chile's "dominant classes" to disempower "workers in the fields and in the city" and to "hammer" and "crush" labor and student movements with a "wave of bloody repression." Global protests helped the students articulate their condemnation of Mexican authoritarianism, demands for national sovereignty, and notions of solidarity with other Latin American countries. But Uni-Son students also argued against Fidel Castro's regime in Cuba and against Communism in general. One decried the way in which Cubans had suffered under Castro, while another criticized those who wanted to see Mexico become "another Cuba or Russia" in order to impose, as in those countries, a "tyrannical," nondemocratic regime that would destroy Mexico's economic and religious institutions. Throughout Mexico, the Cuban Revolution inspired students but also disillusioned them because of its perceived threats to democracy.[54]

Uni-Son, students believed, was the "only place" where they could criticize a government that was incapable of controlling price inflation, had not solved the problems of unemployment, and relied on police repression to keep the rich in power. There they could shine a spotlight on the plight of "farmers without land" and "workers without jobs." Some forty or fifty "millionaires," they said, controlled Sonora. These powerful men sent their children to universities in Mexico City or the United States and therefore cared little about the fate of Uni-Son. The rich even hoped for its demise, students claimed, since that would "condemn future Sonorans to ignorance" and allow state leaders to "freely exploit" them. The alliance between businesspeople and politicians led students to believe—somewhat contradictorily since it suggested that the university served a purpose for them, after all—that Uni-Son had become a mere instrument for the development and advancement of a professional class that had little sympathy for the "social reality of exploitation." New scientific discoveries and technologies only "increased the economic and political power of a dominant minority" that comprised bankers, merchants, and industrialists rather than furthering the "collective interests" of the whole. This so-called progress accrued wealth only to the accounts of the few and was an "inevitable consequence" of "capitalist production." Protesting students claimed that members of Uni-Son's Comité Pro Defensa del Orden Universitario (Committee to Defend Order at the University) voiced the interests of Sonora's aspiring professional class. They accused newspapers like *El Imparcial* and *El Sonorense* of serving as mouthpieces for Sonora's "commercial oligarchy," landowners, and ranchers complicit with "Yankee imperialism." The tactics of these newspapers could not be more "coarse," the students said; they articulated the interests of only *priístas* and *panistas*, businesspeople, and religious leaders who saw student activism at Uni-Son as a clear sign of Sonora's "communist infiltration."[55]

Even if local particulars shaped student activism in Tucson and Hermosillo, and even if a transnational denunciation of postwar society might have lent greater power to their individual and collective voices, youth on both sides of the border criticized the discriminations and inequalities that resulted from Arizona's and Sonora's postwar development. Their parents had struggled in the region's fields and mines or, as labor representatives, had organized workers in these places. These youths arrived at universities in Tucson and Hermosillo because their parents, who themselves had struggled to succeed, instilled in them the belief that education would lead to progress. In a real way, it did. More people of Mexican descent attended college than ever before, many of them with support from newly established fellowships. But in the context of widespread student activism around the world, universities in Arizona and Sonora became sites of protest against rampant injustices on both sides of the border. These universities symbolized postwar growth, modernization, and even enlightenment. Businesspeople and politicians had spent decades selling the idea that progress and harmony characterized the postwar decades. However, student movements during the 1960s and 1970s eroded such notions by maintaining that profits and political power for some had led to discrimination, political corruption, and economic inequality. The tensions that were both cause and effect of their censure spread across the borderlands during the late twentieth century, a contentious period of regional history that rendered postwar assertions of progress relics from the past.

By the early 1980s, several university-sponsored programs demonstrated progress in international relations between Arizona and Sonora and for people of Mexican descent in Tucson. Yet students on both sides of the border simultaneously critiqued their academic institutions and postwar borderlands society in general and revealed cracks in the Sunbelt borderland that widened as the twentieth century wore on. Developments at the U of A and Uni-Son during the 1960s and 1970s were representative of the region's transition from an era when ideas about state-led economic growth, modernization, and progress dominated public discourse to an era shaped by neoliberal economies and social, political, and cultural tensions and conflicts.[56]

A steady stream of research had brought together academics from both sides of the border, whose work expanded knowledge about the borderlands and encouraged mutual understanding between the United States and Mexico. The Guadalajara Summer Program remained one of the university's most popular study-abroad opportunities, and the university had developed an alumni base in Sonora and other Mexican states. In response to pressure from Chicanos and Tucson's broader Mexican-descent community, the U of A and Arizona's state legislature increased funding for programs that benefited so-called minority students. In 1978, President Schaefer allotted a meager $5,000 for the recruitment of "Hispanic" students, but for the 1981–1982 academic year the state legislature designated almost $500,000 to develop such initiatives.[57]

The founding of the MASRC and of a Hispanic alumni association, in particular, demonstrated gains from two decades of mobilization. The MASRC had been in the planning stages since 1968, and throughout the 1970s students and professors discussed what a Chicano, Raza, or Mexican American studies program might look like. In 1981, the Mexican American Studies and Research Center became a reality, and in 1983 it received state funding. The University of Arizona Hispanic Alumni Association was established in 1982, when a group of "Hispanic community and business leaders"—former members of the Los Universitarios social club—held a meeting attended by Arizona governor Bruce Babbitt, U of A president Koffler, and more than seventy Mexican Americans from Tucson. It was an event that, according to one article, could not have happened twenty-five years earlier because there would not have been enough alumni to attend. One Mexican American considered the event a celebration of progress. "That night," he said, "we saw how far we've come since the end of World War II." Columnist Ernesto Portillo added, "It's a good indicator of progress when, every day, an individual or a community raises its goals, its vision, and its aspirations." The U of A, he concluded, is "our university, period."[58]

The appointment of Edie Auslander to the board of regents as the first Mexican American woman to hold that position, as well as the Arizona Historical Society's Mexican American Heritage Project, which set out to collect photographs and oral histories from Tucson's residents of Mexican descent, seemed to confirm progress. The project marked a significant turnaround for an organization that, during the early twentieth century, sanitized Arizona's histories of ethnic and racial conflict. Although the historical society was not formally linked to the university, most of its researchers were university affiliates. Anthropologist Tom Sheridan directed the effort and from its collected materials wrote his seminal study of Tucson's Mexican and Mexican American communities, *Los Tucsonenses*.[59]

Despite these signs of advancement, more than ten years after Chicanos and the HEW charged the U of A with institutional racism, the situation they observed had barely changed. Several professors of Mexican descent believed that the financial support MASRC received was a mere "illusion"; it did not come with an ideological commitment to or an understanding of the center's work. In 1982, shortly after the MASRC opened, President Koffler stated that the center would be a place where students of

Mexican descent could "feel culturally comfortable." Many students and professors took offense, claiming that Koffler had undermined the center's teaching and research agendas. That same year, the university halved the new center's budget, leading its director, Macario Saldate, to present President Koffler with a "10-year history of academic neglect of Hispanics at the UA." Because of community pressure applied by more than two hundred "Hispanic leaders," the center received more than $200,000 for the 1982–1983 academic year. The incident nevertheless reinforced the belief that the university acted only when forced to do so.[60]

Moreover, the U of A student senate cut MEChA's budget, citing the organization's political activities and calling on the group to "alter" its "intent." Ironically, Tucson newspapers had recently published articles about the successes of several MEChA alumni who had studied at the university during the early 1970s. Instead of "picketing 'the system,'" as they once had done, now they were "making the system work" for them. Baldenegro was the director of Tucson's Youth Services Bureau; Grijalva was a board member of the Tucson Unified School District; and Guadalupe Castillo taught history at Pima County Community College. At the same time, recruitment efforts also suffered. As Sunnyside School District board member Camilo Castillo put it, "I see more Army recruiters . . . than I see university recruiters." Despite more than a decade of social and political activism, the conditions that had inspired their engagement still remained.[61]

Meanwhile, the U of A and Uni-Son became models for cross-border collaboration during decades that gave rise to greater tensions between the United States and Mexico. Professors in departments at Sonoran universities had earned their doctoral degrees in Tucson. One newspaper article stated, "When Mexican engineers gather for cocktails in Cananea, Sonora, they often salute the school that endowed them with their skills—the University of Arizona." Describing how university exchanges minimized separations caused by the border, the article stated that Arizona and Sonora are "fused by an intricate web of educational ties." The U of A and Uni-Son therefore would remain "sister institutions" despite episodes of conflict that threatened to divide them.[62]

Divisions within and between Arizona and Sonora became more pronounced and moved well beyond universities on both sides of the border. The transformation of local, national, and global economic and political conditions during the 1970s and 1980s led to greater conflicts throughout the Americas. Transnational connections and the cross-border diplomatic efforts of men like Alex Jácome and Ignacio Soto endured. Their quest for profits and harmony continued, and shoppers, tourists, students, and families moved between Arizona and Sonora daily. But in the minds of many, these actors no longer embodied cross-border relations between Arizona and Sonora. Changing commercial relationships and mounting debt transformed borderland economies, and undocumented immigrants, smugglers, and refugees—who migrated to the area in response to these shifting circumstances—claimed increasing attention and were seen as dangerous, illegal threats.

5

VIOLENCE AND SANCTUARY

After Isabel García graduated from the University of Arizona's law school in the early 1970s, the Arizona-Sonora borderland became the focus of national and international attention when Mexican migrant workers were kidnapped and tortured, and Central Americans sought refuge from violent civil wars. García and others immediately established advocacy organizations to support them. Greatly influenced by her parents' experience organizing Mexican and Mexican American laborers in and around Tucson, she dedicated her career to fighting for immigrants' rights. Fewer Latin Americans settled in Arizona than in California or Texas, but the state was hardly the "backwater" that immigration scholars have described. The growing number of documented and undocumented immigrants of Latin American descent incited both a nativist backlash and the formation of equally forceful movements for immigrants' rights. Battle lines formed along axes of sovereignty and the rule of law on one side and of social justice and human rights on the other, shaping Arizona's border debates into the twenty-first century.[1]

The shifting economies and politics of Arizona's and Sonora's Sunbelt borderland created the immigration and border debates of the 1970s and 1980s, which were characterized by the decline of an extended period during which rhetoric about cross-border relations focused on the promotion of growth, modernization, and progress. To be sure, in the late twentieth century cross-border exchanges of the sort celebrated from the 1940s through the 1960s persisted. More tourists traveled between the United States and Mexico. Animals, grains, and produce continued to stream into the United States from Sinaloa and Sonora. Mexican shoppers, even if their flow temporarily decreased in the late 1970s, remained loyal customers of stores in Nogales and Tucson. Students from Sonora still received degrees from the University of Arizona, while those from Tucson visited Nogales and Puerto Peñasco. Yet global, hemispheric, and national economies and politics led to important transformations in the commercial, consumption, and migration patterns of the Arizona-Sonora borderland. These changes created friction throughout the region.

The transition from a state-driven to a neoliberal economy characterized by the increasing power of private development and investment by foreign corporations, in addition to increasingly tense Cold War politics, marked this new era of domestic and international conflict. The U.S. and Mexican governments decreased their investments in Arizona's and Sonora's agricultural and livestock sectors, as the economies of both states shifted toward the service sector. Meanwhile, the mechanization of farm and ranch work and soil exhaustion led to rising levels of unemployment, especially among the poorest members of society. The Mexican growers and ranchers who became wealthy during the postwar era—Jácome's Mexican clientele, in other words—became increasingly indebted as they earned less yet tried to maintain the lifestyles to which they were accustomed, spending lavishly on automobiles, homes, clothes, and travel. As one scholar wrote, the "crisis in private agricultural circles" of the late 1960s and early 1970s stemmed "in large part from the inability of the wealthy to adjust their standard of living." In the emerging world of consumer credit on both sides of the border, these middle-class spenders in a sense were ideal "consumer-citizens," demonstrating how U.S. and Mexican debt economies from the 1970s forward shaped the lives of borderland residents. But the increased indebtedness of individuals and nations alike destabilized borderland economies and deepened the economic, political, and ethnic inequalities that had led to protests at the University of Arizona and La Universidad de Sonora.[2]

In Sonora and other Mexican border states, the establishment in 1965 of the Border Industrialization Program (BIP) was intended to alleviate some of the financial problems caused by agricultural decline. The BIP led to the development of *maquiladoras*, or Mexican border factories owned by international corporations that assembled raw materials into finished products for distribution around the world. The premium these factories placed on cross-border exchange built on the postwar logic of borders that were open for commercial trade but also foreshadowed the signing of the North American Free Trade Agreement (NAFTA) in 1994, when neoliberal logic reached its apex in the United States and Mexico. The cross-border commerce created by the *maquiladora* industry helped set in motion the migrant streams of the late twentieth century, as did shifting

Cold War dynamics in Central America. Brutal U.S.-backed regimes and guerrillas repressed leftist movements and worked to destabalize leftist governments. Cities throughout the Americas offered sanctuary to refugees from political violence. Many borderland residents and politicians in the United States reacted to the new migrations by calling for increasingly restrictive immigration policies that focused on preventing unauthorized immigration, human smuggling, and drug trafficking.

Until the 1970s, migration between Arizona and Sonora was, by and large, a regional phenomenon, but increased migration during that decade from other areas of Mexico and Central America altered the demographic landscape of both states. Up to three-quarters of Mexicans and Mexican Americans in Arizona traced their roots to Sonora. But the end of the Bracero Program in 1964, passage of the 1965 Immigration and Nationality Act (Hart-Celler), establishment of the BIP in the same year, and the financial and political crises of the 1970s brought an increasing number of immigrants from countries throughout the Americas. Sonora historically had one of the lowest rates of emigration of any Mexican state, a number that included migrants who traveled to other areas of Mexico and those who left for other countries. In the 1970s, however, an increasing number of Sonorans left their state, both with and without documentation. As a result, Arizona's foreign-born Mexican population doubled in a decade. The state still received a fraction of the undocumented immigrants that settled in California and Texas, yet their presence incited waves of anti-immigrant sentiment and violence.[3]

Increased Mexican immigration reversed population trends in Arizona that had shaped the state since the early twentieth century. Whites became Arizona's majority population in the 1920s, and the gap between white and Mexican populations widened as a result of World War II–era and postwar migrations. But higher birthrates among Mexicans and Mexican Americans and the rise of Mexican immigration altered these dynamics. People of Mexican descent constituted an ever-greater percentage of Arizona's population, and demographers expected them to surpass the state's white population sometime during the twenty-first century. Many whites came to believe that Mexicans threatened their livelihoods and took over their communities.[4]

As the region's shifting economic and political contexts led a greater number of Mexican and Central American immigrants into Arizona, whites, people of Mexican descent, native peoples, anti-immigration forces, immigrant rights advocates, and the United States and Mexico increasingly debated immigration and border policy. Citizens and the U.S. and Mexican governments alike had confronted these issues in earlier periods as well. In virtually all moments of economic or political crisis during the twentieth century, the U.S. government sought to restrict immigration by deporting Mexicans seen as financial burdens or political threats and by requiring Tohono O'odham and others seeking to cross the border to carry cards that verified their right to move between Arizona and Sonora. As one historian notes, U.S. and Mexican authorities worked together to police the border. However, beginning in the 1970s, the U.S.-Mexico border became increasingly militarized as conservatives and vigilantes lobbied the U.S. government to hire more border patrol officers, erect more fencing along the U.S.-Mexico border, and punish employers who knowingly hired undocumented immigrants. Legislators worked these ideas into bills debated between 1972 and 1986, when the Immigration Reform and Control Act (IRCA) was passed. At the same time, vigilantes armed themselves to protect the border, and immigrant rights advocates opposed restrictive policies, arguing for labor protections and citizenship for undocumented workers. The increasingly contentious tone of national debates had grave consequences for U.S.-Mexico relations and people of Mexican descent living in the United States. Even though undocumented immigration seemed to be a domestic debate about how to protect U.S. borders and national sovereignty, it was in fact the result of transnational political economies. Undocumented immigration was only one symptom of the postwar rise and decline of Arizona's and Sonora's Sunbelt borderland.[5]

The Political Economy of Rising Anti-Immigrant Aggression

From the 1960s forward, the Arizona-Sonora borderland experienced dramatic economic transformations that ultimately shaped immigration and border debates. Borderland economies shifted toward service industries in Arizona and toward service and manufacturing industries in Sonora embodied by *maquiladoras*. Hundreds of thousands of Mexican migrants moved to northern Mexico's borderlands to work in these sectors; many of them crossed into the United States to seek employment. The economic conditions of the 1970s unfolded against a backdrop of global political change. Markets collapsed, inflation spiked, and international debt increased, while the Cold War in the Americas entered a particularly tense period shaped by the anti-Communist, U.S.-backed repression of leftist movements. Changing economies, politics, and demographics led to anti-Mexican sentiment throughout the borderlands.

In 1965, the Mexican government established a program enabled by the economic visions of postwar businesspeople and politicians on both sides of the border. The BIP led to the construction, from Baja California to Coahuila, of *maquiladoras,* which became a central feature of borderlands economies into the twenty-first century. The border region's postwar economic development had established infrastructures that paved the way for *maquiladoras;* new construction operations built them, while expanded agricultural and livestock industries nourished their workers, and international highways carried materials and finished products to and from the factories.

The BIP had several advantages for Mexican and U.S. governments and businesses, fulfilling postwar dreams of cross-border trade. Mexico also expected the program to alleviate a job crunch created by the mechanization of agriculture and ranching and the conclusion of the Bracero Program, which sent hundreds of thousands of migrant guest workers back to Mexico. Unemployment reached 50 percent in some Mexican border communities. The jobs created by the *maquildoras* paid more than others, reinforcing notions of northern Mexico's higher quality of life in comparison to other parts of the country. For the international corporations that owned them, the *maquiladoras* had obvious benefits, including a cheap labor supply and taxes levied only on the profit margin of goods produced in Mexico. As a result, many global corporations moved some or all of their manufacturing operations to the Mexican border, thereby opening the region to rising forces of globalization that shifted the production of goods from so-called developed to underdeveloped areas of the world. Business owners also expected the factories to lift regional economies in general, since they would increase revenue for restaurants, groceries, other retailers, and construction companies that built new homes for plant employees.[6]

Because of their perceived benefits, the number of *maquiladoras*—and Sonora's dependence upon them—increased rapidly and transformed the state's economy. Sonora's first two factories opened in 1967, and by 1968 twelve *maquiladoras* employed 550 workers in Nogales, Agua Prieta, and San Luis Río Colorado. Between 1970 and 1990, the number of plants increased from thirty to more than one hundred, and the number of workers they employed increased from 2,700 to some 37,000. *Maquiladoras* also expanded beyond the border itself and, indeed, throughout Mexico. A network of plants formed between Hermosillo and Tucson, which became a free-trade zone that distributed *maquiladora*-produced goods across the United States. The biggest factory in Sonora's interior, the Ford Motor plant that opened in 1984 and employed University of Arizona alumni María Eugenia Flores and Humberto Acuña, produced more than a hundred thousand cars per year during the mid-1980s. The Sonoran government constructed a gas pipeline to meet Ford's energy needs, created industrial parks, and provided the company with water, cheap electricity, and tax benefits. Ultimately, one Sonoran scholar wrote, the cross-border exchange facilitated by the *maquiladoras* converted the Arizona-Sonora borderland into an "industrial corridor" that lessened Sonora's economic dependence on agriculture, while at the same time maintaining its dependence on the United States.[7]

Although the *maquiladoras* had some positive effects, they also had negative consequences both for employees and for regional businesses in general. The factories created tens of thousands of jobs not only for laborers but also for professionals. Half of all economic activity in Nogales and Agua Prieta depended on the *maquiladoras*, and in Naco the factories employed 65 to 80 percent of all residents. Yet they also revealed a darker side of economic development. Employees worked long hours, often without breaks. Eighty to 90 percent of them were women, and many became victims of sexual harassment and other forms of violence. The factories also highlighted deep social and class divisions. As cities expanded—both as a result of and to accommodate the *maquiladoras*—their poorest neighborhoods, where many employees lived, became overpopulated, infrastructurally strained, and polluted, with no drinking water, sewers, electricity, or paved roads. The broader export economies favored large-scale operations able to mass-produce goods, and as corporations took control, labor movements waned. Finally, Sonorans spent half of their earnings in Arizona, thereby depriving Sonoran businesses of income. Even though Arizona companies operated one-third of Sonora's *maquiladoras* or provided their supplies, and even though Sonoran businesses benefited from the *maquiladoras*, profits generally followed their parent corporations back to their international headquarters.[8]

As Sonora's *maquiladoras* grew, shifting economic and political contexts created tensions between the United States and Mexico that overshadowed praise for the benefits brought by cross-border exchange. Tourism industries still promoted cross-border travel, and during the early 1980s, hundreds of thousands of Arizonans and Sonorans crossed the border every month. Even though Jácome's had closed, Mexican consumers still visited Tucson's shopping malls. Local department stores like Goldwater's and national chains like Montgomery Ward and J.C. Penney continued to advertise in *El Imparcial* and accept payment in pesos despite the currency's instability. In the late 1970s, University of Arizona economists and the Arizona Office of Tourism began studying the habits of Mexican shoppers and found that they came from all class backgrounds. The vast majority lived in Sonora, while a small percentage came from Jalisco, Sinaloa, and Baja California. The working-class Mexicans who visited Arizona tended to live in border cities, cross by foot, stay for less than a day, and spend less money than members of "professional," "technical," and "managerial" groups, who traveled greater distances by car or airplane, stayed longer, and went primarily to Tucson and Phoenix. In total, Mexican shoppers spent more than $300 million in Arizona every year, including almost $10 million in local and state taxes. In the thirteen years after the survey, between 1978 and 1991, yearly border crossings by day laborers, tourists, shoppers, and families with relatives on the other side increased from 13.7 million to 19.4 million. While these factors pointed to the continued cross-border exchanges many considered hallmarks of the postwar period, much attention also shifted to the conflicts that shaped border debates into the twenty-first century.[9]

Economic travails in the 1970s and 1980s shaped debates about immigration and the border. In the United States, stagflation, rising levels of unemployment, and market instabilities caused by oil shortages shaped the lives of many Americans. Mexicans also suffered significant economic blows, both for domestic reasons and because of the global financial malaise. Sonora's *maquiladora* and mining industries experienced gains, but agriculture suffered from soil exhaustion, forcing scientists to develop new techniques. Without recognizing how deeply intertwined the two national economies had become—through labor exchanges, international loans, tourism, and trade—many in the United States increasingly saw Mexico as a risky partner. The Mexican government devalued the peso, which led to price hikes, capital flight, increased import costs, and even more political pressure on the already-beleaguered PRI. As during earlier economic downturns, Mexico sought to lessen its dependence on the United

States, this time by seeking to establish financial partnerships with Asia, Europe, and Canada. Moreover, Mexico's birthrate increased dramatically after World War II, leading to social spending that, by 1982, amounted to half of Mexico's GDP. Finally, new oil discoveries in 1977 fed optimism that Mexico's economy would stabilize and the government could cover mounting expenses, but in 1981 oil markets crashed, forcing Mexico to default on its debt. Mexico's postwar economic "miracle" was over.[10]

Shifting national and international economies were inseparable from increasingly tense Cold War relations throughout the Americas. The United States had wound down postwar economic-development programs south of the border. The conflict in Vietnam challenged its authority. Moreover, capitalist development widened inequalities instead of narrowing them, leading to the rise of leftist regimes. Between 1975 and 1979, Marxist movements took control of eleven Latin American countries. The United States cooperated with right-wing Latin American leaders eager to topple them, forming, in 1975, a "continental alliance against the Left," called Operation Condor. The increased polarization of U.S.–Latin American affairs caused tensions between U.S. and Mexican leaders, who expressed sympathy for leftist movements and denounced U.S. hegemony at the same time that they strove for harmonious U.S.-Mexico relations. Their posturing both angered U.S. officials and strengthened Mexico's bargaining position. Concurrently, the United States and Mexico negotiated shifting domestic politics. In Mexico, from the 1960s forward, the conservative PAN party challenged the PRI in municipal and state elections, particularly in central and northern states, including Sonora. In the United States, many Americans considered the Carter administration weak on the economy and passive toward Communism—instead of arguing for containment, Carter advocated the protection of human rights in Central America—which helped Ronald Reagan win the presidency in 1980. Under Reagan, direct state sponsorship of anti-Communist violence increased throughout the region.[11]

Sweeping economic and political transitions affected the Arizona-Sonora borderland and ultimately led to the emergence of Mexican immigration as a deeply divisive issue. First, they led to significant demographic shifts. Until the 1970s, migration in and between Arizona and Sonora maintained an overwhelmingly regional character, and Sonora had one of the lowest emigration rates of any Mexican state both because salaries in Sonora remained higher than elsewhere in the country and because people could work in the United States without moving there permanently. In 1973, only 2.6 percent of undocumented immigrants came from Sonora. By 1978 that number stood at 3.7 percent and by 1984 had grown to more than 5 percent. In little more than a decade, Sonora moved from twelfth to sixth place among Mexican states sending the greatest number of undocumented immigrants to the United States, behind Chihuahua, Michoacán, Baja California, Jalisco, and Guanajuato. Many Tohono O'odham, although displaced from their homelands, also moved within the region instead of to other parts of the United States or Mexico. These regional migration patterns changed during the 1970s, however, as former *braceros* and new migrants from central and southern Mexico sought work on both sides of the Arizona-Sonora border.[12]

In general, Sonora and Arizona experienced increased migration from outside the region during the 1970s and 1980s. By the end of the period, more than 16 percent of Sonora's population had been born in another Mexican state. Migrants to Sonora worked in the fishing and tourism industries of Guaymas and Puerto Peñasco; the fields surrounding Hermosillo and San Luis Río Colorado; and the *maquiladoras* of Nogales and Agua Prieta. Border cities had higher proportions of non-Sonorans living in them than other areas of the state, which offered evidence that many migrants planned temporary stays there before crossing over to the United States. Indeed, the number of Mexicans entering Arizona increased dramatically between 1970 and 1990; the Mexican and Mexican American population reached 17 percent of the state as a whole. Southern Arizona's communities of Mexican descent represented 26 percent of the area's population as a whole, compared with 14 percent of central Arizona and 5 percent of northern Arizona. Many of them still came from Sonora; one survey found that 60 percent of Sonoran emigrants named Arizona as their destination. However, compared with earlier periods, many more Mexicans came from other parts of Mexico, and Latin American migrants increasingly arrived from countries beyond Mexico, especially war-torn El Salvador and Guatemala.[13]

Tohono O'odham also continued to move throughout the border region in response to shifting economic contexts, although their migrations became increasingly unidirectional: from Sonora to Arizona. With assistance from the Mexican government—and, in particular, Hermosillo's land colonization commission, the state agency responsible for disbursing public lands—*mestizo* farmers and ranchers continued to displace Sonoran O'odham from their small *rancherías* near Caborca, Quitovac, and Pozo Verde. Some of them moved to Sonoran cities, where they worked in factories and sold crafts to tourists from the United States. But many more moved to Arizona, where they benefited from BIA services, settled with family members, and found employment as ranchers, agricultural workers, and domestics. They earned, on average, eight to ten times more than they had in Sonora. As a result, Arizona's O'odham population increased steadily from the mid-1960s forward, with a commensurate decline in Sonora. From the mid-twentieth century to 1990, Arizona's O'odham population increased from 7,200 to more than 17,000, whereas Sonora's declined from 400 to fewer than 50. The Mexican census in 1990 counted none.[14]

Longtime borderland residents and new migrants confronted local economies hampered by the global financial downturn and, more immediately, the Mexican peso devaluations of the late 1970s and early 1980s, which resulted from the country's debt crisis. Arizona's and Sonora's cattle, mining, tourism, and retail industries suffered. Economic turmoil hit border communities particularly hard, leaving them devastated. Governor Babbitt called them "economic disaster areas." Many Mexican consumers could no longer afford to shop in the United States, which left in shambles the Arizona businesses that relied on them. "My family still goes over," one Mexican shopper said, "but we mostly just look now." An Arizona department-store owner said that the devaluations had a "very depressing effect on the Mexican people—they are in no buying mood." Grim financial reports confirmed the impact of the devaluations on Arizona's border counties. Retail sales in Nogales fell between 40 and 70 percent. Santa Cruz County, with Nogales as the county seat, had the highest rate of unemployment in Arizona even before the 1976 devaluation, but afterward, joblessness rose by 2 percent in less than a month, to almost 20 percent. More than five hundred retail employees lost their jobs as a direct result of the devaluations; pedestrian and automobile traffic entering the United States declined sharply.[15]

The decreased flow of capital between the United States and Mexico negatively affected borderlands institutions beyond retail shops, including universities, ranches, and banks. Many Mexican students were forced to drop out of Pima County Community College and the University of Arizona because they could no longer afford tuition. Wary of Mexico's economic situation, ranchers sold their cattle and deposited the proceeds in U.S. banks. Others followed suit by selling their land and homes and transferring money to the United States. According to the *Tucson Citizen*, Sonora's "big money" families had always invested in the United States, but the devaluations led more Sonorans to make deposits. Sonoran businesspeople also left their home state, became "migrant capitalists," as one Sonoran historian has called them, started new businesses, and created thousands of jobs in Arizona. From 1977 to 1987, the number of Mexican-owned businesses in Arizona more than doubled, as did their sales and hiring. Because Mexican banks lost $3 billion, the Mexican government ordered a temporary suspension of all buying and selling of foreign currencies and gold. While well-to-do Mexicans sheltered themselves from the effects of the peso devaluations, working-class Mexicans had no assets to convert into dollars. This fact led to an even wider gap between Mexico's haves and have-nots, as one political cartoonist described them, inspiring him to ask, "Pancho Villa, where are you?" The cartoon suggested that Villa, the Mexican revolutionary hero—by reputation, a Robin Hood figure who stole from the rich and gave to the poor—would have protected poor Mexicans.[16]

Government officials, financiers, and merchants in Arizona proposed several solutions to the woes caused by the devaluations, demonstrating their recognition of the profound interdependence of Arizona's and Sonora's border economies. One Nogales department-store owner lowered his shop's prices. Governor Raúl Castro suggested that merchants should offer short-term credit to Mexican consumers by maintaining store accounts, as Jácome's had for decades. When Governor Babbitt, Castro's successor, pleaded Arizona's case to the White House, the U.S. government granted "economic dislocation" loans of up to $100,000 each for retailers who were able to prove that the devaluations had affected their businesses. For his part, Senator Goldwater suggested that the United States should invest directly in Mexico in order to bolster the country's economy. Mexico was, after all, our "biggest customer" in Latin America, he stated. The country's troubles also led to more qualitative observations about dilapidated borderland economies. Once grand monuments, like the 1964 customs gateway in Nogales, had become symbols of disrepair. A construction designed as a "show window" into Mexico, the gateway was now "filthy," projecting a message for tourists that said, "Do not enter this country."[17]

The simultaneous rise of immigration and decline of borderland economies sparked heated debates on both sides of the border. Because larger states like California and Texas received more immigrants, some scholars have argued that Arizona was irrelevant to immigration debates until the final years of the twentieth century. Yet the Arizona-Sonora borderland became a focal point of national and international debates in the 1970s and 1980s. Immigration and border politics there unfolded within the context of national tensions over these issues, but events in the borderland stretching from Tucson to Hermosillo, in particular, shaped the way Mexicans and Americans thought about immigrant rights, human rights, sanctuary, illegality, and the border more broadly.

Between 1972 and 1986, the U.S. Congress debated several comprehensive immigration-reform proposals, most notably the 1972 Rodino Bill—named after New Jersey's Democratic senator, Peter Rodino—Jimmy Carter's 1977 Alien Adjustment and Employment Act, and IRCA, which eventually passed on July 1, 1986. These proposals emerged as the result of increasing pressure to curb the rise of undocumented immigration after the mid-1960s. The end of the Bracero Program in 1964 terminated a guest-worker initiative that had provided for the legal, albeit temporary, migration of Mexicans to the United States. During the two decades of the program's existence, Mexican immigrants also crossed illegally, but the number who did so increased dramatically after its conclusion. With or without the Bracero Program, Mexicans still sought jobs in the United States. Congress passed the Hart-Celler Act in 1965, which—although technically restrictive since it capped the number of immigrants from particular countries at 120,000 per year—offered family-reunification provisions that led to greater immigration from Latin America, Asia, and elsewhere.[18]

The proposals debated between 1972 and 1986 contained many of the same provisions, which ultimately led to the articulation of a four-pronged approach to undocumented immigration that remained unchanged into the twenty-first century. The centerpiece of the Rodino Bill was sanctions against employers who knowingly hired undocumented immigrants. The Alien Adjustment and Employment Act kept Rodino's employer sanctions but also introduced highly controversial citizenship-adjustment provisions—derisively referred to as "amnesty"—which proposed to grant citizenship to millions of immigrants. Both proposals failed to pass Congress because of opposition from conservatives and liberals alike. After his election, Reagan revived debates about immigration reform with a proposal that combined employer sanctions and amnesty provisions, in addition to increased funding for the U.S. Border Patrol and an amendment to the existing work-visa program. Shifting national and international politics, as well as a delicate compromise among Latinos, enabled the passage of IRCA in 1986.

The points of contention over the various proposals remained fairly consistent throughout the 1970s and 1980s. Many conservatives supported employer sanctions despite objections from employers who relied on undocumented Mexican labor. They claimed to support legal migration but opposed unauthorized immigration by rearticulating old arguments that undocumented Mexicans took jobs from American citizens and burdened social-service programs. They vociferously opposed provisions that offered undocumented immigrants a path to citizenship, arguing that amnesty incentivized undocumented migration, rewarded undocumented migrants for breaking the law, and devalued U.S. citizenship because Americans and legal immigrants had earned it, whereas undocumented Mexicans would get it for free.

Liberals countered these conservative arguments. They generally opposed employer sanctions, claiming that they led employers to discriminate against all Latinos based on accent or appearance. They also refuted the ideas that Mexican immigrants took American jobs and burdened social-service programs by arguing instead that the United States relied on Mexican workers to fill positions U.S. citizens did not want and that Mexican immigrants gave more to the U.S. economy than they took by paying sales, Social Security, and other taxes even though they did not receive benefits from these revenues. Finally, they supported amnesty but wanted more immigrants to be able to take advantage of citizenship adjustment provisions than Carter or Reagan proposed. Carter's proposal set January 1, 1970, as the date from which undocumented immigrants had to reside continuously in the United States in order to be eligible for citizenship adjustment, while Reagan's proposal designated January 1, 1982. Liberals argued that both dates were arbitrary and maintained that those who came afterward, and were therefore ineligible, would constitute a "subclass" of people living in the United States. They proposed dates much closer to when the legislation would be passed. Finally, conservatives and liberals both agreed to increase financial support for the U.S. Border Patrol even though they disagreed about the effectiveness of stationing more officers along the international line.[19]

In Arizona, politicians, police, vigilantes, immigrant advocates, and ordinary citizens debated the immigration proposals circulating around the nation. Governor Babbitt became a sounding board for the full spectrum of arguments Arizonans made about immigration. He received letters—or manifestos—and ultimately advocated positions that recognized the rights of migrant workers regardless of their citizenship status. Babbitt filed away news articles about the dangers of population growth and the need to create opportunities for disadvantaged U.S. citizens rather than undocumented Mexicans. He also puzzled at how the Ku Klux Klan and César Chávez's United Farm Workers both argued for a "tightly restricted border," although for different reasons. A well-known priest and historian, Charles Polzer of Tucson, told Babbitt that he advocated an "almost open border," and Manuel García, a Mexican American attorney from Tucson, urged Babbitt to consider that it was "intolerable and immoral" to "bring in trainloads of poor people from a less developed country to pick our crops for substandard wages." A Tucson group called the Mexican Americans for Legalizing Aliens insisted that Mexican immigrants did not take jobs from Americans and instead contributed to the economy by paying taxes and shopping in Arizona stores. Babbitt listened to all of the arguments his constituents made and then delivered public proclamations supporting immigrant rights. He lamented their impoverished living conditions, the abuses they suffered, and their lack of legal protections. Such declarations drew ire from conservatives in Arizona and praise from Mexican officials, who appreciated his "humanitarian approach" to immigration.[20]

Arizonans also weighed in at hearings held in connection with Carter's 1977 proposal, organized by Senator Dennis Deconcini and Congressman Morris Udall, both from Arizona. The hearings, which took place in Nogales and Tucson, reflected a great diversity of opinions on immigration. Border Patrol agents, ranchers, university professors, teachers, graduate students, and immigrant rights advocates all testified, and after two days, an exasperated Udall said of the seemingly widespread disapproval of Carter's bill, "There is no one here to claim this monster." He struggled to make sense of the contradictory positions he heard. Some witnesses supported pieces of Carter's proposals, but nobody supported all of them, and many supported none. Law-enforcement officials believed amnesty was an outrage that mocked the rule of law, while those concerned about the "humanitarian aspects" of immigration believed that "amnesty is totally inadequate."[21]

Representatives of the Manzo Area Council, an immigrant-rights organization based in Tucson, offered some of the most provocative solutions. Established in 1972 as a federally funded War on Poverty program, the Manzo Area Council originally served poor Mexicans and Mexican Americans in Tucson, offering basic welfare services, senior-citizens assistance, and youth programs regardless of citizenship status. By the time of the 1977 hearings, the group had come under intense scrutiny from public officials, who argued that the Manzo Area Council improperly used public funds to support undocumented immigrants. On April 9, 1976, the U.S. Border Patrol—in coordination with the Immigration and Naturalization Service (INS) and the U.S. Attorney General—raided the organization's offices. After poring through hundreds of files, Border Patrol officers went to the homes of Manzo Area Council clients and deported more than fifty of them. Although the group was cleared of charges, it lost federal funding. A crucial source of support had been taken away, but independence from the government allowed the group to pursue a more aggressive strategy for protecting the human rights of all migrants. At the hearing in Nogales, attorney Margo Cowan, one of the organization's founders, lobbied for what she called an immigrant's "bill of rights," which would guarantee equal pay, unemployment insurance, disability payments, and permanent-resident visas. The Mexicans there agreed with her, arguing that migrant workers and their families should have the same rights as all American workers; receive equal pay and Social Security benefits; and have protection under United Nations resolutions that declared that all nations must respect the human rights of migrant workers.[22]

The Manzo Area Council remained southern Arizona's strongest voice for immigrant rights into the 1980s. After the hearings in Nogales, its members called for protections against deportation, the right to housing, and freedom from harassment by police. The group also suggested that, as integral members of U.S. communities, undocumented immigrants should be allowed to vote. These proposals would constitute the "most revolutionary immigration package of the century," Cowan said. Beyond its proposals, the Manzo Area Council established a foundation for all immigrant-rights organizations in Tucson from the 1970s forward and enlisted advocates—many of them women like García, Castillo, and Cowan—who anchored the city's immigrant-rights movement for the next several decades. The group framed its arguments in terms of human rights and combated the anti-Mexican sentiment that was spreading throughout the borderlands and the United States more broadly.[23]

Overall, national immigration debates led to a rising tide of anti-Mexican aggression. Many viewed Latinos as a national threat that undermined U.S. economy and culture, including white social and economic privilege and English monolingualism. Latinos increasingly became victims of scapegoating and physical violence. Border Patrol officers harassed them regardless of their citizenship status, based on their "physical and speech characteristics." Authorities were more likely to ask Latinos for identification and search their automobiles. In Texas, police murdered people of Mexican descent, and a *Washington Post* article claimed that, between 1976 and 1979, "at least 15 killings and more than 150 incidents of alleged brutality against Mexican Americans, mainly by law-enforcement officials" had occurred. One Mexican American attorney argued that such violence demonstrated the "continuing pattern of disregard for the civil rights and lives of our people." Because national sentiment was so fiercely anti-Mexican, civil rights groups, including the Mexican American Legal Defense and Educational Fund (MALDEF), opposed Rodino's and Carter's proposals, arguing that no immigration reform was better than laws that led to even greater discrimination against Latinos. While a broad base of elected Latino officials and civil rights workers led the opposition to immigration reform in the late 1970s and early 1980s, by the time of IRCA's passage in 1986, this coalition had broken down in the face of mounting pressure to solve problems that allegedly stemmed from undocumented immigration, including a high rate of unemployment, poverty, welfare, and crime.[24]

In Arizona's borderland, anti-Mexican agitators singled out undocumented immigrants as the cause of the area's troubles. Local newspapers blamed Mexicans for several burglaries there in the late 1970s. In Douglas, the sheriff's department recorded 122 burglary calls between January and August 1976, which corresponded with $135,000 in stolen property. Local authorities refused to entertain the possibility that U.S. citizens had committed the crimes, claiming that Mexican immigrants accounted for 85 to 90 percent of them. The Douglas sheriff himself said, "Most of our problems have come from Mexico."[25]

Law-enforcement officers and other community members believed that the ability to recognize Mexicans as culprits came from years of experience and that they could identify crimes committed by Mexican immigrants through certain cultural traits. "They kind of stick out," said a Douglas police sergeant, explaining that their muddy shoes and wet pant legs were signs that they had recently "been in the ditch at the border." Also, missing pillowcases, which immigrants supposedly used to "carry out the loot," and a "raided refrigerator," left empty by immigrants who had taken all the food, became telltale signs that Mexicans had committed the crime. Such notions drew on more than a century of stereotypes about greedy, desperate, and hungry Mexicans as bandits and thieves who robbed U.S. citizens and then fled to Mexico to evade prosecution. However, one article acknowledged that these assumptions were just "street talk" and, despite whatever claims individuals made, there were "no figures" available for the "number of aliens who burglarize Douglas homes."[26]

Still, entire communities armed themselves, and vigilante groups formed to police the border and propose their own immigration reforms. In early 1977, for example, sixty-five residents of southeastern Arizona established the Bisbee Junction Security Group, which called on the U.S. government to solve the problem of undocumented immigration. Rather than the criminality of Mexican immigrants or Mexico's economic decline, the group blamed the U.S. government itself. Members of the group believed that Mexican bandits hoped for arrest because they could get "medical or dental care" in U.S. prisons. "We're the people who are being robbed by these guys," one group member said, because they paid for "all these fringe benefits for them." So the group wrote its own four-point proposal that called for the erection of a "new and better" border fence, with updated monitoring technologies, including motion sensors; construction of a road the length of the border "so the fence can be patrolled and fence-jumpers quickly caught"; and creation of a "special strike force to track and capture illegal aliens." Although too extreme for the moment, their ideas gained currency in later years, fueled by new waves of vigilante organizations that policed the border and committed violence—from the Ku Klux Klan to Civilian Military Assistance to the Minuteman Project—and carried out in conservative border policies.[27]

Friction along the Border

Two episodes in particular demonstrated how anti-immigrant aggression on the one hand and immigrant-rights advocacy on the other shaped the Arizona-Sonora borderland in the 1970s and 1980s. First, on August 18,

1976, white ranchers kidnapped and tortured three Mexican workers near Douglas, Arizona. Second, beginning in the late 1970s, organizations in Tucson assisted Central American refugees who fled violence in their home countries. Both episodes sparked regional, national, and international controversies. In terms of their personnel, ideologies, and legacies, they established the grounds on which immigration and border debates would be fought into the early twenty-first century not only in Tucson and southern Arizona, which became ground zero for such contests, but also across the United States as a whole.

In Elfrida, Arizona, a town in Cochise County, farm work awaited twenty-five-year-old Manuel García Loya, twenty-four-year-old Eleazar Ruelas Zavala, and eighteen-year-old Bernabe Herrera Mata. Originally from other parts of Mexico—Chihuahua, Sinaloa, and Durango, respectively—at the time they held jobs in Hermosillo. Each had worked in the United States before, and they knew they would earn more in Arizona than by staying home. The path to Elfrida took them across private ranchland owned by the Hanigans, a family that had lived in the area for decades, working their ranch, operating Dairy Queen ice-cream stores, and serving as leaders in the state's Republican Party. Their encounter with the Mexican workers focused attention on issues of violence against immigrants.[28]

Soon after the Mexican workers crossed into Arizona, Thomas and Patrick Hanigan spotted the migrants from their pickup truck as the three walked across the Hanigans' land. After briefly questioning the workers about why they had entered the United States, the Hanigan brothers bound them, forced them into their truck, and drove them to the Hanigans' ranch house to alert their father, George Hanigan. The migrants later claimed that they believed the Hanigans were U.S. Border Patrol officers. The three ranchers then drove the workers into the fields, where they robbed them of $36, beat them, directed racist remarks at them, dragged them across the desert floor, suspended them from a tree, held a knife to their genitals, and burned their feet. Mexican newspapers claimed that the Hanigans also cut their hair to the scalp. After several hours, the ranchers cut the men loose and instructed them to go back to Mexico. As the workers ran south, the ranchers fired several rounds of birdshot that planted hundreds of pellets in their backs. The migrants made it to Agua Prieta, where doctors treated their wounds and reported the incident to Mexican police, who then notified Raúl Aveleyra, the Mexican consul in Douglas. Reporters, investigators, lawyers, nuns, and other government officials visited the men in the hospital. Aveleyra filed charges of kidnapping, robbery, and torture against George, Thomas, and Patrick Hanigan.[29]

Between 1976 and 1981, the Hanigans stood trial three times; twice for violating the workers' civil rights, and finally for interfering with interstate commerce since the migrants were on their way to work. Before the first trial, held at a state-level court in Bisbee, George Hanigan died of a heart attack. Mexican Americans in Douglas believed that God had punished him, but the all-white jury acquitted his sons Thomas and Patrick Hanigan. The second trial concluded in 1980, when a hung jury at a federal court in Tucson acquitted the brothers again. Finally, in 1981, a second federal trial in Phoenix convicted and sentenced Patrick Hanigan to three years in prison but acquitted Thomas Hanigan for a third time. During the five years it took to achieve partial justice, the Hanigan case enraged

Eleazar Ruelas Zavala, Manuel García Loya, and Bernabe Herrera Mata. (Copyright 1977 Norah Booth. All Rights Reserved. Antonio D. Bustamante Papers, Chicano/Chicana Research Collection, Arizona State University Libraries.)

many borderland residents, Mexican American civil rights organizations, immigrant-rights advocates, and Mexican officials who viewed the incident as a human-rights issue affecting U.S.-Mexico relations. As the *Washington Post* put it, the Hanigan case "heightened tensions along the border," created "embarrassing political problems for the Carter administration," and intensified Mexican American claims that they were "victims of a rising tide of violence." It was a "good case in point," one Douglas City Council member said, that federal laws were needed to ensure the security of all immigrants.[30]

In all three trials, the ranchers claimed they had stopped the Mexican workers because they believed them to be the same men who, earlier that summer, had stolen pistols from their ranch house. The Hanigans maintained that they held the workers only to reclaim their property, but some of the most damning evidence against them demonstrated that they turned this defensive position into offensive sport. Patrick Hanigan's ex-wife testified that, for several weeks before the incident, her former husband "went on almost nightly patrols looking for wetbacks." Both brothers, she said, had planned to "pick them up, knock them around, steal whatever money they had, and turn them in to the Border Patrol." Another witness, a waitress at a hotel in Douglas, testified that she had overheard Patrick Hanigan say, "We fixed those . . . wetbacks." The workers also correctly identified the Hanigans in Douglas High School yearbooks from 1972 and 1976, when Patrick and Thomas Hanigan graduated. Finally, "without prompting as to direction," the workers led Mexican consul Aveleyra from Agua Prieta to the Hanigan ranch. Given such evidence against them, the Hanigans found it difficult to convincingly portray themselves as innocent residents of a border community besieged by "illegal aliens."[31]

Nevertheless, the incident's immediate aftermath frustrated those who demanded punishment. The U.S. authorities said they had moved as quickly as possible to prosecute the perpetrators of the crime, but it took them more than a week to make an arrest even though the Hanigans were considered suspects almost immediately. The La Raza Law Students Association in Washington, D.C., wondered why it took so long to bring charges against the Hanigans, and UFW President César Chávez wrote letters demanding prosecution. Mexican newspapers expressed optimism when the initial grand jury hearing determined that enough evidence existed to try the ranchers. An article in *El Imparcial* mistakenly reported that the grand jury had found the Hanigans guilty, claiming that they could each receive up to eighteen years in prison and the victims could receive $100,000 each as a cash settlement. Instead, those hopeful of a conviction were disappointed when the jury in Bisbee found the ranchers not guilty.[32]

If the incident had been a national news story before the trial, the acquittal of Thomas and Patrick Hanigan in October 1977 inspired widespread mobilization by Mexican American civil rights organizations and immigrant-rights advocates, as well as scathing criticism from Mexico. Given the area's rising anti-Mexican sentiment, lawyers for the migrants predicted that their clients could not receive a fair hearing in southeastern Arizona, where the Hanigans wielded political and economic influence. It did not help that the presiding judge removed the six Mexican Americans originally slated to serve on the jury, allowing the objection made by the Hanigans' attorney that these jurors were eager to convict his clients. Still, many considered the jury's composition unfair given Douglas's Mexican and Mexican American majority. As the jury deliberated, demonstrators from Tucson, Bisbee, and Douglas celebrated mass and called for an end to border violence.[33]

Upon hearing the jury's verdict, the Mexican consul in Douglas famously claimed that it opened "hunting season" against "every illegal alien" in the United States. Immigrant-rights attorney Margo Cowan agreed, arguing that the verdict "set a violent precedent of sanctioned aggression" against "the whole Chicano people in the Southwest." Cowan called a meeting at Tucson's San Agustín Cathedral to discuss how her organization and other immigrant-rights advocates would respond. More than 150 Arizonans and Sonorans attended, representing religious, political, and community groups. They decided that the Manzo Area Council would collect signatures for a petition demanding a federal retrial and that the group would also sponsor a boycott of Douglas merchants. To advertise the action, the Manzo Area Council bought airtime on Mexican radio stations, posted placards on telephone poles, and placed quarter-page manifestos in Agua Prieta newspapers. One sign said, "Boycott! Mexicans Unite! Don't Buy from U.S. Border Cities until Justice Is Served in the Hanigan Case! Defend Your Race!" Others organized their own protests. Some carried signs outside the Douglas Dairy Queen—owned by the Hanigans—advising shoppers to not buy ice cream there. Children told their friends that "the ice cream is not good." Meanwhile, just days after the court's decision, Knights of the Ku Klux Klan leader David Duke traveled to Tucson to urge Klan supporters to head to Douglas and support the ranchers.[34]

Beyond the borderlands, the Hanigan case drew attention from Mexican American civil right organizations across the United States. Law student Antonio Bustamante established the National Ad Hoc Coalition on the Hanigan Case just one month after the not-guilty verdict, on November 16, 1977. Originally from Douglas, he had firsthand experience with the area's long history of racial antagonism. His coalition brought together several prominent groups, including LULAC, the National Council of La Raza, the National Association of Farmworkers Organizations, the American G.I. Forum, MALDEF, and La Raza National Bar Association. In earlier periods, the differing politics of these groups may have precluded their alliance, but in the late 1970s, a diverse array of civil rights organizations united in opposition to restrictive immigration and border policies. Although they did not always hold the same views, opposing the torture of Mexican workers meshed with their interest in drawing attention to racism against all peoples of Mexican descent, regardless of citizenship. The coalition spearheaded a letter-writing campaign to state and federal officials, asking them to intervene on behalf of the Mexican workers. In response to the pressure, the U.S. Department of Justice (DOJ) announced that it would indict Patrick and Thomas Hanigan on federal charges.[35]

Mexicans claimed that the incident inflicted deep humiliation on them personally and on Mexico in general. Farm workers protested in Mexico City's Plaza de la Constitución, and, in response, Mexico's assistant secretary of foreign relations assured them that their government would seek a severe punishment. Mexican president Echeverría, referring to the incident's ethnic and racial motivations, called it a "consequence of irresponsible attitudes." Another official expressed disappointment that individuals motivated by "dark prejudices and barbarous instincts" committed such violence. Summarizing what many Mexicans felt, an editorial in a Mexico City newspaper said that the incident had left a "nasty aftertaste of bitterness." It inspired *corridos* about the ranchers and their victims and comic books that chronicled the poor treatment of Mexicans in the United States. Some compared them to the last Aztec emperor, Cuauhtémoc, whose feet were burned by Spanish conquistadors. As an article in the *New York Times* explained, officials in Sonora and Mexico City "seized upon [the Hanigan incident] as an extreme example of

United States treatment of Mexican migrants." For their part, the workers thought it was ironic that U.S. and Mexican government officials paid so much attention to their case, considering their general neglect of the working poor on both sides of the border.[36]

To many Mexicans, the plight of the three workers became ensnared within the larger web of U.S.-Mexico relations. Mexico's interior minister claimed that the incident was a reminder of the "painful exchange of undocumented migratory workers," who frequently became subjects of "racial sadism" and "exploitation" in the United States. A Mexican newspaper explained how the Hanigan incident had "exacerbated" the problems of all "Mexican braceros, whose presence in the United States is considered illegal and has unleashed a massive deportation campaign against all undocumented workers." The author of the article wrote what many Mexican Americans felt, that the Hanigan case, and the mistreatment of Mexican migrant workers in general, affected all people of Mexican descent.[37]

Mexicans also noted the hypocrisy in claiming that Mexican immigrants stole jobs and drained the U.S. economy. "We need to remember," one Mexican wrote, "that the Mexican migrant laborer is, in fact, a contributor to the U.S. economy; he doesn't deprive U.S. citizens of jobs since, unfortunately, he works in such tedious and unpleasant jobs that U.S. citizens will not take them." The author reminded readers that Mexicans had served the United States as *braceros* from 1942 to 1964 and as soldiers in the U.S. military during World War II and in Korea and Vietnam. Others noted how U.S. citizens in Mexico also caused trouble. After the Hanigans tortured their victims, Mexican newspapers criticized American gunrunners and white drug addicts from Tucson who stole a car and tried to hide in Mexico.[38]

In this period of rising hemispheric tensions—when an increasing number of Marxist movements in Latin America met a fiercely conservative U.S.-sponsored backlash and Mexicans became victims of violence in the United States—communities on both sides of the border sought an immediate resolution to the case in order to avoid further conflict. To this end, U.S. and Mexican officials engaged in tense exchanges about civil wars in Central America and undocumented migration to the United States. Members of the U.S. House of Representatives ignited a controversy when they claimed that Mexico supported Communism. Moreover, the United States sparked López Portillo's ire by backing out of a deal to purchase natural gas from Mexico even though Mexico had already spent millions of dollars constructing a pipeline for its transport. When López Portillo and Carter met at the White House, the Mexican president cited the Hanigan incident as a case in point for his reluctance to allow Mexicans to participate in temporary labor exchanges. Then when Carter visited Mexico, he vowed to protect the "basic human rights" of all migrants to the United States. Contemplating the incident's significance within this heated climate, one Mexican author argued that it provided one more explanation for the "friction along the border."[39]

Meanwhile, some government officials and businesspeople, still heeding the Good Neighbor rhetoric of the early Cold War, articulated the need for cross-border friendship and cooperation. Arizona governor Raúl Castro denounced the crime in the strongest of terms, calling it "an inhumane situation" and a "return to the days of slavery." Still, the U.S. ambassador to Mexico said, it "ought not tarnish the good relations that exist between the two countries." Businesspeople and regional boosters responded by doing what they had always done; in the midst of the Hanigan trials, the Arizona-Mexico Commission planned its 1980 meeting in Guaymas to promote tourism to the city, while Tucson and Ciudad Obregón declared themselves sister cities and held celebrations attended by mayors Lewis Murphy and Adalberto Rosas López. Even though the Hanigan case undoubtedly raised the level of tension between the United States and Mexico, the two countries continued to work to resolve their problems because of the "inevitable union that geography imposes upon us," as one editorial explained.[40]

In Arizona, Mexicans and Mexican Americans remained engaged with the Hanigan case into the early 1980s as the federal trial in Tucson neared. They believed that they, too, experienced the rise of anti-immigrant sentiment and violence throughout southern Arizona. By the time of the trials, Mexican Americans had spread across Tucson, although the vast majority of them remained on the city's southwest side. With expanded educational and job opportunities, a greater percentage attended college and worked as professionals, although they continued to lag behind whites educationally and economically. People of Mexican descent opened a greater number of businesses than ever before, particularly in service, retail, and construction industries, but most were small operations that struggled to break even. Moreover, most people of Mexican descent came from families that had lived in Tucson for several generations. In 1970, 80 percent of Mexican Americans in Arizona had been born in the United

States. Because of these mixed signals of incorporation, many Mexican Americans struggled to preserve their rights. The U.S. Border Patrol increasingly raided their neighborhoods, descending on churches and soccer games. Recognizing that they suffered collateral discrimination as a result of increasingly harsh immigration and border policies, many Mexican Americans protested the raids and supported the efforts of civil- and immigrant-rights groups.[41]

Recognizing the symbolic importance of the trial for all peoples of Mexican descent, civil rights organizations encouraged Mexicans and Mexican Americans throughout the region to follow the trial closely. National media claimed that the trial in Tucson would be a "test of the government's concern about Mexican Americans." Mexicans and Mexican Americans on both sides of the border jammed the phone lines of Spanish-language radio stations to express their views on the case. Picketers marched outside the courthouse, while others gathered in hotel rooms to watch television together, awaiting the jury's verdict. When the jury could not reach one, thereby acquitting the Hanigans for a second time, Mexican newspapers reported that hundreds of people marched in protest. Expecting violence, the Tucson Police Department was put on "alert" status, and the DOJ sent community-relations experts to calm tensions. Although no riots ensued, a U.S. prosecutor said the verdict had a "chilling effect" on interracial relations in Arizona.[42]

Federal officials announced almost immediately that the U.S. government would prosecute the Hanigans again, but the third trial—or second federal trial—would be moved to Phoenix because Judge Richard Bilby believed that Tucson was too contentious a venue. "Deep, bitter divisions" existed in Tucson, he said, citing a poll that had found that "100 percent of the Hispanics and 64 percent of the Anglos surveyed expressed the opinion that the brothers were guilty." Some Tucsonans supported the Hanigans. One woman believed that the "Mexican men were where they had no business of being so they got just what was coming to them." Advocating vigilantism, she concluded, "If more people would do the same, maybe we would not be bothered with so many illegal aliens." Because of such tensions within Tucson, as the site of the third trial Bilby chose Prescott, a rural, majority-white town a hundred miles north of Phoenix. He believed Prescott would be far enough from the border to be free of the biases of southern Arizona's Mexican and Mexican American populations even though anti-Mexican bias had already worked in favor of the defendants in Bisbee and Tucson. He sought to keep the location secret, but those interested in the case figured it out. They initiated a letter-writing campaign and walked door to door delivering fliers representing their respective positions, which increased local tensions and caused the judge to move the trial once more, this time to Phoenix.[43]

The guilty verdict delivered there brought little consolation to the victims or people of Mexican descent because the jury acquitted Thomas Hanigan for a third time. Moreover, many saw Patrick Hanigan's sentence of only three years in prison as shamefully merciful considering his crime. Most aggravating was that it took three trials spread over five years to achieve one conviction. Patrick Hanigan did not begin serving his sentence until May 27, 1983, when he arrived at the prison in Safford, Arizona, nearly seven years after he had robbed and tortured the three workers. In an ironic twist, weeks after the jury acquitted Thomas Hanigan, Arizona authorities charged him with possessing and transporting 574 pounds of marijuana. Residents of the border region had long cited rampant drug smuggling by Mexican cartels in their arguments for tighter border enforcement and immigration restriction. It must have troubled them that Thomas Hanigan had committed such a crime himself, especially considering their vigorous defense of his character.[44]

The Hanigan case established an important legal precedent and has received more attention from legal scholars than from historians. Prosecutors first argued that the ranchers had violated the workers' civil rights, but the state court in Bisbee claimed that "illegal aliens" did not have rights to violate. According to the *Washington Post,* civil rights law required that an "alleged victim of brutality be a citizen or that the alleged attacker be a law enforcement official." Neither was true in this case. Like vigilantes, the Hanigans may have taken the law into their own hands, but they were not law-enforcement officers. At the suggestion of Mexican American civil rights attorneys, the DOJ prosecuted the Hanigans under the 1951 Hobbs Act, which prohibited interference with interstate commerce. In arguing that the ranchers had prevented the workers from reaching jobs in Elfrida, the Hanigan case became the first to apply the Hobbs Act to immigrant workers, presenting Mexican labor as a commodity to be traded and depersonalizing the violence the ranchers committed. On the other hand, the Hanigan case was also the first instance of the U.S. government suing U.S. citizens on behalf of undocumented migrants, adding to the "arsenal of protections for illegal aliens," as the *New York Times* stated.[45]

Lawyers for the Hanigans pushed back against the application of the Hobbs Act to the case against their clients, arguing that protecting undocumented immigrants was not the purpose for which it had been established. Some lawyers within the DOJ argued that the agency bent the law in order to try the ranchers. Arizonans expressed their frustration as well. When federal prosecutors announced their decision to try the ranchers under the Hobbs Act, one man asked, "Who is sponsoring this anti-Hanigan coalition . . . Mexico or Russia?" He continued, "With this Hobbs Act nonsense, anyone I catch vandalizing my property can say he's on his way to Elfrida and he'll get off. If this case stands, illegals can go where they want with impunity." Others believed that Attorney General Benjamin Civiletti, by prosecuting the ranchers, sought to improve his image among Mexican Americans, who had protested his nomination and confirmation because he had neglected cases of civil rights abuse pertaining to them. Their criticism led Civiletti to make a "nomination-hearing pledge" to respond to violence against Mexican Americans and other Latinos. He insisted, however, that the decision to prosecute the Hanigans had nothing to do with politics.[46]

Beyond the legal precedents set by the Hanigan case, the torture and its aftermath marked a crucial turning point for immigration politics in the Arizona-Sonora borderland. Linked with broader national debates about anti-Mexican discrimination and immigration reform, the Hanigan case signaled a move toward a particularly tense, militarized period in the recent history of the U.S.-Mexico borderlands. As the economy declined, the United States experienced increasing levels of undocumented immigration, and, as a result, many Americans targeted Mexicans like García Loya, Ruelas Zavala, and Herrera Mata. The federal government responded by debating immigration reform and building steel walls in the border cities where most immigrants crossed; monitoring vigilante groups who patrolled the border and detained Mexicans; and cracking down on civil- and immigrant-rights organizations who worked to protect Mexicans and Mexican Americans.

Rising immigration debates also shaped the context in which borderland residents reacted to the deaths of thirteen Salvadoran immigrants who perished in the Sonoran Desert's Organ Pipe National Monument while seeking refuge from civil wars in their home country. Immigrant-rights organizations like the Manzo Area Council immediately supported Central American refugees, and religious organizations in Tucson became the first in the United States to call for similar groups around the country to offer them sanctuary. Sparking a conflict between immigrant-rights workers and the federal government, the sanctuary movement—as the coordinated efforts of religious organizations to shelter Central American refugees became known—kept national and international attention focused on Tucson as an epicenter of debates on immigration and the border. Rather than a new form of immigrant-rights advocacy, as it frequently has been portrayed, the sanctuary movement was part of a longer tradition of migrant assistance in the Arizona-Sonora borderland.

As the United States propped up brutal military juntas and sought to depose leftist movements and governments in Central America, refugees from El Salvador, Guatemala, and Nicaragua streamed into the Arizona-Sonora borderland. Between 1974 and 1996, more than a quarter million Central Americans were killed, and more than one million fled their homes to seek shelter from violence and unrest. Some moved to Costa Rica or Honduras, and many others journeyed to Mexico, the United States, and Canada. Describing its local impact, one Sonoran historian called their movement a "migration flow theretofore unknown" to the area. Before the arrival of Central American refugees, Arizona's and Sonora's Latino communities were overwhelmingly Mexican and largely Sonoran. But between 1979 and 1981, Central American migration increased five-fold. Although the sanctuary movement began as a local effort to offer shelter to victims of violence, it also sparked an internationally charged debate about immigrant and refugee rights, church-state relations, and the Reagan administration's foreign policy toward Latin America.[47]

Central American immigration patterns in Mexico, the United States, and Canada shifted according to the asylum and immigration policies of the receiving countries; the financial resources available to immigrants; the likelihood of encountering violence during or after the journey; and whether individuals or groups of immigrants already had connections in one of the countries. Mexico was an attractive destination for Guatemalan immigrants because of its proximity. More than 750,000 Guatemalans sought shelter there. Canada, on the other hand, was extremely far from home, but refugees had a greater chance of receiving political asylum there than in the United States, which, during the 1970s and 1980s, granted asylum to only 3 percent of all Salvadorans and Guatemalans who applied. Canada, meanwhile, granted asylum to 80 percent. The sanctuary movement in Tucson began as Central Americans dispersed throughout North America.[48]

Area residents became acutely aware of Central American refugees in the summer of 1980, following the death of the thirteen Salvadorans in the Sonoran desert. Twenty-six had started out making the trek; the survivors awaited deportation in a Tucson jail. Unlike many Mexican immigrants during the 1970s and 1980s—who were poor and from rural areas—these victims of El Salvador's civil war hailed from diverse socioeconomic backgrounds. They were doctors, university students, factory workers, and salesmen. The refugees together paid $20,000 to smugglers who helped them cross the border but then abandoned them. As the refugees died of heat exhaustion and thirst, they consumed deodorant, lotion, and urine in an effort to stay alive. Some who did not know what to expect of the journey wore high heels, and the soles of one woman's feet were badly injured. The survivors feared that their families in El Salvador would face reprisals if their identities were revealed, so they demanded that the bodies be cremated before being returned to El Salvador.[49]

The thirteen Salvadorans who died in Arizona represented the hundreds of thousands of Central Americans who, out of desperation, migrated to the United States. The majority of them entered through Arizona, California, and Texas, both because overland journeys were relatively cheap in comparison to flights and because repressive regimes had a harder time monitoring refugees fleeing by foot than by plane. Many passed through the U.S.-Mexico borderlands on their way to other areas of the United States and Canada, but those who did stay there became integrated into communities on both sides of the border. In Sonora, Central Americans settled in coastal towns, where they worked in agricultural fields and factories. In Tucson, many made their homes on the city's historically Mexican and Mexican American southside, reshaping the city's Latino communities. Some became students, workers, and citizens. Fifty members of one Guatemalan family came to reside in Tucson.[50]

On March 24, 1982, John Fife and other leaders of Southside Presbyterian Church, while seated beside a Salvadoran man and in front of more than twenty reporters, announced that the church congregation would provide sanctuary to Central American refugees. The declaration had been months in the making. In November 1981, Fife told the members of Southside Presbyterian that, at the church's annual meeting in January 1982, they would vote on whether to declare sanctuary. Between November and January, the church organized several meetings in anticipation of the vote to discuss the idea of sanctuary's Judeo-Christian underpinnings, as well as U.S. immigration law and foreign policy. At the January meeting, the majority of congregants voted for sanctuary, while the few who opposed it wrote letters to the FBI to inform the agency of the church's intentions.[51]

In fact, a decade of migrant assistance and immigrant-rights advocacy in Tucson had laid the foundation for this declaration. Lawyers and religious leaders in Tucson had supported Latin American migrants since the early 1970s by arranging for social services, doctors, legal representation, work opportunities, and interpreters to assist families and individuals who fled poverty in Mexico or escaped Anastasio Somoza's dictatorship in Nicaragua or Carlos Humberto Romero's in El Salvador. These networks established the infrastructure that sanctuary workers relied on in the 1980s and also their arguments, which focused on refugee, immigrant, and human rights. The Manzo Area Council worked with Mexicans throughout the 1970s, and when Central Americans began to arrive in Tucson, the organization served them as well. "Literally, a Salvadoran woman walked in with a bullet lodged in her ribcage," Isabel García recalled, and that "started the Central American work." Presbyterians like John Fife and James Corbett have received most of the credit, but organizations like the Manzo Area Council and its female leaders, including García, Castillo, and Cowan, formed the core of immigrant-rights advocacy in Tucson from the 1970s forward.[52]

The Manzo Area Council increasingly responded to appeals for help from Central American refugees. By the beginning of 1981, the organization represented thirty non-Mexicans, who told Cowan and Castillo about conditions in their home countries, journeys that ended in Arizona, and co-nationals apprehended by the U.S. Border Patrol and detained in California. These stories demonstrated their entanglement within the broader world of U.S. and Mexican immigration enforcement. In 1977, the Border Patrol apprehended more than 7,000 Salvadorans and 5,000 Guatemalans, numbers that were higher than ever before but that paled in comparison with the number of Mexicans arrested. By the early 1980s, approximately 95,000 Salvadorans and 63,000 Guatemalans had settled in the United States. The Border Patrol apprehended some 17,000 and 10,000 of them, respectively, in addition to more than 1 million Mexicans. Meanwhile, in Mexico, the country's migratory services agency arrested some 300 Central Americans every month and set up detention centers in Mazatlán and elsewhere. Moved by their stories, Cowan and Castillo drove from Arizona to Guatemala to observe the situation firsthand. When they returned, they visited the California detention centers and organized "bond outs" in Tucson—fundraisers to bail Central Americans out of jail. Released from prison, the refugees settled in Tucson or other cities with large Central American populations, like Houston and Los Angeles.[53]

Following the Manzo Area Council's lead, religious communities in Tucson also assisted refugees by declaring their churches sanctuaries. Saint Mark's Presbyterian Church became one of the first after Southside Presbyterian, and then sixty-five Catholic and Protestant churches formed the Tucson Ecumenical Council Task Force on Central America (TECTF) to research U.S. refugee policy and the wars in Central America. The TECTF also published newsletters about how to assist refugees, asking Tucsonans to offer their homes, food, and transportation and to help them find jobs. Several other organizations formed as well, including the Tucson Committee on Human Rights in Latin America and the Tucson Ecumenical Council for Legal Services for Central Americans. In committing to offer sanctuary, they cited the influence of the famous liberation theologian, Archbishop Oscar Romero, shot and martyred in 1980 as he said Mass in El Salvador. To some Tucsonans, religious organizations had veered off course by participating in politics so explicitly. Some "church people," one resident wrote, have "gone off the deep end to become activists" and should "receive swift rebuff." Adding to his rant, he claimed that Central Americans brought "diseases and parasites" with them and argued that they might cause "another AIDS-type scourge." Despite such extremist reactions, sanctuary supporters heightened awareness of U.S.–Latin American affairs in general and U.S. interventions in Central America in particular.[54]

Tucson's religious leaders networked with others throughout the United States and Mexico, making the sanctuary movement a transnational effort. Cadres of volunteers from across the United States traveled to Tucson, and religious leaders in Sonora formed partnerships with their counterparts in Arizona, providing food and shelter along the path from Central America to the United States. Five churches in Berkeley, California, declared sanctuary on the same day that Southside Presbyterian did, and within a year, Tucson's "underground" network of sanctuary workers was connected with others in Chicago, Los Angeles, San Francisco, Seattle, New York, Boston, Nogales, Hermosillo, and Mexico City. In Sonora, religious leaders like Dagoberto Quiñones and María del Socorro Pardo played pivotal roles in facilitating the travels of refugees through the state. James Corbett cultivated their cooperation. Like Cowan and Castillo, he

Sanctuary movement poster. (Courtesy of Darlene Nicgorski Papers on the Sanctuary movement, Special Collections, Honnold/Mudd Library, Claremont Colleges.)

traveled to the Guatemala-Mexico border to observe the situation there. He also personally led refugees from Guatemala all the way to Tucson. Corbett had heard of Quiñones's work in Sonoran shelters, which offered Mexicans and Central Americans food and a place to sleep. He asked Quiñones whether he would consider joining his network, and Quiñones agreed, claiming it was God's work. He accepted money from sources in Arizona to support his migrant centers and even walked with groups of refugees from Sonora to Tucson and ranches in southern Arizona.[55]

Sanctuary workers on both sides of the border believed that Central American refugees were candidates for asylum under the 1980 Refugee Act, but they still evaded immigration authorities and hid them in safe locations around the United States. Corbett and Socorro Pardo taught Central Americans how to appear Mexican. Playing on the idea that, to many Americans, Latin American migrants seemed interchangeable, they believed that, if the refugees were caught, the U.S. Border Patrol would deport them to Mexico—most likely Nogales—rather than to their home countries. Corbett taught them northern Mexican idioms and Nogales street names, while Socorro Pardo taught the women how to dress and wear their hair. According to one Sonoran scholar, such activities led to friction between Sonoran sanctuary workers and Mexican police, whom religious leaders accused of abusing refugees. The sanctuary movement also created tension within Sonora's religious hierarchy, which sanctuary workers accused of being too passive in dealing with the Central American crisis and also led to accusations that sanctuary workers skirted international immigration laws.[56]

The controversy over the sanctuary movement turned on the question of whether Central Americans ought to be considered refugees or migrants. Sanctuary workers argued that Central Americans fleeing war-torn homelands were refugees and therefore could not be denied asylum. The inconsistent application of the Refugee Act frustrated them greatly. Cuban exiles were considered refugees because they fled the regime of Fidel Castro, a foe of the U.S. government, whereas Central Americans were denied refugee status because they fled regimes supported by the Reagan administration. The United States, sanctuary workers believed, was responsible for creating the refugee crisis because of its financial and military support of right-wing dictators throughout Latin America. Guatemala's Efraín Ríos Montt adopted a "policy of scorched Communists," and under his rule, some four hundred Guatemalan villages disappeared along with many thousands of inhabitants. He harassed, intimidated, beat, and murdered Guatemalans who tried to leave the country and ordered planes and helicopters to fly above refugee camps in Mexico to intimidate them. Still, the United States backed him, as it did other Central American leaders whose violent acts gave their countries an "apocalyptic" feel. Fife therefore considered the U.S. refusal to grant Central Americans refugee status to be "illegal and immoral."[57]

Because Reagan supported anti-Communist regimes in Central America, he could not consider Central Americans as refugees; doing so would have been tantamount to acknowledging U.S. complicity with governments that abused their own citizens. Reagan sent a delegation to Central America to observe and report on conditions there, but despite testimony from refugees that detailed harassment, torture, murder, and the destruction of entire villages, the officials returned to the United States and argued that conditions were not as bad as the refugees claimed. Their assertions led the administration to insist that Central Americans were economic migrants looking for jobs rather than political refugees escaping violence; thus the United States was able to skirt the provisions of the Refugee Act, which did not require the United States to accept migrants seeking work.[58]

Given the stakes of the debate about classifying Central Americans as refugees or economic migrants, the sanctuary movement in Tucson became a front line of the U.S.–Latin American Cold War during the 1980s. Reagan argued that the situation in Central America was part of the broader East-West struggle. He wanted to stop Communism south of the border before it spread to the United States. Vigilante groups made the same argument when they patrolled the Arizona-Sonora border. Meanwhile, sanctuary workers emphasized that a combination of moral conviction and political opposition to U.S. interventions in Central America guided their actions. In defiance of the Reagan administration, they claimed to answer to higher principles of justice and human rights rather than to the U.S. government. The U.S. "legal system," they said, occupied a "lower level" of justice than the work they did. They shared one belief in common with their critics: "America" itself was on trial. Either the sanctuary workers were innocent, which meant that they could practice their "religious values freely without government interference," and, by implication, that U.S. foreign policy in Latin America was unjust, or sanctuary workers were guilty, which meant that "no person, religious or otherwise, was higher than the laws of the land." This drama unfolded in courtrooms in Arizona and throughout the United States.[59]

It did not take long for federal prosecutors to indict sanctuary workers for smuggling immigrants into the United States. In 1984, Stacey Lynn Merkt of Brownsville, Texas, became the first sanctuary worker convicted of smuggling Central Americans, and the indictment of eleven sanctuary workers in Arizona and Sonora quickly followed. An undercover FBI agent had infiltrated Southside Presbyterian's sanctuary movement, collecting evidence against its volunteers. In July 1986, a jury in Tucson convicted eight of the sanctuary workers brought to trial, including Fife and two Sonorans, Socorro Pardo and Quiñones. Corbett and two other defendants were acquitted, newspapers said, only because some evidence against them was not permitted in the hearings. The conviction of two Sonoran sanctuary workers was controversial not only because the United States had charged Mexicans for crimes allegedly committed in Mexico but also because the INS had positioned spies in Sonora to collect evidence against them. One Sonoran historian called it "espionage" and a challenge to Mexican sovereignty. Quiñones considered his extradition to be the latest example of U.S. aggression against Mexico and claimed that he attended the trial only to protest U.S. interventions in Latin America. Although the court handed down light punishments, including suspended sentences, probation, and a warning to not help Central American refugees—or any undocumented immigrants—in the future, many decried the decision as unconscionable. As they left the courtroom, sanctuary workers sang "We Shall Overcome," a song popularized by the African American civil rights movement, and vowed to continue their "border ministry."[60]

Although the U.S. government expected prosecutions to discourage participation in the sanctuary movement, the "courtroom drama," one scholar has argued, in fact brought it more attention and helped recruit even more volunteers. Segments on national television programs like *60 Minutes* and *Frontline* were sympathetic to sanctuary workers and sparked even more interest in the movement as a whole. By late 1987 the number of declared sanctuaries had reached the hundreds, including two states, twenty-eight cities, and 430 "distinct religious bodies." The movement had more than seventy thousand volunteers. National news media, including *Newsweek* and the *Economist*, linked the sanctuary movement to the moral crusades of earlier generations, drawing comparisons with the "underground railroad" of the nineteenth century under headlines such as "This Is a Freedom Train" and "John Brown Is Back."[61]

As sanctuary workers stood trial in Tucson, President Reagan signed the Immigration Reform and Control Act. The signing ceremony took place on July 1, 1986, after debates that had lasted fifteen years and spanned three presidential administrations. Even before his election to office, in July 1980, Reagan had visited Sonora and mentioned a desire to work on immigration reform. While talking with reporters there, he called Mexico the United States' most important ally and stated that undocumented immigrants had a right to work in the country. He proposed a law less than a year later that combined amnesty, employer sanctions, and increased border enforcement. Reagan also discussed with President López Portillo the possibility of a new guest-worker program, but they could not agree on the details. The INS Commissioner was pessimistic about the possibility of real reform, believing that undocumented immigrants would continue to cross the border regardless of policy. "Every president does the same study" when entering office, he claimed, noting that Reagan's proposal was essentially the same as Carter's. Reagan forged ahead, and after several years of deliberation in Congress, the IRCA passed by a vote of 238 to 173 in the House and 63 to 24 in the Senate.[62]

Many in the United States opposed the law—especially its employer sanctions and amnesty provisions—but the steady increase in Mexican immigration, rising anti-immigrant sentiment, and growing influence of Latino elected officials and civil rights organizations created immense pressure for compromise. From 760,000 in 1970, the Mexican population of the United States had increased to 4.4 million by the late 1980s, a number roughly equivalent to the entire populations of Chihuahua and Sonora. Reagan claimed that IRCA would "improve life" for Mexican newcomers who "hide in the shadows" without "access to the benefits of a free and open society." After its implementation, he said, Mexicans could "come into public light and, if they wish, become Americans." Reagan also argued that IRCA would help the federal government control the border and protect U.S. sovereignty not only against the threat of undocumented immigration but also against the vigilante groups who organized their own border patrols. As a result of the law's combination of amnesty and increased enforcement, millions of Mexicans applied for naturalization, and the INS budget jumped by 130 percent.[63]

Despite national trends toward increased anti-immigrant sentiment and border militarization, many who opposed IRCA suggested alternatives, including an open border and a guest-worker program with a "minimum wage, health benefits, transportation, job training, and protections against employer abuse." Others proposed that other countries make direct investments in Mexico and, with *maquiladoras* in mind, suggested that U.S. companies should move their "production capacity" to Mexico, which would save money and create jobs there. Both ideas relied on the long-standing belief that a thriving economy on one side of the border benefited the other as well. But neoliberal ideologies of globalization, such as the shifting of manufacturing to developing countries while keeping corporate profits in the United States, were also at play. The ultimate outcome of such policies, some hoped, would be open borders throughout North America, echoing Barry Goldwater's predictions for the twenty-first century and foreshadowing arguments that would support NAFTA in the 1990s. Border Patrol officers, one reporter claimed, would become "friendly Mexican assistance agents," and Mexico, the United States, and Canada would form a "coherent political and economic unit."[64]

As with earlier immigration-reform proposals, Arizonans and Sonorans debated IRCA vigorously. Because they relied on undocumented workers and opposed government impositions, many Tucson employers rejected IRCA's employer-sanctions provisions. Mexican American Chamber of Commerce members feared that the law would deprive growers, contractors, and restaurants of employees. Moreover, most Tucsonans of Mexican descent predicted that employer sanctions would lead to discrimination against anyone with "dark skin" and a last name like "Martinez or Rodriguez." When an early version of the bill passed in 1984, hundreds took to the streets in Tucson, wearing on their shoulders brown triangles made of cloth that symbolized how the law would stigmatize all Latinos. Local and state politicians like Governor Babbitt also objected to the negative effect the law would have on U.S.-Mexico relations, leading one Arizonan to complain about Babbitt's "willingness to subordinate American interests to those of Mexico's corrupt regime." Such sentiments revealed the growing tension between the United States and Mexico over immigration policy, as well as Babbitt's sensitivity to this reality.[65]

During early debates about IRCA, Babbitt expressed dismay over both the increase in anti-immigrant sentiment and the state of U.S.-Mexico relations more broadly. After almost a decade, he said, "We appear to be no closer to a solution." No new ideas had been proposed, and each of IRCA's provisions forced "uneasy compromises" that disappointed everyone to some degree. He recognized the difficulty of reaching an agreement. Immigration struck at the "heart of our self-definition, at our very conception of democracy and Americanism." The United States was a nation of immigrants or a land of laws; even though not necessarily mutually exclusive, many found these ideas difficult to reconcile. Babbitt himself believed that the core of the problem was "our continuing inability as a society to come to grips with Mexico." Even though the United States and Mexico were "inextricably linked" through "tourism, trade, investment, agriculture, technology—and migration," many U.S. citizens increasingly emphasized sovereignty, separation, and unilateralism. This discourse was often expressed in racist, xenophobic terms. In response, Babbitt wrote, "we" must "jettison the fear and hysteria" that have "dominated our thinking about illegal immigration" and "overcome our anxieties born of uncertainty and misunderstanding." The "historical relationship" between the two countries, he concluded, has shaped the "formation of our own national character." In the most impassioned plea from any of Arizona's political leaders during the late twentieth century, he spoke of developing "new attitudes" and a sense of "responsibility" toward Mexico and of dealing with our neighbor "honestly and directly."[66]

Mexicans shared Babbitt's concern about deteriorating U.S.-Mexico relations. While Reagan and his ambassador to Mexico argued that IRCA offered Mexicans the protection of U.S. laws, Mexican officials and labor unions worried that immigrants would continue to experience discrimination and that immigration lawyers would exploit applicants for naturalization or report them to immigration authorities. Moreover, as thousands of Mexican citizens returned to Mexico because they had not resided continuously in the United States since the beginning of 1982, Mexican officials knew they could not guarantee them employment. These fears came to pass: the law simply did not work. As many had predicted, Mexicans continued to enter the United States illegally, discrimination against Latino employees abounded, and unemployment and poverty in Mexico grew along with the country's population. One Mexican senator therefore concluded that IRCA represented "a new aggression against our country." Mexicans in general felt that increased border restrictions and employer sanctions were a direct attack on them. Even the law's amnesty provision, they believed, would offer a path to citizenship for some—but would send back the rest and seal the border behind them.[67]

After fifteen years of debate, IRCA was to be a grand compromise that solved immigration problems once and for all. It purported to address what many considered the core problems associated with undocumented immigration: employers who knowingly hired undocumented immigrants, a subclass of people living in the United States without citizenship, and a porous international border. The Hanigan case and the sanctuary movement highlighted particular aspects of immigration debates—including migrant abuse, anti-Mexican vigilantism, church-state disputes, and shifting Cold War politics—and placed the Arizona-Sonora borderland in the eye of a national and international storm. They also gave rise to Arizona's and Sonora's modern immigrant and human-rights movements, forged through resistance to harsh and uncompromising state policies. Even though the Manzo Area Council disbanded after IRCA's passage, its members formed other organizations, including No More Deaths, the Mesilla Organizing

Project, Coalición de Derechos Humanos, and Alianza Indígena sin Fronteras, which led immigrant- and human-rights struggles into the twenty-first century. But if these episodes spanning the 1970s and 1980s presaged the ongoing immigration debates of the future, they also invoked the language of regional history, including ideas about frontier justice and horse and cattle cultures beyond those celebrated by La Fiesta de los Vaqueros.

During the Hanigan and sanctuary movement trials, many observers referred to both the ranchers and sanctuary workers as cowboys, revealing the complicated legacies of regional ranching traditions. In their comparisons, they highlighted tensions between local and federal authorities and competing notions of frontier justice. When Bustamante testified about patterns of violence against Mexicans along the border, he referred to acts committed by the Hanigans as a "time-honored cowboy custom." A representative of the DOJ's civil rights division used more sarcastic language in her condemnation of the ranchers. "What big brave cowboys these guys are," she said. "Armed with shotguns," she continued, they "terrorize . . . defenseless young men" and "rob them of their money, their clothes, and their dignity." She powerfully undercut their bravado, honor, and masculinity, the very qualities that supposedly defined borderlands horsemen. For his part, the judge who convicted Patrick Hanigan said, "Nobody has the right to do to another human being what was done to those three men . . . The days of the Old West are gone." Meanwhile, Fife and Corbett were described as different sorts of cowboys. One newspaper account said that Fife, by helping refugees, was practicing "his own version of justice on the frontier." For violating U.S. immigration law in the name of loftier values, the *Denver Post* called Corbett a "new kind of outlaw in the American West."[68]

Even though the ranchers and sanctuary workers inspired comparisons with cowboys, vigilantes, or frontier bandits, they did not represent a "new kind of outlaw." The description also fit borderlands horsemen like the Mexican revolutionary Francisco "Pancho" Villa. During the Mexican Revolution and beyond, Villa was the very embodiment of competing notions of frontier justice. Like the Hanigans, Villa frequently committed wanton acts of violence against his enemies, took the law into his own hands, and meted out justice however he saw fit. But like sanctuary workers, Villa also pursued a vision of justice that protected the poor and defenseless against state-sponsored violence. Villa's legacy demonstrated how representations of various borderlands horsemen during the Hanigan and sanctuary trials made sense.

Rising tensions over undocumented immigration, articulated in terms of moral authority versus lawlessness, characterized the period from the 1970s forward. During the postwar era, many borderland residents clung to representations of the region's frontier past. However, with his statement that "the days of the Old West are gone," the judge implied that the modern West must follow a code of order and progress. Tucson's rodeo and parade had intertwined these two traditions by harnessing and incorporating both the spirit and memory of the region's modernization, progress, and racial harmony. The 1981 gift to Tucson by the Mexican government of a fourteen-foot statue of Villa, however, unsettled such ideas and became a reminder of the obstacles standing in the way of social, racial, and political peace. Tucsonans who opposed the Villa statue considered the Spanish missionary Eusebio Francisco Kino a more fitting representative for the area. During the late 1980s, they successfully lobbied to have a Kino statue erected in Tucson as a counterpoint. Located not even two miles apart, the bronzed likenesses of Kino and Villa offered different ways of thinking about the city's borderland relationships during the late twentieth century. One promoted ideologies that had long bolstered the Sunbelt borderland, and the other became a reminder of its enduring injustices.

6

TWO HORSEMEN

The arrival in Tucson of two larger-than-life statues sparked debates about regional history that demonstrated how Tucsonans thought of their city in an era of growing conflict. In June 1981, a crane lifted the veil from a fourteen-foot-tall statue of Francisco "Pancho" Villa. Then in January 1989, another, even larger equestrian statue was unveiled just a few miles away. It was a fifteen-foot-tall monument to Eusebio Francisco Kino, a Jesuit missionary. The Villa statue—even though its sponsors saw it as a symbol of international friendship—highlighted long histories of borderlands conflict and, more immediately, rising discrimination and inequality on both sides of the border. On the other hand, the Kino statue, a direct response to that of Villa, demonstrated the enduring faith of businesspeople, politicians, and boosters in Sunbelt borderland ideologies, such as cross-border economic development and trade, despite the disparities they had produced. According to supporters of the Villa statue, the bronze horseman symbolized Tucson's historical relationship with Mexico and inspired Mexicans and Mexican Americans in the city to continue their struggles for justice, whereas supporters of the Kino statue hoped that their hero would help refocus attention on international peace and prosperity, which, to them, defined the core of the Arizona-Sonora borderland's character.

Sculpted by the same Mexican artist, the statues therefore represented strikingly different visions of the Sunbelt borderland, demonstrating how debates about the border were also debates about the past, both distant and recent. At particular moments throughout the twentieth century, people on both sides of the border, for different purposes, had invoked the legacies of these borderlands icons. In general, Tucsonans feared Villa or saw him as a Robin Hood–like figure who fought for the poor, while Kino was a figure whom Arizonans and Sonorans invoked when they explained the arrival of civilization or promoted economic development. After Villa killed Americans in Columbus, New Mexico in 1916, many Tucsonans believed that he would attack their city next. For their part, Chicano movement participants saw Villa as an inspirational figure who fought for justice and equality as they did. When the Mexican debt crisis widened the gulf between the haves and the have-nots, and as Mexican policies continued to favor already wealthy elites despite the rhetoric of state and national leaders about the need for social progress and harmony, poor Sonorans borrowed Villa's name in their ongoing movements to secure land. Meanwhile, many Arizonans and Sonorans considered Kino the founder of the Pimería Alta as they knew it. In addition to building missions, he introduced cattle, implemented new agricultural techniques, and converted native peoples to Christianity. Tucsonans commemorated him with rodeo-parade floats, businesspeople saw his mission of progress mirrored in their own experiences, and regional boosters in the early twentieth century—as their California counterparts had done for their own missions—established a commemorative trail so tourists could follow the path the missionary had blazed.[1]

If the Villa and Kino statues evoked tensions over how Tucsonans interpreted regional history, they also represented the fragile state of U.S.-Mexico relations in the late twentieth century. Conflicts over economic issues, international migration, and the militarization of the border threatened to push the countries apart. The United States experienced an economic downturn in the 1970s, but, as one Sonoran historian wrote, Mexico's neighbor transferred "the cost of its crisis to the poorer capitalist countries." As Mexico's biggest foreign investor, the United States—both the government and the country's private banks—exerted a great deal of influence on the Mexican economy by deciding whether, when, or how much money to lend the country. In the decades after World War II, Mexico adopted the strategy of borrowing foreign capital in order to finance its economic development; as a result, by 1980, it had become one of the world's most indebted nations. The inability to meet its debt obligations, along with plummeting oil prices and a 1985 earthquake in Mexico City, led to the country's economic crises and created a power imbalance that caused widespread resentment when U.S. lenders demanded neoliberal reforms as the condition for their support. After the August 1982 debt crisis, Mexico increasingly adopted neoliberal economic policies, reversing high trade barriers that had been put in place during the mid-twentieth century to protect domestic industries and permitting increased foreign ownership of Mexican companies.[2]

As evidenced by the Hanigan case and the sanctuary movement—one ending and the other beginning just as the Villa statue was unveiled—transnational migration also led to increased tensions between the United States and Mexico. Borderlands economies, including Sonora's and Arizona's *maquiladora* and service industries, had in fact prompted immigration to the area, inviting Mexican immigrants from the country's interior to Sonora and from Sonora to Arizona. Declining economies on both sides of the border had led to greater unemployment and even more immigration as Mexicans left desperate situations in their homeland to seek better lives across the border. Their increased presence in the United States unleashed a nativist backlash. Mexicans and Mexican Americans with or without papers became targets of violence, and the Mexican government criticized the United States for its failure to protect Mexican workers. The shifting political economies of work, migration, and border enforcement also affected the O'odham who moved between Sonora and Arizona, as U.S. Border Patrol agents and other authorities sought to limit their crossings within their homelands. At the same time, U.S. support for violent, right-wing, military dictatorships in Central America created international and domestic friction both because many Mexicans sympathized with leftist movements and opposed U.S. intervention and because the wars created a refugee crisis in the United States. As a result of this tension, the United States no longer believed that Mexico could guarantee "order and stability" along the border, heightening the atmosphere of conflict.[3]

Nevertheless, cross-border economic ties simultaneously pulled the United States and Mexico closer together. Commercial exchange—tourism, export-import businesses, and investment—remained vital to the economies of both countries. Demonstrating the area's continued importance as an engine of economic growth, people kept streaming into the borderlands, hoping to find opportunities there. The population of U.S. and Mexican border states had grown by 60 and 90 percent, respectively, between 1960 and 1980. Also, Mexican emigration alleviated Mexico's unemployment situation, and the Mexican government relied on support from international banks to solve the country's financial problems. For better or worse, neither the United States nor Mexico could move forward without the other. The Villa and Kino statues reflected these broader regional and international tensions.[4]

The response to the statues also spotlighted Tucson's growing domestic troubles in the 1980s. Despite postwar advances and civil rights movements, a majority of Mexicans and Mexican Americans still experienced significant discrimination. Villa was a symbol of postwar borderlands conflict, which included the social, political, and economic disparities between whites and people of Mexican descent. Mexicans and Mexican Americans latched on to him as inspiration for their continued struggles and as a symbol of Tucson's Mexican past and its enduring connections with Mexico. Instead of a region defined by its conflicts, however, supporters of the Kino statue sought to reaffirm the Sunbelt borderland's dominant message, that the Arizona-Sonora borderland, because of their hero and his twentieth-century followers, stood for modernization, economic development, and free enterprise. In promoting these ideals, they did not entirely ignore Tucson's ethnic and racial histories, arguing that Kino, through his fair dealings with the Pimería Alta's native peoples, served as a model for the realization of prosperity. They ignored the border region's persistent inequalities and discriminations, which by the late twentieth century had caused the O'odham and other native peoples to reject the legacies of Spanish colonialism and call for greater autonomy from the U.S. and Mexican nation states. Opposition to and support for the Villa and Kino statues therefore demonstrated that late twentieth-century border debates in Arizona and Sonora went beyond undocumented immigration by also encompassing historically based definitions of community and regional identity.

Francisco "Pancho" Villa

More than six hundred people gathered to celebrate the unveiling of the Pancho Villa statue, including surviving Mexican revolutionaries, Villa's seventh of eight wives, Chamber of Commerce representatives, Mexican American civil rights leaders, consular officials, and customs agents. Tucson's renowned Mariachi Cobre serenaded the crowd, which then listened to speeches by Governor Babbitt and Luis Dantón Rodríguez, the Mexican official sent by President López Portillo. Rodríguez spoke about goodwill between Arizona and Mexico and about Villa's fight to stamp out abuse, oppression, and dictatorship. He stayed mum, however, about Villa's less savory deeds. In closing, Rodríguez personally thanked "Señor" Babbitt, whom he called an "amigo de México." A few Mexican Americans waged a peaceful demonstration against Tucson mayor Lewis Murphy, who opposed the statue and did not attend. From a footbridge over the park, they hung a sign that read "Villa sí, Murphy no!" Despite one reporter's fear that "anti-Villa elements" would disrupt the ceremony, there was not a "single sign of opposition." To the rhythm of a *bajo sexto*—an acoustic Mexican bass—attendees marched out of the park and proceeded to the Arizona Inn for lunch. There they dined on "Turkey Breast Ambassador" or a "White House Sandwich with Peace Garnish."[5]

Since 1981, those entering Tucson via the Broadway exit on Interstate 10 have encountered the Villa statue as the first monument they see. Between the adobe remnants of the presidio and the copper-tinted windows of the modern skyscrapers, it stands in one of Tucson's most visible public squares, formerly known as La Placita. Some still remember the plaza as the site of the original San Agustín Cathedral and as a gathering point for

Statue of Pancho Villa. (Photograph by author.)

Tucson's Mexican and Mexican American communities. The Villa statue stands just steps from where Jácome's Department Store and the Pioneer Hotel once thrived. Its stillness belies a turbulent life pulsing beneath its bronze façade. From his downtown pedestal, Villa faces Mexico as he rears back in the saddle of his favorite steed, Siete Leguas. They seem ready to gallop to Sonora or grind to a halt in Arizona, presenting an uncomfortable juxtaposition of motion and fixture. Their ambivalence, as well as Villa's gaze toward Mexico, suggests tensions that riddled the Arizona-Sonora borderland in the late twentieth century.[6]

While festivity and goodwill characterized the unveiling ceremony, the statue, even before it arrived in Tucson, sparked a controversy that divided the city. One historian wrote that Tucsonans greeted it with a "mixture of love and hate, of respect and contempt." Some regarded Villa as a cold-blooded killer both in Mexico and the United States and therefore resented the statue's prominent placement downtown. Others considered it a fitting tribute to a figure who fought for the poor against the rich and as a monument that would inspire Mexicans and Mexican Americans who continued to struggle for equality in Tucson. But the controversy over the Villa statue was about more than Villa's legacy; it became a symbol of the Arizona-Sonora border region's debates about immigration and cross-border relations by demonstrating that these vexing issues resonated with the Sunbelt borderland's deep histories of conflict and exchange.[7]

As they prepared for the statue's journey to Tucson, Mexican officials insisted that the bronze monument demonstrated their goodwill toward the United States. Mexico's Agrupación Nacional Periodista (ANPE), a professional association of journalists, first proposed the gift. Augustine García, Governor Babbitt's aide in Tucson, said that an ANPE representative asked Babbitt whether he would accept the statue. Babbitt responded vaguely that he would not reject it and then forgot about it. However, the ANPE representative returned to Mexico and put his plan into action. In addition, ANPE executives convinced the Mexican government of the project's worth by arguing that it would strengthen relations with their "brothers to the north." López Portillo offered his blessing and financial support, and ANPE commissioned Julián Martínez, Mexico's so-called sculptor laureate, to cast Villa in bronze. The artist had been born in Valencia, Spain, in 1921 and moved to Mexico in 1937 as an exile from the Spanish Civil War. He constructed the $260,000 statue at the Fundidora Artística in the state of Mexico. Before it embarked for Arizona, an ANPE representative, in a letter to López Portillo, praised the statue as a work of "perfection," noting, in particular, its "authentic Mexicanness and revolutionary effect." In closing, he wrote, "We're certain that the statue will be received by the North American public with great enthusiasm."[8]

Many in Tucson were, in fact, enthusiastic about the statue's arrival in their city. Phoenix was the original destination, but in March 1981 Babbitt wrote Murphy to say that, "given your community's geographical location to and close ties with Mexico, both historically and culturally," it would be placed in Tucson. Murphy supported the statue before he opposed it. "We are pleased that we have been given this option and would like to accept your most generous offer," he responded. Explaining the statue's placement in Tucson, some said that prominent Mexican Americans, including members of the Jácome family, lobbied to have the statue there. They had spent lifetimes developing close relations with Mexico, and for them it would be a symbol of their binational work. Babbitt concurred. When he sent invitations to attend the unveiling ceremony, he said the statue would inspire "friendship and goodwill." His correspondence after the unveiling confirmed his sentiment. In a letter to one Tucsonan, he wrote, "Our relations with our neighbors to the south were further enhanced by the historical and commemorative unveiling ceremony." Echoing language more typical of the Good Neighbor era, a Tucson city councilman wrote, "May this statue serve as a reminder that the people of the Americas are truly neighbors and that our destinies are so closely related." Finally, a Mexican man who claimed to have fought with Villa wrote that Babbitt's acceptance of the statue demonstrated that Arizona "was a state where people respect Mexicans."[9]

Despite optimistic proclamations about cross-border friendship, by the early 1980s U.S.-Mexico relations had entered a particularly tense period shaped by economic and political conflicts. Racked by foreign debt, Mexico devalued its currency and had difficulty servicing its loans, which hurt U.S. and Mexican economies, particularly along the border, and gave the United States the upper hand in negotiating Mexico's way out of the crisis. Many Mexicans felt the pain of their "unequal partnership." Nevertheless, U.S. and Mexican officials were compelled to solve these problems together since the economies of their countries were interconnected. The United States imported Mexican animals, vegetables, oil, and manufactured goods while at the same time exporting produce and grains from the United States to meet Mexico's growing domestic needs.

Furthermore, U.S. sources were Mexico's principal financiers—providing two-thirds of the country's total foreign investment—and cross-border tourism was vital to both countries as the number of visitors crossing the border in both directions increased steadily from the 1960s forward. By the early 1980s, when the Villa statue was unveiled, Mexicans accounted for 16 percent of all visitors and 25 percent of all tourist expenditures in the United States, outranking every other country except Canada in both areas. They spent 70 percent of their money in border cities. A temporary decline of cross-border commerce after 1982 notwithstanding, economists believed that the border region would become "progressively more important to the U.S. economy." For their part, Sonora's governors during the 1980s, Samuel Ocaña García and Rodolfo Félix Valdés, continued to invest in livestock, agriculture, tourism, mining, and, especially, manufacturing and service industries that were geared toward export. Ocaña acknowledged the difficulties caused by the 1982 crisis, as Mexican capital fled the country and U.S. lenders were reluctant to invest there, but he persistently argued that attracting domestic and foreign investments was the only way that Sonora could advance.[10]

Cross-border political relations also became more tense with the rise of undocumented immigration, abuse of Mexican migrant workers, and U.S. interventions in Central America. After 1965, the number of Mexicans who entered the United States without papers increased dramatically, as did the number of apprehensions by the U.S. Border Patrol. Between the mid-1960s and the end of the 1970s, apprehensions rose from 60,000 to 900,000 per year. Anti-immigrant forces claimed that the invasion of undocumented Mexicans posed a new threat to the United States and blamed Mexico for not controlling the situation. Meanwhile, immigrant advocates argued that Mexicans, regardless of whether here legally, helped the U.S. economy. In the *New Yorker*, writer Octavio Paz blamed much deeper histories for the tension between the United States and Mexico. The two countries were neighbors "condemned to live alongside each other," he wrote, and from the fifteenth century on, the "history of our relationship" was "the history of mutual and stubborn deceit."[11]

And so, as Mexicans criticized the United States' aggressive behavior throughout the hemisphere, including toward its own country, many in Arizona considered the Villa statue as another in a long line of Mexican deceits. Indeed, critics wondered whether it was a practical joke on the "gullible gringos" of Arizona, the result of barroom banter by a few Mexican journalists. It was an odd gesture of goodwill, they believed, considering Villa's history of violence within his own country and especially in the United States. To them, Villa was a bandit who crossed the border to rob and murder U.S. citizens. Angry Tucsonans quipped that the "American press" should offer Mexico a statue of General John Pershing, who, with thousands of U.S. troops, hunted Villa south of the border. They also proposed a statue of General Winfield Scott, who took Chapultepec Hill in the final battle of the U.S.-Mexico War. Others compared the Villa statue in Tucson to a statue in downtown Honolulu of Mitsuo Fuchida, the Japanese commander who led the attack on Pearl Harbor. Both men had violated U.S. sovereignty, and to honor Villa with a statue was tantamount to vindicating him.[12]

The Villa statue outraged some Tucsonans, who remembered the Mexican revolutionary for acts of violence he and his troops committed in the U.S.-Mexico borderlands, especially the December 1915 massacre at San Pedro de la Cueva, Sonora, and his raid on Columbus, New Mexico, in March 1916, just a few months later. The first left scores of Sonoran civilians dead, including women and children; the second was a six-hour skirmish between *villistas* and U.S. soldiers that led to the deaths of eighteen Americans and more than one hundred Mexicans. These events took place during some of the darkest months of Villa's career, characterized by his increasing isolation and hostility toward the United States.

If Villa had become an enemy of the United States by the end of the Mexican Revolution, in earlier years he was widely admired. Although the United States ultimately recognized the government of his rival, Venustiano Carranza, Villa seemed to promise several advantages, including his vow—on which he later reneged—that he would not reclaim property owned by U.S. citizens or attack U.S. corporations. Moreover, Villa had forged close relationships with U.S. merchants, who supplied his troops with arms, ammunition, cattle, and horses. He also carefully cultivated his image in the United States by writing adulatory letters to U.S. officials, cutting movie deals with Hollywood studios, and sitting for interviews in which he proclaimed his admiration of the United States.[13]

The Arizona-Sonora borderland had figured prominently in the Mexican Revolution and in Villa's own career, feeding the stories Arizonans told about their state's relationship to Mexico throughout the twentieth century. Merchants in Tucson and Phoenix provisioned Sonoran leaders. In addition, U.S.-owned mining companies sought to protect their operations in Cananea and other Sonoran cities, while Sonorans, seeking refuge from violence, fled to Arizona. Finally, revolutionary factions waged battles in Sonoran border towns. In 1913, Emilio Kosterlitzky led a force of four hundred men against federal troops in Nogales. In 1914, José María Maytorena's troops fought Calles's and Obregón's soldiers in Naco. Villa himself suffered his most fateful defeat along the border between Arizona and Sonora. In 1915, three thousand *carrancistas* crushed more than eight thousand villistas in Agua Prieta, which reduced Villa to waging guerrilla warfare in the mountains of Chihuahua. He blamed the loss on President Wilson, who permitted Carranza's troops to enter the United States and stage their attack from there. Villa believed that the collusion between Carranza and Wilson signaled U.S. support for Carranza's constitutionalist movement and also that Mexico would have to allow U.S. troops to enter the country if and whenever they wanted. Confirming his fears, U.S. troops under General Pershing soon entered Chihuahua to hunt Villa.[14]

Villa's crushing defeat in Agua Prieta and Carranza's efforts to win U.S. support led him to commit the acts of violence for which many Arizonans remembered him. In December 1915, Villa took out his frustration on the Sonoran town of San Pedro de la Cueva, where he murdered seventy-four civilians in what many have considered his most appalling act. When he attacked Columbus a few months later, his movement had reached its low point. At one time, Villa had commanded more than fifty thousand soldiers, but in early 1916 his troops numbered only a few hundred. He increasingly attributed his—and Mexico's—misfortunes to the United States. After his defeat at Agua Prieta, according to historian Friedrich Katz, Villa demonstrated a "new attitude" toward Mexico's northern neighbor. For months before the Columbus Raid, he had escalated violence against U.S. interests in Mexico, including the confiscation of William Randolph Hearst's ranch in Chihuahua and the murder of seventeen U.S. mining engineers. He delivered a manifesto in Naco, Sonora, in which he accused Carranza of entering into a secret pact with Wilson, which, he said, would accomplish the complete "sale of our country by the traitor Carranza." Instead of attacking Carranza directly, he planned to "attack the Americans in their own dens."[15]

Villa's raid on Columbus had immediate and long-term consequences for the U.S.-Mexico borderlands, culminating in the reactions to the Villa statue in Tucson. First, the raid brought the United States and Mexico to the brink of war. Within a week, Wilson ordered thousands of troops to pursue Villa. In February 1917, in part because of the likelihood that the United States would be drawn into World War I, the so-called punitive expedition left Mexico, having failed, as Katz wrote, "even to catch sight of its elusive prey." Ironically, Pershing's failure benefited Villa as both the sight of U.S. soldiers marching through Chihuahua and their execution of Villistas converted the beleaguered revolutionary into a powerful symbol of national resistance to the United States. Yet Villa also undermined Mexico's position, as the United States imposed several preconditions for withdrawing its troops.

The Columbus Raid also left its mark on Tucson and the Southwest more broadly as many wondered whether Villa would target their communities next. To defend Tucson, militias formed, including one made up of faculty at the University of Arizona, charged with protecting the campus. The controversy over the Villa statue demonstrated the Columbus Raid's long-term impact. Decades after the attack, one newspaper article argued that Tucson was unable to defend itself against Villa after all. "What Villa did not accomplish in life," it read, "he was able to do in death—he got to Tucson."[16]

If the revolutionary violence Villa committed against Sonora and New Mexico made the statue seem an unlikely gesture of goodwill, it made more sense from the perspective of a Mexican government that had spent years rehabilitating Villa's reputation within Mexico. Ever since the Mexican Revolution ended, the Mexican government had sought to control the revolution's meaning. Mexican presidents Obregón and Elías Calles, both from Sonora, first established the idea of a "revolutionary family," which rhetorically unified the leaders of the Mexican Revolution. In 1929, Calles and his supporters worked to establish the Partido Nacional Revolucionario, a precursor to the PRI that claimed the mantle of the revolution. By the 1960s and 1970s, the massacre at Tlatelolco, student movements like the one at la Universidad de Sonora, and increasing financial insecurity and economic inequality destabilized the party and led to rising levels of opposition. Histories of the Mexican Revolution reflected these changing attitudes toward the PRI. They "undermined the orthodoxy of revolutionary synthesis," one historian explained, by "portraying the Zapatista and Villista peasant revolutions as the genuine Mexican Revolution." The PRI sought to neutralize the threat posed by opposition parties by appropriating figures such as Zapata and Villa and incorporating the revolution's working-class and agrarian movements into official commemorations. In

1966, Mexico recognized Villa as a revolutionary hero for the first time when it authorized the engraving of his name in gold in the Chamber of Deputies next to the names of Madero, Venustiano Carranza, and Emiliano Zapata. In 1976, the government disinterred Villa from his grave in Parral, Chihuahua, and moved his body to the Monument to the Revolution in Mexico City, where he became the only nonpresident to lie alongside Madero, Carranza, Elías Calles, and Lázaro Cárdenas. The move to Mexico's "sacred temple of the nation," one historian wrote, signaled the government's decision to "heal the wounds of memory."[17]

The Villa statue in Tucson therefore represented Mexico's effort to bolster the PRI during the years of increasing challenges to its authority. It also represented an attempt to reach out to Mexican nationals abroad and "forge patriotism" among them, as the famous Mexican anthropologist Manuel Gamio put it in 1916. López Portillo effectively renewed Gamio's appeal through his emissary's comments at the 1981 unveiling ceremony, delivered before many Mexicans and Mexican Americans, that "every day we need to do whatever is necessary to listen to the voice of our people, to respect them, and to serve them, increasing their liberties, fighting for their rights, and improving every day." Demonstrating the link between Villa and Mexican patriotism, during the late 1970s the Mexican government erected Villa statues throughout Mexico—in Durango, Chihuahua, Zacatecas—including a statue similar to the one in Tucson that sits on a traffic island along Avenida División del Norte in Mexico City. Thus, when they sent the statue to Tucson, Mexicans planned an elaborate send-off for their rejuvenated hero before loading him on a flatbed truck for the eighteen-hundred-mile trek from the capital city to Arizona.[18]

From the outset, the statue's journey north was rough. Government representatives had to reschedule the official send-off when the weight of the statue snapped a cable that was supposed to hoist it onto the delivery truck. López Portillo, his cabinet, military units, and the Arizona delegation sent to Mexico to accept the gift had planned to attend the ceremony. However, the fall caused the figure of Villa to break off from his horse, forcing Mexico to plan a second send-off, which also did not go as planned. Drivers took the wrong route and realized that the statue was too tall to go through an underpass. Finally, a downsized celebration sent the statue on its way in late April 1981. Heading north to Tucson, the Villa statue passed through Ciudad Juárez and El Paso, twin border cities along the Chihuahua-Texas border. Several thousand people gathered on the Mexican side, where they greeted Villa "with enthusiasm," happy to catch a glimpse of the revolutionary icon. When the Villa statue entered Ciudad Juárez, an ANPE representative reiterated its purpose. Villa, he said, "who once brought violence to the United States, now in bronze brings a message of peace." As the Villa statue crossed the border, representatives of the United States and Mexico, in a performance of international friendship, met on the bridge between their two countries to embrace and exchange pleasantries.[19]

The opponents of the Villa statue in Tucson anxiously followed news of its progress after leaving Mexico City, steeling themselves for its arrival and expressing their misgivings in language that demonstrated their distaste for Villa. Anticipating the unwelcoming reception awaiting the statue upon arrival in Tucson, one reporter wrote, when the figure approached the border between Chihuahua and Texas, the "fierce warrior" saw the "tall buildings of El Paso in the country to which he brought death and destruction 65 years ago." In the weeks before the unveiling ceremony, constituents from all across Arizona flooded Governor Babbitt's office with letters that expressed their displeasure. A man from Tucson did not understand how Babbitt could accept a monument to a man who "by any count was a multiple murderer." Another wrote that the "offer of this statue by Mexico was an insult to intelligent U.S. citizens while the acceptance was sheer stupidity." A woman from Globe, Arizona, thanked Babbitt for "sparing my sweet mother from seeing this." She claimed that Villistas had killed her father and kidnapped her mother before the attack in New Mexico. Her mother, she wrote, watched them scalp, cook, and eat American ranchers. Babbitt responded simply, "I thank you for taking the time to share your comments concerning this most controversial figure in history."[20]

For other Tucsonans, the Villa statue struck at their sense of the city's postwar progress and modernization. City officials and businesspeople had spent decades hawking the benefits of economic growth and order. In a sense, Villa was a symbol of a bygone era, when conflict, more than peace and prosperity, defined the Arizona-Sonora border region. But he was also a symbol of more recent conflicts over Chicano civil rights, undocumented immigration, and tense U.S.-Mexico relations more broadly, which demonstrated that neither peace nor prosperity represented the experience of all borderland residents. After Tucson's mayor, Lewis Murphy, considered the meaning of these issues, he decided to oppose the statue despite his earlier support. In consequence, he announced that he would not attend the unveiling ceremony. When a reporter asked him whether he had a prior commitment or out-of-town business, Murphy said, "No, I'll just be unavailable."

Another Tucsonan filed a lawsuit to have the statue removed from the city. Local businessman Byron Ivancovich argued that it constituted an illegal use of tax revenue, but because Babbitt had used "privately donated money" from a "special governor's fund," the argument had no merit. Ivancovich tried another tack, arguing that the statue would drive tourists from the area by "glorifying a murderer and a rapist," "corrupting public morals," and "creating an eyesore." It would therefore be bad for his financial interests in downtown real estate. A Pima County judge decided against him in April 1983, almost two years after the statue's unveiling.[21]

When arguments based on civic order and business interests failed, Ivancovich and other Tucsonans appealed to history, sentiment, and the statue's psychological impact on them. Before the judge refused Ivancovich's claim, the plaintiff's lawyer criss-crossed the Southwest, collecting testimonies from contemporaries of the Columbus Raid, seeking to reinforce the idea that Villa was a cold-blooded killer. Ivancovich also claimed that the statue had caused him great emotional distress because it undermined his sense of the city he and his ancestors had built. Like the white settlers in *Arizona*, they were "pioneers," whose entrepreneurship led to Tucson's growth from the late nineteenth century onward. However, instead of paying tribute to people like them, here was a statue that affirmed Tucson's relationship with Mexico and, he claimed, violence committed against the United States. For these same reasons, another Tucsonan said that the statue sent him into a "state of shock."[22]

Historians at the University of Arizona lent their expertise to opponents of the Villa statue. Like others, they based their arguments on the violence he committed in Sonora and New Mexico. But they also argued that other regional icons would have been more appropriate. In a letter to Governor Babbitt, Franciscan historian Kieran McCarty suggested replacing the Villa statue with one of Kino. Babbitt thanked McCarty for the suggestion, adding that the next time he was "called upon to look a Mexican gift horse in the mouth" he would consider it carefully. Bernard "Bunny" Fontana, Charles Polzer, and Bernardo Acedo—three more historians of the Southwest—returned to the issue of violence. Acedo, whose family had roots in Sonora, had written a thesis about the San

Pedro de la Cueva massacre that led him to conclude that "Villa was more heartless villain than hero." He noted that the city of Hermosillo had refused to place a Villa statue there because of Villa's atrocities against Sonora.[23]

While criticism or praise of the Villa statue often depended on the ethnicity of the beholder, Acedo's remarks demonstrated that Mexican heritage did not necessarily predict a favorable view. The attitudes of Mexicans and Mexican Americans toward Villa could depend on where in Mexico their families originated; whom their family had supported during the Mexican Revolution; and their social, political, and class positions on both sides of the border. During the Mexican Revolution, Villa's base of support was Chihuahua, but he was not universally liked there. Likewise, he made enemies in Sonora because of his violent campaigns in the state, but many there sympathized with him as well. What was true during Villa's own lifetime remained true into the late twentieth century: he had a wide array of allies and enemies. During the Mexican Revolution, thousands of Chihuahuans and Sonorans had immigrated to Arizona and other areas of the Southwest. By the early 1980s, several generations of their families had settled there. The stories they told about the revolution influenced the way Mexicans and Mexican Americans viewed Villa. As Fontana noted, "If you were to wander around the barrios, you would find that Villa is not popular with Sonorans and people who have roots in Sonora." Similarly, broadcast journalist Raúl Aguirre remembered when angry descendants of Obregón supporters had barged into the offices of Tucson's Spanish-language radio station, KXEW, and threatened to "kick the deejay's ass" after he praised Villa. Others, of course, felt differently.[24]

For many Mexicans and Mexican Americans, the statue was a source of pride and inspiration, evoking their sense of struggle in a city that many had considered home for a long time even though some Tucsonans still saw them as foreigners. Babbitt acknowledged that, in some sense, the statue was for them. In letters to Mexican American constituents in Tucson, he recognized that their communities continued to suffer discrimination, especially in the "fields of employment, education, and civil rights." After decades of fighting for equality, the vast majority of Mexican Americans still earned less than whites, far fewer graduated from college, and many lived in the city's poorest communities, where they experienced police harassment based on their appearance. To address this situation, Babbitt wrote, the "cultural and social heritage" of Mexicans and Mexican Americans, through figures like Villa, "must be integrated into the make-up of Arizona's unique character if we are to achieve racial equality."[25]

If Villa was a symbol of Tucson's Mexican and Mexican American heritage, communities on both sides of the border also turned to the figure of Villa to express their frustration that, after decades of fighting for equality, little seemed to have changed. In Arizona, partially as a result of the Chicana and Chicano movement for civil rights, more Mexican American officials than ever before held elected positions in the 1970s and 1980s, including, for a brief period, the governorship. Yet many wondered whether these politicians represented their interests or those of the middle and upper classes. In their search for leaders, some Mexican Americans saw Villa as a role model. One Mexican American author, for example, wrote a short story titled "And Where Was Pancho Villa When You Really Needed Him?" about her experiences in a Tucson public school. In her story, teachers at the school had "low expectations" for their Chicana and Chicano students, whose grades were higher than they deserved and who had "unrealistic" aspirations for themselves. After enduring such discriminations, the protagonist of the story hoped for a daring hero to help her, so she "waited for Pancho Villa to come charging into the room." In the story, her fantasy became a reality as students and administrators returned to school the next day to find their classroom in ruins. Villa had destroyed it in order to create something new. Meanwhile, Sonorans claimed that Villa would have protected them against the economic crises caused by two peso devaluations, and landless communities in the state formed a group they called the "Francisco Villa movement," which protested the government's granting of land to wealthy Sonorans instead of poor people like them.[26]

One Mexican American man from Tucson whose family came from Sonora summed up Villa's legacy of fighting for poor people: "We don't have many people like that anymore." Edward Tapia defended the statue after a group of vandals painted a yellow stripe and the word "trash" on it. He saw the markings every morning on his way to work. When he reported the graffiti to Tucson's Parks and Recreation Department, officials failed to act, so he cleaned the statue himself. Once word of his action spread, people called him anonymously and asked, "Why don't you get on the horse and ride off to Mexico?" He ignored them and instead told stories about "old-timers" like his Sonoran father-in-law, who told him that

Villa "fought for *campesinos*, and anybody who fights for the poor is great." Another Sonoran, Heleodoro Rendón-García, said that Villa "never killed a man unjustly," and he had known since he was a "young boy" that Villa would be "seen as a hero."[27]

In addition to a figure that inspired various campaigns for justice, Villa also reminded Mexican Americans in Tucson of prior efforts to erase the history of their community and its relation to Mexico. The 1940 film *Arizona*, about Tucson's first white settlers, offered one example, and the urban-renewal project that razed Barrio Libre during the late 1960s provided another. Literary scholars and historians have argued that landscapes possess historically encoded significance and that space produces and reinforces social relations. It was understandable, therefore, that the Villa statue's placement in Veinte de Agosto Park, in the heart of the urban-renewal zone, suggested the social and historical claims of belonging made by Mexicans and Mexican Americans in Tucson. In response to a "one-man protest" of the Villa statue, immigrant-rights attorney Isabel García—a University of Arizona alumna and founding member of groups like the Manzo Area Council and the Coalición de Derechos Humanos—saw it through the lens of U.S. westward expansion and conquest. At a counterprotest by "Villa supporters," she argued that the statue should have a home in Tucson because "this area should be part of Mexico." Tucson, she continued, "was all our land," and "your people stole it."[28]

The reactions of Tucsonans who opposed and supported the Villa statue demonstrated that Villa-as-symbol continued to shape the culture and politics of the Arizona-Sonora borderland, a region whose public image was increasingly defined by heated debates about immigration and the border. Many Mexicans and Mexican Americans mobilized historically and regionally around notions of Villa's life and legacy to inspire ongoing struggles for social, political, and economic justice. However, those who continued to place faith in the Sunbelt borderland's core ideologies of development and order by and large opposed the Villa statue. These ideas were antithetical to Villa's nature, they believed. The figure of Eusebio Francisco Kino helped them reconcile this tension. Kino embodied the economic ideals of Arizona's and Sonora's Sunbelt borderland, but, according to Kino's supporters, he also fought for justice. Many claimed that he brought civilization to the area and developed it economically. He was a visionary and a peacemaker—not a warrior, like Villa. In Kino's own time, his supporters said, he achieved harmony through his many good works among the Pimería Alta's native peoples. He would help heal a conflicted border region in the late twentieth century, just as he had transformed it centuries earlier. So the legend went, and the legend was eventually cast in bronze by the same Mexico City sculptor who just a few years earlier had cast Pancho Villa.

Eusebio Francisco Kino

Kino had appealed to generations of Arizona and Sonora borderland residents. The romantic version of his legacy held that the Jesuit missionary, who arrived in the Pimería Alta in the late seventeenth century, brought Western civilization to the region by converting indigenous peoples to Christianity, establishing more than two dozen missions over the course of three decades, and introducing cattle and new agricultural techniques. He was a progenitor of regional history, a figure that latter-day businesspeople and politicians turned to as the inspiration for their twentieth-century quests for prosperity. A Kino statue, they believed, would be a symbol of the Arizona-Sonora borderland that was far superior to the Villa monument that occupied downtown Tucson. Unable to have the Villa statue removed, its opponents instead commissioned a statue of Kino to serve as a counterweight. It would represent their vision of regional history by echoing the ideological underpinnings of Arizona's and Sonora's Sunbelt borderland, which, they believed, was still Tucson's path to the future.

The Kino statue was, in fact, made in triplicate, and the other two went to Segno, Italy, and Magdalena de Kino, Sonora. Kino had been born in Segno in 1645. He crossed the Atlantic from Spain to Mexico in 1681 and then established two dozen missions in Arizona and Sonora between 1687 and 1707, including Tucson's San Xavier del Bac. He died in Magdalena in 1711. Kino was buried in the chapel he had established, though archaeologists from Arizona and Sonora discovered his grave only in 1966. When Kino first arrived in Mexico, he was instructed to learn about California and convert its native peoples to Christianity. Biographies, films, and other historical accounts of his life have not only narrated his failed efforts to reach the Pacific Coast but also described how he paved the way for later Spanish missionaries, including Junipero Serra. The three statues cast during the late 1980s would be monuments to his life and work. The first was unveiled in January 1989 in Tucson, the site of Kino's northernmost mission. The second was unveiled in May 1989 in

Magdalena, the site of Kino's death, and the third in the summer of 1991 in Segno, his birthplace. Kino's supporters called these "Three Statues for Three Centuries."[29]

If University of Arizona historians played a key role in articulating opposition to the Villa statue, they played an equally important part in explaining why a Kino statue would be better. After the unveiling of the Villa statue, McCarty, Fontana, and Polzer began lobbying for a monument to honor Kino because of his legacy as a proselytizer, developer, modernizer, and civilizer of the area and also because of his reputation for treating the area's native peoples with respect. Kino, not Villa, McCarty said, was part of Arizona's "authentic history." For his part, Polzer lobbied for the Kino statue to such an extent that, by 1987, newspapers were calling it the "brainchild" of this "premier Arizona historian."[30]

University historians and other Kinophiles—the boosters, businesspeople, and politicians, who, along with academics, promoted Kino as a regional and an international hero—explicitly thought of a monument honoring Kino as a rebuff to the Villa statue. The Kino statue in Tucson, they hoped, would loom over the Villa statue and erase the pain that

Unveiling of Eusebio Francisco Kino statue, downtown Tucson in background. (Arizona Historical Society, Tucson Photo Files, Case 38, 78210.)

some associated with the experience of seeing Villa in their city. When plans for the Kino statue were first announced in 1987, one newspaper article explained, "The Villa statue has been a sore point among some Tucsonans." Polzer advanced the argument that it had divided Tucson, whereas the Kino statue would unite the city. In a revision of the story told by those directly involved in the planning for the Villa statue, he claimed that the Mexican revolutionary was intended to appeal to Mexicans and Mexican Americans only. Polzer said it was the result of concerted efforts by Arizona's Mexican American governor, Raúl Castro, and López Portillo's predecessor, President Echeverría. His narrative made the decision to bring the Villa statue to Arizona seem like the result of plotting by Mexicans and Mexican Americans on both sides of the border rather than the effort of a broader, more representative swath of Tucson as a whole. Unlike the Villa statue, he argued, the Kino statue would become a "clear rallying point," a common cause that would bring the community together.[31]

Polzer also ventriloquized Julián Martínez, the Mexico City sculptor who crafted both the Villa and Kino statues, arguing that Martínez regretted that Tucson had "wound up," or gotten stuck with, the Villa statue. According to Polzer, Martínez believed that the city "deserved something much better, such as a statue of Father Kino." While many Tucsonans claimed that the trio of U of A historians had come up with the idea of a Kino statue, Polzer claimed that Martínez proposed it in order to make up for the Villa travesty. Martínez was a self-avowed Kinophile. He had sculpted Kino before, including two twin statues that stood in the capitol buildings of Arizona and Sonora, in Phoenix and Hermosillo, respectively. By the mid-1980s, Polzer recalled, Martínez had been telling him for "several years" that he wanted to "sculpt Kino again."[32]

Even though the Kinophiles believed that their statue would be a perfect fit for Tucson, they had a hard time obtaining popular and financial support. Polzer promoted the statue all over Tucson, giving speeches on television and radio and at the Arizona Historical Society. The Pathfinder Project, a nonprofit organization founded in 1977 to support historical preservation and commemorative projects, tried to raise $100,000, the cost of the statue, which was a bargain in comparison to the Villa statue's $260,000 price tag. The cost was substantially less for this second work because Martínez donated his time and transportation companies covered shipment. The group solicited investors on both sides of the border, in Arizona and Sonora. Its members believed fund-raising in Tucson would be easy, since it was a city of 600,000 residents, which would mean "$10 from 10,000 of us," "$5 from 20,000 of us," or "$1 from 100,000 of us." But the group failed to secure sufficient private donations. By October 1987, when the fund-raising campaign was to end, Project Pathfinder had procured only $11,000. The campaign was extended to December but failed again. A plea for contributions televised during the final game of the World Series yielded a single $2 donation. Banks and television and radio stations offered advertising assistance, but to no avail. Ultimately, the Pathfinder Project relied on government funds and donations from wealthy businesspeople. The City of Tucson contributed $24,000; the Pima County Board of Supervisors, $24,001; Valley National Bank, $5,000; and the remaining amount came from fourteen anonymous businesspeople.[33]

The Pathfinder Project's failure to find support from a broad range of Tucsonans demonstrated that the Kino statue was the pet project of businesspeople and politicians. The process of financing the Kino statue and the cast of actors who dedicated themselves to the cause highlighted stark contrasts with the process of bringing the Villa statue to Tucson. Unlike the Villa statue, the Kino statue benefited from local government support. Although Mayor Murphy, in the end, did not welcome the Villa statue, he gave his full support to the one of Kino and even opened the city's coffers to help pay for it. He also offered city land and renamed the road near where the Kino statue would sit, calling it "Kino Parkway." The Pathfinder Project's chairman claimed that, without Murphy's help and donations from "Tucson business leaders," the project "probably would have failed." These Tucsonans continued to invest in narratives of regional history crafted by promoters of Arizona's and Sonora's Sunbelt borderland in the decades after World War II, promoting modernity and progress even as inequalities and discrimination undermined such notions.[34]

With the scale of Tucson's Kino statue, the Kinophiles aimed to ensure that the monument to their hero would overshadow the Villa statue. A full foot taller, the Kino statue literally towered over the one of Villa. In addition, they hoped that the Kino statue would make the Villa statue also seem irrelevant and—as they understood regional history—completely iconoclastic. Kino-statue supporters knew that their monument's appeal would depend on their ability to make it represent their own version of the past, which promoted growth, prosperity, and romantic notions of interracial harmony. These ideals, they believed, contrasted with the violence and conflict for which the Villa statue stood. As a promotional pamphlet put it, the Kino statue would "tell a story and present something more than just another likeness of the missionary explorer." It represented a regional hero whose legacy would inspire Tucsonans to come together and bridge the divides that separated them, which the Villa statue had only widened.[35]

Beyond the physical scale of the statue, its component materials helped the Kinophiles reinforce their message about Kino's deserved place in Arizona-Sonora borderland lore. Martínez in fact inscribed on the statue their version of Kino as a civilizer, modernizer, and international and intercultural peacemaker. Martínez worked with members of Kino's family to choose the design; used "forensic data" taken from Kino's remains to determine the statue's features; and blended into the statue soil gathered from Italy, Arizona, and Sonora. Martínez then worked to capture Kino's tireless work ethic and his relationship with native communities. Most statues of Kino—including the ones Martínez had made earlier—depicted Kino at around the age of sixty. However, this time the artist, with urging from the Arizona Historical Society, decided to represent Kino in his fifties, at the pinnacle of his career and around the time that Tucson's iconic San Xavier del Bac mission was being constructed. Kino and his horse sat tired but upright, reflecting both their "arduous" journey and their determination. Portraying the missionary's career as an explorer and a mapmaker, bronze Kino carried in his saddlebags a telescope and various astronomy instruments. With the abalone shells Kino held close to his chest, Martínez suggested Kino's "devotion and inspiration to the native peoples he had come to serve."[36]

The moment for a Kino statue therefore seemed opportune; this was a time when Tucson and the Arizona-Sonora borderland needed to reestablish a sense of harmony after more than a decade of growing tensions. Still, borderland residents ever since the early twentieth century had found meaning in his career and legacy. Interest in Kino developed with help from California scholars who, in the late nineteenth and early twentieth centuries, began noting the significance of the state's Spanish past. Carey McWilliams argued that popular manifestations, such as mission trails and reconstructed town plazas, formed part of California's "Spanish fantasy heritage." Borderlands historian Herbert Eugene Bolton, a professor at Berkeley, published Kino's little-known autobiography in 1919, translating Kino's *Favores celestiales* as *Kino's Historical Memoir of Pimería Alta.* Later, in 1932, Bolton wrote a popular account titled *The Padre on*

Horseback. Historians like Hubert Howe Bancroft had "chastised" Spanish colonizers for their "adherence to backwards economic and religious beliefs," one historian wrote, adding that religious scholars "wrote about the missions and the missionaries in a heroic, hagiographic mode." Bolton instead noted the missions' "broad impact and the enduring legacies" in economic, social, and cultural terms. His ideas helped Tucsonans think of Kino as the connection between the area's past and their own modernizing efforts in the present.[37]

As Bolton wrote, regional boosters, religious leaders, and scholars in the Arizona-Sonora borderland simultaneously promoted their own monuments to Kino. They excavated his missions and published "numerous studies, travelogues, articles, and pamphlets" about Kino's work and legacies. Frank Lockwood—English professor and predecessor of McCarty, Fontana, and Polzer at the U of A—sparked Tucson's early Kinophilia. Lockwood was an expert in early nineteenth-century British and American literature, but after moving to Tucson from the Midwest he became fascinated by regional history. Upon encountering Bolton's work, he remarked, "Order came out of chaos, and light shone in the darkness." During the late 1920s, Lockwood organized the Kino Memorial Committee to cultivate interest in erecting a monument to their hero. In 1936, after years of delay attributed to the Great Depression, the committee succeeded in creating a "plaque and commemorative space" at Tucson's city hall. It was Tucson's first twentieth-century Kino monument.[38]

The members of the Kino Memorial Committee "traced a line" from the present to the past, between Kino—who, they believed, was their ideological antecedent—and their own modernization efforts. Demonstrating how racial thinking about Italians and Spaniards had changed by the 1930s, they called Kino Arizona's "first white settler." Lockwood wrote in his 1934 book, *With Padre Kino on the Trail*, that Kino was not only a "spiritual captain" but also "an explorer, a ranchman, a builder, and a statesman." As tourism by car increased, boosters profited from Kino commemorations by establishing an international tour of the missions he founded, which also nurtured "good spirit" with the "Mexicans of Sonora," according to one Arizona politician. Letters to Lockwood demonstrated that Sonorans felt the same way. One sent from Magdalena said, "We are all here with you . . . in making a big success of your chain of Father Kino's Missions." Kino's legacy in the region, Arizonans and Sonorans believed, had the potential to sew back together a Pimería Alta divided by the Gadsden Purchase. As Lockwood wrote, people on both sides of the border were interested in "re-uniting" the region and "once more drawing together Northern Sonora and Southern Arizona as Father Kino knew it." Such symbolic efforts continued into the postwar era.[39]

Promotions of Kino as a hero in both the United States and Mexico again reached high tide during the mid-1960s, when the Sunbelt borderland's service and manufacturing economies reached new heights and as businesspeople and politicians on both sides of the border preached the benefits of international friendship. Two episodes in particular highlighted Kino commemorations during the 1960s: first, in 1965, Arizona's political representatives donated a Kino statue to the National Statuary Hall in the U.S. Capitol; second, in 1966, after a search that lasted decades, Kino's remains were discovered in Magdalena, Sonora. These two pivotal moments in the evolution of Kinophilia resulted in the erection of Tucson's Kino statue two decades later.

A grand ceremony in the U.S. Capitol, attended by national and international representatives, was held on Valentine's Day in 1965, a fitting date to express the affection Arizona's and Mexico's business, political, and religious leaders felt for Kino. By the early twenty-first century, the National Statuary Hall featured one hundred statues in total, or two per state. Arizona's other statue is that of John Campbell Greenway, a leader of Arizona's mining and railroad industries during the early twentieth century. Greenway also served as a member of Theodore Roosevelt's Rough Riders in the Spanish-American War. The statue of him was dedicated in 1930, only four years after he died. In attendance at the Kino dedication ceremony were Governor Samuel Goddard; John Rhodes, an Arizona congressman who later served as the Republican Party's minority leader; and Stewart Udall, a former Democratic senator from Arizona, who at the time served under President Johnson as secretary of the interior. Also attending were civic and religious leaders from Tucson; Kino's descendants in the United States; and Italian and Mexican ambassadors. Carl Hayden, longtime U.S. senator from Arizona, delivered the main address, reciting Kino's accomplishments in the Pimería Alta.[40]

Sonoran ceremonies held in connection with the discovery of Kino's remains in Magdalena demonstrated that celebrations of Kino in the mid-1960s were binational affairs. In 1966, the "long search" for Kino's remains ended at the site of the mission he built in Magdalena, a town that originally was called Buquivaba but by the 1960s had incorporated his name:

Magdalena de Kino. The search for Kino's remains dated to the 1930s, during the first wave of regional Kinophilia. One Sonoran wrote in a letter to Lockwood that, "according to manuscripts here at my disposal, the grave of Father Kino is here in this Church at the right side of the Altar in a special crypt that I have found." It took another thirty years to confirm the finding. On June 20, 1968, Sonora passed a law proclaiming that Sonorans would celebrate the discovery of Kino's bones every year. Like promotions of Kino during the 1930s, these two episodes during the 1960s became opportunities to highlight Kino's role as a modernizer of the Arizona-Sonora borderland. At the dedication ceremony in Washington, D.C., Senator Hayden claimed that Kino first made Arizona "known to the civilized world." He said that the Kino statue in the nation's capitol "enshrined" Kino as one of an "exclusive group who were makers of our Nation's history."[41]

Finally, twentieth-century Kinophilia peaked in the 1980s as scholars, businesspeople, and local and state governments geared up to celebrate the three-hundredth anniversary, in 1987, of Kino's arrival in the Pimería Alta. In 1981, shortly before the Villa statue was unveiled in Tucson, articles in Hermosillo's *Revista de Historia* noted that Kino experienced great hardships as a result of native rebellions, yet he still planted trees and domesticated cattle and served as both a peacemaker and a worker. In 1983, the owner of Mazón's department store in Hermosillo—Alex Jácome's contemporary—declared his admiration for the Spanish missionary: "Kino showed us how to conquer the desert, the arid lands, the uninhabitable." In 1986, *El Imparcial* proclaimed that Kino was the "designer of the economy of our region." Celebrations were held in Hermosillo, Cucurpe, Caborca, Imuris, and Tubutama, Sonora, as well as at San Xavier del Bac, near Tucson. Ambos Nogales held an international celebration along the border, which was attended by the governors of Arizona and Sonora. The Sonoran government announced plans to inscribe his name in gold on the state's capitol building. Similar expressions of Kino's civilizing and modernizing influence shaped the ideas of Kinophiles like Polzer, who sought to bring Tucson together in common cause by holding up the figure of Kino as a symbol that would reunite Tucson and Arizona and Sonora.[42]

Leading up to the unveiling of Kino's statue, Kinophiles worked to ensure that Tucsonans would understand the monument's meaning in the same way they did. They called Kino a cartographer, a scientist, an architect, a farmer, a rancher, an astronomer, and a developer. They saw the chronology of Arizona history as "before Kino" and "after Kino." One article said that Kino "rode through a primitive land . . . with nary a road sign in sight," but then the missionary transformed the area. When Pima County funded the statue, the Republican county supervisor argued that Kino was a "lot more" than a missionary: "he opened up—he developed—this area, all the way from Mexico right up to our great city." The Kino statue, its supporters believed, would therefore reinforce the ideologies of a Sunbelt borderland that, by the late twentieth century, had buckled under the weight of social, political, and economic conflicts. As the owner of Mazón's department store in Hermosillo put it, offering his own diagnosis of Mexico's problems, his country suffered from "social apathy" and lacked "enterprising spirit, the sense of individual and social responsibility." Kino, he believed, stood for the opposite: hard work and ingenuity. "We need authentic role models" like him, he concluded.[43]

To bolster the idea that Kino had civilized the area and therefore to legitimize their own promotions of growth and industry, Kinophiles went beyond the argument that Kino had done great things in the Pimería Alta, maintaining in addition that he was the first man to do great things there. Noting his work as a cartographer, one article claimed that Kino was the "first to put Tucson . . . on a map." He had introduced cattle and sheep. He "brought Christianity" and "Western civilization" to the region. He opened Arizona and Sonora to "European settlement." The director of the Arizona Historical Society argued that Kino's work formed the "base" of Tucson's "existence as a community." Suggesting Kino's part in origin stories about the United States, one article stated, "Most of us think of George Washington and Thomas Jefferson when the term 'founding fathers' comes up, but there are some Arizonans who would like us to think of Father Eusebio Kino." Finally, placing Kino alongside other American icons, another article said, "Just as Texas has its Sam Houston and Virginia its George Washington," residents of Arizona and Sonora had Kino. Because of such ideas about Kino's central role in settling the area, many called him the "most important person in Arizona history."[44]

Even though a monument to Kino seemed a fitting tribute to a man whom many saw as a leader who brought peace and productivity, the Kinophiles, when praising their hero, did not address the social, economic, and racial tensions that continued to divide the Arizona-Sonora borderland. These realities made unqualified promotions of civilization, progress, and modernity seem romantic, at best. In a sense, Kinophiles deserved credit for moving debates about the Arizona-Sonora borderland beyond simple portrayals of the area as a drug- and crime-ridden landscape. Moreover, recognizing Kino as Arizona's founder marked a significant departure from the version of regional history projected in the 1940 film *Arizona*, which made it plain that white immigrants in the nineteenth century were the bringers of civilization. Half a century later, a Jesuit missionary from Italy via Spain was seen as the area's most important historical figure. Kino's supporters called him a "white settler," and a newspaper article said he was "mom-and-apple-pie all the way."[45]

But Kino's figure also demonstrated a regionally specific multiculturalism that romanticized the area's ethnic and racial relations. Even though Mexican, Mexican American, and native communities faced violence, discrimination, and inequality, newspapers claimed that the Kino statue demonstrated Tucson's gratitude for "the nations and the families that have honored our desert living." Expressions of regional multiculturalism in fact marked the greatest difference between earlier outbreaks of Kinophilia and its expression in the 1980s. During the 1930s and 1960s, Kinophilia offered an opportunity for businesspeople, politicians, and boosters to imagine their kinship with this civilizing and modernizing hero, demonstrating how their status on both sides of the border depended on their adherence to a particular set of beliefs represented by Kino. Kinophilia during the 1980s established this connection as well, while at the same time highlighting Kino's relationship with native peoples, in part because movements for social justice and civil rights, even if their successes remained contested, had forced recognitions of the Arizona-Sonora border region's ethnic and racial pluralism. The fact that Kinophiles incorporated language that was central to these movements—they noted, for example, that Kino had opposed slavery and that he was a humanitarian—demonstrated their influence.[46]

Throughout the post–World War II era, ever since regional boosters promoted La Fiesta de los Vaqueros as an event that displayed multiracial harmony, many Tucsonans publicly dismissed ethnoracial tensions within their communities and throughout the Arizona-Sonora borderland. In Kino-statue promotions, such efforts came across as paternalism toward the area's native peoples. Polzer described how Kino "brought civilization" to the "Indians." He "taught" them "farming techniques and introduced livestock." Sonorans articulated their own version of multiculturalism in the language of *mestizaje*, an ideology of racial hybridity first conceived in a moment of postrevolutionary nation building, which endured into the late twentieth century. Kino, one article said, "made possible our *mestizaje*, leaving as our inheritance a rich material and cultural patrimony." Sonoran praise of Kino's treatment of indigenous communities also seemed paternalistic. The missionary "guided" native peoples in farming and livestock breeding and helped them build homes and grow crops. He had worked to "free" the Pima Indians from "slave conditions imposed by New Spain's mine owners." In consideration of his good deeds among them, they became his "staunch Indian friends." They gave him their treasured abalone shells, which first signaled to Kino that land connected the Pimería Alta and California and that California was not an island. They "loved him so much."[47]

Despite such narratives of Kino's heroism and good deeds among the Pimería Alta's native peoples, many O'odham increasingly rejected the cultural hegemony and violence of the Spanish colonial period, as well as its lasting legacies. To many, Kino embodied Spanish colonialism. Leading up to three-hundredth anniversary celebrations of Kino's arrival in the area, Sonorans, much as they debated whether Villa was a hero or a bandit, debated whether Kino was a missionary or a colonizer. From the Spanish colonial period forward, narratives endured that Europeans had encountered "not always friendly" and "hostile" Indians. Unfriendly and hostile were descriptive terms applied most frequently to Apaches rather than O'odham, but even if O'odham were peaceful and friendly, they were still called "primitive." Such stereotypes fed antagonism between O'odham and Mexicans in Sonora, and among O'odham, Mexicans, and whites in Arizona. Even more damaging, though, was the fact that dispossessions of their land continued into the late twentieth century. *Mestizo* farmers in Sonora continuously encroached upon their settlements, leasing them or poaching them outright. In the mid-twentieth century, Sonoran O'odham lived in some twenty settlements, but by the end of the century they only inhabited eight. Moreover, only a single family lived in each of these localities, whereas between two and five families had lived in them in the mid-twentieth century. The vast majority of Sonoran O'odham had left their rural villages for work on Arizona's Sells Reservation, or in cities such as Tucson, Caborca, or Hermosillo, where they sold bread and tortillas, worked on ranches and mines surrounding these cities, or performed cheap manual labor. To survive, some worked for Mexican drug cartels, which benefitted from their family connections on both sides of the border and their familiarity with the routes and terrain of the Arizona-Sonora border region. Arizona's O'odham faired marginally better, in part because the reservation structure granted them access to medical care and federal employment with the Bureau of Indian Affairs. Still, in the late 1980s, the O'odham officially changed the name of their tribe from "Papago"—which meant "bean eater," the name given them by their enemies and adopted by Kino—to Tohono O'odham, which meant "desert people." Believing that the United States and Mexico had failed to protect their land and rights, indigenous peoples throughout the Americas, including many O'odham, fought for greater autonomy.[48]

Nevertheless, the Kinophiles' belief that a Kino statue would bridge differences between borderland residents became, to them, increasingly compelling as the modern transformation of their city—including rising numbers of immigrants and debates about the border—threatened to tear it apart. "In a city where most of us are from somewhere else," one article explained, the "incredibly rich, native heritage of this place we now call home tends to blur, to get lost." The Kino statue could "change all that." Mayor Tom Volgy, Murphy's successor, articulated the same sentiment. He said that, in the "midst of all the growth and change that is taking place in the community," the statue would serve as a "reminder that this is a community of great history, culture, and traditions." Describing the ideals that Kino represented as solutions to the ills of the late twentieth century seemed somewhat paradoxical since Kinophiles asked their hero, as symbol, to return the city to an imagined peaceful time when it was more united.[49]

After carefully crafting Kino's image, businesspeople and politicians eagerly awaited the statue's arrival in Tucson, where it would serve both as a counter to the statue of Villa and as a symbol that would reunite the region despite growing international and domestic tensions. When the Kino statue was completed, newspapers dramatized its difficult trip from Mexico City in language that evoked Kino's arduous journeys through the borderland some three centuries earlier. The statue headed north from Martínez's foundry, but instead of taking the most direct route to Tucson, it traveled along the same path Kino had followed through the Pimería Alta. The procession stopped in Hermosillo, Cananea, and Nogales, Sonora, and Tubac, Tumacácori, and San Xavier, in Arizona. Kino had established missions in most of these places. Mexican and U.S. officials gathered at the border. Mexican highway-patrol officers met the statue near Cananea and escorted it to Nogales, Arizona. From there, Department of Public Safety officers accompanied the statue to Tucson, where police took over once the statue reached the city limits. Pathfinder Project personnel speculated that it would be "quite a parade" by the time the statue reached its destination.[50]

After several years of planning, promoting, fund-raising, sculpting, and traveling, the Kino statue was finally unveiled on January 13, 1989, at a ceremony heavy with symbolism. The Arizona Historical Society, which sponsored the event, published a pamphlet containing historical essays, lists of Kino's deeds, and quotations from Kino's journals from his time in the Pimería Alta. The missionary had written of his development efforts, including the introduction of cattle, harvesting of crops, and conversion of souls to Catholicism. Arizona's Democratic governor Rose Mofford attended the ceremony, along with dignitaries from Mexico and Italy. The head of Sonora's tourism industry, Félix Álvaro Obregón—a descendant of Sonora's former governor and Mexico's former president, Villa's main rival in Sonora—opined that Tucson had chosen the perfect location for the Kino statue, alongside a road that symbolized the "many roads Kino opened in the territory" and next to a school, which, Orbegón explained, symbolized the "padre's side as a teacher."[51]

During a decade of great changes in the Arizona-Sonora borderland, Kinophiles looked to the Spanish missionary as a symbol of order and peace, which contrasted greatly with the conflict and division they saw as Villa's legacy and also with the conflicts they saw engulfing their city. Supporters of the Kino statue implicitly contrasted Kino and Villa when they said Kino brought peace instead of war. Kino embodied "humility, peace, endurance, and vision." He took an "unusually peaceful approach" to his conversion work. He preached "values of love, peace, tolerance and well-being." He stood for "peace and progress." Finally, explaining how Kino could be seen as the anti-Villa, another newspaper article claimed that "Kino was not a conqueror, he was a peacemaker." These articulations of Kino's legacy offered a sanitized version of regional history by ignoring the conquest, violence, and inequality that also defined the borderland's past from Kino's time to the present. These were the realities that Villa combated, the revolutionary's admirers believed. However, they contrasted with the sense of regional history shared by Kinophiles on both sides of the border as they contemplated the present state of the Sunbelt borderland they and their predecessors had created.[52]

Arizona's and Sonora's Sunbelt borderland had, in fact, depended on the "peace and progress" that one Kinophile claimed as the Spanish missionary's key achievements. According to the Kinophiles, these values synced well with their notions of how they themselves had helped develop the region after World War II. Kino was their forebear in the project of modernizing the borderlands. His values, they believed, were the same values that civic organizations promoted during La Fiesta de los Vaqueros. They were the same ones that Arizona and Sonora politicians promoted whenever they gave speeches and attended ceremonies across the border. They were the same ones that Jácome had spent a lifetime promoting and that led many faculty members at universities in Arizona and Sonora to collaborate. Finally, they were the same ones preached by Arizona and Sonora politicians and tested by incidents such as the Hanigan case in order to maintain peaceful ties despite rising tensions. For these reasons, they hoped to make the Kino statue "as familiar to Tucson motorists as a favorite uncle."[53]

The meanings of the Villa and Kino statues continued to resonate into late twentieth and early twenty-first centuries. Kinophiles continued to honor their hero as the Arizona-Sonora borderland became increasingly mired in national and international immigration debates. Father Kino remained in the news, competing with frequent stories about the threats that immigrants, drugs, and their proximity to the border posed to residents of the area. First, the news media covered unveiling ceremonies for the Kino statues in Sonora and Italy. Just as Sonorans and Italians made the trip to Tucson for the unveiling ceremonies there, so Tucsonans traveled to celebrations in these places. In advance of the Italian ceremony—which would cost Tucsonans $2,800 per person, or $3,000 per couple—Polzer again recited Kino's good works in a public lecture at the Arizona Historical Society. Second, the news media covered later efforts by Kinophiles to have their hero beatified. McCarty, Fontana, and Polzer had initiated this quest, but other U of A scholars, such as folklorist James "Big Jim" Griffith, carried the effort forward by sending dozens of boxes of Kino material to the Vatican for the pope's consideration. While Kino offered a model of peace and order that was disconnected from competing historical narratives of native resistance to Spanish colonialism, promotions of Kino at the turn of the twenty-first century ignored enduring realities of violence and injustice.[54]

Because discrimination and inequality continued to plague the Arizona-Sonora borderland, Pancho Villa remained a figure that many borderland residents turned to when they confronted the conditions that continued to shape their lives, including residential segregation, employment discrimination, and disparate educational opportunities. They looked for a figure like Villa to help them find solutions to their problems. As during the 1970s and 1980s, when Mexicans and Mexican Americans conjured the figure of Villa to help them struggle against the peso devaluation, land monopolies by wealthy Mexican landowners, and the discriminations that motivated Chicanos, Tucsonans continued to invoke Villa's legacy. In the wake of the controversy over the Villa statue, Raúl Aguirre highlighted Villa's enduring meaning for U.S. history. He said he wanted to "keep the Villa controversy alive" because the "famed *guerrillero* stuck a small knife in the soft underbelly of the United States . . . and he got away with it." For him, Villa's presence in Tucson was a valuable reminder of the limits of U.S. power, one that delivered a message of resistance for many people of Mexican descent living in the United States. "Villa will live," Aguirre said, "Viva Villa!" An editorial in a Tucson newspaper added that Villa would always loom large in the U.S.-Mexico borderlands regardless of whether a statue of him stood in Tucson. To the extent that poverty, violence, and racism continued to circumscribe the lives of many borderlands residents, Villa would remain an important icon. As the author put it, "In the Southwest, Villa is never very far away."[55]

In the decade before and, especially, after the placement of the Villa and Kino statues in Tucson, the Arizona-Sonora borderland became a focal point of national debates about the border. Even as NAFTA seemed to promise expanded opportunities for regional businesspeople—who, in their full-throated promotions of cross-border commercial exchange, were the ideological heirs of men like Jácome and Soto—Arizona voters passed California-style legislation that sought to deny undocumented immigrants access to education, health care, and other public services. Operation Hold the Line in Texas and Operation Gatekeeper in California pushed Mexican immigrants into Arizona's dangerous desert. Arizona's corridor of exchange became a corridor of death as increasing numbers of immigrants died of dehydration and exposure to the desert's intense heat. Political opinion grew increasingly divided, and Latinos throughout the state increasingly became victims of discrimination. Anti-immigrant activist Don Barrington, as he announced the formation of an Arizona-based spin-off of

California's anti-immigrant group, Save Our State (SOS), stood in front of the Villa statue and said, "That fellow on the horse is an example of a Mexican national who didn't give a damn about the border." He blamed unauthorized immigrants in Arizona for burdening the economy, draining social services, and siphoning away tax dollars and claimed they had led to an increase in rapes, murders, and drive-by shootings in the state. These claims had been debunked in the 1970s, but they persisted nevertheless. Barrington's comments comparing Villa to an undocumented Mexican immigrant revealed that the statue continued to serve as a lightning rod in arguments about the border.[56]

Looking back from the twenty-first century, it is tempting to place the Villa and Kino statues neatly in separate camps of Mexican sympathizers and opponents; pro-immigrant and anti-immigrant; law-breaking and law-abiding; or resistant to and complicit with discrimination. Indeed, these are some of the most dangerous fault lines in the Arizona-Sonora borderland, and in some ways they sum up how contemporaries saw the Villa and Kino statues. But the statues also reveal new things about the Arizona-Sonora border region. Or, rather, they reveal very old aspects of this borderland that have become overshadowed by the divisions of the late twentieth and early twenty-first centuries. Instead of seeing the Villa and Kino statues as representative of regional divisions, it is more helpful to see them as giant weights that hold together seemingly fractured geographies and communities. Like borderlands history itself, the statues suggested many different meanings—about racial divisions and interethnic friction; social justice and inequality; nationalism and regionalism; and state control and instability. The dynamic, almost magnetic tension the statues created through their relation to one another shaped characterizations of the city and its surrounding border region and offered broader possibilities for understanding a borderland that, only on the surface, seems defined by the politics of undocumented immigration. The Villa and Kino statues demonstrated that border politics remained deeply shaped by the stories that people told about their community and its transnational relationships.

CONCLUSION

By way of explaining the recent history of the U.S.-Mexico border, many have claimed that it hardened or took its modern form during the early twentieth century, and that it has become increasingly militarized ever since. Such assertions are, to a degree, undeniably true. After the formation of the U.S. Border Patrol, the Great Depression, and a series of anti-immigrant movements spread across the twentieth century, undocumented Mexicans have become the victims of rising levels of discrimination and violence. Increased drug and human smuggling from the 1970s forward have further contributed to widespread negative perceptions of the border and Mexicans in general. Mexican Americans and other U.S. Latinos—often cast as "illegal immigrants" regardless of their status—also suffer from anti-immigrant sentiments and policies. In the late twentieth century, U.S.-Mexico relations became more tense as neoliberal economies symbolized by NAFTA benefited the United States more than Mexico, and wealthy business owners more than the working-class or indigenous communities of each country. In response, *mestizos* and native peoples in Chiapas turned to the Mexican revolutionary Emiliano Zapata for inspiration in their struggles. If Villa had seemed an uplifting symbol for marginalized Mexicans and Mexican Americans in Tucson, Zapata became an advocate for the landless poor in Mexico during the 1990s. These developments, however, tell only part of the story. Another, the one told here, is how the U.S.-Mexico borderlands after World War II defied simple claims about the opening or closing of the border.

In the decades following World War II, the Arizona-Sonora borderland remained a space shaped by its diverse cross-border exchanges. Businesspeople and politicians in Arizona and Sonora forged a Sunbelt borderland characterized by massive investments in and promotions of growth, modernization, and progress. Borderland economies evolved as a result of international collaborations, and economic developments on one side of the border greatly affected the other. In these decades of dramatic economic transformation, the populations of Arizona and Sonora exploded, and cities in both states grew as many thousands of immigrants came to work in defense and manufacturing industries and in factories related to the agricultural and ranching operations that surrounded cities. Cross-border expressions of friendship influenced by Roosevelt's Good Neighbor policy shaped the way a regional elite described cross-border relations because they established solidarity against international political threats, smoothed the way for commercial exchange, and appealed to Mexican Americans in Arizona. Entrepreneurs like Alex Jácome and Ignacio Soto grew wealthy through the expansion of postwar borderland economies and rose to inclusion among the elite of each state. But the vast majority of borderland residents—especially many native people on both sides of the border and a majority of Mexican Americans in Arizona—remained economically, politically, and socially marginalized. Labor and civil rights organizations fought alongside them against ongoing class and racial discrimination.

Even though most businesspeople and politicians—Jácome's and Soto's ideological heirs—continued to promote cross-border unity through economic, cultural, and social exchanges, from the late 1960s and early 1970s forward, economic and demographic patterns changed again, giving rise to the immigration and border debates that rocked Arizona into the twenty-first century. The end of the Bracero Program, the Hart-Celler Act, rising levels of unemployment and indebtedness despite the growth of *maquiladoras*, and civil wars in Central America led to increased Latin American migration into the Arizona-Sonora borderland. These factors coincided with the hemispheric escalation of Cold War tensions and financial crises on both sides of the border, as well as a marked rise in violence and discrimination against immigrants and other Latinos in the United States regardless of their citizenship status. Arizonans tortured Mexican immigrants and called Central American refugees Communists and economic threats. Immigrant and civil rights groups defended them and helped determine the shape of the IRCA. By the late twentieth century, conflicts on both sides of the border made postwar notions of progress seem romantic. Many Arizonans and Sonorans struggled to determine what kind of community theirs would become. Would the international line and other borders of race and class make divisions seem insurmountable, or would Arizonans and Sonorans redouble their efforts to forge cross-border friendship and solidarity while simultaneously acknowledging that these pursuits had not, in the past, always led to social justice and equality?

In the early twenty-first century, these questions yielded mixed answers. On the one hand, cross-border exchange continued, and the economies of Arizona and Sonora remained as connected as ever. People throughout the region continued to visit Tucson every February to celebrate La Fiesta de los Vaqueros. Arizona tourists still traveled to Sonora's cities and beaches, while Sonorans visited Tucson, Phoenix, and other destinations. Even though Jácome's department store had closed decades earlier, Mexican consumers spent more than $300 million per year at Arizona's big-box stores, malls, shopping centers, and resorts. University students in Tucson and Hermosillo still participated in exchange programs, and Kinophiles on both sides of the border worked to have their hero beatified by the Vatican. These cross-border relationships seemed to point to the recognition among Arizonans and Sonorans that their futures remained tied to each other.

On the other hand, University of Arizona students invited criticism for disrespecting Mexican culture by flinging tortillas into the air at their commencement ceremonies instead of graduation caps. The Occupy movement in Tucson camped for months in the park where the Villa statue has sat for thirty years, demonstrating that Pancho Villa remained a symbol of social and class conflict. Indigenous groups in Arizona and Sonora continued to struggle against centuries-old patterns of violence and neglect. The U.S. Border Patrol increasingly policed O'odham lands searching for drug- and human-smuggling activities, and made it more difficult for them to cross the border, even within tribal lands. Along with the proliferation of harsh immigration laws and the growing presence of the U.S. Border Patrol in Tucson, these realities made it seem that the Arizona-Sonora borderland would remain a space besieged by conflict.[1]

More than any other single issue, the immigration of undocumented Mexican workers defined the U.S.-Mexico borderlands in the public sphere. Even though IRCA was supposed to offer a permanent solution, critics had almost immediately labeled the law a failure. Ongoing debates led to the articulation of increasingly punitive proposals in the 1990s and beyond, as undocumented immigrants continued to enter the United States and, as many had predicted, Latinos became victims of the bill's employer sanctions. Fearful employers refused to hire immigrants, even those in the United States legally. In 1994, Californians passed Proposition 187, a law that would have denied undocumented immigrants access to basic health and education services. Several states tried to pass versions of the law even though the California Supreme Court had rejected it. Both IRCA and Proposition 187, designed to stop the flow of undocumented immigration, instead impeded historical patterns of circular migration. Many undocumented immigrants remained in the United States rather than returning to Mexico, fearing they would not be able to come back.[2]

National leaders followed up on IRCA by proposing and enacting laws that militarized the border and made enforcement their top priority. Rather than protecting immigrant rights, Operation Gatekeeper led to the construction of border fencing and the placement of more U.S. Border Patrol officers along the California border. Operation Hold the Line did the same in Texas. The Illegal Immigration Reform and Immigrant Responsibility Act of 1996 made it easier to deport undocumented immigrants and created the controversial 287(g) program, which authorized some local and state police to enforce immigration laws. The terrorist attacks of September 11, 2001, increased demands for border enforcement based on the logic that Middle Eastern terrorists might bring weapons across the border. U.S. Senators, including Democrat Ted Kennedy and Republicans James Sensenbrenner, John Cornyn, John McCain, and John Kyl, proposed bills that, among other things, would have mandated harsh prison sentences for undocumented immigrants, permitted the use of drones to track them, and limited the ability of U.S. citizens to offer them aid. These built on familiar proposals such as increased border patrols, a new guest-worker program, and an electronic employment-verification system akin to employer sanctions. No proposal passed Congress, however, and, in early 2013, IRCA remained the last comprehensive immigration reform act.

Arizona played an expanding role in national debates about immigration and the border. Voters passed their own version of Proposition 187 and the U.S. government Operation Safeguard, which aimed to crack down on undocumented immigration through Nogales, Sonora, and mimicked Gatekeeper and Hold the Line. As Gatekeeper, Hold the Line, and Safeguard increased enforcement in border cities, immigrants increasingly crossed through the Sonoran desert, where thousands died of heat exhaustion. By the late 1990s, more undocumented immigrants entered the United States through Arizona than any other point along the U.S.-Mexico border. Border Patrol officers arrested hundreds of thousands of them every year, and the Tucson sector of the Border Patrol, which moved its headquarters in the early twenty-first century to the northern edge of Davis-Monthan Air Force Base, became the busiest in the nation in both undocumented immigrant apprehensions and marijuana seizures. New vigilante organizations formed their own border patrols, most notably the Minuteman Project. Governor Janet Napolitano declared a state of emergency because of the fiscal burden that undocumented immigration placed on Arizona. Maricopa County sheriff Joe Arpaio conducted raids in Mexican and Mexican American communities and forced detained migrants to live in open-air prisons under inhumane conditions. Meanwhile, groups like the Coalición de Derechos Humanos and No More Deaths combated the state's rising anti-immigrant sentiment, along with newer groups like Puente Arizona. By the early twenty-first century, Arizona had become the front line of immigration and border conflicts, or "ground zero," as one leading scholar put it.[3]

Rising anti-immigrant sentiment in the state targeted both Mexicans and Mexican Americans. Many were quick to blame Mexicans for the murder of rancher Robert Krentz only a few miles from where the Hanigans tortured their victims. The charge was never proven. Governor Jan Brewer signed the anti-immigrant law, S.B. 1070, one month later, and even though the bill had been in the works for some time, many suspected that Krentz's murder was its immediate impetus. Brewer falsely claimed that Mexican cartels had dumped beheaded bodies in the Arizona desert, thereby feeding fears of Mexican violence and criminality. Despite the reality of a conservative state legislature that had defunded health and education spending, she blamed Mexicans for the state's failing hospitals and schools. Less than two weeks after she signed S.B. 1070, Brewer signed House Bill 2281 (H.B. 2281), which outlawed ethnic studies classes in Arizona from kindergarten through twelfth grade. Mexican and Mexican American communities saw this latest bill as another effort to erase their history and culture. By outlawing ethnic studies classes, Arizona threatened to prevent future generations from even learning about S.B. 1070 or H.B. 2281. Both bills came at a moment when white Arizonans felt more threatened than ever by changing demographics that promised to make them a minority sometime in the twenty-first century. In addition to being punitive measures against Latin Americans and Latinos living in the United States, the bills also weakened the transnational ties that have connected Arizona and Sonora for almost two centuries. In a basic sense, this book shows that Arizona was not always this way.

As debates became increasingly polarized—with people on all sides of the issue growing more and more entrenched in their own positions, articulating tired arguments, and offering little reason to hope for accord—Sonora-based artists Alberto Morackis and Guadalupe Serrano sought to spark a new dialogue with their sculpture *Border Dynamics*. They crafted four humanlike figures that were fourteen feet tall and weighed nine hundred pounds each. They posed the figures leaning against a border wall made from the same leftover Vietnam-era steel that reinforced the actual U.S.-Mexico border fence. The figures are visually striking. Their fiery flesh and angular composition resemble José Clemente Orozco's *Prometheus* mural at California's Pomona College, which also encourages viewers to continually question knowledge as they acquire and produce it. The sharp edges and rigid steel of their bodies evoke the fixity and narrow-mindedness of those on both sides of the international line who were uncompromising in their views of cross-border relations. But their flesh, contemplative expression, and name—"dynamics," a word that means the forces responsible for creating change and causing motion—also suggest flexibility. The figures therefore demand a critical rethinking of the Arizona-Sonora border and borders in general.

Morackis and Serrano had worked together since the 1990s, using as their studio a bullfighting ring two miles south of the border, in Nogales, Sonora. Together they formed the group "Taller Yonke," or "Junk Shop." Both held part-time jobs in *maquiladoras* and schools, but by the early twenty-first century they were working full time as artists, receiving a monthly commission from the Municipio de Nogales to create public art. Morackis and Serrano built *Border Dynamics* piece by piece and then welded it together just before the installation along the border. With the same floodlights that the Border Patrol used to spot undocumented immigrants entering the United States, the artists bathed their pieces in light at a small unveiling ceremony in January 2003. After several months in Sonora, *Border Dynamics* moved to Tucson when the University of Arizona purchased the piece. Ever since, the sculpture has stood on campus.[4]

The Beyond Borders Binational Art Foundation, the nonprofit organization that commissioned *Border Dynamics*, originally planned to display the piece on both sides of the U.S.-Mexico border, with two of the four figures pressing up against the border wall in Nogales, Sonora, while

Border Dynamics. (Photograph by author.)

the other two leaned against the wall in Nogales, Arizona. But just before the sculptures went up in the United States, a Border Patrol officer in Arizona informed the foundation's director that all four figures had to stay in Mexico. Because there was a drug- and human-smuggling tunnel at the spot where the artists planned to place the sculpture, the officer claimed, *Border Dynamics* would interfere with the patrol's surveillance efforts. The officer also cited safety and security concerns, such as the risk that immigrants might use the sculptures to ease their entry into the United States. They might jump the fence and shimmy down the figures, perhaps cutting themselves on the sculpture's jagged steel edges.[5]

The meaning of *Border Dynamics* varied according to the placement of the figures on one side of the border or the other and on each viewer's perception of the border. The figures might represent immigrants seeking to cross the border to find jobs in the United States or Mexicans reinforcing the barrier between the United States and Mexico in an effort to limit U.S. influence. They might also represent vigilantes trying to protect Arizona against the so-called Mexican invasion or businesspeople who metaphorically toppled the border with their easy crossings. At the University of Arizona, two figures pressed against one side of the wall while two pressed against the other instead of having all four figures on one side, as in Nogales. Placed on the same side of the wall, the figures operated in concert, but pushing on both sides, they demonstrated the tensions between them and emphasized the necessarily binational character of immigration and border debates.[6]

The material and composition of the figures also informed their meaning. Their rusting steel, sharp angles, and resin flesh represented both the hard labor that Mexicans performed in the United States and also the set views of immigrant-rights advocates and anti-immigrant vigilantes, who were entrenched at opposite sides of a discourse on civil and human rights. Lacking skin—and more important, skin color—the figures alluded to the raceless, humanist, and universal impulses of the piece, evoking Morackis's sentiment that "every border" dividing people "is the same." Their hardened flesh hinted at the emotions that got buried as immigrants struggled to reach the United States, as well as the tough façade with which politicians, border residents, and others have approached border issues.[7]

As an integrated whole that nevertheless enabled contradictory interpretations, *Border Dynamics* embodied the complexity of immigration and border debates in the twenty-first century. The flesh and steel of the figures and the force they exerted on both sides of the border revealed the dual meaning of dynamics—motion and change—and therefore critiqued the state of border debates. Instead of rigidly opposed views that never met eye to eye, *Border Dynamics* called for a new conversation based on principles of flexibility and change. As Morackis has said, "People on both sides think of the border as a bad place," but "it's also a point of shock, a point of discovery."[8]

Like *Border Dynamics*, this book seeks to start a new conversation about the border. By focusing on the recent history of the Arizona-Sonora Sunbelt borderland, it only begins to reveal the history of the U.S.-Mexico borderlands since World War II. At a time when many Americans increasingly pronounce the dangers posed by our border with Mexico and by Mexican immigrants in general, vibrant cross-border exchanges between Arizona and Sonora demonstrate that the border has always signified many things at once even though public discourse in the early twenty-first century has by and large characterized it as a single and hard dividing line between countries, races, and civilizations. As *Border Dynamics* suggests, though, we imbue the border with meanings that are flexible and can change.

In the twenty-first century, contradiction and polarization seem to characterize all aspects of life in the U.S.-Mexico borderlands. The U.S. economy depends on undocumented Mexican laborers, yet U.S. citizens have sought to bar their entry. Virtually all politicians and media portray Mexican immigrants as undocumented laborers. Even if they emphasize different characteristics—that they are hard workers or violent criminals—they nevertheless ignore the cultural, educational, and other exchanges that also constitute transnational migration between the United States and Mexico. An unexceptional fact about both countries throughout the postwar era has been their support for wealthy elites at the expense of working-class communities on both sides of the border, enabling the interpretation that the border is less a divide between two nations and more a line separating haves and have-nots.

People on both sides of the international line must acknowledge these contradictions, recognize their reliance upon migrant labor for the food they eat and the clothes they wear, and strive to find the points at which the border—both arguments about it and the thing itself—is most flexible and open to change. Even as immigration and border debates seem hopelessly bogged down by black-and-white disputes, postwar histories of cultural and commercial exchange between Arizona and Sonora can reorient conversations around the multiple points of unity, division, affiliation, kinship, and alienation that have characterized the U.S.-Mexico borderlands. An acknowledgment that dynamics between the United States and Mexico are far more complicated than public debates have recognized will not by itself solve the many challenges presented by the border, but it is a necessary beginning point if there is hope for a just future for all people within and beyond both nations.

NOTES

Prologue

1. Edwin Schallert, "Gala Film Event Held in Tucson," *Los Angeles Times,* November 16, 1940.
2. "Just 'Any Old Rock' Didn't Do for 'Arizona,'" *Los Angeles Times,* September 29, 1940, C4; "Magnitude of Movie Filming Readily Apparent in Tucson," *Arizona Daily Star,* May 3, 1940; "Film Company Built Old Tucson in 1940," *Arizona Daily Star,* November 2, 1952; Columbia Pictures production booklet, "The Winning of a Mighty Empire Inspires the Making of a Great Picture," Arizona Historical Society (AHS); "Fletcher Boys Deliver Goods," *Arizona Daily Star,* May 3, 1940.
3. "'Premiere' Arizona, Aquí," *El Tucsonense,* July 16, 1940, 2; "Festejos previos al premiere 'Arizona,'" *El Tucsonense,* October 8, 1940, 1; Sidney Osborn to Mayor Dyer of St. Thomas, Ontario, Canada, June 24, 1941, Box 19, Folder 5, Governors Files (Osborn), Arizona State Library, ASL (Osborn Papers); "Just 'Any Old Rock' Didn't Do for 'Arizona'"; Columbia Pictures production booklet, "The Winning of a Mighty Empire Inspires the Making of a Great Picture."
4. Leslie Marmon Silko, *Almanac of the Dead* (New York, 1992); Clarence Budington Kelland, *Arizona* (New York, 1939), 11, 43.
5. Samuel Truett, *Fugitive Landscapes: The Forgotten History of the U.S.-Mexico Borderlands* (New Haven, CT, 2006), 1–12; Rocío Guadarrama, José Ramírez, Ricardo León, Oscar Conde, Cristina Martínez, and Lourdes Martínez, *Historia General de Sonora: Historia Contemporánea, 1929–1984,* vol. 5, ed. Ernesto Camou Healy et al. (Hermosillo, 1997, 3rd ed.), 23–26, 119–120, 143–163; Thomas Sheridan, *Arizona: A History* (Tucson, 2012, rev. ed.); *Arizona,* DVD, directed by Wesley Ruggles (Los Angeles, 1940), 1:57.
6. Phoebe Titus, quoted in official program for *Arizona* premiere, November 15–16, 1940, AHS.
7. "Magnitude of Movie Filming Readily Apparent in Tucson"; "Erection of Movie Set to Start Monday," ephemera file, "Places—Arizona—Tucson—Movies," AHS; "Arizona Film Location Work Goes Swiftly," ephemera file,

"Places—Arizona—Tucson—Movies," AHS; "The Winning of a Mighty Empire Inspires the Making of a Great Picture"; Corky Simpson, "Wanted Alive: Old Tucson Studios," *Tucson Citizen,* August 8, 2003; "De interés a mexicanos de esta ciudad," *El Tucsonense,* March 22, 1940; Hedda Hopper, "Hedda Hopper's Hollywood," *Los Angeles Times,* June 8, 1940; August Wieden to Lewis Irvine, April 18, 1940, Box 14, Folder 9, Governors Files (Jones), ASL (Jones Papers); casting card from Columbia Pictures, Box 14, Folder 9, Jones Papers.

8. "Comisiones nombradas para fiesta mexicana de premiere 'Arizona,'" *El Tucsonense,* October 11, 1940; "'Premiere' Arizona, Aquí"; "Festejos previos al premiere 'Arizona,'" *El Tucsonense,* October 8, 1940, 1; "Comité Hisp-Amcn. del premiere 'Arizona' tiene junta hoy a las 7:30," *El Tucsonense,* September 24, 1940, 1; "'Dia Mexicano' de premiere 'Arizona,'" *El Tucsonense,* August 2, 1940; "Gala Film Event Held in Tucson"; Bonnie Henry, "Filming of 'Arizona,'" in *Another Tucson* (Tucson, 1992), 216; "How Press Agent Got Taste of the Old West," *Tucson Daily Citizen,* January 9, 1970.
9. Rachel St. John, *Line in the Sand: A History of the Western U.S.-Mexico Border* (Princeton, NJ, 2011), 39–62; Daniel Lewis, *Iron Horse Imperialism: The Southern Pacific of Mexico, 1880–1951* (Tucson, 2007), 3–14; Truett, *Fugitive Landscapes,* 55–132; Guadarrama et al., *Historia General de Sonora,* vol. 5, 25, 35, 54, 56–58, 60–61, 75, 95.
10. C. L. Sonnichsen, *Tucson: The Life and Times of an American City* (Norman, 1982).

Introduction

1. Senate Bill 1070, Forty-Ninth Legislature, second regular session, 2010, 3.
2. Randall Archibold, "Arizona Endorses Immigration Curbs," *New York Times,* April 14, 2010, A16; Brady McCombs, "Dupnik Says He Will Enforce AZ Immigration Law If 'Forced' to Do So," *Arizona Daily Star,* April 28, 2010; "Ley Arizona, potencial apartheid," *El Imparcial,* July 16, 2010; Randall Archibold, "Arizona Law Causes Split for Border Governors," *New York Times,* July 6, 2010, A1; Adam Liptak, "Blocking Parts of Arizona Law, Justices Allow Its Centerpiece," *New York Times,* June 25, 2012, A1.
3. Douglas Massey, "How Arizona Became Ground Zero in the War on Immigrants," in *Illegals in the Backyard: State and Local Regulation of Immigration Policy,* ed. G. Jack Chin and Carissa Hessick (forthcoming); Jeremy Adelman and Stephen Aron, "From Borderlands to Borders: Empires, Nation-States, and the Peoples in Between in North American History," *American Historical Review* 104(3) (June 1999): 840–841; Mae Ngai, *Impossible Subjects: Illegal Aliens and the Making of Modern America* (Princeton, NJ, 2004), 131; Truett, *Fugitive Landscapes,* 9; Kelly Lytle-Hernández, *Migra! A History of the U.S.*

Border Patrol (Berkeley, 2010). 84; Katherine Benton-Cohen, *Borderline Americans: Racial Division and Labor War in the Arizona Borderlands* (Cambridge, MA, 2011), 17; St. John, *Line in the Sand*, 9; Sheridan, *Arizona*, 299.

4. Michelle Nickerson and Darren Dochuk, Introduction, *Sunbelt Rising: The Politics of Space, Place, and Region*, ed. Michelle Nickerson and Darren Dochuk, 4, 8–9 (Philadelphia, 2011); Elizabeth Tandy Shermer, *Sunbelt Capitalism: Phoenix and the Transformation of American Politics* (Philadelphia, 2013).
5. John Crow, *Mexican Americans in Contemporary Arizona: A Social and Demographic View* (San Francisco, 1975), 263–264.
6. Gerald Nash, *The American West Transformed: The Impact of the Second World War* (Bloomington, 1985), chap. 2; Sheridan, *Arizona*, 270–273; Guadarrama et al., *Historia General de Sonora*, vol. 5, 152; Louise Walker, *Waking from the Dream: Mexico's Middle Classes after 1968* (Stanford, CA, 2013), 1.
7. U.S. and Mexican census data from 1940 to 1970; Walter Nugent, *Into the West: The Story of Its People* (New York, 1999), 255–257; Rubén Salazar, "Fence, River Divide U.S., Mexico Cultures," *Los Angeles Times*, January 7, 1962, J1.
8. Shermer, *Sunbelt Capitalism*; Nickerson and Dochuk, *Sunbelt Rising*, 1–28; Andrew Needham, "Sunbelt Imperialism: Boosters, Navajos, and Energy Development in the Metropolitan Southwest," in Nickerson and Dochuk, *Sunbelt Rising*, 240–264; Micaela Larkin, "Labor's Desert: Mexican Workers, Unions, and Entrepreneurial Conservatism in Arizona, 1917–1972," PhD diss., University of Notre Dame, 2008; Michael Logan, *Fighting Sprawl and City Hall: Resistance to Urban Growth in the Southwest* (Tucson, 1995).
9. Guadarrama et al., *Historia General de Sonora*, vol. 5, 47, 145, 152; Adrian Bantjes, *As if Jesus Walked on Earth: Cardenismo, Sonora, and the Mexican Revolution* (Boulder, 1998), 123–149; Cynthia Hewitt de Alcántara, *Modernizing Mexican Agriculture: Socioeconomic Implications of Technological Change, 1940–1970* (Geneva, 1976).
10. Peter Smith, *Talons of the Eagle: Dynamics of U.S.-Latin American Relations* (New York, 2008, 3rd ed.), 113–140; Deborah Cohen, *Braceros: Migrant Citizens and Transnational Subjects in the Postwar United States and Mexico* (Chapel Hill, 2011), 1–20; Lytle-Hernández, *Migra!*, 125–150.
11. James Officer, "Sodalities and Systemic Linkage: The Joining Habits of Urban Mexican-Americans," PhD diss., University of Arizona, 1964, 73–74; Geraldo Cadava, "Borderlands of Modernity and Abandonment: The Lines within Ambos Nogales and the Tohono O'odham Nation," *Journal of American History* 98(2) (September 2011): 377.
12. Officer, "Sodalities and Systemic Linkage," xv–xvi, 1, 68; Eric Meeks, *Border Citizens: The Making of Indians, Mexicans, and Anglos in Arizona* (Austin, TX, 2007), 155–179; Crow, "Mexican Americans in Contemporary Arizona," 29, 42, 44, 57–58, 60, 70–71, 77.

13. Walker, *Waking from the Dream,* 73–140.
14. Jaime Pensado, "The (Forgotten) Sixties in Mexico," *The Sixties* 1(1) (2008): 83–90; Cadava, "Borderlands of Modernity and Abandonment"; Yemile Mizrahi, *From Martyrdom to Power: The Partido Acción Nacional in Mexico* (South Bend, IN, 2003); Greg Grandin, *Empire's Workshop: Latin America, the United States, and the Rise of the New Imperialism* (New York, 2006).
15. See http://www.inegi.org.mx/default.aspx; Mae Ngai, *Impossible Subjects: Illegal Immigrants and the Making of Modern America* (Princeton, NJ, 2004), 258; María Cristina García, *Seeking Refuge: Central American Migration to Mexico, the United States, and Canada* (Berkeley, 2006), 13–43.
16. Massey, "How Arizona Became Ground Zero in the War on Immigrants"; Christine Marie Sierra, "In Search of National Power: Chicanos Working the System on Immigration Reform," in *Chicano Politics and Society in the Late Twentieth Century,* ed. David Montejano (Austin, TX, 1999), 131–153.
17. Officer, "Sodalities and Systemic Linkage," 68; Crow, "Mexican Americans in Contemporary Arizona," 17; U.S. census reports from 1970 to 2010, http://www.census.gov/prod/www/decennial.html, accessed August 30, 2011; "Tucson Population by Race & Ethnicity: 1860–2015," http://cms3.tucsonaz.gov/planning/data/demographic/, accessed August 31, 2011; Guadalupe Castillo and Margo Cowan, *It Is Not Our Fault: The Case for Amending Present Nationality Law to Make All Members of the Tohono O'odham Nation United States Citizens, Now and Forever* (Sells, AZ, 2001); Catherine Elsworth, "Whites Becoming a Minority in Urban US," *Telegraph,* August 9, 2007.
18. On the nexus of politics and culture in the making of U.S.-Latin American relations in the twentieth century, see Gilbert Joseph, Catherine LeGrand, and Ricardo D. Salvatore, eds., *Close Encounters of Empire: Writing the Cultural History of U.S.-Latin American Relations* (Durham, NC, 1998).

1. Defending the Borderland

1. "Problema Fronterizo," *El Tucsonense,* July 19, 1940, 1.
2. Lytle Hernández, *Migra!,* 104–106.
3. Nash, *American West Transformed,* 17–36; Sheridan, *Arizona,* 270–273; Guadarrama et al., *Historia General de Sonora,* vol. 5, 152; Lytle Hernández, *Migra!,* 112; Ignacio Almada, *Breve histora de Sonora* (Mexico City, 2000), 146.
4. Shermer, *Sunbelt Capitalism,* 71–90; Guadarrama et al., *Historia General de Sonora,* vol. 5, 151.
5. Charles Kelly, "Arizona's Harsh Terrain, Climate Toughened GIs," *Arizona Republic,* August 27, 1989; *Arizona Daily Star* article quoted in Sonnichsen, *Tucson,* 260; Barbara Hollins-Lewis and Josie Huerta Herrera, in *They Opened Their Hearts,* ed. Sherri Wagoner and Rita Maria Magdaleno, 30, 92 (Tucson, 2005).

6. Frank Condron, "Leave the Lady Be," *Collier's*, July 27, 1940.
7. "Gral. Camacho en Hermosillo," *El Tucsonense*, May 21, 1940; "Almazán en Nogales, es aclamado," *El Tucsonense*, June 14, 1940; "Se une Mexico a Estados Unidos, facilitan fondos para armar a Mex.," *El Tucsonense*, June 21, 1940.
8. Ricardo Rubio V. to a Mexican agent in Nogales, Sonora, November 1, 1940; anonymous to the office of Información Política y Social, under the Secretaría de Gobernación, October 31, 1940; J. Gutiérrez to Cipriano Arriola, October 28, 1940. Letters from Box 192, Folder 2.1/311.1/5, Investigaciones Políticas y Sociales, Archivo General de la Nación (AGN), Mexico City (IPS).
9. Friedrich Katz, *The Life and Times of Pancho Villa* (Stanford, CA, 1998), 564–566; Mario García, *Desert Immigrants: The Mexicans of El Paso, 1880–1920* (New Haven, CT, 1981), 191–196; Brian DeLay, *War of a Thousand Deserts: Indian Raids and the U.S.-Mexican War* (New Haven, CT, 2008), 141–164; Benton-Cohen, *Borderline Americans*, 52–71; St. John, *Line in the Sand*, 39–62; "Confidential Biographic Data" on Abelardo Rodríguez, January 25, 1939, Record Group 84, Box 6, U.S. Consulate, Nogales, Mexico, Classified General Records, National Archives and Records Administration, Washington, DC (Nogales Classified Records, NARA); Pierre Boal, "Problems in Mexico of Especial Interest to the United States," October 11, 1937, Record Group 84, Box 1, Nogales Classified Records, NARA.
10. "Un pacto de defensa mutua con los EE.UU.," *El Imparcial*, March 8, 1941; Miguel Acosta, "México en la crisis Guerra Mundial," *El Imparcial*, February 5, 1941, 2.
11. "Circunstancias que obligan a Mex. a ceder, para arreglo con los E.U.," *El Tucsonense*, January 16, 1940; "Mexico listo a ayudar a E.U., en la defensa de todo el continente," *El Tucsonense*, July 23, 1940, 1; "Arreglo global entre México y Estados Unidos," *El Imparcial*, February 6, 1941; "El arreglo con E.U. se hara respetando la dignidad y los intereses de la nación," *El Imparcial*, February 13, 1941; "Un pacto de defensa mutua con los EE.UU."
12. "Editorial, el mensaje presidencial," *El Imparcial*, December 12, 1941.
13. Daniel Masterson with Sayaka Funada-Classen, *The Japanese in Latin America* (Urbana, IL, 2004), 117–118; "Contingentes de tropas llegan a Nogales, Ariz.," *El Imparcial*, December 10, 1941; "Tropas mexicanas cruzan la línea internacional rumbo a Mexicali," *El Imparcial*, December 10, 1941; "Mexico rompió ayer con Alemania e Italia," *El Imparcial*, December 12, 1941.
14. Lawrence Armstrong to Cordell Hull, October 28, 1939, Record Group 84, Box 2, Nogales Classified Records, NARA; Byron White to Joseph McGurk, November 24, 1941, Record Group 84, Box 2, Nogales Classified Records, NARA; Raymond Phelan to Hull, May 29, 1942, Record Group 84, Box 3, Nogales Classified Records, NARA; Phelan to Hull, June 30, 1942, Record

Group 84, Box 3, Nogales Classified Records, NARA; Phelan to Hull, July 31, 1942, Record Group 84, Box 3, Nogales Classified Records, NARA; Phelan to Hull, September 1, 1942, Record Group 84, Box 3, Nogales Classified Records, NARA; Ben Zweig to Hull, March 1, 1944, Records Group 84, Box 5, Nogales Classified Records, NARA; Zweig to Hull, September 6, 1944, Records Group 84, Box 5, Nogales Classified Records, NARA; "La prensa americana habla de las 'mordidas' que reciben los turistas," *Accion*, Nogales, March 2, 1945.

15. "Wings over the Southwest Desert," *Standard of California* (Spring 1944), ephemera file, "Arizona—History—World War, 1939–1945," AHS; " 'Old Blood and Guts' Remembered," *Tucson Citizen*, November 22, 1990; Sonnichsen, *Tucson*, 272; Matt Bischoff, *The Desert Training Center/California-Arizona Maneuver Area, 1942–1944: Historical and Archaeological Contexts* (Tucson, 2000), 1; Sheridan, *Arizona*, 278, 280; Shermer, *Sunbelt Capitalism*, 75.
16. Sidney Osborn to John DeWitt, June 23, 1942, Box 21, Folder 7, Governors Files (Osborn), ASL (Osborn Papers); Osborn to Carl Hayden, June 26, 1942, Box 21, Folder 7, Osborn Papers.
17. Osborn to John DeWitt, June 23, 1942; Osborn to Carl Hayden, June 26, 1942; DeWitt to Osborn, June 26, 1942. Letters from Box 21, Folder 7, Osborn Papers.
18. Jack van Ryder to Osborn, March 30, 1942, Box 21, Folder 8, Osborn Papers; Albert Shropshire Jr. to Franklin D. Roosevelt, February 28, 1942, Box 15A, Folder 10, Osborn Papers; Shropshire to Osborn, March 3, 1942, Box 15A, Folder 10, Osborn Papers; Osborn to Shropshire, March 10, 1942, Box 15A, Folder 10, Osborn Papers; Shropshire to Osborn, April 1, 1942, Box 15, Folder 10, Osborn Papers; Osborn to Shropshire, April 9, 1942, Box 15A, Folder 10, Osborn Papers; Linda Gordon, *The Great Arizona Orphan Abduction* (Cambridge, 2001), 266.
19. Osborn to Anselmo Macías Valenzuela, February 2, 1942; Enrique Encinas to Osborn, February 9, 1942. Letters from Box 15A, Folder 10, Osborn Papers.
20. Elpidio Perdomo to Robert Jones, September 2, 1939, Box 12, Folder 31, Governors Files (Jones), ASL (Jones Papers); Loaiza to Osborn, January 15, 1943, Box 25, Folder 4, Osborn Papers; Osborn to American Steel Company, February 2, 1943, Box 25, Folder 4, Osborn Papers; Osborn to Loaiza, February 2, 1943, Box 25, Folder 4, Osborn Papers.
21. Mohave Chamber of Commerce to Franklin D. Roosevelt, May 27, 1940, Box 12, Folder 3, Jones Papers; Frank Lackland to Jones, September 19, 1940, Box 12, Folder 3, Jones Papers; Julian Velarde to Osborn, August 6, 1943, Box 28, Folder 20, Osborn Papers; Lytle Hernández, *Migra!*, 113; Guadarrama et al., *Historia General de Sonora*, vol. 5, 151–152, 154, 160; Fernando Lozano Ascencio et al, *Sonorenses en Arizona: Proceso de formacion de una region binacional*, (Hermosillo, 1997), 43.

22. "Strategic Realm for War Industry," *Standard of California* (Spring 1944), from ephemera file, "Arizona—History—World War, 1939–1945," AHS; Guadarrama et al., *Historia General de Sonora*, vol. 5, 152–153.
23. Emily Edmonds-Poli and David Shirk, *Contemporary Mexican Politics* (Lanham, MD, 2009), 58, 70; "Inauguration of General Román Yocupicio," 1937, Record Group 84, Box 1, Nogales Classified Records, NARA; "Confidential Biographical Data" on Abelardo L. Rodríguez; Lewis Boyle to Armstrong, January 19, 1939, Record Group 84, Box 2, Nogales Classified Records, NARA; Armstrong, "Brigadier General Román Yocupicio," January 30, 1939, Record Group 84, Box 2, Nogales Classified Records, NARA; Guadarrama et al., *Historia general de Sonora*, vol. 5, 151–152, 159; Almada, *Breve historia de Sonora*, 147.
24. Julian Velarde, report on Puerto Peñasco, 1936, Box 28, Folder 20, Osborn Papers; John Akers to Osborn, May 25, 1942, Box 20, Folder 18, Osborn Papers; William Shipley to Osborn, October 18, 1945, Box 33, Folder 10, Osborn Papers; Shipley to Osborn, May 23, 1946, Box 33, Folder 10, Osborn Papers; Guadarrama et al., *Historia general de Sonora*, vol. 5, 156, 183.
25. "Está por iniciarse la erección de nuestra planta de cemento," *El Imparcial*, July 28, 1945; "Reina optimísmo en Saric," *El Imparcial*, April 26, 1945; Guadarrama et al., *Historia General de Sonora*, vol. 5, 76, 152, 154–155.
26. Guadarrama et al., *Historia general de Sonora*, vol. 5, 154, 161.
27. Anselmo Macías Valenzuela, *Informe rendido por el C. Gral. Ansemo Macías V., gobernador constitucional del estado de Sonora, al H. Congreso del Estado*, from September 1, 1939, to March 31, 1940 (Hermosillo, 1940), 15; Miguel Acosta, "México en la Crisis Guerra Mundial," *El Imparcial*, February 5, 1941, 2; "Los Edos. Unidos van a fomentar en México las carreteras," *El Imparcial*, December 18, 1941, 1; "La Carretera Panamericana y los EE.UU.," *El Imparcial*, January 20, 1942, 1; Osborn to Ernest McFarland, December 22, 1942, Box 80, Folder 13, Osborn Papers.
28. Guadarrama et al., *Historia General de Sonora*, vol. 5, 152–153.
29. Enriqueta de Parodi, "Sonora, la entidad del futuro," *El Imparcial*, February 15, 1944.
30. "Editorial, el mensaje presidencial," *El Imparcial*, December 12, 1941; "Por el bien de la patria . . . hay que producir más!" *El Imparcial*, March 12, 1942; Parodi, "Sonora, la entidad del futuro"; Guadarrama et al., *Historia General de Sonora*, vol. 5, 151, 156.
31. Nogales Chamber of Commerce to Osborn, February 27, 1943, Box 25, Folder 17, Osborn Papers; Nogales, Sonora Merchants Association to Nogales, Sonora Chamber of Commerce, April 9, 1943, Box 25, Folder 17, Osborn Papers; Temple Penrod to William Nielander, June 2, 1943, Box 25, Folder 17, Osborn

Papers; Estela Jácome, interview by the Arizona Historical Society, March 21, 1990, 21–23, AHS; Alva Torres and Edward Madrid, in *They Opened Their Hearts*, 15, 48.

32. Mario de la Fuente, with Boye De Mente, *I Like You, Gringo—But!* (Phoenix, 1972), 71–73.
33. Don Smith to Osborn, March 9, 1942, Box 19, Folder 14, Osborn Papers; G. Howland Shaw to Armstrong, May 7, 1942, Record Group 84, Box 1, Nogales Classified Records, NARA; Felipe Cano to Osborn, December 28, 1942, Box 25, Folder 4, Osborn Papers; John Flores to Osborn, April 22, 1943, Box 25, Folder 4, Osborn Papers; proclamation of Anselmo Macías Valenzuela, June 22, 1943, Box 25, Folder 4, Osborn Papers; Jesús Trias to Osborn, September 9, 1943, Osborn Papers; Junta Patriótica to Osborn, September 20, 1943, Box 25, Folder 4, Osborn Papers; award presented to Osborn by Alejandro Villaseñor, September 15, 1947, Box 39, Folder 6, Osborn Papers.
34. Osborn to Antonio Uroz, December 19, 1942, Box 25, Folder 4, Osborn Papers; Raúl Michel to the mayor of Clifton, Arizona, May 20, 1943, Box 25, Folder 4, Osborn Papers; Osborn to Uroz, April 15, 1944, Box 25, Folder 4, Osborn Papers.
35. Kelly, "Arizona's Harsh Terrain, Climate Toughened GIs."
36. Alfred Atkinson to University of Arizona Board of Regents, January 27, 1942, Box 20, Folder 41, Osborn Papers; Alex Jácome to Osborn, January 7, 1943, Box 25, Folder 4, Osborn Papers; Bonnie Henry, "Davis-Monthan Air Force Base, It's Been Home to Some High-Flying History," *Arizona Daily Star*, May 20, 1987; Bonnie Henry, "The Homefront," in *Another Tucson* (Tucson, 1992), 97–102.
37. "Expansion for Airport Looms," *Arizona Daily Star*, August 7, 1940; Henry, "Davis-Monthan Air Force Base"; Sonnichsen, *Tucson*, 263.
38. Hal Marshall, "Tucson Leans Heavily On D-M Payrolls," *Arizona Daily Star*, May 13, 1956; Josie Huerta Herrera, in *They Opened Their Hearts*, 92; Sonnichsen, *Tucson*, 263, 268.
39. Jácome, interview; "Personal Memories from Davis-Monthan," from ephemera file, "Arizona-History-World War, 1939–1945," AHS; Pearlie Mae Purdie, in *They Opened Their Hearts*, 38.
40. "Soldier Given Death Penalty," *Arizona Daily Star*, October 12, 1942; Ken Burton, "Last Man Hanged in Tucson Now No More than a Dusty Military File," *Arizona Daily Star*, September 6, 1977; Josie Huerta Herrera, in *They Opened Their Hearts*, 92–93.
41. Gerardo Licón, "Pachucas, Pachucos, and Their Culture: Mexican American Youth Culture of the Southwest, 1910–1955," PhD diss., University of Southern California, 2009, 43–44, 145.

42. Lytle Hernández, *Migra!*, 103; "Hoy empieza registro de los extranjeros," *El Tucsonense*, August 27, 1940; Gilbert Ronstadt, interview by the Arizona Historical Society, 2–3; "Excursion de Tucson," *El Tucsonense*, February 13, 1940; "Para turistas que vayan de E.U. a México," *El Tucsonense*, July 2, 1940; "No hay restricciones en la frontera para el turismo de los Estados Unidos," *El Imparcial*, December 20, 1941; "Ayer comenzo en los E.U. el registro de mexicanos," *El Imparcial*, February 17, 1942; "Border Staff Is Handling New Burdens, U.S. Patrol Has Duty of Guarding against Enemy Alien Entries," *Arizona Daily Star*, February 20, 1942; "Aliens Roundup Moves Rapidly," *Arizona Daily Star*, February 23, 1942; "Notice to American Citizens," *El Imparcial*, March 14, 1942.
43. Louis Hudgin to Jones, June 28, 1940, Box 12, Folder 31, Jones Papers; Y. C. White to Hudgin, June 29, 1940, Box 12, Folder 31, Jones Papers; "Jim" of Nogales to Y. C. White, June 29, 1940, Box 12, Folder 31, Jones Papers; Jones to Hull, August 8, 1940 Box 12, Folder 31, Jones Papers; Resolution no. 34 of the Arizona Cattle Growers Association, February 6, 1943, Box 25, Folder 4, Osborn Papers; S. Deborah Kang, "Crossing the Line: The INS and the Federal Regulation of the Mexican Border," in *Bridging National Borders in North America: Transnational and Comparative Histories*, ed. Benjamin H. Johnson and Andrew R. Graybill, 183–187 (Durham, NC, 2010).
44. Osborn to DeWitt, June 23, 1942, Box 21, Folder 7, Osborn Papers; Masterson, *Japanese in Latin America*, 113–114; Eric Boime, "'Beating Plowshares into Swords': The Colorado River Delta, the Yellow Peril, and the Movement for Federal Reclamation, 1901–1928," *Pacific Historical Review* 28(1) (2009): 27–53.
45. Sharon Cosner, "Citizens Who Became Prisoners," publication and date unknown, from ephemera file, "Arizona-History-World War II, 1939–1945," AHS; Anne Denogean, "Bitterness Doesn't Go Away," *Tucson Citizen*, February 21, 1997; Sheridan, *Arizona*, 279.
46. Masterson, *Japanese in Latin America*, 120, 122, 126; Andy Eisen, "Entangled Borders: International Security and the Relocation of Japanese in Mexico during World War II," unpublished paper, presented at the Newberry Seminar in Borderlands and Latino Studies, March 25, 2010.
47. "Resumé of Conditions in Mexico during March, 1942," Record Group 84, Box 3, Nogales Classified Records, NARA; Masterson, *Japanese in Latin America*, 127; Rodolfo de los Cobos, "Strictly Confidential" memorandum based on stay in Altar, Sonora, September 22–26, 1942, Record Group 84, Box 5, Nogales Classified Records, NARA; Ben Zweig to George Messersmith, September 28, 1944, Record Group 84, Box 5, Nogales Classified Records, NARA; Guadarrama et al., *Historia General de Sonora*, vol. 5, 75, 83; "Sacados todos los extranjeros, ahora los Mexicanos han recobrado sus tierras en la Baja California," *El Imparcial*, January 17, 1942; Lytle Hernández, *Migra!*, 70–75.

48. U.S. Federal Census of 1930; Armstrong to George Messersmith, June 18, 1942, Record Group 84, Box 3, Nogales Classified Records, NARA; "Army Reports Pima County's Dead in World War II," *Arizona Daily Star,* June 27, 1946; "Five Tucson War Dead Being Returned from European Area," May 6, 1948, from ephemera file, "Arizona-History-World War II, 1939–1945," AHS; "Jácome's Celebrating 50th Anniversary This Weekend," March 16, 1946, from ephemera file, "Places-Arizona-Tucson-Business-Department Stores-Jácome's," AHS; Richard E. Wilbur, "End of War Lifted Gloomy Veil That Had Settled over Tucson," *Tucson Citizen,* August 14, 1985; Crow, "Mexican Americans in Contemporary Arizona," 33; Laura L. Cummings, *Pachucas and Pachucos in Tucson: Situated Border Lives* (Tucson, 2009), 37. It is likely that some of these ninety soldiers were Tohono O'odham or Yaqui Indians since members of these communities also had Spanish surnames.
49. Walter White to Osborn, November 5, 1942, Box 15A, Folder 14, Osborn Papers; "Indians on Warpath for Uncle Sam," *Standard of California* (Spring 1944): 3; Commission of the National Baptist Convention to Osborn, September 19, 1945, Box 34, Folder 1, Osborn Papers; Dolores Melton Smith to Dan Garvey, November 16, 1949, Box 45, Folder 30, Governors Files (Garvey), ASL (Garvey Papers); Wilbur, "End of War Lifted Gloomy Veil"; *They Opened Their Hearts,* 31, 33, 37.
50. Manuel Herrera and Patrick Franco, quoted in *They Opened Their Hearts,* 70, 98; "Memorial Day Tributes 2004," *Arizona Daily* Star, May 31, 2004; Sonnichsen, *Tucson,* 266–267; Lorena Oropeza, *¡Raza Si! ¡Guerra No! Chicano Protest and Patriotism during the Viet Nam War Era* (Berkeley, 2005), 11–46.
51. Christine Marín, "La Asociación Hispano-Americana de Madres y Esposas: Tucson's Mexican American Women in World War II," in *Renato Rosaldo Lectures Series Monograph,* vol. 1, series 1983–1984 (Summer 1985): 5–18; Bonnie Henry, "Hispanic Troops Were Happy to Get Chatter from Home," *Arizona Daily Star,* June 9, 1991; "Visitas de los soldados a las familias de Hermosillo," *El Imparcial,* April 21, 1944; "Pisaron hoy tierra mexicana los veteranos del escuadrón," *El Imparcial,* November 16, 1945; "Recibirá Hermosillo los restos de un héroe de la guerra," *El Imparcial,* January 13, 1949, 1.
52. "About the Boys at the Homefront," *La Alianza* (October 1944), 7; "Silver Star," *La Alianza* (January 1945), 6; Benito Xavier Pérez-Verdía, "La participación bélica en México," *La Alianza* (January 1945), 11; "Año nuevo," *La Alianza* (January 1945), 1; Lydia Otero, *La Calle: Spatial Conflicts and Urban Renewal in a Southwest City* (Tucson, 2010), 35.
53. Armstrong to Osborn, April 10, 1942, Box 76, Governors Subject Files, "Foreign Relations, 1941–1950," ASL; John Flores to Osborn, April 22, 1943, Box 25, Folder 4, Osborn Papers; Wirt Bowman to Osborn, November 3, 1943, Box 26, Folder 13, Osborn Papers; Juanita Villegas Bernal, interview by the Arizona

Historical Society, May 18, 1985, 54; Harry T. Getty, *Interethnic Relationships in the Community of Tucson* (New York, 1976); Officer, "Sodalities and Systemic Linkage"; Aracely Carranza et al., *Don't Look at Me Different/No me veas diferente* (Tucson, 2000), 16–17; Sheridan, *Arizona,* 278, 292.

54. Beulah Head to Evan Flory, September 22, 1942, Box 15A, Folder 14, Osborn Papers; Consolidated Vultee to Henry Arneson, November 20, 1943, Box 22A, Folder 10, Osborn Papers; "Strategic Realm for War Industry," *Standard of California,* Spring Bulletin, 1944, from ephemera file, "Arizona—History—World War II, 1939–1945," AHS; Ruben Moreno and Evelyn Gump, in *They Opened Their Hearts,* 45, 52; Sonnichsen, *Tucson,* 272; Zaragosa Vargas, *Labor Rights Are Civil Rights: Mexican American Workers in Twentieth-Century America* (Princeton, NJ, 2005), 220.
55. Lily Oliveras Valenzuela, interview by the Arizona Historical Society, July 5, 1984, 6, AHS; Sheridan, *Los Tucsonenses,* 181; Vargas, *Labor Rights Are Civil Rights,* 220.
56. Vicki Ruiz, *From out of the Shadows: Mexican Women in Twentieth-Century America* (New York, 1999), 82, 84; Zaragosa Vargas, *Crucible of Struggle: A History of Mexican Americans from the Colonial Period to the Present Era* (New York, 2010), 261; Beatrice Amado Kissinger, in *A Legacy Greater than Words: Stories of U.S. Latinos and Latinas of the WWII Generation,* ed. Maggie Rivas-Rodríguez, 187 (Austin, 2006); Josie Huerta Herrera, in *They Opened Their Hearts,* 92; "Local Girls Work on Planes," May 30, 1943, from ephemera file, "Arizona—History—World War II, 1939–1945," AHS; Bonnie Henry, "Hispanic Railroad Women," in *Another Tucson,* 111–112; Lily Oliveras Valenzuela, interview by the Arizona Historical Society, July 5, 1984, 2–3.
57. Juanita Villegas Bernal, interview by the Arizona Historical Society, May 18, 1985, 36–37, AHS. All of the following biographical information is drawn from pages 1, 13, 16–17, 22, 35, and 53–54.
58. Vargas, *Crucible of Struggle,* 262–263.
59. Raymond Phelan to Hull, September 30, 1942, Record Group 84, Box 3, Nogales Classified Records, NARA; Lozano Ascencio et al., *Sonorenses en Arizona,* 44; Carlos Ronstadt to Osborn, May 12, 1943, Box 25, Folder 4, Osborn Papers; Osborn to Carlos Ronstadt, May 13, 1943, Box 25, Folder 4, Osborn Papers; Lytle Hernández, *Migra!,* 111, 114.
60. Pima County Board of Supervisors to Osborn, September 5, 1941, Box 17, Folder 23, Osborn Papers; Gladstone Mackenzie to Osborn, September 6, 1941, Osborn Papers; Berkeley Bunker to Sidney, June 16, 1942, Box 17, Folder 23, Osborn Papers; Clarence DeHoff to Lon Jordan, February 9, 1943, Box 24, Folder 17, Osborn Papers; Osborn to Carl Hayden, February 19, 1943, Box 24, Folder 17, Osborn Papers; Earl Maharg to Osborn, April 7, 1943, Box 24, Folder 17, Osborn Papers; Arizona Farm Bureau Federation to Osborn, April 23, 1943, Box 24, Folder 17, Osborn Papers.

61. Raúl Grijalva, interview by author, August 9, 2007.
62. Ibid.; Ernesto Portillo Jr., interview by author, June 11, 2007.
63. U.S. Consulate in Nogales, Sonora, "Labor Report, September 12, 1945, Record Group 84, Box 6, Nogales Classified Records, NARA; Guadarrama et al., *Historia General de Sonora*, vol. 5, 153.
64. Osborn to Armstrong, April 19, 1942, Box 76, Governors Subject Files, "Foreign Relations, 1941–1950," ASL; Parodi, "Sonora, la entidad del futuro"; "Resultados y esperanzas," *El Imparcial*, January 1, 1942; Osborn to Fred McCormick, April 8, 1942, Box 20, Folder 38, Osborn Papers; "Exposición regional del noroeste de México," *El Imparcial*, July 28, 1945; Rodríguez, quoted in Guadarrama et al., *Historia General de Sonora*, vol. 5, 152.
65. Strictly confidential memo, February 26, 1941, Record Group 84, Box 2, Nogales Classified Records, NARA; U.S. Consulate in Nogales, Sonora, "Labor Report," September 12, 1945; "Las condiciones de vida del proletariado industrial de Sonora," *Accion*, August 6, 1945; Bantjes, *As if Jesus Walked on Earth*, 123–150; Guadarrama et al., *Historia General de Sonora*, vol. 5, 151, 154, 308.
66. Osborn to Antonio Uroz, August 11, 1943, Box 25, Folder 4, Osborn Papers; "La guerra nos une más," *El Imparcial*, March 28, 1944; Lic. Benito Xavier Pérez Verdía, "El pensamiento de América," *El Imparcial*, March 24, 1945; "El día de las Américas," *El Imparcial*, April 13, 1945; "Así somos los latinos," *El Imparcial*, August 3, 1945.
67. George Chambers to Osborn, November 8, 1944, Box 26, Folder 3, Osborn Papers; "El informe que rinde el Presidente Sr. don Ignacio Soto," *El Imparcial*, September 16, 1945; Sheridan, *Arizona*, 287.
68. "Derechos aduanales y otras barreras existentes seran pronto suspendidas," *El Imparcial*, January 27, 1942; Guillermo Ibarra, "La verguenza del racismo," *El Imparcial*, October 10, 1945; "Instrumentos de Washington en las Américas," *El Imparcial*, October 10, 1945.
69. Frank Nevares to Osborn, January 27, 1946, Box 34, Folder 1, Osborn Papers; Vargas, *Labor Rights Are Civil Rights*, 203–206.

2. La Fiesta de los Vaqueros

1. The rodeo was canceled for two years during World War II but otherwise has been an annual event. Shermer, *Sunbelt Capitalism*, 83–90; Nickerson and Dochuk, *Sunbelt Rising*, 1–18.
2. "Tucson Celebrates 31st Fiesta de los Vaqueros," *Arizona Daily Star*, February 23, 1956; William Deverell, *Whitewashed Adobe: The Rise of Los Angeles and the Remaking of Its Mexican Past* (Berkeley, 2005), 51; "Big Parade Heralds Opening of 29th Rodeo," *Arizona Daily Star*, February 19, 1954; Dean

Prichard, "Champ Cowboys Vie in 4-Day Go," *Arizona Daily Star,* February 19, 1954.

3. Shermer, *Sunbelt Capitalism,* 52, 239.
4. Daniela Spenser, "Standing Conventional Cold War History on Its Head," in *In from the Cold: Latin America's New Encounter with the Cold War,* ed. Gilbert Joseph and Daniela Spenser, 388 (Durham, NC, 2008); Lytle Hernández, *Migra!,* 171–195; "Mrs. Conan" to Dan Garvey, March 13, 1950, Box 45, Folder 1, Garvey Papers; Watson Miller to Ernest McFarland, May 18, 1950, Box 45, Folder 1, Garvey Papers.
5. Almada, *Breve historia de Sonora,* 141; Shermer, *Sunbelt Capitalism,* 4–5, 51–55.
6. Vivien Keatley, "Rodeo-Happy Tucson," Western Way Feature Files Collection, MS 1059, Box 19, Folder 278, AHS; Alex Kimmelman, "Luring the Tourist to Tucson: Civic Promotion during the 1920s," *Journal of Arizona History* 28 (1987): 135–154; Dina Berger and Andrew Grant Wood, eds., *Holiday in Mexico: Critical Reflections on Tourism and Tourist Encounters* (Durham, NC, 2010), 1, 6, 11; Phoebe S. Kropp, *California Vieja: Culture and Memory in a Modern American Place* (Berkeley, 2008); John L. Mortimer, "Texas 'Charro Days,'" *New York Times,* January 25, 1942, 1; Carey McWilliams, *North from Mexico: The Spanish-Speaking People of the United States* (Westport, CT, 1990, 2nd ed.), 43–53.
7. Sheridan, *Arizona,* 280; Guadarrama et al., *Historia General de Sonora,* vol. 5, 157; Cadava, "Borderlands of Modernity and Abandonment," 377.
8. Otero, *La Calle,* 41–58.
9. Ferd Lauber, "*La fiesta de los vaqueros,*" 1925–1987 (Tucson Arizona, 1990), 2.
10. Richard Slatta, *Cowboys of the Americas* (New Haven, CT, 1990), 210; Gary Williams, interview by author, July 23, 2006; Lauber, "*La fiesta de los vaqueros.*"
11. *Arizona Daily Star* article, from ephemera file, "Places—Tucson—Celebrations—Rodeo—1930s," AHS; Chamber of Commerce, 1947 rodeo program.
12. Slatta, *Cowboys of the Americas,* 7, 212; Kathleen Sands, *Charrería Mexicana: An Equestrian Folk Tradition* (Tucson, 1993), 61–86; Terry Jordan, *North American Cattle-Ranching Frontiers: Origins, Diffusion, and Differentiation* (Albuquerque, 1993), 128, 132; Mary Lou LeCompte, "The Hispanic Influence on the History of Rodeo, 1823–1922," *Journal of Sport History* 12(1) (1985): 21–38. The Cowboys' Turtle Association was renamed the Rodeo Cowboys Association in 1945 and the Professional Rodeo Cowboys Association in 1974.
13. J. J. Wagoner, *History of the Cattle Industry in Southern Arizona, 1540–1940* (Tucson, 1952), 7, 9–10, 16–17, 23; Jordan, *North American Cattle-Ranching Frontiers,* 138–145.

14. Slatta, *Cowboys of the Americas*, 222; U.S. Consulate, Nogales, Sonora, "Labor Report," September 12, 1945, 3, Record Group 84, Box 5, Nogales Classified Records; Ben Zweig to Cordell Hull, March 1, 1944, Record Group 84, Box 5, Nogales Classified Records.
15. "Zona sanitaria contra la fiebre aftosa," *El Imparcial*, January 22, 1947, 1; "Oponense a que se levante una cerca en la frontera," *El Imparcial*, February 26, 1947, 1; "Será amplísima la ayuda para combatir la aftosa," *El Imparcial*, February 13, 1947, 1; "Condiciones del mercado de la carne mexicana en los E.E. U.U.," *El Imparcial*, January 31, 1952, 1; "226,743 cabezas de ganado fueron exportadas en 1955," *El Imparcial*, February 11, 1956, 1.
16. Abelardo Rodríguez, *Informe rendido ante la H. XXXVIII legislatura constitucional del estado*, from September 1, 1945, to August 31, 1946 (Hermosillo, 1946), 20–22; "Convención de ganaderos que se celebra en Nogales, Arizona," *El Imparcial*, February 11, 1949, 1; "Ganaderos de Arizona, en Hermosillo," *El Imparcial*, February 26, 1960, 1; "Background & History of the Arizona-Sonora Committee," Box 178, "The Arizona-Sonora Committee Background & History, 1959," 6, Governors Subject Files (Fannin), ASL; "Reanudó Sonora las exportaciones de ganado en pie al mercado en E.U.," *El Imparcial*, February 3, 1980, 1A.
17. "Major Development Looming at Airport, CC Official Asserts," *Arizona Daily Star*, April 8, 1954; Hal Marshall, "Tucson Leans Heavily On D-M Payrolls," *Arizona Daily Star*, May 13, 1956; Sheridan, *Arizona*, 277, 284–285, 287, 289, 291; Shermer, *Sunbelt Capitalism*, 100–112, 225–269.
18. Ignacio Soto, *Informe rendido ante la H. XL legislatura constitucional del estado*, from September 1, 1953, to August 31, 1954 (Hermosillo, 1954), 9–10; Guadarrama et al., *Historia General de Sonora*, vol. 5, 154, 157–160; Almada, *Breve historia de Sonora*, 148–149, 150; Hewitt de Alcántara, *Modernizing Mexican Agriculture*.
19. Slatta, *Cowboys of the Americas*, 210; Bolton, quoted in Wagoner, *History of the Cattle Industry in Southern Arizona*, 10.
20. Sidney Osborn to Rollo Ashby, June 30, 1943, Box 25, Folder 4, Osborn Papers; Alfonso Acosta V. to Dan Garvey, October 13, 1948, Box 39, Folder 6, Osborn Papers; "Ayuda de mexicanos de Arizona," *El Imparcial*, January 21, 1949, 1; Jesús Franco to Garvey, January 26, 1949, Box 45, Folder 1, Garvey Papers; Rudolf Zepeda to Garvey, January 31, 1949, Box 45, Folder 1, Garvey Papers; Horacio Sobarzo to Garvey, January 31, 1949, Box 45, Folder 1, Garvey Papers; Juan Martínez to Garvey, March 8, 1949, Box 45, Folder 1, Garvey Papers; Soto to David Aepli, April 30, 1953, Box 98, "Mexico, Sonora," Governors Subject Files, ASL.
21. "Ayuda de Mexico para combatir el trafico de drogas en E.E.U.U.," *El Imparcial*, February 14, 1953, 1; Lytle Hernández, *Migra!*, 212–213; Rudolf Zepeda to Ignacio Soto, February 5, 1951, Box 98, "Mexico, 1943–1954,"

Governors Subject Files (Pyle), ASL; Soto to Pyle, February 15, 1951, Box 98, "Mexico, 1943–1954," Governors Subject Files (Pyle), ASL.

22. "Infame explotación venian sufriendo cuatrocientos braceros de Mexicali," *El Imparcial*, February 18, 1954, 1; "Explotan a los pobres braceros en Empalme," *El Imparcial*, February 11, 1956, 1; "400 braceros estuvieron en Palacio hoy," *El Imparcial*, February 26, 1957, 1; "Exhortan a los braceros contra los 'coyotes,'" *El Imparcial*, February 3, 1960, 1; "Grave acusación contra el alcalde de Empalme," *El Imparcial*, February 20, 1960, 1; "Reanudaran la contratación de braceros en marzo pxmo. en el centro de Empalme," *El Imparcial*, February 27, 1960, 1.
23. "Cuerpo de perros para perseguir a los espaldas mojadas," *El Imparcial*, February 21, 1956, 1; Maricopa County farm workers to Sidney Osborn, March 7, 1946, Box 32, Folder 14, Osborn Papers; Charles Pickerell to Osborn, April 11, 1946, Box 32, Folder 14, Osborn Papers; Ann Tinnon to Ernest McFarland, November 13, 1946, Box 32, Folder 14, Osborn Papers; Osborn to Pickerell, November 19, 1946, Box 32, Folder 14, Osborn Papers; Shapard to Fred Wilson, May 19, 1950, Box 45, Folder 1, Garvey Papers; William Larson to Howard Pyle, March 3, 1951, Box 98, "Mexico, 1943–1954," Governors Subject Files (Pyle), ASL; Pyle to John Daffner, April 20, 1953, Box 54, Folder 3, Pyle Papers; "Crítica al Gob. de Washington por su sistema en el manejo de la contratación braceril," *El Imparcial*, February 24, 1954, 1.
24. Club de Leones of Nogales, Sonora, to Garvey, May 23, 1949, Box 45, Folder 1, Garvey Papers; Junta Patriótica Mexicana to Garvey, August 29, 1949, Box 45, Folder 1, Garvey Papers; Soto to "Ciudadanos de Sonora," June 30, 1950, Box 45, Folder 1, Garvey Papers; Garvey to Soto, September 9, 1950, Box 45, Folder 1, Garvey Papers; Eliseo Ruiz Russek to Howard Pyle, September 8, 1951, Box 98, "Mexico, 1943–1954," Governors Subject Files (Pyle), ASL.
25. "Fabulosa cosecha de tomate en Guaymas," *El Imparcial*, January 31, 1959, 1; remarks of Frank Boykin of Alabama, April 12, 1960, Box 171D, "Shrimp Imports, 1960," Governors Subject Files (Fannin), ASL; Sidney Osborn to Abelardo Rodríguez, October 19, 1946, Box 33, Folder 10, Osborn Papers; "Arizona recibe con festejos al Gobernador Lic. Sobarzo," *El Imparcial*, January 4, 1949, 1; "Cordial agasajo en Arizona a Sonorenses," *El Imparcial*, January 30, 1950, 1; Dan Garvey to Gilberto Flores Muñoz, February 5, 1950, Box 45, Folder 1, Garvey Papers; Frank Minarik to Dan Garvey, August 4, 1950, Box 45, Folder 1, Garvey Papers; "Optimists May Underestimate Tucson's Growth Potential," *Arizona Daily Star*, February 24, 1955.
26. Gonzalo Guerrero Almada to Dan Garvey, February 27, 1950, Box 45, Folder 1, Garvey Papers; Pyle to José Muguerza, February 17, 1954, Box 98, "Mexico, 1943–1954," Governors Subject Files (Pyle), ASL; Enrique de Alba, "Huéspedes de honor en el rodeo de Tucson," *El Imparcial*, February 14, 1950, 1;

"Entrevista de los gobernadores de Sonora y Arizona," *El Imparcial*, February 20, 1951, 1; "Encabeza Soto la 'parada' de los vaqueros," *El Imparcial*, February 23, 1950, 1; "Acedo Romero se encuentra en Tucson," *El Imparcial*, February 23, 1955, 1; "S. Gutierrez en comisión a Tucson," *El Imparcial*, February 20, 1959, 1.

27. R. L. Rodríguez to Sidney Osborn, April 8, 1946, Box 33, Folder 10, Osborn Papers; "Lunch ofrecido ayer a excursionistas de Phoenix," *El Imparcial*, February 12, 1948, 1; Osborn to Abelardo L. Rodríguez, September 9, 1947, Box 39, Folder 6, Osborn Papers; "Intensa actividad realiza El Comité Arizona-Sonora," *El Imparcial*, January 23, 1948, 1; schedule of Sonoran agriculturalists during their visit to Arizona, September 3–5, 1953, Box 98, Governors Subject Files (Pyle), "Mexico, Sonora, Governor Ignacio Soto, 1951–1954," ASL.
28. "Visita del Gobernador Rotario a Hermosillo," *El Imparcial*, February 26, 1947, 1; "Interesante sesión-cena del Club Rotario de Hermosillo," *El Imparcial*, January 18, 1949, 1; "Hermosillo y Phoenix nuevamente unidos en lazos de amistad al través de sus respectivos clubes rotarios," *El Imparcial*, February 22, 1954, 1; "Cena de gala del Club Rotario local, en su XX aniversario," *El Imparcial*, February 15, 1955, 1; "Salió hoy a Nogales, Tucson, y Agua Prieta, el Gobernador Soto," *El Imparcial*, February 23, 1955, 1; "Brillantes orientaciones rotarias expuestas por el Gobernador Soto," *El Imparcial*, March 1, 1955, 1.
29. Kaye Lynn Briegel, "Alianza Hispano-Americana, 1894–1965: A Mexican American Fraternal Insurance Society," PhD diss., University of Southern California, 1974, 64, 94–95; "La Historia de la Alianza Hispano Americana," *La Alianza* (January 1944); "The Alianza Hispano-Americana: A Brief History," *La Alianza* 46(2) (February 1953): 3.
30. "Noticias de México," *La Alianza* (January 1945): 7; "El nuevo presidente de la Logia Fundadora," *La Alianza* (February 1945): 5; Ralph Estrada, "Fraternally Yours," *La Alianza* (February 1955): 2.
31. "Éxito artistico y cultural el concierto de la A.H.A.," *El Imparcial*, March 1, 1946, 1; "Actividades de la Alianza Hispano Americana Local," *El Imparcial*, March 1, 1947, 1; "Visitantes al gran evento del sabado," *El Imparcial*, January 24, 1951, 1; "Inauguración del casino de Hermosillo," *El Imparcial*, January 27, 1951, 1; "Bodas de plata de la Alianza de Nogales," *El Imparcial*, February 19, 1953.
32. Rodeo programs of 1948 and 1951, published by the Tucson Chamber of Commerce, AHS; "Ride 'em Cowboy," *La Alianza* 46(2) (February 1953): 12.
33. Eduardo "Lalo" Guerrero, *Lalo: My Life and Music* (Tucson, 2002), 73–74; Licón, "Pachucas, Pachucos, and Their Culture," 120, 147–148.
34. Thomas Robinson to Cordell Hull, January 30, 1937, Record Group 84, Box 1, Nogales Classified Records; Anselmo Macías Valenzuela, *Informe rendido por el C. Gral. Anselmo Macias V. al H. Congreso del Estado*, from September 1, 1939, to March 31, 1940 (Hermosillo, 1940), 16; Abelardo Rodríguez, *Informe rendido ante la H. XXXVII Legislatura Constitucional del Estado*, from

September 1, 1943, to August 31, 1944 (Hermosillo, 1944), 62; Sidney Osborn, speech at Western Governors' Conference, November 19–20, 1945, Box 31, Folder 11, Osborn Papers.

35. "Condena el gobierno del estado toda especulación contra el turismo," *El Imparcial*, February 20, 1950, 1; Meade Cole to Rafael Aveleyra, July 13, 1951, Box 98, "Mexico, Sonora, Governor Ignacio Soto, 1951–1954," Governors Subject Files, ASL; "Piden más facilidades para viajar entre México y Estados Unidos," *El Imparcial*, February 3, 1953, 1; "Simpatía para los turistas," *El Imparcial*, February 28, 1955, 4.

36. "Solemne inauguración de la carretera," *El Imparcial*, January 16, 1950, 1; "Condena el gobierno del estado toda especulación contra el turismo," *El Imparcial*, February 20, 1950, 1.

37. "Regio baile de aniversario en el casino Aliancista," *El Imparcial*, January 3, 1947, 1; "Carnaval!" *El Imparcial*, January 25, 1947, 1; "Atractivo programa presenta el Comité de Carnaval," *El Imparcial*, February 15, 1947, 1; "Formaron el Comité de Carnaval," *El Imparcial*, January 14, 1948, 1; "Actividades del Carnaval 1950," *El Imparcial*, February 3, 1950, 1; "Hermosillo celebra jubiloso una de las más brillantes fiestas de carnestolendas," *El Imparcial*, February 20, 1950, 1.

38. "Distinguidos visitantes de Arizona," *El Imparcial*, February 13, 1947, 1; "Caravana de buena voluntad salió esta tarde de Arizona," *El Imparcial*, January 14, 1950, 1; "200 tucsonenses vienen a Carnaval," *El Imparcial*, January 17, 1950, 1; "Estan reservados los hoteles de Hermosillo para el Carnaval," *El Imparcial*, January 24, 1950, 1; "Actividades del Carnaval de Hermosillo," *El Imparcial*, January 27, 1950, 1; "Caravana de Nogales al Carnaval," *El Imparcial*, January 31, 1950, 1.

39. Alfonso Almada, "La industria turística en Sonora," *El Imparcial*, February 23, 1950, 3; "Condena el gobierno del estado toda especulación contra el turismo," *El Imparcial*, February 20, 1950, 1; Hector Sánchez, the Sonoran tourism commissioner, to Pyle, January 25, 1951, Box 98, "Mexico, 1943–1954," Governors Subject Files, ASL.

40. Jesús Siqueiros, "Noticias de México," *La Alianza* (January 1946), 7.

41. Abelardo Rodríguez, *Informe rendido ante la H. XXXVIII legislatura constitucional del estado*, from September 1, 1946, to August 31, 1947 (Hermosillo, 1947), 12; Ignacio Soto, "Al pueblo de Sonora," *El Imparcial*, January 14, 1949, 5; "Auge del turismo hacia Sonora," *El Imparcial*, January 4, 1950, 1; "Hermosillo progresa, dice un turista," *El Imparcial*, January 31, 1953, 1; Leopoldo Cecena, "Ignacio Soto, el hombre símbolo," *El Imparcial*, February 13, 1948, 3.

42. Alfonso Almada, "La industria turística en Sonora, II," *El Imparcial*, February 25, 1950, 1; "Simpatía para los turistas."

43. Patricia Preciado Martin, ed., *Beloved Land: An Oral History of Mexican Americans in Southern Arizona* (Tucson, 2004); Thomas E. Sheridan, *Del*

Rancho al Barrio: The Mexican Legacy of Tucson (Tucson, 1983); Cummings, *Pachucas and Pachucos in Tucson*, 74–76, 90–92.

44. Carlotta Sotomayor, quoted in Preciado Martín, *Beloved Land*, 6; Sheridan, *Los Tucsonenses*, 32; Bianca Premo, "Recreating Identity: Recreation on the Arizona-Sonora Border," *Studies in Latin American Popular Culture* 16 (1997): 45.
45. Fred Emery, "'Growing Pains' Years Are Over for Tucson," *Arizona Daily Star*, February 24, 1955; "Ariz. Economic Growth Exceeds National Gains," *Arizona Daily Star*, February 23, 1956; "Tucson's Spendable Income Approaches Half-Billion," *Tucson Daily Citizen*, July 7, 1959, 12; Tucson Chamber of Commerce, *Facts and Statistics, Tucson, Arizona* (Tucson, 1964–1965); Sheridan, *Arizona*, 285.
46. Otero, *La Calle*, 9, 73–77; Clifton Abbott, "Rodeo Goes Collegiate," Western Ways Feature Files Collection, MS 1056, Box 16, Folder 229, AHS; "Prize Offered to Owner of Widest 'Bows,'" *Arizona Daily Star*, February 2, 1954.
47. "Whiskers Will Be in Style at Fiesta," *Tucson Citizen*, from 1948 Rodeo Parade Scrapbook, in possession of Rodeo Parade Committee (all scrapbooks referenced hereafter belong to the Rodeo Parade Committee); "Tucson School Solves Hairy Problem, Silky Rodeo Whiskers for Sale," 1953 Rodeo Parade Scrapbook; "Bowlegs May Bring Reward," January 17, 1953, in 1953 Rodeo Parade Scrapbook.
48. Slatta, *Cowboys of the Americas*, 211; "Go Western Tomorrow," *Tucson Citizen*, February 9, 1951; Vivien Keatley, "Tucson's 'La Fiesta de los vaqueros'" Western Way Feature Files Collection, MS 1059, Box 19, Folder 278, AHS; "Tucsonians to Don Western Garb Jan. 29," *Tucson Citizen*, date unknown, from 1948 Rodeo Parade Scrapbook; "Jailed Dudes Shrug Off No Western Garb," *Tucson Citizen*, February 7, 1953.
49. "That Western Look," *Tucson Citizen*, February 15, 1958; no title, *Arizona Daily Star*, February 8, 1953, from 1953 Rodeo Parade Scrapbook; Frances Reynolds, "Crowd of 30,000 Persons Sees Colorful Spectacle," *Arizona Daily Star*, February 21, 1948.
50. "All-Horse Rodeo Parade May Be on Last Legs," publication unknown, February 22, 1956, from 1956 Rodeo Parade Scrapbook; "Dress Western to Back Rodeo," *Arizona Daily Star*, February 5, 1950.
51. "Rodeo Cowboy, Professional Athlete in the World's Roughest Sport," *Tucson Citizen*, February 10, 1954; "32 Beauties Pitch Curves for Sake of Old Pueblo," *Arizona Daily Star*, February 23, 1956; Olga Nájera-Ramírez, "Mounting Traditions: The Origin and Evolution of la Escaramuza Charra," in *Chicana Traditions: Continuity and Change*, ed. Norma E. Cantú and Nájera-Ramírez (Urbana, 2002).
52. Sheridan, *Arizona*, 286; Margot Canaday, *The Straight State: Sexuality and Citizenship in Twentieth-Century America* (Princeton, NJ, 2009), 138.

53. Mrs. Joe Hernandez, "That Matter of Names," *Arizona Daily Star,* September 21, 1945; Fred G. Holmes to Dan Garvey, December 28, 1948, Box 45, Folder 30, Garvey Papers; William Harrison to Garvey, February 23, 1949, Box 45, Folder 30, Garvey Papers; Officer, "Sodalities and Systemic Linkage," 74–92; Cummings, *Pachucas and Pachucos in Tucson,* 5, 69; Sheridan, *Arizona,* 283, 293, 295–297.
54. Papago Tribal Council, *Papago Development Program* (Chilocco, OK, 1949), 43–44, 48, 53, 61–62, 65, 80; "Papago Rehabilitation Bill: Hearings before the Subcommittee on Indian Affairs of the Committee on Public Lands," August 1950 (Washington, DC, 1950).
55. Meeks, *Border Citizens,* 213; *Papago Development Program,* 61–62, 65; Henry Manuel, Juliann Ramon, and Bernard Fontana, "Dressing for the Window: Papago Indians and Economic Development," in *American Indian Economic Development,* ed. Sam Stanley, 511–578 (The Hague, 1978); Robert Hackenberg and C. Roderick Wilson, "Mobility and Modernization: The Migration Process in Papago Indian Adaptation," August 1969, Bureau of Ethnic Research Projects, Record Group 8, Box 1, Folder 16, ASM; Cadava, "Borderlands of Modernity and Abandonment," 371–380.
56. "Pasan centenares de comunistas mexicanos a los Estados Unidos," *El Imparcial,* February 12, 1954, 1; "Nuevas reglas en la ley de inmigración en Edos. Unidos," *El Imparcial,* February 2, 1953, 4; Mario García, *Mexican Americans: Leadership, Ideology, and Identity,* 1930–1960 (New Haven, CT, 1989), 199–227; David Gutiérrez, *Walls and Mirrors: Mexican Americans, Mexican Immigrants, and the Politics of Ethnicity* (Berkeley, 1995), 152–178.
57. García, *Mexican Americans,* 25–61; Benjamin Johnson, *Revolution in Texas: How a Forgotten Rebellion and Its Bloody Suppression Turned Mexicans into Americans* (New Haven, CT, 2005), 176–205; Stephen Pitti, *The Devil in Silicon Valley: Northern California, Race, and Mexican Americans* (Princeton, NJ, 2003), 149–172.
58. "Ancient Custom of Indians Is Broken by Segundo's Election," *Arizona Daily Star,* September 21, 1947; "Indians Revamp Customs," date and publication unknown, from ephemera file, "Indians of North America—Tohono O'odham—People, Segundo, Thomas A.," AHS; "Papago Tribal Leader among Crash Victims," date and publication unknown, from ephemera file, "Indians of North America—Tohono O'odham—People, Segundo, Thomas A.," AHS; Adolfo Quezada, "Papago Leader Segundo Strived to Aid His Tribe," *Tucson Citizen,* May 11, 1971.
59. Meeks, *Border Citizens;* Julie Greene, "Segundo's Horse Waits at Gravesite," *Tucson Citizen,* May 13, 1971.
60. "Registro para rodeo de Tucson gratis a todos," *El Tucsonense,* February 16, 1940; "18th Annual 1942 Rodeo," publication and date unknown, from

ephemera file, "Tucson—Celebrations—Rodeo—1940s," AHS; rodeo programs from 1946, 1948, 1951, and 1953, published by the Tucson Chamber of Commerce, AHS; Julian Tuthill, "Tucson," *La Alianza* 48(5) (May 1955): 12.

61. Rodeo programs for 1946 and 1947.
62. "Indian No Grow Beard, Scalp Big White Chief for Whiskers," *Arizona Daily Star,* February 13, 1953; Elliott Young, "Red Men, Princess Pocahontas, and George Washington: Harmonizing Race Relations in Laredo at the Turn of the Century," *Western Historical Quarterly* 29(1) (Spring 1998): 48–85.
63. LeCompte, "The Hispanic Influence on the History of Rodeo, 1823–1922." Lists of rodeo entrants appear in rodeo programs, and the percentage of Spanish-surnamed riders is based on my own calculation.
64. "Baile, mañana sabado, a candidatas a reina de nuestra raza en el rodeo," *El Tucsonense,* February 9, 1940; "Candidata a reina mxcna. del pxmo. rodeo de Tucson," *El Tucsonense,* February 13, 1940; 1948 Rodeo Parade Scrapbook.
65. Bernie Roth, "Pioneer Days Return at Tucson's Rodeo Parade," *Arizona Daily Star,* January 30, 1955; "Crowds Line Streets to See Wild West Tucson on Parade," from 1947 Rodeo Parade Scrapbook; Ed Dougherty, "30,000 See Postwar Parade," from 1946 Rodeo Parade Scrapbook.
66. Roth, "Pioneer Days Return at Tucson's Rodeo Parade."
67. "Parade Entry Application," in the 1946 Rodeo Parade Scrapbook. In 1948 one woman, referred to as "Mrs. Anthony Tappero," was a parade judge. The 1940 Federal Census lists her name as Ruby Juanita Tappero and her husband's name as Antonio.
68. Reynolds, "Crowd of 30,000 Persons Sees Colorful Spectacle"; Ramón Gutiérrez, *When Jesus Came, the Corn Mothers Went Away: Marriage, Sexuality, and Power in New Mexico, 1500–1846* (Stanford, CA, 1991), 47, 70.
69. Melissa Amado, "Hispanic Businesses in Tucson since 1854," (Tucson, 1988), 12.
70. "Parade Draws Praise from City Visitors," *Tucson Citizen,* February 21, 1953; Tucson Chamber of Commerce, *Welcome Visitor, Official Guide to Tucson,* 1957 Rodeo Parade Scrapbook; "18th Annual 1942 Rodeo"; "Tucson Feature Is Rodeo Parade," *Tucson Citizen,* February 12, 1952; "Geronimo Rides Again," February 22, 1957, 1957 Rodeo Parade Scrapbook.
71. Philip Deloria, *Playing Indian* (New Haven, CT, 1998), 128–153; "Rip-Roarin' West Will Be Depicted in Rodeo Parade," 1950 Rodeo Parade Scrapbook; Bernie Roth, "103,000 Watch Fiesta Parade," 1957 Rodeo Parade Scrapbook; Roger O'Mara, "100,000 Turn Out for Fiesta Parade, Top Prize Goes to Indians," *Arizona Daily Star,* February 21, 1958; "18th Annual 1942 Rodeo."
72. Deverell, *Whitewashed Adobe,* 49–90; "Parade Draws Praise from City Visitors"; "The Rodeo Parade," op-ed in *Arizona Daily Star,* February 14, 1954.

73. See "Art of the Charrería: A Mexican Tradition," a web catalog for an exhibition at the Autry Museum of the American West, Los Angeles, CA, from May 5, 2002, through October 20, 2002, http://theautry.org/explore/exhibits/charreria.html, accessed July 31, 2011.

3. Jácome's Mission

1. Bonnie Henry, "Jácome's Has Been Gone since '80, but Many Fond Memories Linger On," *Arizona Daily Star,* December 20, 1989; June Webb-Vignery, *Jácome's Department Store: Business and Culture in Tucson, Arizona, 1896–1980* (New York, 1989), 105.
2. Lizabeth Cohen, *A Consumer's Republic: The Politics of Mass Consumption in Postwar America* (New York, 2003), 62–111; Hewitt, *Modernizing Mexican Agriculture,* 145–146, 177–178.
3. Officer, "Sodalities and Systemic Linkage," 74.
4. Julio Moreno, *Yankee Don't Go Home!: Mexican Nationalism, American Business Culture, and the Shaping of Modern Mexico* (Chapel Hill, NC, 2007), 172–206.
5. Shana Bernstein, *Bridges of Reform: Interracial Civil Rights Activism in Twentieth-Century Los Angeles* (New York, 2011), 182.
6. Gutiérrez, *Walls and Mirrors,* 152, 165, 176, 178; Almada, *Breve historia de Sonora,* 150–152.
7. The thirty-year lease agreement the Jácomes entered into with Tucson businessman Albert Steinfeld, who was also a competitor in the department-store business, stipulated that the Jácomes could not open a store within fifteen miles of downtown. When they accepted the agreement in 1950, the Jácomes did not anticipate the downtown's demise. "This Is New in Tucson; Firm to Aid Competitor," *Wall Street Journal,* August 21, 1950, 5.
8. Herbert Eugene Bolton, "The Mission as a Frontier Institution in the Spanish-American Colonies," *American Historical Review* 23(1) (October 1917): 42–61; Webb-Vignery, *Jácome's Department Store,* 105–106.
9. Officer, *Hispanic Arizona,* 17–18, 121, 359–360; Sheridan, *Los Tucsonenses.* Jácome's became formally known as "Jácome's Department Store" during the twentieth century. When the store opened in 1896, it was named "La Bonanza," and then "Jácome & Carillo's," "Jácome & Manzos," and "Jácome's Stores, Inc."
10. Webb-Vignery, *Jácome's Department Store,* 35, 46.
11. Ibid., 25.
12. "Expanded Jácome's to Open," *Arizona Daily Star,* September 8, 1957; Jack Carson, "Jácome's Plans Two-Story Addition on Stone Avenue," *Tucson Daily Citizen,* April 6, 1956; "Jácome's Story a Story of Tucson," from ephemera file, "Places—Arizona—Tucson—Business—Department Stores—Jácome's,"

Arizona Historical Society, Tucson, Arizona; Webb-Vignery, *Jácome's Department Store*, 140–141.

13. Felipe Jácome, interview by author, December 11, 2006; Officer, "Sodalities and Systemic Linkage," 145.
14. Webb-Vignery, *Jácome's Department Store*, 19, 98; Otero, *La Calle*, 39; Alison Isenberg, *Downtown America: A History of the Place and the People Who Made It* (Chicago, 2005), 166–202, 255–311.
15. Harry T. Getty, "Interethnic Relationships in the Community of Tucson," PhD diss., University of Chicago, 1950, 114.
16. Ibid., 113; Macario Saldate, interview by author, March 10, 2008; Webb-Vignery, *Jácome's Department Store*, 118; Alex Jácome, "The Jácome Story: Part IV, Old Hands and New Faces," *Arizona Daily Star*, September 1, 1957; "3 Employees Have 28 Years' Service," date and publication unknown, from ephemera file, "Places—Arizona—Tucson—Business—Department Stores—Jácome's," AHS.
17. Shermer, *Sunbelt Capitalism*, 102; Guadalupe Castillo, interview by author, January 30, 2007; Vicki Ruíz, *From out of the Shadows: A History of Mexican Women in the United States*, 1900–1995 (New York, 1998), 55–58.
18. Webb-Vignery, *Jácome's Department Store*, 22–23, 68; Jácome to Mr. and Mrs. Robert Fish, of Los Altos, CA, September 19, 1957, Box 2, Folder 1, Jácome's Department Store Records, University of Arizona Special Collections, Tucson, Arizona (Jácome Papers).
19. Webb-Vignery, *Jácome's Department Store*, 48–49, 63; Alex Jácome, "The Jácome Story: Part I, How It Began," *Arizona Daily Star*, August 11, 1957; Alex Jácome, "The Jácome Story: Part II, Going Broke in Style," *Arizona Daily Star*, August 18, 1957; Jácome, "The Jácome Story: Part IV, Old Hands and New Faces"; Alex Jácome, "The Jácome Story: Part V, It's Fun to Be Nice to People," *Arizona Daily Star*, September 7, 1957.
20. Estela Jácome, interview by AHS, March 21, 1990, 34–35, transcript at AHS; Alex Jácome Jr., interview by author, March 6, 2007.
21. "Cele Peterson: 50 Years of Fashion, Helping, Caring," *Tucson Citizen*, October 8, 1981; J. C. Martin, "Clothing Enterprise Pays Off for Tucsonan," *Arizona Daily Star*, October 9, 1981; Cele Peterson, interview by AHS, 1980, transcript at AHS.
22. "Jacome's Features Work of 3 Artists," from ephemera file, "Places—Arizona—Tucson—Business—Department Stores—Jácome's," AHS; Jácome Jr., interview.
23. Truett, *Fugitive Landscapes*, 85.
24. Hewitt, *Modernizing Mexican Agriculture*, 177; Ignacio Soto, *Informe rendido ante la H. XL legislatura constitucional del estado*, from September 1, 1953, to August 31, 1954 (Hermosillo, 1954), 9–10; "Electricidad para el pueblo

sonorense," *El Imparcial,* November 12, 1964, 1; "Inauguró obras públicas el Sr. Presidente," *El Imparcial,* November 12, 1964, 2; Cadava, "Borderlands of Modernity and Abandonment," 367–371; "Obras por $200 millones inauguradas en Nogales," *El Imparcial,* November 14, 1964, 8; Estela Jácome, interview by AHS, March 21, 1990, 17.

25. José Vázquez, interview by author, January 13, 2007.
26. Bonnie Henry, "Downtown's Pioneer Hotel, Only Its Façade Remains to Evoke Memories," *Arizona Daily Star,* March 25, 1987; "Hotel Known Worldwide," *Arizona Daily Star,* date unknown, from ephemera file, "Places—Arizona—Tucson—Business—Hotels—Pioneer—(1929–1974)," AHS; Pioneer Hotel breakfast menu, from ephemera file, "Places—Arizona—Tucson—Business—Hotels—Pioneer—(1929–1974)," AHS.
27. Jácome, Tucson Optimist Club speech, undated, Box 1, Folder 46, Jácome Papers; "Murió en Tucsón Alex Jácome Sr.," *El Imparcial,* January 15, 1980, 1; Arcadio Valenzuela to Jácome, September 1, 1965, Box 2, Folder 6, Jácome Papers; Jácome to Arcadio Valenzuela, September 4, 1965, Box 2, Folder 6, Jácome Papers; Jácome to Belisario Moreno, July 23, 1968, Box 2, Folder 7, Jácome Papers; Jácome's advertisement, *El Sonorense,* November 25, 1964, 9; Jácome's advertisement, *El Imparcial,* February 25, 1958, 7; Jácome's advertisement, *El Imparcial,* February 16, 1955, 5; Jácome's advertisement, *El Imparcial,* February 21, 1958, 7; Estela Jácome, interview by AHS, March 21, 1990, 17–18; Cele Peterson, interview by author, October 4, 2006; Alex Jácome Jr., interview by author, January 13, 2007; Webb-Vignery, *Jácome's Department Store,* 44.
28. Vázquez, interview.
29. Raúl Deabenie Q., in Enrique "Pepys" de Alba, "Del diario de un moderno," undated article, from Estela Jácome's scrapbooks, in possession of the Jácome family. Though the article is undated, the year was almost certainly 1956 because the author mentioned a recent tragic airplane crash in the Grand Canyon that killed 128 people, which occurred on June 30, 1956.
30. Ibid.
31. Jácome, Tucson Optimist Club speech.
32. Fannin to Jácome, August 27, 1959, Box 1, Folder 33, Jácome Papers; Kenneth Knauer to Arizona delegation of the Arizona-Mexico West Coast Trade Commission, September 30, 1959, Box 1, Folder 30, Jácome Papers.
33. "Murió en Tucsón Alex Jácome Sr."
34. Jácome to Luis Echevarría Álvarez, November 12, 1969, Box 2, Folder 8, Jácome Papers.
35. Guide to Davis-Monthan, November 15, 1960, Box 193, Governors Subject Files, "Tucson (Mineral Location) & (D-M AFB) 1959–1961," ASL.
36. Armando Landgrave García to Jácome, March 30, 1967, Box 2, Folder 7, Jácome Papers.

37. Jácome to Germán Salazar Girón, November 15, 1965, Box 2, Folder 6; Germán Salazar Girón to Jácome, November 30, 1965, Box 2, Folder 6; Rodolfo León Manzo to Jácome, June 13, 1975, Box 2, Folder 11; John T. Boyer, MD, to Jácome, January 31, 1978, Box 2, Folder 12. Letters from Jácome Papers.
38. Ignacio Soto to Jácome, September 30, 1957, Box 2, Folder 2; immigration papers filed by Jácome, Box 2, Folder 1; Jácome to U.S. Consulate, Juárez, Chihuahua, Mexico, May 27, 1957, Box 2, Folder 1. Materials from Jácome Papers.
39. Jácome to Paul Fannin, September 24, 1959, Box 1, Folder 33; Paul Fannin to Jácome, September 30, 1959, Box 1, Folder 33; Barry Goldwater to Richard Nixon, vice president of the United States, December 13, 1956, Box 1, Folder 34; Morris K. Udall to Jácome, January 22, 1962, Box 2, Folder 20. Letters from Jácome Papers.
40. Goldwater to Jácome, December 20, 1966, Box 1, Folder 35, Jácome Papers; Seth Fein, "New Empire into Old: Making Mexican Newsreels the Cold War Way," *Diplomatic History* 28(5) (November 2004): 711, 742; Jácome, Tucson Optimist Club speech; Julio Moreno, *Yankee Don't Go Home!*, 152–228.
41. Jácome to Goldwater, June 3, 1957; Goldwater to Jácome, July 2, 1957. Letters in Box 1, Folder 34, Jácome Papers.
42. See Peter Iverson, *Barry Goldwater: Native Arizonan* (Norman, OK, 1997); Robert Alan Goldberg, *Barry Goldwater* (New Haven, CT, 1995); Rick Perlstein, *Before the Storm: Barry Goldwater and the Unmaking of the American Consensus* (New York, 2009); Lisa McGirr, *Suburban Warriors: The Origins of the New American Right* (Princeton, NJ, 2002).
43. Barry Goldwater, "Arizona's Next Fifty Years," *Tucson Daily Citizen*, February 14, 1962.
44. Jácome to Goldwater, May 18, 1957, Box 1, Folder 34, Jácome Papers; Felipe Jácome, interview by author, December 11, 2006.
45. Estela Jácome, interview by author, December 21, 2006; advertisement announcing store closing on Election Day, from personal collection of Estela Jácome, in the Jácome family's possession.
46. Jácome to Goldwater, October 27, 1958, Box 1, Folder 34, Jácome Papers.
47. Jácome to Goldwater, March 27, 1962, Box 1, Folder 35, Jácome Papers; Jácome to Newsweek, Inc., July 23, 1964, Box 1, Folder 35, Jácome Papers.
48. Enrique de Alba to Jácome, August 1964, Box 2, Folder 3, Jácome Papers; "Barry seguirá luchando," *El Imparcial*, November 5, 1964, 1.
49. Undated letter from Carlos Ronstadt to Jácome; Roy Laos Jr. to Jácome, August 8, 1957. Both letters in Box 1, Folder 41, Jácome Papers.
50. "One Big Market," op-ed in the *Arizona Republic*, June 18, 1965; Alex Jácome Jr., interview by AHS, April 2, 1980, 9–10, transcript at AHS.

51. Jácome to Paul Fannin, July 5, 1967, Box 1, Folder 33; Jácome to Goldwater, February 1, 1973, Box 1, Folder 36; Jácome to Goldwater, April 27, 1970, Box 1, Folder 36; Jácome to Dennis DeConcini, June 13, 1979, Box 1, Folder 32; DeConcini to Jácome, July 13, 1979, Box 1, Folder 32; Jácome to John Rhodes, January 31, 1974, Box 2, Folder 11. Letters from Jácome Papers. Also see Webb-Vignery, *Jácome's Department Store*, 12, 134; interview with Alex Jácome Jr. by author, February 14, 2007.
52. Jácome to Goldwater, April 27, 1970, Box 1, Folder 36, Jácome Papers.
53. Cummings, *Pachucas and Pachucos in Tucson*, 134, 139; Otero, *La Calle*, 5, 7, 38, 91, 118; Sheridan, *Arizona*, 298; Kropp, *California Vieja*, 207–260; Matt García, *A World of Its Own: Race, Labor, and Citrus in the Making of Greater Los Angeles*, 1900–1970 (Chapel Hill, NC, 2001), 17–46; Eric Ávila, *Popular Culture in the Age of White Flight: Fear and Fantasy in Suburban Los Angeles* (Berkeley, 2004), 145–184.
54. Meeks, *Border Citizens*, 211–220.
55. Ibid., 211; Cadava, "Borderlands of Modernity and Abandonment," 376–377; Augustine Jácome, in Webb-Vignery, *Jácome's Department Store*, 36; William Barton, "New Giant Telescope to Be Set Up," *Los Angeles Times*, April 11, 1956, A1; "Arizona Will Get U.S. Observatory," *New York Times*, December 14, 1957, 7; "'Long Eyes' to Probe Skies over Tucson," *Chicago Daily Tribune*, May 15, 1960, D9; John Young, "Mountaintop Home of 'the Men with Long Eyes,'" *New York Times*, March 15, 1970; James Pearre, "Stareway to the Stars," *Chicago Tribune*, April 25, 1976, G24.
56. Guadalupe Castillo, interview by author, January 30, 2007; Patricia Preciado Martin, interview by author, October 12, 2006.
57. Tucson advertisements, *El Imparcial*, December 23, 1970.
58. "Relato de la nefasta jornada," *El Imparcial*, December 21, 1970, 1; Douglas Kreutz and Gabrielle Fimbres, "Pioneer Hotel Tragedy: Others Linked to '70 Fire," *Tucson Daily Citizen*, July 28, 1986; María León, "Alega acusado inocencia," *El Imparcial*, December 20, 1970, 14A; Sam Negri, "The Pioneer Hotel Fire," *Arizona Republic*, December 19, 1986.
59. "Trece Hermosillenses perecieron en la tragedia del Hotel Pioneer," *El Imparcial*, December 21, 1970, 1; "Solidaridad en el dolor de los deudos," *El Imparcial*, December 21, 1970, 1; Charles Bowden, "After 12 Years, Pioneer Fire Still Burns in Memory," *Tucson Daily Citizen*, December 20, 1982; José Alberto Healy Noriega, "En la cueva del terror," *El Imparcial*, December 22, 1970, 1–2; "Su esposa y 5 hijos perdió el Mayor Luken," *El Imparcial*, December 21, 1970, 8.
60. "Fire Decimates Three Prominent Mexico Families," December 21, 1970, from ephembera file, "Places—Arizona—Tucson—Business—Hotels—Pioneer—Fire,"

AHS; "Patética recepción en el Campo Aéreo," *El Imparcial*, December 21, 1970, 8.

61. Ernie Heltsley, "Mass Said for Fire Victims," *Arizona Daily Star*, December 22, 1970.
62. Jay Hall, "Memorial Mass Commemorates Deaths of 28," *Tucson Daily Citizen*, December 24, 1970; "Hotel Fire Brings Grief to 2 Nations," December 20, 1970, from ephembera file, "Places—Arizona—Tucson—Business—Hotels—Pioneer—Fire," AHS; Cemento Portland Nacional Advertisement, *El Imparcial*, December 21, 1970, 2.
63. Roy Drachman, "Up in Flames, Pioneer Fire Destroys Last of Strong Downtown Symbols," *Tucson Citizen*, April 16, 1988.
64. Carla McClain, "'I Told Him I'd Work for Nothing If That Would Help,'" *Tucson Daily Citizen*, February 28, 1980; "Murió en Tucsón Alex Jácome Sr.," *El Imparcial*, January 15, 1980, 1; Alex Jácome Jr., interview by author, January 9, 2007; Castro, quoted in Webb-Vignery, *Jácome's department store*, 152.
65. Bonnie Henry, "Jácome's Has Been Gone since '80, but Many Fond Memories Linger On," *Arizona Daily Star*, December 20, 1989; McClain, "'I Told Him I'd Work for Nothing If That Would Help'"; Leyla Cattan, "Jácome's Cierra," *El Imparcial*, February 28, 1980, 1, 6.

4. Student Movements

1. "Background & History of the Arizona-Sonora Committee," 1; "Contingente de la UNI-SON irá a Arizona," *El Imparcial*, March 2, 1959, 1; "Extraordinario interés por la conferencia Ariz.-Sonora," *El Imparcial*, February 3, 1959, 1; "Propaganda a la conferencia Sonora-Ariz.," *El Imparcial*, February 26, 1959, 1.
2. Walker, *Waking from the Dream*, 6; Shermer, *Sunbelt Capitalism*, 200–218; Douglas Martin, *The Lamp in the Desert: The Story of the University of Arizona* (Tucson, 1960), 25.
3. Leyla Cattan, "Aunque palidamente, los hispanos sí han estado presente en la UA," *Arizona Daily Star*, January 9, 1985.
4. Walker, *Waking from the Dream*, 1–2; Shermer, *Sunbelt Capitalism*, 302–335; Grandin, *Empire's Workshop*.
5. Martin, *Lamp in the Desert*, 52–53; John P. Schaefer, *President's Report, University of Arizona*, 1973–74 (Tucson, 1974), 5; John P. Schaefer, *President's Report, University of Arizona: A Decade of Progress*, 1963–1973 (Tucson, 1973), 5.
6. Abelardo Rodríguez, *Informe rendido ante la H. XXXVII legislature constitucional del estado*, from September 1, 1943, to August 31, 1944 (Hermosillo, 1944), 62–63; Ignacio Soto, *Informe rendido ante la H. XL Legislatura constitucional del estado*, from September 1, 1951, to August 31, 1952 (Hermosillo, 1952), 24–25; Ignacio Soto, *Informe rendido ante la H. XXXIX Legislatura constitucio-*

nal del estado, from September 1, 1950, to August 31, 1951 (Hermosillo, 1951), 30–31.

7. John P. Schaefer, *President's Report, University of Arizona, 1975–76* (Tucson, 1976), 30–31; John P. Schaefer, *President's Report, University of Arizona, 1976–77* (Tucson, 1977), 35; Richard Harvill, Preface, *Lamp in the Desert;* Schaefer, *Decade of Progress, 1963–1973,* 5.
8. Martin, *Lamp in the Desert;* Sidney Osborn to Alfred Atkinson, January 21, 1942, Box 20, Folder 21, Osborn Papers.
9. "An Arizona-Sonora Research Report," report by University of Arizona professors, 1955, Special Collections, University of Arizona.
10. "An Arizona-Sonora Research Report," 2; "Background & History of the Arizona-Sonora Committee," 1.
11. Article in *El Imparcial,* attached to letter from Norberto Aguirre to Alex Jácome, November 28, 1953, Box 2, Folder 9, Jácome Papers; Jácome to Carlos Ibarra Altamirano, July 14, 1958, Box 2, Folder 3, Jácome Papers; Jácome to Robert Hull, January 20, 1966, Box 2, Folder 6, Jácome Papers; Ignacio Soto to Jácome, September 7, 1966, Box 2, Folder 6, Jácome Papers; *Tucsotarian,* June 26, 1974, Box 2, Folder 28, Jácome Papers.
12. James Officer, "A Proposal for a Joint Economic Survey of Arizona and Sonora" (Tucson, 1960), 1–3, Box 29, Folder 398, Officer Papers, AHS.
13. Ibid., 11; "Laboratorio de biología marina en P. Peñasco," *El Imparcial,* November 12, 1964, 1; Thomas Sheridan, interview by author, February 21, 2008.
14. "Pascua Yaqui Office of Economic Opportunity, 1960–1981," Series VI, Boxes 1–8, Edward Spicer and Rosamond Spicer Papers, ASM; Raymond Thompson, interview by author, March 20, 2008; "Palabras del Sr. Raymond Thompson durante la sesión plenaria de La primera reunión sobre antropología e historia del Noroeste de Mexico," January 19, 1974, in author's possession.
15. Robert Hackenberg, *Papago Population Study: Research Methods and Preliminary Results* (Tucson, 1961); William Kelly, *The Papago Indians of Arizona: A Population and Economic Study* (Tucson, 1963); Thomas Weaver and Theodore Downing, eds., *Mexican Migration* (Tucson, 1976); Raymond Thompson, "Anthropology at the University of Arizona, 1893–2005," *Journal of the Southwest* 47(3) (Autumn 2005): 327–374; "Courses Taken/Taught," Accession #91–10, Box 2, Spicer Papers; 1967 spring enrollment list, Anthropology 212, "Peoples of Mexico," Accession #91–10, Box 2, Spicer Papers; Felipe Jácome, interview by author, April 8, 2008.
16. "Sigue adelante el intercambio de estudiantes de dos universidades," *Boletín Informativo de la Universidad de Sonora* 2(17) (March 1966); Macario Saldate, interview by author, March 10, 2008.

17. "Four Foreign Programs Expect 800," *Arizona Daily Wildcat*, May 18, 1967; Renato Rosaldo, *Progress Report of the Intensive Summer Program of the University of Arizona at the Guadalajara Summer School* (Tucson, 1960), 3.
18. Rosaldo, *Progress Report*, 31; Macario Saldate, interview by author, March 10, 2008.
19. Rosaldo, *Progress Report*, 1, 30.
20. Ibid., 2.
21. *Boletín del Departamento de Extensión Universitaria* 3(5) (año escolar 1963–1964), "Boletines," Archivo histórico, la Universidad de Sonora, Hermosillo, Sonora (AH Uni-Son).
22. Macario Saldate, interview by author, March 10, 2008; Patricia Preciado Martin, interview by author, March 18, 2008. After she married, Patricia Ann Preciado became Patricia Ann Martin. She published under the name Patricia Preciado Martin.
23. Martin, interview by author, March 18, 2008.
24. Don Thornton, "Mexican Beaches Attract 250; No Damage or Arrests Reported," *Arizona Daily Wildcat*, February 7, 1966; Stan Gordon, "Sand and Sun Point to Fun at Rocky Point," *Arizona Wildcat*, May 12, 1965.
25. Frank Sotomayor, "Students Behave 'Like Savages,' Newspaper Says," *Arizona Wildcat*, February 1, 1965.
26. Ibid.; "Students Warned to Obey U.S.-Mexico Laws," *Arizona Wildcat*, January 14, 1965.
27. Cartoon, *Arizona Daily Wildcat*, February 3, 1965.
28. Francisco Marmolejo, interview by author, March 12, 2008.
29. María Eugenia Flores, interview by author, April 2, 2008. All remarks by Flores come from this interview. Apartment advertisements, *El Imparcial*, June 28, 1981, 10.
30. Marmolejo, interview.
31. Flores, interview; Humberto Acuña, interview by author, March 18, 2008. All quotations by Acuña come from this interview.
32. Felipe Jácome, interview by author, April 8, 2008.
33. Salomón Baldenegro, interview by author, September 11, 2012.
34. Angélica Pence, "MEChA to Celebrate 30 Years of Activism," *Arizona Daily Star*, October 4, 1997; Cummings, *Pachucas and Pachucos in Tucson*, 157; Meeks, *Border Citizens*, 175–179.
35. "Harvill's Answer to Charges of Discrimination," *Druid Free Press*, September 24–October 1, 1969.
36. Ibid.
37. Meeks, *Border Citizens*, 159–160, 164; Jack O. Waddell, *Papago Indians at Work*, Anthropological Papers of the University of Arizona, no. 12 (Tucson, 1969), 3–5, 12–16, 23.

38. "Mexican-American Students Lacking?" *Tucson Citizen*, April 19, 1978; "Minority Plan," *Tucson Citizen*, November 8, 1982; John Spagnoli, "UA Posts Largest Minority-Student Increase in 8 Years," *Tucson Citizen*, November 16, 1983; Pence, "MEChA to Celebrate 30 Years of Activism"; Edward Lempinen, "UA Report on Minorities Urges Better Recruiting, Ethnic Studies," *Arizona Daily Star*, December 5, 1980; Raúl Gámez, "New Start, programa para ayudar a universitarios de minorías," *Tucson Citizen*, April 25, 1984.
39. Bob Svejcara, "UA Lacks Strong Minority Hiring," *Arizona Daily Star*, May 3, 1983; "Dismal Record at UA," *Tucson Citizen*, May 5, 1983; Lori Stiles, "Educators Zero In on Hispanics' Problems," *Lo Que Pasa*, November 7, 1983.
40. The children of Carlos C. Jácome to the University of Arizona Board of Regents, Box 1, Folder 40, Jácome Papers; Adolfo Quezada, "League Makes Many Dreams Come True," *Tucson Citizen*, August 24, 1979; "Scholarship Fund Drive to Begin," *Arizona Daily Star*, July 17, 1969.
41. "Minority Plan," *Tucson Citizen*, November 8, 1982; Leyla Cattan, "Los jóvenes de secundaria y los cursos en la UA," *Arizona Daily Star*, June 4, 1982.
42. "Walkout!" *El Coraje* 1(1) (March 1969); "Chicanos on the Move," *El Coraje* 1(2) (April 1969).
43. "Coraje," "Commitment Gap," and "A Call to Reason," in *El Coraje* 1(2) (April 1969); Officer, "Sodalities and Systemic Linkage," 108–109.
44. Dick Fowler, "El Rio Coalition Refused by City," *Arizona Daily Star*, August 10, 1970; Bill Kimmey and Neal Savage, "Group Back at El Rio," *Tucson Daily Citizen*, September 7, 1970; "A Park, Yes, but Golf Will Stay at El Rio," *Tucson Daily Citizen*, September 11, 1970; Bill Kimmey, "El Rio Meetings End," *Tucson Daily Citizen*, October 2, 1970; Felipe Jácome, e-mail to author, February 13, 2007; Alex Jácome Jr., interview by author, February 14, 2007.
45. Guadalupe Castillo, interview by author, March 20, 2008.
46. Alex Jácome, "Should Be Ashamed," *Arizona Daily Star*, April 29, 1970; Jácome to Alexandra DeGrazia, September 24, 1958, Box 1, Folder 46, Jácome Papers; Jácome to Paul Fannin, March 17, 1970, Box 1, Folder 33, Jácome Papers; Jácome to Luis Garibay, February 25, 1974, private collection of Estela Jácome; Jácome to Adam Schantz, August 1975, private collection of Estela Jácome; Webb-Vignery, *Jacome's Department Store*, 135–136; Macario Saldate, interview by author, March 10, 2008. "Chingado" translates loosely as "fucker."
47. "Call to Reason," *El Coraje;* Martin, interview; Isabel García, interview by author, March 18, 2008.
48. "'Chicanos' pretenden crear en E.U. la 'Republica de Aztlán,'" *El Imparcial*, August 3, 1986, 12A; Humberto Acuña, interview by author, March 18, 2008; María Eugenia Flores, interview by author, April 2, 2008.
49. Castillo, interview; Baldenegro, interview.

50. Jaime Pensado, "Student Politics in Mexico in the Wake of the Cuban Revolution," in *New World Coming: The Sixties and the Shaping of Global Consciousness,* ed. Karen Dubinsky et al, 332, 335 (Toronto, 2009); Jaime Pensado, "The (Forgotten) Sixties in Mexico," in *The Sixties: A Journal of History, Politics, and Culture* 1(1) (2008): 84; "Estado de Sonora, información de Hermosillo," February 26, 1967, Box 460, Folder 1, IPS; "Estado de Sonora, información de Hermosillo," March 1, 1967, Box 460, Folder 1, IPS; "Tensa situación en Hermosillo" and "Queremos estudiar, señor presidente," Box 1517A, Folder 491, IPS; "Represión fascista en la universidad," Folder "Micos," AH Uni-Son; "Cambio de 'poderes' en el estado," September 13, 1973, Folder "Diciembre 1973," AH Uni-Son; Walker, *Waking from the Dream,* 23–44.
51. Letter from Magdalena, Sonora, October 1973, Folder "Derecho," AH Uni-Son; "Cambio de 'poderes' en el estado"; "A la población de Hermosillo y del estado," September 12, 1973, Folder 22, "Manifiestos," February 22, 1972, to January 21, 1974, AH Uni-Son; "Editorial, PREFACIO responde a las necesidades actuales del movimiento estudiantil," *Prefacio* 3 (no date): 1–2; Pensado, "Student Politics in Mexico in the Wake of the Cuban Revolution," 336; "Manifiesto, las fuerzas más retrógradas del estado impiden el desarrollo de la universidad," Folder "Recortes de Periódico," AH Uni-Son.
52. "A quien sirvió realmente la revolución?" November 20, 1973, "Diciembre 1973," AH Uni-Son; Pensado, "Student Politics in Mexico in the Wake of the Cuban Revolution," 336; "Al pueblo de Magdalena, a los estudiantes," September 28, 1973, "Derecho," AH Uni-Son.
53. "Al pueblo de Magdalena, a los estudiantes"; "La lucha en el Yaqui, y la necesidad de la organización independiente de obreros, campesinos, y estudiantes," *Prefacio* 3 (no date): 3–4, 6; FEUS, "Dos de octubre, Tlatelolco," October 1973, *Expediente* 22, "Manifiestos," February 22, 1972, to January 21, 1974, AH Uni-Son.
54. "Recuerdan los sucesos del 68 en la Uni-Son," *El Sonorense,* October 3, 1972, 1; "La lucha de los estudiantes de Sinaloa," Folder 38, "Universidad de Sinaloa," December 1, 1971, to February 27, 1973, AH Uni-Son; Mario Cruz Sánchez G., "Vietnam: Impulsa la lucha revolucionaria mundial," *Prefacio* 2 (May 7, 1972): 6; "La situación en Chile," November 20, 1973, *Expediente* 21, AH, Uni-Son; "Sigue la ofensiva reaccionaria contra la universidad," "Diciembre 1973," AH Uni-Son; Guillermo Moreno Figueroa, "La patria desgarrada," Luis Mártinez, "Comunismo señuelo para los crédulos," *El Ahuizote* 1(5) (December 1972); Pensado, "Student Politics in Mexico in the Wake of the Cuban Revolution," 330–331.

55. "Organización, objetivos, y contenido del cogobierno en la escuela de derecho," "Derecho," AH Uni-Son; "Carta abierta de los estudiantes de la Uni-Son a los padres de familia y al pueblo," December 10, 1973, AH Uni-Son; *Historia general de Sonora*, vol. 5, 213–218; "La lucha en el Yaqui, y la necesidad de la organización independiente de obreros, campesinos y estudiantes," 3; "A los maestros y estudiantes, a la opinión pública," 3–4, Expediente 22, "Manifiestos," February 22, 1972, to January 21, 1974, AH Uni-Son.
56. For a discussion of this transition in the United States and Mexico more broadly, see Bethany Moreton, *To Serve God and Wal-Mart: The Making of Christian Free Enterprise* (Cambridge, 2010); Daniel Rodgers, *Age of Fracture* (Cambridge, 2012); Walker, *Waking from the Dream*.
57. Beverly Medlyn, "'First Step' Stirs Call for More Hispanics at UA," April 21, 1978, from ephemera file "Mexican-American News Clippings," AHS; Bob Svejcara, "Schaefer Asks to Quadruple Minority-Student Funds," *Arizona Daily Star*, June 17, 1981; Bob Svejcara, "Regents Vote $488,000 for UA Minority Program," *Arizona Daily Star*, July 12, 1981.
58. "'First Annual Event' of the Mexican American Studies & Research Center," March 25, 1986, SCUA; Raúl Gámez, "El 'Centro' de la universidad es centro de atención," *Tucson Citizen*, July 28, 1982; Judy Katrowitz, "UA Hispanic Alumni Association launched," *Tucson Citizen*, June 27, 1983; John Huerta, "Qué estamos pidiendo de Koffler y de la Universidad de Arizona?" *Tucson Citizen*, October 2, 1982; Ernesto Portillo, "Ya viene la Sociedad de Ex-Alumnos de U of A," *Tucson Citizen*, November 20, 1982
59. Jacoby, *Shadows at Dawn*, 238–239.
60. Shannon Travis, "Mexican-American Center Won't Be Closed, UA Says," *Tucson Citizen*, July 15, 1982; Bob Svejcara, "UA Hispanic Center May Be on Verge of Vanishing," *Arizona Daily Star*, July 11, 1982; Doug McDaniel, "Mexican-American Studies Wins Big in UA Budget," *Tucson Citizen*, October 11, 1982; Macario Saldate, interview by author, March 10, 2008.
61. Student senators, "MEChA Needs to Alter Intent If Senate Is to Provide Funds," *Arizona Daily Wildcat*, November 9, 1983; Maria Vigil, Douglas Kreutz, and Louis Sahagún, "Salomón Baldenegro: A Chicano Activist Mellows (a Little)," *Tucson Citizen*, November 22, 1980; Patrisia Gonzales and Shannon Travis, "UA Programs Focus on Minorities," *Tucson Citizen*, September 9, 1982; Judy Kantrowitz, "Recruiting Minorities at UA Takes New Tack," *Tucson Citizen*, April 22, 1983.
62. Keith Rosenblum, "To a Degree, Learning Links Tucson and Mexico; Peripatetic Professors, Students Cross Borders to Teach Each Other," *Arizona Daily Star*, July 5, 1987.

5. Violence and Sanctuary

1. Massey, "How Arizona Became Ground Zero in the War on Immigrants."
2. Hewitt de Alcántara, *Modernizing Mexican Agriculture*, 178–179, 248; Walker, *Waking from the Dream*, 73–140.
3. Lozano Ascencio et al., *Sonorenses en Arizona*, 100–102, 95–96, 129–130.
4. Ibid., 100–101.
5. Lytle Hernández, *Migra!*.
6. Guadarrama et al., *Historia General de Sonora*, vol. 5, 197, 213; Lozano Ascencio et al., *Sonorenses en Arizona*, 45; Almada, *Breve Historia de Sonora*, 163–168.
7. Lozano Ascencio et al., *Sonorenses en Arizona*, 140, 45–46; Jon Levine, "On the Border: Managing the Mexican Twin Plants," *Today's Business* (October 1980), 16; "Sobre asuntos migratorios y fronterizos," *Boletín Informativo* 9 (November–January, 1979–1980): 11; Latin America Area Center, University of Arizona, "Arizona's Relations with Northern Mexico, Fifty-First Arizona Town Hall" (Phoenix, 1987): 49, 128; Jim Kolbe, "Made in Mexico, Good for the U.S.A.," *New York Times*, December 13, 1987; Guadarrama et al., *Historia General de Sonora*, vol. 5, 197, 212–213; Leopoldo Santos Ramírez, "Sonora y Arizona en los '80s," *Revista de el Colegio de Sonora* 2 (1990): 363–364.
8. Lozano Ascencio et al., *Sonorenses en Arizona*, 47; Miguel Ángel Fernández, "Regularizarán el crecimiento de la fronteriza Nogales, Son.," *El Imparcial*, June 13, 1981, 1D; Santos Ramírez, "Sonora y Arizona en los '80s," 366–368, 370.
9. Arizona Office of Tourism advertisement, "Venga a ver Arizona ahora," *El Imparcial*, June 15, 1981, 7; Luis Orduño González, "Incrementa Nogales su afluencia turística," *El Imparcial*, July 5, 1981, 1D; El Con advertisement, *El Imparcial*, March 18, 1980, 3C; Ignatius Anthony de Gennaro and Robert J. Ritchey, *The Economic Impact of Mexican Visitors to Arizona* (Tucson, 1978), i–iv; Luis Armas, "Importante temario de la reunión fronteriza," *El Imparcial*, June 24, 1980, 1; Alejandro Silva Hurtado to Babbitt, October 21, 1981, Box 20, Folder 1, Governors Files (Babbitt), ASL (Babbitt Papers); Lozano Ascencio et al., *Sonorenses en Arizona*, 248–249.
10. Hal Brands, *Latin America's Cold War* (Cambridge, MA, 2010), 142, 154, 225; Guadarrama et al., *Historia General de Sonora*, vol. 5, 200, 214–215; Walker, *Waking from the Dream*.
11. Miguel Ángel Vázquez R., "Frontera norte: Notas sobre la importancia de su studio," *La Revista de la Universidad de Sonora* 1 (June 1985): 9; Brands, *Latin America's Cold War*, 97–163, 175, 195–197; Grandin, *Empire's Workshop*, 52–86.
12. Lozano Ascencio et al., *Sonorenses en Arizona*, 82–83, 127, 144.

13. Ibid., 5, 48–49, 84, 87, 89. 137, 140–141; http://www.census.gov/prod/www/decennial.html.
14. Cadava, "Borderlands of Modernity and Abandonment," 371–380; Lozano Ascencio et al., *Sonorenses en Arizona,* 53–54; Guadarrama et al., *Historia General de Sonora,* vol. 5, 311–312.
15. Babbitt to Ronald Reagan, May 3, 1984, Box 408, Folders 4290–4292, 1984, Babbitt Papers; "Floating Peso 'Confuses' Nogales," *Tucson Daily Citizen,* September 13, 1976; "Peso Fall Hurts Border Business," *Tucson Daily Citizen,* October 28, 1976; "Tortured Mexico Pins Hopes on New Leader," *Tucson Daily Citizen,* November 26, 1976; Georgie Anne Geyer "Prognosis for Mexico's Future: Not Good," *Tucson Daily Citizen,* March 11, 1977; "Peso Devaluation Blamed for 500 Border Layoffs," *Tucson Daily Citizen,* November 5, 1976; "Joblessness Up in Santa Cruz," *Tucson Daily Citizen,* December 6, 1976; "U.S.-Bound Traffic Dips in Nogales," *Tucson Daily Citizen,* December 27, 1976; "Nogales: Little Change," *Tucson Daily Citizen,* November 23, 1976.
16. Associated Press, "U.S. Border Towns Feeling Money Pinch," *Sun,* December 15, 1976; "Weak Peso Drives Mexican Cattle to U.S.," *New York Times,* January 3, 1977; Geyer, "Prognosis for Mexico's Future"; "Nogales: Little Change"; Lozano Ascencio et al., *Sonorenses en Arizona,* 173, 252–253; Frank Allen, "Mexico Stops Dollar Trading," *Tucson Daily Citizen,* November 22, 1976; "Tortured Mexico Pins Hopes on New Leader," *Tucson Daily Citizen,* November 26, 1976; Richard Salvatierra, "Devaluation May Not Help Mexico," *Tucson Daily Citizen,* September 16, 1976.
17. "Peso Devaluation Blamed for 500 Border Layoffs"; "Peso Loss Assistance Available," *Tucson Citizen,* November 9, 1977; "U.S. Should Weigh Peso Woes Relief," *Tucson Daily Citizen,* December 27, 1976; Luis Orduño González, "Puerta de México: El gran olvido," *El Imparcial,* June 27, 1981, 1; Cadava, "Borderlands of Modernity and Abandonment," 367–371.
18. Ngai, *Impossible Subjects,* 258.
19. David Gregory and Ambassador Robert McBride, "U.S./Mexican Migration and Bilateral Development Strategies," 1981, Box 21, Folder 11, Special Subjects, Babbitt Papers; Wayne Cornelius, "A Critique of the Carter Administration's Policy Proposals on Illegal Immigration," August 10, 1977, Box 21, Folder 11, Babbitt Papers, ASL; Mexican American Legal Defense Educational Fund (MALDEF), "Statement of Position regarding the Administration's Undocumented Alien Legislative Proposal," September 26, 1977, Box 21, Folder 11, Babbitt Papers; "Testimony of Vilma S. Martinez for Hearings on S.2252 before the Subcommittee on Immigration of the Senate Committee on the Judiciary," May 4, 1978, Box 21, Folder 11, Babbitt Papers.
20. Richard Lamm, "America's Most Difficult Issue: Immigration," December 9, 1980, Box 21, Folder 11, Babbitt Papers; Richard Lamm, "The Search for a

Realistic Immigration Policy," Box 21, Folder 11, Babbitt Papers; "Testimony by Governor Bruce Babbitt to the Select Commission on Immigration and Refugee Policy," February 4, 1980, Box 21, Folder 11, Babbitt Papers; Charles Polzer to Babbitt, June 2, 1981, Box 21, Folder 11, Babbitt Papers; Manuel García to Babbitt, October 8, 1981, Box 20, Folder 1, Governors Subject Files (Babbitt), "Immigration," ASL; Mexican Americans for Legalizing Aliens to Babbitt, October 22, 1981, Box 20, Folder 1, Governors Subject Files (Babbitt), "Immigration," ASL; Mark Acuff, "Immigration Issue Stirs Debate at Border Conference in El Paso," *New Mexico Independent*, October 9, 1981; Alberto Becerra Sierra to Babbitt, May 11, 1981, Box 20, Folder 9, Governors Subject Files (Babbitt), "Mexico," ASL.

21. *Hearings on S. 2252: Alien Adjustment and Employment Act of 1977, to Amend the Immigration and Nationality Act, and for Other Purposes, Part 2* (Washington, DC, 1979), 30–31, 150; "El Diputado Juan José Osorio externó la indignación del país por el brutal trato a tres mexicanos en Douglas, Arizona," *El Nacional*, August 25, 1976, 7.
22. Julia Consuela Gonzales, "From the Barrios to the Border: An Organizational History of the Manzo Area Council and Immigrants' Rights in Tucson, Arizona, from 1972 to 1986" (bachelor's thesis, Yale University, 2005), 12; *Hearings on S. 2252*, 30–31, 150.
23. Cowan, quoted in Gonzales, "From the Barrios to the Border," 48–50.
24. MALDEF, "Statement of Position regarding the Administration's Undocumented Alien Legislative Proposal"; "Testimony of Vilma S. Martinez"; Testimony of Antonio D. Bustamante, *U.S. Senate Hearings on S. 35 of the Civil Rights Improvement Act of 1977* (Washington, DC, 1978), 69; Al Senia, "U.S. Grand Jury in Ariz. Probes Alleged '76 Torture of Aliens," *Washington Post*, July 23, 1979; Gutiérrez, *Walls and Mirrors*, 179–205; Christine Marie Sierra, "In Search of National Power: Chicanos Working the System on Immigration Reform, 1976–1986," in *Chicano Politics and Society in the Late Twentieth Century*, ed. David Montejano, 131–153 (Austin, 1998).
25. "Creciente ola de robos en Nogales por posible banda bien organizada," *El Imparcial*, August 24, 1976, 6A; Christine Marin, "They Sought Work and Found Hell: The Hanigan Case of Arizona," *Perspectives in Mexican American Studies* 6 (1997): 98; Carol Trickett, "Friendly Border Town's Problems," *Yuma Daily Sun*, September 29, 1976.
26. Trickett, "Friendly Border Town's Problems"; Arnoldo de León, *They Called Them Greasers: Anglo Attitudes toward Mexicans in Texas, 1821–1900* (Austin, 1983).
27. Jeff Smith, "Burglary! Border Vigilantes Feared," *Tucson Daily Citizen*, February 4, 1977; Kathleen Belew, "Theaters of War: Paramilitarism, Mercenaries, and the Racist Right from Vietnam to Oklahoma City" (PhD diss., Yale University, 2011).

28. Tom Miller, *On the Border: Portraits of America's Southwestern Frontier* (Tucson, 1992), 145–146.
29. "Despiadado tormento a tres trabajadores mexicanos ilegales en Estados Unidos," *El Nacional*, August 22, 1976, 6; Miller, *On the Border*, 153.
30. Miller, *On the Border*, 157; Senia, "U.S. Grand Jury in Ariz."; *Hearings on S.* 2252, 30–31, 150; "El diputado Juan José Osorio externó la indignación del país."
31. "Ranchers in Alien Torture Case Will Seek to Counter Testimony," *United Press International*, February 16, 1981; Associated Press, "Defendant Spoke of Fixing Wetbacks, Surprise Witness Says," February 12, 1981; Larry López, "One Hanigan Jury Told of 'Wetback Hunts' as Others Deliberate," *Associated Press*, February 20, 1981; Miller, *On the Border*, 150; "Hanigan Jury Hears New Testimony," *Dispatch*, February 11, 1981.
32. Miller, *On the Border*, 157; "Orden de aprehensión contra los torturadores de 'braceros,' veredicto: ¡Culpable!" *El Imparcial*, August 28, 1976, 1–2.
33. Miller, *On the Border*, 164.
34. "Hanigans Found Innocent," *Sun*, October 9, 1977; Miller, *On the Border*, 165; "Mexican Torture Case," *Tucson Citizen*, October 11, 1977; "They Sought Work and Found Hell," 121n71; "Ads in Mexico Propose 'Hanigan Boycott,'" *Tucson Citizen*, October 24, 1977; Gonzales, "From the Barrios to the Border," 35; "Bomba de alto poder hallada en el rancho de los Hannigan," *El Imparcial*, August 29, 1976, 1, 6.
35. Gutiérrez, *Walls and Mirrors*, 179–205; Marin, "They Sought Work and Found Hell," 114, 116; Testimony of Antonio D. Bustamante, 69; Senia, "U.S. Grand Jury in Ariz."
36. "Castigo a victimarios, pero también más fuentes de trabajo para evitar salida de mexicanos," *El Imparcial*, August 26, 1976, 1; "Es injustificable que las autoridades de EU no hayan aprehendido a los responsables de las torturas a tres trabajadores mexicanos," *El Nacional*, August 29, 1976, 12; Miller, *On the Border*, 156; Antonio Murguía Rosete, "Los trabajadores migratorios indocumentados," *El Nacional*, August 24, 1976, 5; "Vejaciones a tres trabajadores mexicanos en Douglas, Arizona," *El Nacional*, August 22, 1976, 1; "El diputado Juan José Osorio externó la indignación del páis"; "Mexican Role Visible in U.S. Trial of Arizona Ranchers," *New York Times*, July 7, 1980.
37. "Governor, Mexico React to Torture," *Daily Dispatch*, August 25, 1976; Murguía Rosete, "Los trabajadores migratorios indocumentados."
38. Murguía Rosete, "Los trabajadores migratorios indocumentados"; Miguel Ángel Fernández, "Intensifican vigilancia aduanal por las vacaciones en Nogales," *El Imparcial*, June 27, 1981, 1D; "Deportarán de México a dos estadounidenses indeseables," *El Imparcial*, August 31, 1976, 1; Rogelio Olivares A., "Estrechan relaciones las policías de Sonora-Arizona," *El Imparcial*, June 3, 1981, D1.

39. "¿Qué se proponen los que vejaron a tres mexicanos?" *El Nacional,* August 24, 1976, 5; "J. L. P. demanda respeto de E.U.," *El Imparcial,* June 27, 1980, 1; Gerardo Canseco, "Indispensable madurar actitudes entre México y Estados Unidos," *El Sonorense,* July 1, 1980, 4A; "Impugnan en EU a los legisladores que nos acusan de ir al comunismo," *El Nacional,* August 27, 1976, 13; "México y EU deben olvidar rencores: JLP," *El Sonorense,* June 27, 1980, 1; Miller, *On the Border,* 167; "Durarán años aún las pláticas con Estados Unidos sobre los indocumentados, declara Jorge Castañeda," *El Nacional,* March 25, 1981.
40. "¿Qué se proponen los que vejaron a tres mexicanos?"; "Governor, Mexico React to Torture"; "La agresión a mexicanos en Arizona, reflejo de la violencia mundial," *El Nacional,* August 25, 1976, 7; "Comisión Sonora-Arizona, vía para mejorar relaciones," *El Imparcial,* July 12, 1986; Jesús Carrasco Sharpe, "Guaymas será la sede de la próxima reunión del Comité Sonora-Arizona," *El Sonorense,* July 5, 1980, 1; "Ciudad Obregón y Tucson se declaran ciudades hermanas," *El Imparcial,* July 3, 1986, 1D; "Indispensable madurar actitudes entre México y Estados Unidos."
41. Gonzales, "From the Barrios to the Border," 2, 21, 23, 30, 35; Lozano Ascencio et al., *Sonorenses en Arizona,* 182, 186, 196–197; Sheridan, *Arizona,* 295.
42. "Border Leaders Hope to Smooth Relations," *Dispatch,* June 25, 1980; "Mexican Role Visible in U.S. Trial of Arizona Ranchers," *New York Times,* July 7, 1980; Latin America Area Center, "Arizona's Relations with Northern Mexico," 134; "U.S. Grand Jury in Ariz. Probes Alleged '76 Torture of Aliens"; "Inician el proceso en contra de quienes torturaron a 3 braceros," *El Sonorense,* June 27, 1980, 1; "Hispanic Groups Seek a New Federal Trial in Arizona Alien Case," *New York Times,* August 4, 1980; "Marchers Call for Retrial," *Washington Post,* August 4, 1980; John M. Crewdson, "Mistrial Declared for 2 Arizonans Charged with Torturing 3 Aliens," *New York Times,* July 30, 1980; "Hispanics React Angrily to Mistrial Ruling in Hanigan Case," *Associated Press,* July 30, 1980; Maria Vigíl, Douglas Kreutz, and Louis Sahagún, "The Academic Connection," *Tucson Citizen,* November 22, 1980; Maria Vigil, Douglas Kreutz, and Louis Sahagún, "Spanish-Language Radio," *Tucson Citizen,* November 22, 1980; Miller, *On the Border,* 171.
43. "Hanigans to Be Tried in Prescott," *Dispatch,* November 4, 1980; Minnie Stella to Babbitt, January 8, 1981, Box 19, Folder 26, Governors Subject Files (Babbitt), "Mexico," ASL; "Paper War Looms in Alien Torture Case," *Associated Press,* December 22, 1980; "Arizona Ranchers Face 3d Trial on Charges of Beating Mexicans," *New York Times,* January 20, 1981.
44. "Two Juries to Weigh Mexicans' Charges," *New York Times,* January 24, 1981; Marin, "They Sought Work and Found Hell," 96; "Acquitted Rancher Is Held on Drug Charges in Arizona," *New York Times,* April 16, 1981.

45. "Hanigans' 2nd Trial to Start Thursday," *Casa Grande, Ariz., Dispatch,* June 25, 1980; Charles Babcock, "2 Arizona Ranchers Indicted; U.S. Charges They Beat, Robbed Three Mexicans," *Washington Post,* October 17, 1979; "New Legal Weapon for Illegal Aliens," *New York Times,* March 1, 1981; Senia, "U.S. Grand Jury in Ariz."; "Inician el proceso en contra de quienes torturaron a 3 braceros."
46. Babcock, "2 Arizona Ranchers Indicted"; Miller, *On the Border,* 169.
47. Maria Cristina García, *Seeking Refuge: Central American Migration to Mexico, the United States, and Canada* (Berkeley, 2006), 1–12; Santos Ramírez, "Sonora y Arizona en los '80s," 371.
48. García, *Seeking Refuge,* 1, 9, 11, 45, 53, 69.
49. Leyla Cattan and Heberto Méndez, "Mueren en el desierto 13 indocumentados," *El Imparcial,* July 7, 1980, 1; "Aliens Fear for Families' Safety," *Dispatch,* July 11, 1980; Hillary Cunningham, *God and Caesar at the Rio Grande: Sanctuary and the Politics of Religion* (Minneapolis, 1995), 13; García, *Seeking Refuge,* 85; "Pide El Salvador castigo a 'polleros,'" *El Imparcial,* July 9, 1980, 1.
50. Ernesto Portillo Jr., "Corbett's Legacy: Aid to Helpless," *Arizona Daily Star,* August 8, 2001.
51. Gonzales, "From the Barrios to the Border," 52–53; Cunningham, *God and Caesar,* 32.
52. Cunningham, *God and Caesar,* 15, 62; Isabel García, quoted in Gonzales, "From the Barrios to the Border," 52.
53. Gonzales, "From the Barrios to the Border," 52–53, 55–56; García, *Seeking Refuge,* 31; Cunningham, *God and Caesar,* 15; Miguel Ángel Fernández, "Estrecha vigilancia para evitar la llegada de 'ilegales' a Nogales, Son.," *El Imparcial,* June 4, 1981.
54. Gonzales, "From the Barrios to the Border," 52; M. Nelson to Babbitt, May 23, 1985, Box 451, Folder 4727, Babbitt Papers.
55. Cunningham, *God and Caesar,* 16, 34; undated letter from the "Task Force for Central America," from ephemera file, "Sanctuary Movement," AHS; Stephanie Innes, "Entrant Aid: From Covert to Overt, New Samaritan Patrol Has Roots in Hidden Sanctuary Movement," *Arizona Daily Star,* July 17, 2002; Dagoberto Quiñones, interview by Benjamín Alonso Rascón, October 4, 2012.
56. Cunningham, *God and Caesar,* 27, 34; Ernesto Portillo Jr., "Corbett's Legacy: Aid to Helpless," *Arizona Daily Star,* August 8, 2001; Tim Steller, "Sanctuary Movement Co-Founder Dies at 67," *Arizona Daily Star,* August 3, 2001; Santos Ramírez, "Sonora y Arizona en los '80s," 371.
57. Brands, *Latin America's Cold War,* 189, 191, 206; Fife, quoted in García, *Seeking Refuge,* 99; Santos Ramírez, "Sonora y Arizona en los '80s," 371.
58. García, *Seeking Refuge,* 2.

59. Ibid., 9, 24, 95; Cunningham, *God and Caesar*, 56; Luis Orduño Gonzalez, "Sentencian a primeros miembros del grupo Santuario," *El Imparcial*, July 2, 1986, 4A; Santos Ramírez, "Sonora y Arizona en los '80s," 371.
60. Robert Reinhold, "Churches and U.S. Clash on Alien Sanctuary," *New York Times*, June 28, 1984; Santos Ramírez, "Sonora y Arizona en los '80s," 371; Cunningham, *God and Caesar*, 59; Peter Appleboime, "5 Given Probation in Alien Smuggling," *New York Times*, July 2, 1986; "Mañana la sentencia en el caso Santuario," *El Imparcial*, July 1, 1986, 4A; Luis Gómez, "Aumenta el flujo de ilegales a los EU," *El Imparcial*, July 2, 1986, 1D; Orduño Gonzalez, "Sentencian a primeros miembros del grupo Santuario," 4A; Daniel R. Browning, "Convicted Vow to Seek Appeals," *Arizona Daily Star*, May 2, 1986.
61. Cunningham, *God and Caesar*, 34, 62; García, *Seeking Refuge*, 93, 107–108; Melinda Beck and Niiki Finke Greenberg, "'This Is a Freedom Train,'" *Newsweek*, April 2, 1984; "Refugees: John Brown Is Back," *Economist*, January 11, 1986.
62. Alejandro Oláis Olivas, "México, el país más importante para EU, ilegales deben tener derecho a trabajar en Norteamérica," *El Sonorense*, July 6, 1980, 1; Tom Beal, "Few Hold Hope for 3-Point Immigration 'Cure,'" March 15, 1981; Michael Gómez to Babbitt, June 11, 1981, Box 20, Folder 9, Governors Subject Files (Babbitt), "Mexico," ASL.
63. "Promulga R. Reagan la ley anti-ilegales," *El Imparcial*, November 7, 1986, 1; "Pretende frenar el flujo de extranjeros," *El Imparcial*, November 7, 1986, 1; Lozano Ascencio et al., *Sonorenses en Arizona*, 65; Gonzales, "From the Barrios to the Border," 69.
64. Gregory and McBride, "U.S./Mexican Migration and Bilateral Development Strategies," 14; Joe González to Babbitt, May 20, 1981, Box 20, Folder 9, Governors Subject Files (Babbitt), "Mexico," ASL; MALDEF, "Statement of Position regarding the Administration's Undocumented Alien Legislative Proposal"; "Testimony by Governor Bruce Babbitt to the Select Commission on Immigration and Refugee Policy"; Mark Acuff, "Immigration Issue Stirs Debate at Border Conference in El Paso," *New Mexico Independent*, October 9, 1981.
65. Gonzales, "From the Barrio to the Border," 61, 63; "No habrá deportación masiva: Pilliod," *El Imparcial*, November 7, 1986, 1; Gary Stark to Babbitt, July 16, 1986, Box 523, Folder 5402, Babbitt Papers.
66. Bruce Babbitt, "Remarks by Governor Bruce Babbitt to Association of Immigration and Naturalization Lawyers," January 23, 1981, Babbitt Papers.
67. "No habrá deportación masiva"; "Psicosis de persecución entre los indocumentados," *El Sonorense*, January 11, 1982; Más del millón de deportados se esperan este año," *El Sonorense*, January 4, 1982, 1; Gregory and McBride, "U.S./

Mexican Migration and Bilateral Development Strategies" 4–5; "Ley Simpson-Rodino, una nueva espina," *El Imparcial*, November 8, 1986, 1.

68. Testimony of Antonio D. Bustamante, 77; "Jury Considers Case of 2 Brothers Charged with Torturing 3 Aliens," *New York Times*, July 25, 1980; "Rancher Sentenced to Prison for 1976 Attack on Mexicans," *Associated Press*, April 20, 1981; "Acquitted Rancher Is Held on Drug Charges in Arizona," *New York Times*, April 16, 1981; *Denver Post Magazine*, August 7, 1983; Cunningham, *God and Caesar*, 52.

6. Two Horsemen

1. Walker, *Waking from the Dream*, 105–140; Kropp, *California Vieja*, 73–88.
2. Santos Ramírez, "Sonora y Arizona en los '80s," 363, 365, 380; Jerry Ladman, "Mexico's Influence on the U.S. Economy," unpublished paper from the conference "The United States and Mexico: Ties That Bind," November 11–12, 1983, 27, Box 408, Folder 4291, Babbitt Papers; Walker, *Waking from the Dream*, 75–103, 173–199.
3. Santos Ramírez, "Sonora y Arizona en los '80s," 363, 365–367, 372–373.
4. Ladman, "Mexico's Influence on the U.S. Economy," 24, 37, 39, 41; Brands, *Latin America's Cold War*, 225; Santos Ramírez, "Sonora y Arizona en los '80s," 363, 365.
5. Babbitt to Lewis Murphy, June 15, 1981, Box 20, Folder 9, Governors Subject Files (Babbitt), "Mexico," ASL; Dantón Rodríguez, "Discurso pronunciado por el Lic. Luis Dantón Rodríguez," June 30, 1981, in possession of Augustine García; Leyla Cattan, "Villa, el drama de la revolución," *Arizona Daily Star*, July 19, 1981; Joe Burchell, "Villa Wins Another Campaign as Statue Gets Spot Downtown," *Arizona Daily Star*, July 1, 1981; Burchell, "Mayor to Be 'Unavailable' at Villa Statue Unveiling," *Arizona Daily Star*, June 26, 1981; Arizona Inn lunch menu for unveiling ceremony, June 30, 1981, in possession of Augustine García.
6. Geraldo Cadava, "Looking a Mexican Gift Horse in the Mouth: The Controversy Surrounding Pancho Villa in Downtown Tucson," unpublished paper, in author's possession; Lydia Otero, "La Placita Committee: Claiming Place and History," in *Mapping Memories and Migrations: Locating Boricua/Chicana Histories*, ed. Vicki Ruiz and John Chávez, 44–68 (Champaign, IL, 2008); Lydia Otero, "The Francisco 'Pancho' Villa Statue: Tucson's Welcoming Mat," unpublished paper, in author's possession.
7. Friedrich Katz, *The Life and Times of Pancho Villa* (Stanford, 1998), 2.
8. Augustine García, interview by author, August 10, 2005; ANPE publication promoting the statue, in possession of Augustine García; Salayandia Najera to José López Portillo, January 9, 1981, Box 19, Folder 23, Governors Subject Files (Babbitt), "Tucson, General Corres., 1981," ASL.

9. Cattan, "Estatuas de Pancho Villa," *Arizona Daily Star,* July 26, 1981; "A Park for Pancho," *Arizona Daily Star,* June 29, 1981; "The Dedication of the Padre Kino Memorial Statue," Tucson, AZ, January 13, 1989, AHS; Babbitt to Murphy, March 6, 1981, Box 19, Folder 23; Murphy to Babbitt, March 12, 1981, Box 19, Folder 23; Babbitt to Dolores Hubik, July 22, 1981, Box 19, Folder 23; Charles Ford to Babbitt, August 3, 1981, Box 19, Folder 23. Letters from Governors Subject Files (Babbitt), "Tucson, General Corres., 1981," ASL. Also see Roberto Fierro Villalobos to Babbitt, August 13, 1981, Box 20, Folder 9, Governors Subject Files (Babbitt), "Mexico," ASL.
10. Ladman, "Mexico's Influence on the U.S. Economy," 2, 12–13, 21, 23, 40, 43, 47; Samuel Ocaña, *Sonora, Tercer Informe de Gobierno* (Hermosillo, 1982), 87; Rodolfo Félix, *Primer Informe de Gobierno* (Hermosillo, 1986); Félix, *III Informe de Gobierno* (Hermosillo, 1988); Félix, *V Informe de Gobierno* (Hermosillo, 1990).
11. Jorge Domínguez and Rafael Fernández de Castro, *The United States and Mexico: Between Partnership and Conflict* (New York, 2001), Introduction; Ladman, "Mexico's Influence on the U.S. Economy," 31, 34, 43, 45; Octavio Paz, "Reflections: Mexico and the United States," *New Yorker,* September 17, 1979, 141–142.
12. George Parker, "Tucson's 'Gullible Gringos,'" *Tucson Citizen,* May 30, 1981; Cattan, "Estatuas de Pancho Villa"; "Park for Pancho"; "Pobre Pancho!" *Arizona Daily Star,* March 30, 1981; José Gonzalo Martínez, "A Practical Joke?" *Tucson Citizen,* July 8, 1981.
13. Friedrich Katz, *The Secret War in Mexico: Europe, the United States, and the Mexican Revolution* (Chicago, 1981), 263; Katz, *Life and Times of Pancho Villa,* 225.
14. Don Coerver and Linda Hall, "The Arizona-Sonora Border and the Mexican Revolution, 1910–1920," in *The Mexican Borderlands,* ed. Félix Almaráz Jr., 77, 79 (Manhattan, KS, 1985); Katz, *Secret War in Mexico,* 284; Katz, *Life and Times of Pancho Villa.*
15. Thomas Naylor, "Massacre at San Pedro de la Cueva: The Significance of Pancho Villa's Disastrous Sonora Campaign," *Western Historical Quarterly* 8(2) (April 1977): 125–150; Katz, *Life and Times of Pancho Villa,* 532–33; Katz, *Secret War in Mexico,* 302, 308; Coerver and Hall, "Arizona-Sonora Border and the Mexican Revolution," 80–82; Katz, "Pancho Villa and the Attack on Columbus, New Mexico," *American Historical Review* 83(1) (February 1978): 109–112, 114.
16. Katz, "Pancho Villa and the Attack on Columbus, New Mexico," 101, 126, 128–129; Katz, *Secret War in Mexico,* 303; Thomas Benjamin, *La Revolución: Mexico's Great Revolution as Memory, Myth, and History* (Austin, 2000), 56; Martin, *Lamp in the Desert,* 128–129; "Tucsonans Feared Villa Would Invade," *Arizona Daily Star,* February 3, 1985.
17. Benjamin, *La Revolución,* 69, 71, 135–136, 150, 159; Katz, *Life and Times of Pancho Villa,* 790–792; "Pancho Villa Finally Official Mexican Hero," *Tucson*

Citizen, November 9, 1976, 135–136; Matt Prichard, "Pancho Villa Crosses over Rio Grande: Statue Making Its Way to Home in Park Here," *Tucson Citizen,* May 14, 1981.

18. "Pancho Villa Finally Official Mexican Hero, Body to Be in Crypt," *Tucson Citizen,* November 19, 1976; Manuel Gamio, *Forjando patria (pro nacionalismo)* (Mexico City, 1916); Dantón Rodríguez, "Discurso pronunciado por el Lic. Luis Dantón Rodríguez."
19. John De Witt, "Non-Violent Pancho Villa a Gift to Arizona," *Arizona Daily Star,* March 21, 1981; Steve Meissner, "Villa Shot out of Saddle," *Arizona Daily Star,* March 26, 1981; Matt Prichard, "Villa Statue on Its Way Here," *Tucson Citizen,* May 7, 1981; Keith Rosenblum, "Pancho Villa Back in the Saddle and Riding toward Tucson Again," *Arizona Daily Star,* April 28, 1981; Steve Meissner, "Viva Villa!," *Arizona Daily Star,* May 15, 1981; Prichard, "Pancho Villa Crosses over Rio Grande," *Tucson Citizen,* May 14, 1981.
20. Prichard, "Villa Statue on Its Way Here"; Donald Trephano to Babbitt, May 15, 1981, Box 20, Folder 9; Mary McCormack to Babbitt, July 22, 1981, Box 20, Folder 9; Babbitt to McCormack, August 24, 1981, Box 20, Folder 9, Letters from Governors Subject Files (Babbitt), "Mexico," ASL. Also see Art Schommer to Babbitt, May 20, 1981, Box 19, Folder 23, Governors Subject Files (Babbitt), "Tucson, General Corres., 1981," ASL.
21. Burchell, "Mayor to Be 'Unavailable' at Villa Statue Unveiling"; Michael Chihak, "Pancho Villa Rides Onward to Downtown, *Tucson Citizen,* June 22, 1981; "Lawsuit Seeks to Block Villa Statue Here," *Arizona Daily Star,* June 2, 1981; Edward Humes, "Tucsonian Fights to Get Villa to Ride out of Town," *Tucson Citizen,* July 20, 1982; Shannon Travis, "Villa to Continue His Ride in City, Removal Denied," *Tucson Citizen,* April 6, 1983.
22. "Lawsuit Seeks to Block Villa Statue Here"; Humes, "Tucsonian Fights to Get Villa to Ride out of Town"; Travis, "Villa to Continue His Ride in City, Removal Denied"; Joe Watt, "Villa-Plagued Veteran Wants Statue Removed," *Arizona Daily Star,* June 22, 1983.
23. Sam Negri, "Critics Fire on Pancho Villa Statue," *Arizona Republic,* November 17, 1982; Kreutz, "Villa's Statue: Disgrace or Honor?" *Tucson Citizen,* May 15, 1981; Otero, "Francisco 'Pancho' Villa Statue."
24. Negri, "Critics Fire on Pancho Villa Statue"; Raúl Aguirre, interview by author, August 22, 2005.
25. Babbitt to Richard Cruz, May 30, 1984, Box 408, Folders 4290–4292, Babbitt Papers.
26. David Montejano, ed., *Chicano Politics and Society in the Late Twentieth Century,* xviii–xx (Austin, 1999); Silviana Wood, "And Where Was Pancho Villa When You Really Needed Him?" in *Puro Teatro: A Latina Anthology,* ed. Alberto Sandoval-Sánchez and Nancy Saporta Sternbach, 176–193 (Tucson,

2000); Carmen Duarte, "Landless Fight for the Right to Realize Dreams," *Arizona Daily Star,* May 22, 1983.

27. Duarte, "Act of Respect for Pancho Villa"; Jim Maish, "Who Was That Fellow Named Pancho Villa?" *Tucson Citizen,* August 1, 1981.
28. Mary Pat Brady, *Extinct Landscapes, Temporal Geographies: Chicana Literature and the Urgency of Space* (Durham, NC, 2002), 8; Otero, "Francisco 'Pancho' Villa Statue"; Phil Hamilton, "Service Will Protest Presence of Villa Statue," *Tucson Citizen,* March 9, 1989; Joe Burchell, "Pancho Villa Statue Draws 1-Man Protest," *Arizona Daily Star,* March 10, 1990.
29. "Dedication of the Padre Kino Memorial Statue."
30. "Three Tributes to Father Kino Worth the Price," unpublished paper, dated August 28, 1987, from ephemera folder, AHS; Kieran McCarty to Babbitt, July 23, 1981, Box 20, Folder 9, Governors Subject Files (Babbitt), "Mexico," ASL.
31. Tom Turner, "Historical Society Commissions Sculptor to Make Kino Statues," *Arizona Daily Star,* August 8, 1987; "Three Tributes to Father Kino Worth the Price."
32. Turner, "Historical Society Commissions Sculptor to Make Kino Statues"; Arthur Rotstein, "3 Nations to Get Kino Statues," *Tucson Citizen,* August 12, 1987; "Dedication of the Padre Kino Memorial Statue."
33. Larry Copenhaver, "Kino Likeness a Reality," *Tucson Citizen,* October 12, 1988; M. Eric Hood, "Historical Group to Seek $48,000 from City for Father Kino Statues," *Tucson Citizen,* October 15, 1987; Deborah Latish, "City Council OKs Kino Statue Funds," *Tucson Citizen,* October 27, 1987; Chris Limberis, "County Joins in Honoring 'Early Developer' Kino," *Arizona Daily Star,* November 4, 1987; Joe Burchell, "Kino Is City's New Roadside Attraction," *Arizona Daily Star,* January 14, 1989; Turner, "Historical Society Commissions Sculptor to Make Kino Statues"; "Three Tributes to Father Kino Worth the Price"; "A Man for All Time," *Arizona Daily Star,* August 30, 1987.
34. Copenhaver, "Kino Likeness a Reality."
35. "Dedication of the Padre Kino Memorial Statue."
36. Turner, "Historical Society Commissions Sculptor to Make Kino Statues"; Rotstein, "3 Nations to Get Kino Statues"; Larry Copenhaver, "Italians Come 4,000 Miles, Fail to See Monument," unpublished paper, no date, from ephemera folder, AHS; "Dedication of the Padre Kino Memorial Statue"; John Jennings, "Tucson to Give Statue Replica to Kino's Italian Hometown," *Tucson Citizen,* June 8, 1991; Enric Volante, "Father Kino's Hometown to Honor Explorer," *Arizona Daily Star,* June 9, 1991.
37. Kropp, *California Vieja,* 6–7; Christopher Schmidt-Nowara, "Meanings of the Spanish Missions: Local Origins and Global Empires, Tucson, Arizona," 3,

unpublished paper delivered at the annual meeting of the Society for Spanish and Portuguese Historical Studies, April 3–6, 2008, in the author's possession.

38. Schmidt-Nowara, "Meanings of the Spanish Missions," 2–4.
39. Ibid., 6–7.
40. *Acceptance of the Statue of Eusebio Francisco Kino, Presented by the State of Arizona*, pamphlet for the proceedings in the rotunda, U.S. Capitol, February 14, 1965, 44.
41. Quoted in Schmidt-Nowara, "Meanings of the Spanish Missions," 6–7; *Revista de Historia* 5 (April–June 1982): 13; "Acceptance of Statue of Eusebio Francisco Kino," address by Hon. Carl Hayden, in *Acceptance of the Statue of Eusebio Francisco Kino*, 41–42.
42. *Revista de Historia*, 2 (April–June 1981): 6; Leyla Cattan, "Mexico's Culture Is under Attack from the North," *Arizona Daily Star*, May 22, 1983, 47; "Festejos por el tricentenario de la llegada del padre Kino," *El Imparcial*, July 2, 1986, 1.
43. Rotstein, "3 Nations to Get Kino Statues"; "Three Tributes to Father Kino Worth the Price"; Chris Limberis, "County Joins in Honoring 'Early Developer' Kino," *Arizona Daily Star*, November 4, 1987; Larry Copenhaver, "After Rough Trip, Kino Statue Due Here Monday," *Tucson Citizen*, December 3, 1988; Enrique Mazón, quoted in Cattan, "Mexico's Culture Is under Attack from the North," 47.
44. "Three Tributes to Father Kino Worth the Price"; "Man for All Time"; Hood, "Historical Group to Seek $48,000 from City for Father Kino Statues"; Latish, "City Council OKs Kino Statue Funds"; "Dedication of the Padre Kino Memorial Statue"; Burchell, "Kino Is City's New Roadside Attraction"; Volante, "Father Kino's Hometown to Honor Explorer"; Rotstein, "3 Nations to Get Kino Statues"; "Three Tributes to Father Kino Worth the Price"; "Kino Fans to Take Statue to Hometown in Italy," *Tucson Citizen*, January 18, 1991; Jennings, "Tucson to Give Statue Replica to Kino's Italian Hometown."
45. "Three Tributes to Father Kino Worth the Price"; "Dedication of the Padre Kino Memorial Statue."
46. "Dedication of the Padre Kino Memorial Statue."
47. *Revista de Historia* 2 (April–June 1981): 6, 13; Rotstein, "3 Nations to Get Kino Statues"; "Three Tributes to Father Kino Worth the Price"; "Man for All Time"; Latish, "City Council OKs Kino Statue Funds"; "Dedication of the Padre Kino Memorial Statue"; Volante, "Father Kino's Hometown to Honor Explorer."
48. "Man for All Time"; Copenhaver, "After Rough Trip, Kino Statue Due Here Monday"; "Festejos por el tricentenario de la llegada del padre Kino"; http://www.sanxaviermission.org/Tohono.html; Cadava, "Borderlands of Modernity and Abandonment"; Itzkuauhtli Benedicto Zamora Sáenz, "Topografías

antropológicas: Territorialidad O'odham y dinámicas regionales del desierto de Sonora," Master's thesis, la Universidad Nacional Autónoma de México, 2006, 58, 70, 103, 108–117, 154–156.

49. Rotstein, "3 Nations to Get Kino Statues"; "Three Tributes to Father Kino Worth the Price"; Burchell, "Kino Is City's New Roadside Attraction"; Volante, "Father Kino's Hometown to Honor Explorer."
50. Associated Press, "Father Kino Statue Starts Mexico City-to-Tucson Trip," *Arizona Republic*, November 27, 1988; Copenhaver, "After Rough Trip, Kino Statue Due Here Monday."
51. Burchell, "Kino Is City's New Roadside Attraction"; Copenhaver, "Kino Likeness a Reality"; "Dedication of the Padre Kino Memorial Statue."
52. "Three Tributes to Father Kino Worth the Price"; Rotstein, "3 Nations to Get Kino Statues"; "Dedication of the Padre Kino Memorial Statue."
53. Burchell, "Kino Is City's New Roadside Attraction"; Copenhaver, "Kino Likeness a Reality."
54. "Kino Fans to Take Statue to Hometown in Italy"; Volante, "Father Kino's Hometown to Honor Explorer."
55. Raul Aguirre, quoted in "Villa's Death Mask Returned," date and publication unknown, from ephemera file, "Places-Arizona-Tucson-Parks-Veinte de Agosto Park (1977–)," AHS; "Respect Others' Heroes," *Tucson Citizen*, July 8, 1981; Maish, "Who Was That Fellow Named Pancho Villa?"
56. Tom Beal, "No Need for a Prop. 187 in Arizona," *Arizona Daily Star*, November 17, 1994.

Conclusion

1. Ray Siqueiros, "Tortilla-Throwing Is an Ugly 'Tradition,'" *People's World Weekly*, March 23, 2002, http://www.peoplesworld.org/tortilla-throwing-is-an-ugly-tradition/, accessed on March 27, 2013.
2. Douglas S. Massey, Jorge Durand, and Nolan J. Malone, *Beyond Smoke and Mirrors* (New York, 2003); Statement of Stephen Pitti, "Shortfalls of the 1986 Immigration Reform Legislation," before the House Committee on Judiciary Subcommittee on Immigration, Citizenship, Refugees, Border Security, and International Law, April 19, 2007.
3. Office of the Border Patrol website, http://cbp.gov/xp/cgov/about/organization/assist_comm_off/border_patrol.xml, accessed on April 18, 2013.
4. Thomas Whittingslow, "Case Study: Beyond Borders Binational Art Foundation (501 C-3)," 1.
5. Thomas Whittingslow, interview by author, March 8, 2006; Ernesto Portillo Jr., "Art's Meaning on the Border Is in the Eye of the Beholder," *Arizona Daily Star*, April 24, 2002; Margaret Regan, "Artistic Warning: A Group including

Tucsonan Alfred Quiróz Hopes to Send a Message about Border-Crossing Deaths with Their Gigantic Nogales Border Art," *Tucson Weekly*, May 13, 2004; Alberto Morackis and Guadalupe Serrano, interview by author, March 11, 2006.

6. Luke Turf, "Border Art," *Tucson Citizen*, January 14, 2003; Alexis Blue, "Straddling a Fragile Border," *Arizona Daily Wildcat*, September 15, 2003.
7. Alberto Morackis, quoted in Anthony Broadman, "Steel Yourself for Reality," *Arizona Daily Star*, September 22, 2003, E1.
8. Ibid.

ACKNOWLEDGMENTS

In many ways, this book is an exploration of the histories that led to my family's settlement in Tucson after World War II. They came from different places: West Virginia, Pennsylvania, Panama, Colombia, Mexico, and the Philippines. My grandfathers, who were tech sergeants in the U.S. Air Force, traveled the hemisphere before landing at Davis-Monthan Air Force Base. When they retired from the military, they held maintenance, dishwashing, and mining jobs. When miners went on strike, women picked up work, cleaning houses to support the family. Grandma Dorla tells stories about her relatives far away, back east, and Grandma Gloria tells stories about her parents, Pete and Anna Lujan. Pete was the first person to sell Pepsi in Safford, Arizona, Grandma Gloria says, and everyone in town spoke of Anna's superior customer service at J. C. Penney's. I am so lucky that all four of my grandparents have seen this story through to the end. In ways that I was not aware of when I began this book, they—and their children, my parents—inspired me to write it.

At Yale University, I had terrific graduate mentors. Stephen Pitti continues to amaze me with his generosity, thoughtfulness, precision, and fun spirit. John Mack Faragher is a sharp critic and great role model, Alicia Schmidt Camacho has always pushed me to think critically about the U.S.-Mexico borderlands, and Gil Joseph helped me consider the possibilities of transnational Mexican history. Also encouraging my work on this book from its earliest stages were other teachers at Yale, including Jean-Christophe Agnew, David Blight, Jon Butler, Seth Fein, Matthew Frye Jacobson, Kellie Jones, and Patricia Pessar. Florence Thomas and Marcy Kaufman of Yale's Department of History; Victorine Shepard in American Studies; Nancy Phillips in Ethnicity, Race, and Migration; and Carl Pullen at Sterling Memorial Library—all of whom made Yale run smoothly for me. I thank them for their patience, guidance, and help.

Chicago is now home, and I have here an extremely supportive and talented group of friends. I could not find better people to work with than the scholars in Northwestern University's Department of History, Program in Latina and Latino Studies and Program in American Studies. From the very beginning of my time here, I have felt their belief in me. Thanks also go to the students in my classes on Latino and U.S.-Mexico borderlands history; Northwestern's College of Cultural and Community Studies; and Valerie Jiménez, Melissa Santana-Rivera, and Melanie Hall, spectacular doctoral students all. It has also been a pleasure to cochair the Newberry Library's Seminar in Borderlands and Latino Studies with Marc Rodríguez, John Alba Cutler, Benjamin Johnson, and Jason Ruiz. Thanks also to Danny Greene, Liesl Olson, and others at the Newberry for supporting such engaging conversations. I have spent one year away from Northwestern, splitting my time as a visiting scholar at Stanford University's Center for Comparative Studies in Race and Ethnicity and as a visiting fellow in Princeton University's Department of History. Many thanks go to Albert Camarillo and Jeremy Adelman for mentoring me and arranging my stay, and to the many other colleagues and friends who made that year a delight.

Organizations and individuals on both sides of the border have helped bring this book to completion. At Yale, I received generous funding from an A. Bartlett Giamatti Fellowship, the Council on Latin American and Iberian Studies, the Beinecke Rare Book and Manuscript Library, the Howard R. Lamar Center for the Study of Frontiers and Borders, and a Robert M. Leylan Dissertation Fellowship. I am also grateful for financial assistance from the Mellon Mays Undergraduate Fellowship Program, the Ford Foundation, the Kinney/Tesoro Foundation, the Social Science Research Council, the Organization of American Historians, Northwestern University's College Fellows Program, and the Woodrow Wilson National Fellowship Foundation. As good as gold, extremely knowledgeable archivists gave generously of their time, especially at the Arizona Historical Society, Special Collections at the University of Arizona, the Arizona State Museum, the Arizona State Library, the Arizona Historical Foundation, the Pimería Alta Historical Society, the National Archives and Records Administration (in College Park, Maryland, and Riverside, California), la Universidad de Sonora, el Colegio de Sonora, Mexico's Acervo Histórico Diplomático de la Secretaría de Relaciones Exteriores, and Mexico's Archivo General de la Nación. Grecia Ramírez helped me in Tucson, and Benjamín Alonso Rascón helped me in Hermosillo.

Since beginning this book, I have received wise feedback from many generous listeners and readers. For inviting me to present pieces of this book at their schools, I thank my hosts at the University of Houston, the University of Michigan, California State University at Fullerton, the University of Southern California, the University of Arizona, Indiana University, Yale University, Harvard University, Princeton University, and Dartmouth College. Thanks also go to the amazing participants in the Tepoztlán Institute for the Transnational History of the Americas. For reading and commenting on parts of my manuscript—or offering their support more generally—I thank Luis Álvarez, Maribel Álvarez, Eric Ávila, Joe Barton, Ned Blackhawk, Alex Bontemps, Brian DeLay, Bill Deverell, María Cristina García, Matt García, Matt Guterl, Dave Gutiérrez, Ramón Gutiérrez, Allyson Hobbs, Karl Jacoby, Emilio Kourí, Benjamin Madley, Kate Masur, David Montejano, Maria Montoya, Katherine Morrissey, John Nieto-Phillips, Dylan Penningroth, Monica Perales, Raul Ramos, Vicki Ruiz, George Sánchez, Chris Schmidt-Nowara, and David Weber. Al Camarillo, Daniel Immerwahr, Benjamin Johnson, Nancy MacLean, Rachel St. John, Sam Truett, and an anonymous reader for Harvard University Press read and commented on the whole manuscript. Kathleen McDermott and Andrew Kinney at

Harvard University Press have been keen and insightful editors, and Carol Hoke and Melody Negron expertly copyedited and produced the book. I cannot thank you all enough.

Many individuals in Arizona and Sonora have shared their time, knowledge, and life histories with me, including Raúl Aguirre, Salomón Baldenegro, Guadalupe Castillo, Augustine García, Isabel García, Erasmo Gómez, Raúl Grijalva, Axel Holm, Patricia Preciado Martin, and Bob Stewart. Special thanks go to members of the Jácome family, who have been astoundingly generous with their time, family photos, papers, and memories. I know that you will not agree with all of my arguments or conclusions, but I hope you feel that I have treated your family—and the life of Alejandro "Alex" G. Jácome in particular—with the utmost respect. Thanks also go to Thomas Whittingslow, founder of Beyond Borders Binational Art Foundation, and to my friends in the Mexican American Studies and Research Center at the University of Arizona. Nicole Guidotti-Hernández, Ben Irvin, Marie Kessler, Erika Korowin, Desika Narayanan, Lydia Otero, Maritza de la Trinidad, and Farzin Vejdani merit special mention for their camaraderie at Wildcat basketball games, during conversations about Tucson, and over many shared meals. Charles Sherry has now mentored two generations of Cadavas.

Love and support from friends has meant everything to me. First, many thanks go to Robert Blakeslee Gilpin, James Lundberg, Robert Morrissey, and Samuel Schaffer, as well as my dear friends Julie Allen, Michael Allen, Mike Amezcua, Amanda Ciafone, Brad Crevier, Nick Demartini, Brian Dunn, Erica Dunn, Lane Fenrich, Brodwyn Fischer, Joseph Fronczsak, Harry Gamboa Jr., Dan Gilbert, Cabray Haines, Gretchen Heefner, Alex Hocherman, Charles Keith, Dorothy Lam, Jason Lipinsky, Brian Lucero, Myra Lucero, Kate Masur, Rebecca McKenna, Matt Nelson, Dylan Penningroth, Brandon Purcell, Beau River, Dana Schaffer, Katie Scharf, Brian Smith, Rachel St. John, Alby Toto, George Trumbull, Jen Van Vleck, Helen Zöe Veit, Wendy Warren, Julie Weise, Ian Wijaya, and Tim Stewart-Winter. In all of academia, the most supportive and congenial people, I think, study the same things I do. Thanks to Latina/Latino and borderlands historians Lori Flores, Mireya Loza, Brian Lucero, Monica Martínez, Ana Minian, Ana Rosas, and Julie Weise. Let us all continue to be there for each other.

Finally, my family deserves all the thanks, love, and appreciation in the world. For welcoming me into their families, thanks go to Dimitri Theodoratos; Marie Belew Wheatley and Michael Ross Wheatley; Bill Belew and Sharon Twenhofel; Jessica and Benjamin Wheatley; Sarah Shelton and Cody Shelton; and Nathan, Alex, and Diana Perry. For raising me or growing up with me, my thanks go to Geraldo Cadava Jr., Gloria Cadava, Dorla Rexroth, Earl Rexroth, Ricky Depugh, Patricia Depugh, Pedro Cadava, Rita Cadava, Ricardo Cadava, and Anna Lujan. I hope you see some of yourselves woven into this work—and into me. Special thanks go to my parents, Eduardo Cadava and Liana Theodoratou, and Arma Depugh and Dave Depugh. Your love has held me up at my least steady moments and also when I am on surer ground. Kathleen Belew, you have read this book too many times already, but that is the least you have done for me. Let us love each other forever and continue the joyous work of making this world, this life, and our new family together everything we want it to be.

INDEX

INDEX